Astaire by Numbers

Astaire by Numbers

Time and the Straight White Male Dancer

TODD DECKER

OXFORD
UNIVERSITY PRESS

Oxford University Press is a department of the University of Oxford. It furthers
the University's objective of excellence in research, scholarship, and education
by publishing worldwide. Oxford is a registered trade mark of Oxford University
Press in the UK and certain other countries.

Published in the United States of America by Oxford University Press
198 Madison Avenue, New York, NY 10016, United States of America.

© Oxford University Press 2022

All rights reserved. No part of this publication may be reproduced, stored in
a retrieval system, or transmitted, in any form or by any means, without the
prior permission in writing of Oxford University Press, or as expressly permitted
by law, by license, or under terms agreed with the appropriate reproduction
rights organization. Inquiries concerning reproduction outside the scope of the
above should be sent to the Rights Department, Oxford University Press, at the
address above.

You must not circulate this work in any other form
and you must impose this same condition on any acquirer.

Library of Congress Control Number: 2022936394

ISBN 978-0-19-764359-4 (pbk.)
ISBN 978-0-19-764358-7 (hbk.)

DOI: 10.1093/oso/9780197643587.001.0001

for
Kelly, David, and James
and for
my Paris colleagues

Contents

INTRODUCTION ... 1
  1. The Clip Reel ... 1
  2. Time on Film and on Paper ... 10
  3. "I Wanna Be a [Cis-Het White] Dancin' Man" ... 15
  4. Outline of the Book ... 24
  5. Four Periods ... 26

ONE: NUMBERS ... 31
  6. Film Musical Actions, Bodies, and Numbers ... 31
  7. Counting Numbers Like Hollywood Did ... 35
  8. 324 Beginnings and 324 Endings ... 40
  9. The Structural Whiteness of the Astaire Corpus and the Studio-Era Film Musical ... 44
  10. Corpus "Nesting Dolls" ... 54
  11. 207 Musical Numbers ... 55
  12. Twenty-Five Fragments ... 57
  13. An Alternate Count: 189 Musical Sections ... 63
  14. 159 Dances: The *Astaire Dancing* Corpus ... 66
  15. Sing, Dance, (Spin,) End—but Modestly ... 72

TWO: SHOTS ... 80
  16. 932 Shots ... 80
  17. ASL and the Longest Shots ... 82
  18. 80 Cutaways and 110 "Inserts" ... 92
  19. "Full Figure" Framings ... 106
  20. 456 Vitruvian Shots ... 107
  21. 82 Context Shots ... 112
  22. 204 Reframed Shots ... 114
  23. Widescreen Adjustments ... 120
  24. Formal Principles, Expressive Resources, Production Conveniences ... 123

THREE: DAYS, HOURS, MINUTES ... 131
  25. "It's a Terrific Job" ... 131
  26. "Astaire Was No Doubt Rehearsing Most of the Time" ... 134

27.	"NG"	147
28.	"NO TIME LOST"	160
29.	"Wet with Persperation [sic]"	166

MIDPOINT: "I Just / Won't / [Don't?] Dance" — 175

FOUR: FRAMES, SETS, CUTS — 184

30.	Shadows on the Wall	184
31.	Frame Awareness	192
32.	A Level View	202
33.	Dance Settings	210
34.	Danced Continuity	216
35.	Object Impermanence	224
36.	On-Set "Jump" Cuts	229
37.	Invisible Match on Action	242
38.	"To Project Intelligence"	246

FIVE: PARTNERS — 251

39.	The Adele Question	251
40.	"Two Equally Matched Individuals"	255
41.	Six Positions for Doubles and Couples	262
42.	Change Partners?	280
43.	The Pan Question	290
44.	MGM "SHOESHINE BOY"	294

SIX: NOISY MASCULINITY — 305

45.	Dancing on Tables for Men	305
46.	Trash-Talk Taps	316
47.	The Matrix of Violent Nondance Dance Moves	323
48.	Silent Yellowface	333
49.	Sarcastic and Aggressive "Routine Tap Steps"	342

CONCLUSION — 351

Appendix One: Astaire Films Corpus	361
Appendix Two: Astaire Dancing Corpus by Number	365
Appendix Three: Astaire Dancing Corpus by Shot	375
Acknowledgments	405
Notes	407
References	425
Index	429

People who make movies tend to be perfectionists, but they also tend to be practical people because making movies is solving a series of very practical questions. The more successful they are, the less time they have to think about the larger theoretical issues.

—Jon Boorstin (1990)

"I don't dig this brooding, analytical stuff," [Astaire] said. "I just dance, and I just act." This, of course, is the impression he has sought to convey through his artless art these many years. He "just" dances, "just" acts, "just" *is*. And perhaps there is no more to Astaire than meets the eye.

—Richard Schickel (1962)

I live in the present and the future—not in the past.

—Fred Astaire (c. 1959)

Within a gesture of apparent perfection, a mortal heart must beat.

—Sara Manguso (2017)

INTRODUCTION

> We may love to imagine that stage performance occupies a real living moment while cinematic performance, recorded on film, thus replayable, abstracts *out of* the living flow; but this is hardly fully true; actors in front of the camera are living their lives, take by take, as they work, and the record—the film—is based on, and contains, this actual, visible living.
>
> —Murray Pomerance (2019)

1. The Clip Reel

Before he set to work creating dance routines for a new film, the musical movie star Fred Astaire reportedly rewatched all his previous films—not in their entirety but just the important parts for his immediate purpose. Astaire only watched the dances. Astaire had a clip reel of all his dance numbers edited into a continuous musical film for screening at home. In 1941, *Life* magazine reported on the clip reel and Astaire's reason for watching it: "To make sure he doesn't repeat himself he runs off reels of his dances from previous pictures."[1] Choreographer Eugene Loring remembered how, before working together for the first time in *Yolanda and the Thief* (1945), Astaire "asked me to see all of the numbers he'd ever done in motion pictures, and he had them magnificently edited. . . . He said he didn't want to repeat himself."[2] Stanley Donen, who directed Astaire in the films *Royal Wedding* (1951) and *Funny Face* (1957), borrowed the clip reel—Astaire kept it in his basement—and confirmed its contents: "He'd cut out all the singing from every number; all that was there was the dancing. It took me three or four days to look at them."[3]

Over the course of his almost twenty-five years in studio-era Hollywood, Astaire's clip reel grew to epic length. Astaire described the extent of the clip reel in 1973, when he was selecting musical numbers for screening at a celebration of his career by the Film Society of Lincoln Center. He told the *New York Times*, "I've counted 200 dances. . . . Now I have to select 40. The film will go from one number to the next—wham!—till people say, 'Let me out!' "[4] Astaire told *Interview* magazine, "You see, I have so many [numbers] that I can't ... something's got to drop out, because you know there's about six hours of stuff."[5] Gossip columnist Joyce Haber mentioned the clip reel skeptically in 1975, with parenthetical quotes from Astaire:

> Let me leave aside the claptrap devised by studio publicists over the years— that he has a personal film library of more than 35,000 feet of film from his musicals, and often watches them ("I certainly don't want to see my own old films; when people tell me at the racetrack 'I saw you on TV at 3 a.m.' well, I'm happy if they want to see them"); that he carries his lunch to the studio in a brown paper bag ("I've never cared about lunch; when I'm working, I may have a cup of soup"); that he never repeated a step in more than 200 dance routines (are there really more than 200 steps in time?).[6]

The numbers Astaire and Haber give—200 routines, six hours, 35,000 feet of film—bear some scrutiny. Just how many dances did Astaire make? And, if edited together, how long would his clip reel be?

By my count—which defines a musical number as any stretch of film where Astaire engages in musical and/or dance actions of any sort—Astaire made 207 musical numbers.[7] Narrowing the count to just the potential contents of his clip reel—only "the dancing"—Astaire danced on the big screen for a grand total of exactly six hours, thirty-four minutes, and fifty seconds. I arrived at this absurdly exact number by counting every second of every dance Astaire made—23,690 seconds in all, composed of 932 shots connected by 778 cuts. (Twenty-two of Astaire's dances are complete in just one shot [average length, 98 seconds].) At the Hollywood standard of twenty-four frames per second, Astaire's 23,690 seconds of dancing translates into about 35,500 feet of film—half again as much as a print of *Lawrence of Arabia* (1962), by Hollywood standards a genuine epic.

Two critics who attended the 1973 Film Society event shared their experience of the abbreviated clip reel Astaire helped assemble. Vincent Canby of the *New York Times* enthused, "Most anthology films obscure the career of a performer by smashing it into fragments. The Astaire film had the opposite effect.... These extraordinary dance-and-song numbers have lives of their own. They're short, ecstatic, romantic fictions with beginnings, middles and ends.... The movies are good, bad, and all right, but the numbers slide effortlessly together to portray a romantic sensibility impossible to define without music and the movement of dance."[8] Alan M. Kriegsman of the *Washington Post* called the Film Society's clip reel "a veritable orgy of viewing pleasures. Just having a chance to watch 29 Astaire song-and-dance numbers from 23 films in a row, without ballast or interruption, nothing but 'the good parts,' was like being the proverbial kid let loose in an ice-cream parlor.... It became a basis for measuring Astaire's achievements, not as isolated triumphs or inspirations, but in relation to each other and from the perspective of his whole career."[9] Ten years after the event, Canby still remembered the clip reel: "The Astaire excerpts had the effect of discovering the dimensions of Mr. Astaire's genius by freeing it from the conventions of narrative filmmaking, allowing us to understand for the first time the exhilarating self-sufficiency of his talent."[10]

This book is about "the good parts": Fred Astaire as found in the complete clip reel of his studio-era dances, all six-and-a-half-plus hours of it. I have my own Astaire clip reel—a digital file on a hard drive (in my basement, backed up in the cloud)—that I have viewed again and again (and again), gathering data shot by shot, cut by cut, second by second. My digital humanities approach to Astaire as screen dancer and film dance maker uses quantitative data of various sorts—objective and descriptive—to analyze Astaire's entire corpus of studio-era film work as an (almost entirely) self-choreographing dancer. Throughout the book, I literally measure—by counting—Astaire's "achievements" or "genius" across the totality of his creative and performance labors in the classical Hollywood musical.

Astaire's dancing body occupies the center point of this study just as it holds the center of the frame for almost all of those over six hours of film dance. The Astaire of the clip reel is a unique and fictive screen-bound being existentially distinct from Fred Astaire the living, breathing human person (born 1899, died 1987). I never met or saw Astaire in person but I have met people who did, including his daughter Ava Astaire McKenzie. I also have a copy of the measurements used by his London bespoke tailors, Anderson and Sheppard, to make his suits. In 2015, I witnessed the cutting of a pattern to these measurements for a suit coat and pants (the cutter expressed surprise at the unusual relationship between Astaire's wide hips and narrow chest and waist).[11] Film writer Murray Pomerance has noted that most people do not know the actual, real-life size of movie stars, and so "the qualities, proportions, and dimensions of a performing body onscreen are thus largely constructions, not facts."[12] This generalization about the cinema, like so many others, doesn't quite apply to the genre of the film musical or to Astaire. The performing body in a musical as Astaire framed it from head to toe is knowable as a fact, at least comparatively by noting Astaire's size relative to the men and women who danced—and still dance—beside him. Astaire's measurements and his height (five feet, nine inches) offer one sort of quantitative data about his body.

A fortunate group of people, by now mostly all passed away, saw Astaire perform live. He was a modestly successful child performer on the vaudeville stage from 1905 to 1916 with his sister Adele. The pair transitioned to the legit theater and by the mid-1920s emerged as genuine stars on Broadway and (even more so) in London's West End. Most people who wrote about seeing the Astaires dance on stage simply marveled at the sight.[13] After Adele's retirement in 1932, Fred did one more stage show (*Gay Divorce*, Broadway 1932, London 1933), and then he went permanently to Hollywood and into the world of film. After this, almost the only audiences who witnessed Astaire dancing live and in person (as opposed to live and on television) were made up of soldiers during World War II who saw Astaire on one of his two USO tours (the first stateside, the second in Europe). In his 1959 autobiography *Steps in Time*, Astaire shared an anecdote about a performance at a Marine base: "It was very hot, about ninety-five, that night. I was dripping, pouring, soaking wet with perspiration after my act and, as I came off stage into the wings, I grabbed a towel and started to mop myself, still breathing heavily. Four big tough Marines standing by open-mouthed seemed transfixed at this sight. One spoke in a deep voice: 'Aw, come on now, it ain't as hard as all that.'"[14] This Marine's reaction suggests a mismatch, perhaps, between his knowledge of Astaire on screen—where the dancer never sweats or gets out of breath—and his direct experience with Astaire's actual body. Or maybe the soldier had a low opinion of men dancing in general and viewed it as decidedly light work—if any genuine (or genuinely masculine) sort of work at all. A notoriously lousy interview subject, Astaire several times over the decades referred to dancing as a "sweat job" and to his work making dances as "Sweat. Days of sweat."[15] Perspiration—never seen in the clip reel—proves a recurring motif in this study, as does the perhaps surprising performance context where Astaire, a straight white man, dances for an audience of men as he did on that Marine base. (Twenty-one dances in the clip reel have entirely or nearly all-male in-film audiences.)

Astaire arrived in Hollywood just as synchronized sound film (introduced in 1927) reached its first technical maturity. The production practices and creative milieu of this still-new medium fit him expressively and temperamentally. Movie audiences adored his work: he was an immediate and lasting movie star unlike any other, a *sui generis* screen talent placed beside Mickey Mouse and Charlie Chaplin within the first years of his film career. When Astaire died in 1987, *New York Times* dance critic Anna Kisselgoff opined, "Ask any foreigner to name one of the great movie stars of all time and 'Fred Astaire,' more often than not, will be the reply. The point is that this image is a dancer's image."[16] Astaire's capacity to embody an entire cultural realm—the movies—and to do so by dancing struck Kisselgoff as his most basic accomplishment. It remains so today. That Astaire embodied a culturally celebrated, mass-mediated straight and white masculinity principally while and by dancing, frequently by himself, warrants early emphasis for the singularity of this achievement. Indeed, Astaire has virtually no creditable peers in terms of the sheer extent of and near-total control over his dances—with the exception of film musical star and director Gene Kelly. However, when compared quantitatively, Kelly proves a distant second: he came on the scene in 1942, nearly a decade after Astaire, and made fewer than half as many dances. Kelly's clip reel clocks in at three hours and seven minutes (well shy of half the length of Astaire's).

Astaire's primary achievement is as a dancer. His principal medium was his own body—more precisely, his body as captured on film, what I will term his screen dance body. Critic and historian David Thomson draws the distinction this way: "Astaire is not a great dancer so much as a great filmed dancer."[17] This book seeks to define the exact nature—the ontological status, the conditions of being—of Astaire's dancing body as captured on the screen. I want to understand as concretely as possible the relationship of Astaire's real dancing body and the studio Hollywood moviemaking machine that captured and repackaged it. This essentially technical process transformed the all-too-human flesh and sweat of Astaire (and those who danced with him) into lasting and powerful moving images of human bodily expression done to music. Crucially, Astaire and his partners *still* dance—albeit in fixed form and in two dimensions. As dancer Mikhail Baryshnikov once lamented, "The problem with Astaire is that he's everywhere—moving."[18] My quantitative approach opens the way to a new understanding of Astaire's body of work and of Astaire's body at work as seen in the clip reel.

Quantitative methods begin with counting. As literary scholar Eric Bulson notes, "The trick, as always, involves knowing where to look for the numbers and then figuring out how to count them and why."[19] What do I count? Astaire's clip reel is the combination of dance choices (how he moved his body) and cinematic choices (how his moving body was captured and presented on film). The technological domain of the cinema offers many countable units: on the image track, I count shots, cuts, ways of framing the dancing body, camera movements, use of cranes, etc.; on the sound track, I quantify the presence (or lack) of foot and body sounds. In the dance domain, I count the content of Astaire's bodily performance in general descriptive ways: what happens in a number (song, dance, song and dance, etc.), where a number takes place, who is involved, ways of transitioning in and out of song and dance, etc. I also catalog Astaire's movements at more detailed levels: his manipulation of objects, his use of familiar dance steps (time steps and double flaps), and his inclusion of nondance actions, such as stomps on toes, kicks in the pants, tripping, shooting, and peering at himself in a mirror. In addition, I quantify the physical relationship between Astaire and his twenty-eight partners—male and female—by determining how much of a given dance involves physical contact between partners (in seconds and types of touching) and a pair's orientation toward each other and toward the camera. This data gathered across the length of Astaire's clip reel forces a reckoning with everything Astaire did and takes my analysis beyond preconceptions or clichés about Astaire's persona, in the process renewing our appraisal of Astaire based on the totality of his work. As Bulson notes, "To read closely with numbers, using computational tools and digital formats, enhances the interpretation since it begins and works through basic facts."[20] My approach to the clip reel extracts "basic facts" and offers a reading of the entirety of Astaire's studio-era dancing on film.

This quantitative data opens the way to new perspectives on Astaire that speak to questions of identity and representation that remain largely unasked in any systematic manner across his long career.[21] Astaire was a straight white male movie star who danced at the highest level of commercial mass media for nearly a quarter century—more if we count his decade dancing on television (not covered here). He enjoyed a position of enormous privilege and power—arguably second to no other individual in classical Hollywood history in terms of realizing his aesthetic goals and controlling his work in front of and behind the camera in the collaborative medium of commercial film (the only substantive comparison may be Charlie Chaplin). Here, a second generalization about film from Pomerance deserves consideration for how it does not apply to Astaire. "The actor's body onscreen, extended through time (by way of shot length or repetitions of presence) and clarified through focus (in close-ups, medium shots, long shots, establishing shots) is not, finally, the property of the actor. Temporal duration by the editor and placement by the director and cinematographer working together are shaped and structured according to the system's, not the actor's, needs. Production trumps expression."[22] For Astaire working in the film musical genre, production was the means to self-expression over which he exercised control, something Canby recognized in the clip reel as Astaire's "self-sufficiency." The opportunity Astaire enjoyed to do this deeply personal creative work as a dance maker and dancer in an industrial context relied fundamentally on his being a man and white and on his presentation as a cis-gender heterosexual. Lacking any of these three identities, his career would have been impossible. Quantifying Astaire's use of the tools of cinema and the way he used his dancing body allows for a nuanced understanding of the three intersectional identity categories Astaire at once boldly, subtly, and idiosyncratically embodies: his whiteness, his maleness, and his straightness.

Astaire's screen dance body was nothing like a real dancing body, but even the most eminent dancers have had trouble nailing down exactly what makes it distinct. Baryshnikov remarked at the 1981 American Film Institute tribute to Astaire, "His perfection is an absurdity that's hard to face."[23] Baryshnikov went on, "You remember the remark by Ilie Nastase about Bjorn Born? He said, 'We are playing tennis. He's playing something else.' It's the same with Fred Astaire. We are dancing, but he's doing something else."[24] At the most mundane level, Astaire's "something else" had technological and economic foundations: he was making dances on film in a commercial context where all he ever had to do, as a dancer, was successfully complete one shot at a time. The average shot length Astaire danced across his career is a modest twenty-five seconds. There is simply no comparison between the tasks set before a screen dancer like Astaire and a stage dancer, such as Baryshnikov, who works in real time and space in front of a real audience within a set dance tradition—whether classical or modern. Astaire danced as himself and created his own rather limited style. British dance critic Alexander Bland commented that Astaire "confined [himself] to a narrow range of dancing outside the general tradition and it is impossible to guess how [he] would have fared in choreography not especially created for [him]."[25] The extent to which creating his own style helped Astaire present as a straight white man proves important.

And yet, Astaire's screen dance body projects a kind of naturalness that dancers, choreographers, and critics who are engaged with dance in the real world—off the screen—take seriously as dance rather than as, quite literally, "something else." Dance historian Beth Genné has detailed the ways choreographer George Balanchine used Astaire as a model for movement and gesture in his dances for the stage.[26] And multiple choreographers have attempted to translate Astaire's screen dance body to real bodies in real space—most notably Jerome Robbins in his 1983 ballet "I'm Old-Fashioned—the Astaire Variations," which directly juxtaposes Astaire and Rita Hayworth dancing on the big screen with comparatively small dancers doing the same dance on the stage below. One explanation for this general view is the extent to which Astaire worked to present his screen body as if it were moving in real time and space, even though it was only intermittently doing so for the duration of each of those 932 shots. The aesthetic norms Astaire adhered to in creating this illusion have been described in the past by Arlene Croce (in relation to Astaire's work with Ginger Rogers at RKO) and John Mueller (who focuses primarily on the choreographic content of Astaire's dancing).[27] In this book, the aesthetic and technological practices that form the foundation of Astaire's "something else" receive concrete and detailed description and analysis in quantitative terms. Before looking at the content of his dance movements, I dwell at length on the cinematic elements of Astaire's film numbers, the precise ways they manifest as movies. It is disingenuous to call Astaire's dancing simply *dancing*. Possible terms mooted by critics have included "Mr. Astaire's super-real dancing" (Kisselgoff) and "the field of dance-photography" (Bland).[28] At Astaire's passing, modern dancer and choreographer Merce Cunningham noted, "I'm not sorry that I saw him only on film" and added that Astaire "perfected 'film dance' as a new art form."[29] Dance scholar Douglas Rosenberg has suggested *screendance* as "an intentionally broad term that may address any and all work that includes dance *and* film." And while Rosenberg acknowledges the term's "inevitable hybridity: tensions between different art genres, between high and mass culture, and between the body and its own mediation," his book defining the term deals almost entirely with noncommercial film: he mentions Astaire, an astoundingly prolific and famous screen dance maker, only once in passing.[30] Dance scholar Erin Brannigan spends a bit more time with Astaire and the commercial musical in her theorization of the term *dancefilm*, but she primarily dwells on the moments when characters in musicals shift from nonmusical to musical mode by way of gestures that are clearly danced (a question dealt with here at the start of Part One).[31] In his 1977 dissertation, Casey Charness borrowed the term *cine-dance* from Mary Jane Hungerford's 1946 dissertation to describe "the interrelationship between camera and dancer in the creation of dance directly for the commercial film musical screen."[32] Charness's method is more discursive than quantitative and he dismisses Astaire's work, giving priority to Gene Kelly and Stanley Donen. Still, close reading of dance and film choices in commercial cinema is his priority. Charness even draws maps of movie sets and camera positions. Quantitative analysis of the Astaire clip reel as an assemblage of shots, connected by cuts and produced within the classical Hollywood studio moviemaking machine, keeps this book intently focused on the technical and aesthetic choices that are the substance of Astaire's screendances, dancefilms, cine-dances, film dances, or whatever we might choose to call them.

Scholars of film style have ignored the special problem of the musical number and the dancing body—neither of which speaks to the questions of narrative that dominate that line of research. The technical solutions Astaire arrived at and mostly stuck with in his dances offer both contrast and complement to the continuity system practiced in the Hollywood studios—indeed, in the dialogue scenes that surround Astaire's numbers in their original narrative feature contexts. Astaire and his collaborators offer a highly focused parallel history of film style, with the visual topic of the dancing (straight white male) body at the literal center. It's worth noting here that about 95% of the clip reel's duration shows Astaire from head to toe. Astaire was completely visible for extended stretches of screen time in a way few other studio-era leading men ever were.

Looking at Astaire's work through quantitative approaches sometimes entails *not* looking at the screen. Bulson's description of the quantitative methods in his study of James Joyce's *Ulysses* applies here as well: "The data sets in this book are relatively small and the computational methods basic.... Someone could potentially use punch cards or some other manual indexing method (as done in the precomputer processing days), but the amount of time required is often enormous and the data, once sifted and structured, would not be as easily manipulated when searching for different results."[33] Most of the data informing this book is included in three appendices, which parse Astaire's clip reel by films, musical numbers, and shots. All the data work is my own, though I was inspired to pursue this approach by collaborative work with an international team of scholars assembled by Marguerite Chabrol and Pierre-Olivier Toulza and based in Paris whom I joined in 2015.[34] My data offers perspectives and insights unavailable otherwise while also directing my analysis toward moments that are statistically common or simply unique in Astaire's clip reel. Still, close reading of the visual and sonic content of Astaire's screen dancing remains at the heart of this project—even if I do so from explicitly quantitative angles.

2. Time on Film and on Paper

A primary fact of Astaire's clip reel is its preservation, in altered form, of actual time—hence the prominence of the word *time* in this book's subtitle. In film studies terminology, Astaire's dancing body is always indexical. In his dances, Astaire's actual body moving in time and space in the past is fixed—in chemical terms, literally so—in the medium of photography. Photography takes three-dimensional space and renders it as a two-dimensional representation of space that can be held in the hand (and run through a projector, etc.). All of Astaire's films were assembled by hand from strips of film in the editing departments of Hollywood studios, and Astaire himself was deeply involved in postproduction completion of his dance numbers: "I used to sit up with the cutters all night doing that," he recalled in 1973 in a thirteen-part BBC radio documentary about his career (a source drawn on throughout this book).[35] His routines prove to be virtuoso examples of Hollywood filmmaking, instances where all involved, and especially the cutters (or editors), faced unusual technical challenges. As the most expensive type of film the studios made, the musical should be understood as the special effects genre of its time, analogous to today's action-adventure spectacles that similarly present (mostly male) bodies in motion (albeit often digitally composited rather than indexical—although hand-to-hand fights easily function as surrogate dances). Indeed, Astaire's clip reel finds a contemporary analog in YouTube supercut videos of highlights from action movies. Astaire's clip reel contains dynamic action movie making of the highest order—some of it containing bona fide special effects, all of it out of the norm for standard Hollywood practices directed at narrative filmmaking.

In several senses, the clip reel is a time machine. Film stock exposed in a camera and successfully developed captures time in physical form. In the case of musical numbers, this captured time in the form of shots (continuous pieces of film composed of thousands of photographs) was then reassembled (edited together) to match prerecorded musical tracks (audio recordings laid down before filming), which, in turn, captured a different span of actual time (usually about a week or so before the time captured on the image track). Prerecorded music tracks served as a foundation or keel (to use a nautical metaphor), to which the individual shots were attached. The technical process of capturing time in the form of images in segments (shots) and then attaching these segments to captured time in the form of sound (prerecorded audio tracks) opened the door on the image-track side to the manipulation not only of time but also of bodies and space. This is the technological essence of the "something else" Astaire was doing.

Viewing Astaire's screen dances, in turn, consumes time. Indeed, Astaire's screen dances were produced to be sold as entertaining stretches of time in a movie theater for the price of admission to the building. As MGM executive Marcus Loew said, "We sell tickets to theatres, not movies."[36] Astaire's numbers were packaged as standout attractions in a specific genre (the musical) of the standard product Hollywood sold (feature-length narrative films). Access to Astaire's dances has changed radically since his time. Today, it's easy to spend hours watching Astaire dancing. Virtually all his numbers are up on YouTube in standalone clips. YouTube is, effectively speaking, a searchable Astaire clip reel, although the ease of letting all the dancing unfold chronologically—in Astaire's words, "from one number to the next—wham!"—is not to be found there (and the quality of some clips is poor). I invite the reader to consult the musical numbers discussed in this book on YouTube or elsewhere as convenient. Yet any such viewing occurs under the caveat that Astaire conceived his screen dances for exhibition on the big screen according to film distribution practices that made each of his films available, as initially released, for a short time only. As Thomson wrote of this period, "A movie was wild and it went away."[37] The situation changed in the mid-1950s, near the end of Astaire's studio-musical career, with the sale of many of Astaire's films to television. The Astaire-Rogers cycle at RKO was among the first batch of Hollywood films made available as content for the new medium.[38] Repeated broadcasts of Astaire's films, one critic wrote in 1980, meant that "we enthusiasts are left to peruse local listings for the sporadic appearance of our idol."[39] In some media markets, old movies were broadcast repeatedly—the *Million Dollar Movie* series in New York City showed the same film twice nightly for a week; Astaire and Rogers's films were in this rotation.[40] Still, Astaire was effectively "wild" until the early 1980s, a situation that prevented the kind of close analysis reliant on total access to the film that I do here. At the tail end of this period, Charness did his dissertation research on films like *Singin' in the Rain* (1952) at the Library of Congress using archival prints viewed on a Steenbeck editing table.

Release of Astaire's films for home viewing on VHS (beginning in the mid-1980s) and subsequently on DVD and via streaming have made him available on demand, turning his clip reel into "an infinitely viewable cultural artifact."[41] As film scholar Gabriele Pedullà writes, "The possibility of viewing old films at one's pleasure created a turning point in the history of moving images comparable to that of the remote control. Rewinding was for some time the reader's prerogative only."[42] Critic D. A. Miller revels in such control over the movie image but wonders at a possible fundamental shift in his activity as a movie watcher. He describes the DVD as "a viewing contrivance" that "performs all those retrievals once merely wished for but now realized as routine functions: pause, step, forward, back, slow, fast, skip, grab, bookmark. . . . [M]y absorbing hours of close viewing in the new cinematheque have given me the most intense experience of cinema in my life, though it may not strictly be cinema that I am watching."[43] Film scholar Jason Sperb raises this problem as well, generalizing across our use of computers to watch earlier audiovisual formats: "Whereas the physical materiality of film projectors, books, or televisions called attention to the act of engaging with said media, computers can cleanly efface the bonds of incongruous media, as well as the sense of how we engage with what we engage with."[44] My perhaps obsessive approach to the clip reel—turning its content into an extensive set of interconnected spreadsheets—was only practically possible once I had digital copies of every Astaire film (not as easy as it might sound). What I'm doing is not, strictly speaking, film watching. I am clearly doing something else. Bulson describes the impact of this approach in literary scholarship: data and visualization "[generates] an estrangement that lets us approach the literary object differently, moving between time and space, up above and down below, to explore the creative process accompanied by quantitative information that anchors our analysis and comparisons."[45] Remarkably, when applied to studio-era film, this estrangement has the potential to return us to the moment in the production process when Astaire and his cutters were assembling his numbers, probably at a Steenbeck machine. Watching so as to extract data along various technical parameters reveals details Astaire's original audiences would have missed—and that he would have counted on their missing. (Astaire said of the changing statue at the back of "The Babbitt and the Bromide" in *Ziegfeld Follies* [1946], "I don't know how many people actually saw it, because they weren't looking at the background as much as what we were doing."[46]) The current regime of total access to these films can make visible that which Astaire assumed could or would not be seen—or, at least, very difficult to catch. Quantitative methods such as I use here force the viewer to slow down, to watch the edges of the frame, to monitor objects, to keep close track of the dance without seeking to recreate it but instead to turn some aspect of its cinematic content and form into data. This sort of watching is tied to the clock: timecode data anchors much of this work.

Crucially, the photographic process behind studio-era motion pictures preserves the actual time Astaire's lived, real body spent dancing. Pomerance writes generally of this phenomenon: "Performances are of the body and from the body, expressed by way of the body. . . . Yet in cinema bodies are also foreign, absent, to us. . . . We are seeing the trace of real life, preserved (see Bazin) in so magical a way that every nuance of life is here but for the palpable presence of the flesh itself (that is given onstage, yet at a forbidding distance). We must find our way toward and into these bodies, especially these bodies offered at such an apotheosis of feeling and being."[47] One way to "find . . . these bodies" is to locate an alternate means of access to the moment of performance for the camera, for instance, by pinning the production of a cinematic moment to a specific date and time. For example, the musical number "Steppin' Out with My Baby" in *Easter Parade* (1948) was shot over three days: November 24 to 26, 1947. Astaire typically shot his numbers in order, so the first day involved the opening vocal and the initial dance section, which has Astaire partner three women in turn. The second day, November 25, saw the completion of the partner dances—a process slowed by having to remove the light-brown, "high yella" makeup from his second partner's legs that was rubbing off on Astaire's white suit. After the lunch break, the *Easter Parade* crew started work on the solo portion of "Steppin' Out," which includes a slow-motion special effects dance for Astaire seen against the chorus dancing in regular motion. The single slow-motion shot was difficult to get—before trying to film this complicated cane-tossing-and-catching combination, Astaire spent an hour and a half in conversation with director Charles Walters and art director Cedric Gibbons. A pause of this length during shooting was very unusual. Finally, at 4:20pm (shooting started at 10am), Astaire attempted the combination on film. Over the next seventy-three minutes he made thirty-two takes. None proved acceptable. At 5:33pm, they called it a day. The assistant director recorded the reason in his daily report: "Mr. Astaire being exhausted we were compelled to stop shooting." At 9:12am the next morning, Astaire was back at it. Four more takes of the troublesome shot followed. By 9:30am the combination was successfully captured on film. In fact, however, it wasn't—Astaire returned to the set on December 1 from 8am to noon and redid the slow motion dance.[48]

The events of those days in November and December 1947—as spliced together to music that was prerecorded before a single shot was taken—can be returned to again and again. I have watched Astaire spin, toss, and catch that cane countless times over the last twenty years: in 2002, when I first worked on Astaire in graduate school; in 2010, when I taught a course on the musical and screened fourteen Astaire films (and virtually all his dance routines) on the big screen in Washington University in St. Louis's commercial-grade movie theater; in 2020 on my home computer while I wrote this book during the Covid-19 lockdown. Each time I watched (or watch) that cane toss and catch, I enter a space where my present and fragments of Astaire's past exist together. Astaire dances for me (and you) here and now; he is present for me (and you) here and now; his screen dance body moves in my (and our) world. In effect, he lives again (albeit in a fixed form). That fixed form might alternatively be understood not as life but as death—a kinetic sort of embalming that, so long as the film is preserved and viewable (in any form), forestalls the operation of time on Astaire's body. His screen dance body is, thus, eternal but also dead—as Sperb describes it, "the perpetual presence of life . . . the presence of a dead man."[49] As philosopher Stanley Cavell wrote, "It is an incontestable fact that in a motion picture no live human being is up there. But a human *something* is, and something unlike anything else we know."[50] This book seeks to foreground the connections between Astaire's carefully constructed simulation of a dancing body (the surviving film dances viewed through a quantitative lens) and the available archival evidence for the real body behind those dances.

The precision with which we know the date and time of that moment of dance from late 1947 relies on the detailed record keeping of the studio system, a quintessentially capitalist context. The studios accounted for the time Astaire labored to make his films down to the minute on time sheets noting his arrival at and departure from the lot, as well as his lunch and dinner breaks. (*Pace* his comment to Haber about not caring about lunch, Astaire *always* took a lunch break, as befits the unionized work environment of the studios, although the salaried Astaire—paid a flat fee per film, sometimes with a profit-sharing percentage—occupied a liminal position between both labor and management and the cast and the creative personnel.) A parallel body of data, mostly drawn from assistant director (or AD) reports, detail the workflow on set during the expensive days when Astaire's dances went before the cameras. This data, part of the vast enterprise of the classical studios, quite literally tracks Astaire's actual working body. I put this seemingly mundane data to use by analyzing what it contains: quantitative and descriptive evidence for Astaire's real body at work. The minute-by-minute nature of these studio records, available for nineteen of Astaire's twenty-nine films, complements the second-by-second timecode data I have extracted from the clip reel. My analyses shift between these two bodies of quantitative data—both of which are mostly measured in units of time—in an effort to understand Astaire's actual and screen-bound bodies as always in contact with each other. As Pomerance writes, "Seeing a spectacle always involves the negation of production, seeing production the negation of spectacle, yet any viewer may shift concentration to see both."[51] This book puts two scholarly methods to work—analysis of quantitative and archival data and close reading of select numbers, shots, cuts, and dance moves—in an effort to see both production and spectacle.

3. "I Wanna Be a [Cis-Het White] Dancin' Man"

Writing in 1998 in anticipation of the close of the twentieth century, *Time* magazine critic Richard Corliss contrasted Astaire with Marlon Brando (both were born in Omaha, Nebraska): "In their distinct ways—grace vs. power, gentility vs. menace, tux vs. torn T shirt—Fred Astaire and Marlon Brando represented the poles of 20th century popular culture. Astaire gave it class; Brando gave it sex."[52] The notion that Astaire did not give his audiences sex is, of course, absurd. Corliss prudishly equates Brando-esque raw or rough sexuality with sex, a schematic reduction that ignores the considerable sexual frisson that attends romance, a register fundamental to Astaire's work. Astaire and Brando's paths crossed at nearly the exact midpoint of the twentieth century, when Brando revised a line of the script for *The Band Wagon* (1953) that referred to him by name. Brando's input raises masculinity questions at the center of this book. In the film, Astaire as Tony Hunter explodes in anger at the artsy pretensions of the ballet and theater folks putting up the Broadway show he is starring in and gives a little speech about who he is. The original script reads, "Now let's get this straight. I am not Nijinsky, I am not Marlon Brando—I'm Mrs. Hunter's little boy, Tony—an entertainer. . . " Brando, communicating through his agent, rewrote the last word, replacing "entertainer" with "song-and-dance man" (as heard in the film). Internal MGM memos noted, "[Brando] will object strenuously if we mention him and retain the original dialogue, as he and his agent feel this would imply Mr. Brando is not an entertainer."[53] Brando, in seeking to keep himself in the category *entertainer*, placed Astaire in a specifically masculine though fraught category: the song-and-dance man. The specifics of being a "man" who sings and dances demand unpacking. As historian John F. Kasson has noted, "Manliness is a cultural site that is always under construction."[54] A man who sings and dances proves an especially difficult building project. Taken as a group, Astaire's dances erect a nuanced monument to assertive if casually confident masculine self-presentation, which always also functions as self-preservation. Importantly, Astaire was directly responsible for almost every detail of this unlikely monument to mid-twentieth-century American manhood made of screen dancing. His control over his screen dance body was near total: always framed as an autonomous figure, Astaire moved under no one else's command. The rare dances when he relinquished control, such as his appearance in yellowface in *Ziegfeld Follies* (analyzed in Part Six), stand out as stark and valuable, even shocking, exceptions. Astaire's position as a leading man proves crucial as well. In a newspaper interview at the very outset of his career as a leading man in the movies, just after the release of *The Gay Divorcee* (1934), Astaire spun his public persona away from dancing, made a claim to control over his work, and even put a number on his contribution to his own success. Reporter Mayne Peak wrote, "I had intended interviewing him from the angle of 'Pavlowa [sic] in Pants.' But he immediately pooh-poohed the idea. 'When you speak of a ballet dancer,' he declared. 'Pavlowa [sic] never spoke a word. I'm an actor. I've always done my shows, had my plays the way I wanted them, and was responsible for 50 percent of their success.'"[55] Brando kept himself in the category *entertainer* by relegating Astaire to the *song-and-dance men*; in reciprocal fashion, Astaire kept himself out of the *dancer* category by invoking other work he did (acting) even though he never would have had a Hollywood career without doing what made him special (dancing). Astaire distancing himself from Pavlova, a great female ballet dancer, is the first of many instances in this book where Astaire's words position what he does as *not* ballet and perhaps also *not* dancing.

But he was, in the end, a dancer. Throughout this study, quantitative methods help isolate exactly how Astaire plied his trade as a song-and-dance man. Along with dancing a solid majority of his dances with female romantic partners—and thereby buttressing his heterosexuality—Astaire also adopted a consistently aggressive, usually inner-directed stance. His command of the

Hollywood moviemaking machine was entirely contingent upon his manifest identity as a straight white male. Each of these intersectional aspects of his identity demands brief initial consideration here, even as each tends to blend into the others.

Shortly after Astaire's death, journalist Sarah Giles gathered reflections on Astaire in a book titled *Fred Astaire: His Friends Talk*. Producer Sam Goldwyn Jr. mused, "Nice man, a really nice man. Who else left a testimony of work like that? He is the only one who has ever totally mastered film."[56] Goldwyn dwells on Astaire's status as a "nice man"—a meaningful credential for understanding Astaire's character as a man—before dubbing him the "only" master of film, a rather shocking but defensible claim. Such mastery, including the very opportunity to develop it, and maleness go hand in hand.

No female dancer could have hoped to be a film musical star for a quarter century. Astaire's nearest female peer, Eleanor Powell, had an eight-year career as a star and made only thirty-eight dance numbers. Her clip reel is one-and-three-quarter hours long. Astaire benefited from Hollywood's enduring bias toward men, which allows male stars to age and remain virile and desirable as partners. Under this unequal system, Astaire constantly required new, always younger female partners—the age gap between them and Astaire steadily increased across his career. Astaire danced romantic duo routines with nineteen women in his twenty-nine studio films from *Flying Down to Rio* (1933) to *Silk Stockings* (1957).[57] The age gap in years between Astaire and his romantic dance partners steadily increased across his career from twelve with Ginger Rogers to thirty-two with Leslie Caron (see chart 1). Astaire certainly wasn't ageless, but because he was a man the fact of his aging was insufficient cause to end his career. His enduring good health and physical resilience also made Astaire's long career possible, as did the decidedly nonstrenuous nature of his dancing, which was near to walking and other everyday movements. The comparatively modest physical demands of his highly individual style extended his dancing career to age sixty-nine. (Still, he was undoubtedly strong: as art director Jack Martin Smith noted of Astaire's use, at age fifty-five, of a trampoline in his solo "Seeing's Believing" in *The Belle of New York* [1952]: "Dangerous number to do. Trampolines are a dangerous rig for a normal person to work on. Fred was good and his ankles were strong so he didn't have any problem."[58])

Nearly two-thirds (59%) of Astaire's dances were partner dances with women where he performed the role of heterosexual male. As social dance scholar Maxine Leeds Craig notes of the early twentieth century (Astaire's

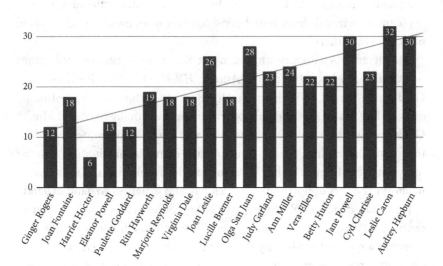

CHART 1 Age gap in years between Astaire and his romantic dance partners (in chronological order of first dance with Astaire)

youth), "Merely by having women in their arms, men certified their 'good' sexuality, that is to say, their desire for women."[59] The sex Astaire and his female partners infer may be sublimated into dance, but representing the physical attraction felt between a man and a woman is primary to the cultural work Astaire did—even if he reportedly did not see himself as a romantic figure. Astaire's daughter Ava remarked to Giles, "Daddy wasn't a romantic, not at all. He was very enigmatic about that sort of thing. He had an amazing ability to make it seem so in films, but that was a job."[60] The notion of Astaire as a man doing a man's job—he described his work this way, as did others—runs across this book. Each duo dance Astaire did and each new woman he took as a partner resecured his heterosexuality, making his dancing demonstrably manly just by virtue of whom he danced with and how. His position as a leading man—despite his looks—further cemented Astaire's heterosexuality. The plot of all his films reinforced his position as a man seeking (and almost always getting) a woman. Male dancers who only did specialty numbers didn't have this sort of external narrative support for their cis het masculinity.

As Craig notes, "Masculinities are in many ways things produced on the surface. Men work to appear masculine to other men."[61] Male peers and critics reflecting on Astaire's persona in the 1970s and 1980s, a period when classical Hollywood icons like Astaire were subject to intense nostalgia, similarly zeroed in on Astaire's masculinity and proclaimed it genuinely manly: meaning not queer. In a handwritten note with the salutation "Dear Friend" for the program book of a major tribute to Astaire in 1975, movie star John Wayne summed up Astaire with the phrase "good taste and masculine grace."[62] Invocation of the word *masculine* works here to qualify qualities (taste and grace) that might otherwise read as feminine. In an interview with Astaire for the *Los Angeles Times*, Philip K. Scheuer expressed his thanks for Astaire's delineation of an appropriately straight masculinity: " . . . we should all salute him for what he represented to his generation: the epitome of elegance without effeminacy."[63] Critic Gregg Kilday, writing in 1981, set aside the euphemisms. "Fred Astaire was—still is, for that matter—an American dandy. An American dandy: At first, it sounded like a contradiction in terms," but, Kilday continues, Astaire managed to take the European dandy type and "turn it straight." "Gene Kelly," he goes on, "was always intent on *demonstrating* his masculinity, but Astaire just *assumed* his."[64] The assumption all three of these male voices share is that proper masculinity equals no trace of queerness—or, to use a term circulating in Astaire's period, effeminacy.

The heterosexuality of men who dance is enduringly suspect. Astaire, of course, knew this. Drawing on taped interviews from the 1980s, Fred and Adele Astaire biographer Kathleen Riley relates Astaire's awareness (circa 1930) of how he was perceived as to sexual identity: "Adele revealed that her brother had once confided in her his desire and determination to get married because 'he didn't want to wake up with the morning papers' and because he knew that many people believed him to be homosexual. He was often, she said, the object of some male's infatuation and even received propositioning letters."[65] Astaire crafted his dances across a period of increasingly public homophobia. The content of his straightness as he danced it shows little adjustment to this cultural shift, but it is noteworthy that he did not engage his male costars as buddies. Film musical scholar Sean Griffin has noted the wartime trend toward "buddy" musicals that involved two men who are "not absolutely or overtly homosexual, but definitely share an intense bond," similar to the Hollywood bromances of the twenty-first century. Griffin mentions Bob Hope and Bing Crosby as well as Gene Kelly and Frank Sinatra as multimusical costars who "seem more closely connected to each other than to any of the women they encounter."[66] Astaire never appeared in such company. Indeed, his two films with Crosby (*Holiday Inn* [1942] and *Blue Skies* [1946]) are studies in underhanded male competition and conflict.[67] Locking in his status as a dancing male star so early in the sound film era surely helped Astaire negotiate later decades. He was, from very early in his career, an exceptional figure: not only a dancer but also a romantic leading man, and a dancer with a modest yet decidedly noisy style, and so—perhaps—not *really* a dancer.

Astaire's monument to manhood and straightness expresses whiteness simply by virtue of its existence. No Black dancer had anything close to Astaire's opportunity to create a screen dance body. His only Black peers in the studio system were Bill "Bojangles" Robinson and the Nicholas Brothers (Harold and Fayard). Robinson made twenty dance numbers in eleven feature films. Once, in the Black-cast *Stormy Weather* (1943), he played a leading role. Robinson's clip reel lasts thirty-five minutes. The Nicholas Brothers made eleven dance numbers—one in each of eleven feature films spread out over fourteen years. Their clip reel is twenty-four minutes long.[68] Astaire averaged seven musical numbers and thirteen-and-a-half minutes of dance *per film* across his twenty-four-year career. Privileged access to the means to make both a personal screen dance body and an iconic straight white male type marks every dance Astaire made simply for the fact that he was empowered to make these dances. The existence of Astaire's clip reel is, in itself, an expression of the power of whiteness in Hollywood. Only whites could be stars in the major Hollywood studios, commercial and cultural entities more properly called white studios—just as literary scholar Richard Jean So, echoing writers Zora Neal Hurston and Toni Morrison, describes the major American publishers as "white publishers" based on the overwhelming statistical prevalence of white authors.[69] As So does for publishing in his book *Redlining Culture: A Data History of Racial Inequality and Postwar Fiction*, here I use statistical data to show the dramatic extent of the studio-era film musical's whiteness and to put a number on racial inequality in the genre. As philosopher Shannon Sullivan writes, "It is a privilege of those who are not racially oppressed to see or treat race as optional. People who are discriminated against because of their race generally do not have a choice of whether to view race as relevant. It is relevant because it is forced upon them by a racist world."[70] The racist world of Hollywood (and Hollywood's white target audience) opened wide its gates to Astaire just as it barely cracked them open for the Nicholas Brothers. Astaire's whiteness is examined here as a component of this larger race-based, racially segregated, thoroughly unequal expressive economy.

My previous book on Astaire, *Music Makes Me: Fred Astaire and Jazz*, dwelt on questions of race in the musical realm. I demonstrated Astaire's affinity for and knowledge of jazz and his consistent, career-long work with Black jazz musicians. Astaire sought out interracial encounters and occasionally crossed the color line in the era of racial segregation and during the height of the mid-century civil rights movement (particularly in his television specials).[71] But attention to Astaire's musical proclivities and occasional musical collaborators does not account for the entirety of his work. In *Music Makes Me*, I posited that Astaire's creative life was "as much about music as it was about dancing and filmmaking."[72] In this book, I focus on his dancing and filmmaking and strive to widen my analysis of Astaire's performance of race by going beyond the paradigm of popular culture whiteness as generated primarily in the use/borrowing/appropriation/stealing of Blackness. Here, I want to understand Astaire's whiteness within and beyond the instrumental use of Blackness. I consider the Astaire of the clip reel through an intersectional paradigm drawn from feminist scholarship that sees identity—everyone's, even that of straight white men—as always multifaceted, specific (not universal), and under construction. As theorist Paul B. Preciado writes, "There is no universal human body, but a multiplicity of gendered, racialized, and sexualized living beings and organic tissues."[73] Astaire's case complicates matters further, given the reciprocal fact of both his actual, historical body (now gone) and his self-fashioned screen dance body (still here in inorganic form).

Astaire's powerful position in mid-twentieth-century culture can be sketched in by way of intersectionality scholars Patricia Hill Collins and Sirma Bilge's four domains of power (structural, cultural, disciplinary, interpersonal).[74] In the structural domain, as a white male, Astaire enjoyed a long period of near-total control over his work at several top Hollywood studios, where he was understood to be a leading man and a creative figure of unique stature. In the cultural domain, for the first two decades of his film career Astaire was presented globally in the only available audiovisual medium at the height of its influence. He was a colossus within the juggernaut that was the movies: what today seems like a decidedly second-rate Astaire vehicle, *Let's Dance* (the only one of his films never released on DVD and generally unavailable to stream), on its initial release in 1950 played three weeks at the Paramount Theatre in Times Square with a stage show featuring Nat "King" Cole. Astaire understood the power of the movies, telling a reporter in 1936, "I actually *have* been discovered by a great body of people who never heard of me or saw me when I was on the stage. And I'm darned proud and happy to have been discovered by them. They're American. I'm an American—and the more people I can dance for, who enjoy my dancing, the better off I am and the happier I am."[75] Astaire's Americanness cannot be underestimated as an element of his cultural power permitting him to dance like he wanted and to present himself as an "outlaw" (his word; unpacked at length in the midpoint section). Critic Jack Kroll's obituary for Astaire in *Newsweek*—which opens with the sentence, "All right, wrap up the 20th century: Fred Astaire is gone."—made the point that, contra British sophistication and "flippancy," Astaire's "white tie and tails, spinning and whirling with supernal grace, was the haberdashery of innocence."[76] I resist notions of "innocence" or "outlaw" with relation to Astaire: he was a figure of tremendous structural and cultural power and the substance of his work expresses this privileged position. But this power was limited. Mechanisms within the disciplinary domain dictated who Astaire could dance with and how he could dance: Jim Crow racial segregation ruled out professional Black performers as partners (he only ever danced beside the Nicholas Brothers on fragmentary home movies captured on the streets outside the soundstages where Hollywood made its movies). Compulsory heterosexuality policed any suggestions of effeminacy in his style and required ever more dances with women (there was no escaping the imperative to couple up). Collins and Bilge define the interpersonal domain as "how individuals experience the convergence of structural, cultural, and disciplinary power." Astaire's structural and cultural power elevated him to a position of unprecedented control; he seems not to have struggled with disciplinary limits, especially since his whiteness and maleness allowed him to partake freely of Black expressive registers—such as jazz and tap dance. This book is not concerned with Astaire's inner life. Nor will I pin down his straight white masculinity as a fixed or essentialized identity. Intersectionality scholars understand identity as something one *does*, not something one *has*.[77] This book seeks to understand how Astaire *did* his straight white masculinity in the creation of his screen dance body and as evident in that body as found in the clip reel.

Masculinity scholar R. W. Connell offers a complementary way to understand Astaire's position. Connell writes, "Masculinity as an object of knowledge is always masculinity-in-relation."[78] Never defined along positivist or essentialist lines, masculinity for Connell functions as a "category of possibility" that is constantly under renegotiation, a "configuration of practice ... simultaneously positioned in a number of structures of relationship, which may be following different historical trajectories."[79] Alone among dancing men of his time, Astaire enjoyed singular conditions to carve out the possibilities for a straight white male dancer. This book isolates Astaire's film dances as one of many "projects of masculinity" of the mid-twentieth-century decades. Connell's observation that "white men's masculinities, for instance, are constructed not only in relation to white women but also in relation to black men" proves apropos to this study of Astaire and his partners and chimes with intersectionality as a theoretical lens.[80] Similarly, Connell's emphasis on the body informs this study of Astaire: "Bodies, in their own right as bodies, do matter.... There is an irreducible bodily dimension in experience and practice; the sweat cannot be excluded."[81] This book leverages production records to document Astaire's sweat, working thereby toward an understanding of Astaire that goes beyond his carefully maintained sweat-free screen image.

Astaire, of necessity given his job as a musical movie star in the classical era, made an extravagant visual and aural spectacle of his masculinity, his whiteness, and his cis-het-ness. He did this by default but also with intention, care, and close attention to the dangerous edges of these identity categories. His negotiation of the edges of whiteness, straightness, and maleness proves as important as his definition of a refined and idealized version of each category. Astaire's intersectional identity deserves head-on consideration: how exactly did this particular cis-het white man get away with dancing—for a mass audience, no less—his masculinity, heterosexuality, and whiteness across the middle decades of the twentieth century? Looking systematically by way of quantitative methods at Astaire's clip reel reveals something of the ontological assumptions behind his powerful presence—a presence that participates fully if always idiosyncratically in the mighty structures of being and power that are whiteness, maleness, and heteronormativity. This book is a sustained effort to describe and to name the constitutive elements of Astaire's cis-gender presentation of his male body, his performance of heterosexual/heteroromantic identity, his whiteness, and his masculinity. This is not a comparative study and I do not spend a lot of time looking at other film musical dancers beside Astaire. On occasion, however, I do place Astaire's choices in their larger Hollywood context.

4. Outline of the Book

This book has six parts. Each brings a quantitative approach to the analysis of Astaire's clip reel. Each part is made of relatively short sections averaging about 2,500 words in length. This structure facilitates the presentation of quantitative data and the making of targeted arguments supported by data. Parts and sections are referenced by number throughout the text.

Parts One and Two, "Numbers" and "Shots," offer a fresh approach to the Astaire films and the Hollywood film musical genre as a whole. I begin by breaking Astaire's film musicals into their component parts: separating the nonmusical from the musical segments; parsing the musical segments down to the dance routines that make up the clip reel; and finally working at the level of the shot. Defining the six-and-a-half-hour corpus of Astaire's dancing in objective, time-based terms is a primary task of these initial two parts. Basic timecode data, such as the number and length of the shots in each routine, yields a variety of ways to think through Astaire's dancing as an object composed of cinematic parts, redefining his dancing as a thing made of shots. This data helps define norms—in some ways Astaire was very consistent in his approach over time—but also identifies anomalies and shifts in his approach to basic problems. Parts One and Two present a complete rethinking of Astaire's entire corpus through quantitative, timecode-derived categories and lay the conceptual and practical foundation for the remainder of the book. In addition, these two parts demonstrate how the genre of the film musical is particularly amenable to quantitative methods that attend to aspects of time. The screen dance body proves an eminently measurable entity.

Part Three, "Days, Hours, Minutes," continues the focus on cinematic elements and turns to the assistant director reports used by the studios to monitor Astaire's body at work in real time making dances on film. These documents, together with pay records, schedules, and memos, offer evidence that allow us to view and hear Astaire's dances as the labor of an actual body. Going beyond anecdotal remembrances or publicity pabulum, these studio documents functioned as integral parts of the daily moviemaking process during the intense days of production (when the film was being shot). As reports direct from the shop floor, their contents reflect the most immediate demands of the studio system—monitoring efficiency and keeping track of who was to blame for any waste of time.

Parts Four, Five, and Six apply a quantitative approach to the content of Astaire's screen dancing (the ways he moved his body), with specific attention to his intersectional identity as represented on screen. (A short midpoint section preceding Part Four reorients the book from cinematic to dance details.) Part Four, "Frames, Sets, Cuts," examines how Astaire used framing and cuts to magnetize the camera and the frame around his dancing body, a body that exercises sovereign—indeed, generative—control over space and a multitude of objects. The all-controlling power of the white body is everywhere on display as Astaire's normative mode of being in this world he creates, a world that is white by virtue of his access to the tools to create it. Looking closely into the cuts, however, this dancing body and the space it produces and controls emerge as closely crafted fictions only possible on screen, fantasies of control that project an ownership over space that is more idea than reality. Part Five, "Partners," compares Astaire's duo dances with men and with women. The quantitative methods used here turn on the basic relationship of two bodies to each other, especially the question of whether they touch or not. This analysis draws out the substantive content of Astaire's performance of heterosexuality and reveals the extent to which his duo dances, with women and with men alike, embody nuanced views of human partnerships, some of which transcend received gender hierarchies. A close reading of his only partner dance with a Black man situates this unique number within Astaire's normative practices when dancing with white men and women. Dancing with Leroy Daniels, a bootblack recruited from Los Angeles's Skid Row for "A Shine on Your Shoes" in *The Band Wagon*, required Astaire to answer the question of how a white male dancing movie star might move to music with a Black man in a public place as represented in the classical style. Part Six, "Noisy Masculinity," considers a variety of ways Astaire presents himself as a man by identifying select hypermasculine moves and counting their occurrence in the clip reel. His use of foot sounds is measured by the second. Close cataloging of Astaire's use of weapons (canes, mostly), aggressive nondance dance steps (such as kicks to the rear), and familiar tap steps (time steps and double flaps) brings decidedly not tasteful and graceful aspects of his persona to the fore. Astaire's use of noise is revealing on this account: he is (almost) always the alpha dog and much of the time he's barking. For contrast, Astaire's astonishing foray into a fully exoticized, nonwhite masculinity in "Limehouse Blues" from *Ziegfeld Follies* is explored in detail as well. The book closes with a look at Astaire's repeated in-film acts of looking at himself in the mirror. This action echoes the labors of the rehearsal hall, when he looked at his actual body and imagined how it might translate to the screen. Such looking allegorizes the unseen work of self-examination in the creation of a straight white male dancing persona such as Astaire's. I also consider further directions for quantitative methods as applied to Hollywood film.

Parts One and Two are foundational to my quantitative approach and work as a pair. Parts Three through Six (and the midpoint essay on the discourse surrounding Astaire's dancing) could be read in any order or as stand-alone studies of their given topics. Given that the book ranges freely over the entirety of Astaire's long career, the text of each part gives release dates on first mention of each film title and indicates on first mention of each musical number the film in which it appears.

5. Four Periods

The corpus of twenty-nine Astaire films considered in this book begins with *Flying Down to Rio* and closes with *Silk Stockings*. Appendix One contains basic information about these films and my grouping of the corpus into four periods. I exclude Astaire's first Hollywood musical, MGM's *Dancing Lady* (1933), because he appears only briefly (as himself) and does only one complete dance with the film's star Joan Crawford (within an extended production number to which Astaire is largely incidental). The films Astaire made after the demise of the studio system, including his only poststudio musical, *Finian's Rainbow* (1968), are not of interest here, nor do I examine his television specials (which are discussed at length in my earlier book). This book is about Astaire's years as a star in the classical Hollywood era.

The elapsed time between the release of *Flying Down to Rio* (December 1933) and *Silk Stockings* (May 1957) is just shy of twenty-three years and five months (or 282 months). Imagine you lived through this quarter century—perhaps you did—and that you consistently went to the movies, as Americans did in historically high numbers, especially for the first two decades of Astaire's film career. Assuming you lived near a movie palace or neighborhood cinema—the studios Astaire worked at, chiefly RKO and MGM, mostly catered to urban audiences—how often could you expect a new Astaire picture to open? On average, a new Astaire musical hit the nation's theaters every nine months. There were some longish dry spells: twenty-seven months separated *The Sky's the Limit* (July 1943) from *Yolanda and the Thief* (November 1945)—of course, there was a war going on at the time. This gap between films was appreciably longer than the sixteen months separating the openings of *Blue Skies* (December 1946) and *Easter Parade* (May 1948), during which time Astaire very publicly retired from the screen then quickly returned for a third decade making screen dances. Sometimes two films came out in quick succession—*Three Little Words* in July, then *Let's Dance* in August of 1950; *Funny Face* in March, followed by *Silk Stockings* in May of 1957 (this second pair coming after a twenty-one-month absence for Astaire from the now much bigger, widescreen format). Astaire's 1930s at RKO, paired for nine films with Ginger Rogers plus one without her, stands out as his most intense in terms of sheer productivity. From *The Gay Divorcee* (October 1934) to *The Story of Vernon and Irene Castle* (March 1939), Astaire's audience never waited more than eight months between films; the RKO average was a new Astaire film every six months. This consistent output fed the intensity of Astaire and Rogers's following: they were ubiquitous in a way Astaire alone never really was in later decades.

From Astaire's perspective, the interval between the releases of his films was less important than the amount of time it took to make a film and the span of time off between films. As he stipulated in one contract, "After completion of all services required in each photoplay, and prior to the commencement of his services in the next photoplay, Fred Astaire is entitled to a rest period of 6 weeks."[82] Available data across the entirety of the Astaire corpus gives an average of six months from the end of production on one film to the start of production on the next. But this measure, reliant on production dates, misses the essential fact of Astaire's career: he made his musical numbers in a protracted process that took weeks and weeks of rehearsal on his own and with trusted assistants in rehearsal halls on the studio lots. Before he went into production on a film—literally stepping in front of the camera—Astaire had already put in substantial time. For the narrative musical films with daily studio data (leaving out the revue film *Ziegfeld Follies*), Astaire averaged forty-two days of rehearsal (seven six-day studio-standard workweeks) before shooting began. Further rehearsal after shooting on a film had begun brings his total average rehearsal days per film up to fifty-eight. On average, Astaire spent twenty weeks total—nearly half a year—on each of his films. This was not the experience of the normal studio-era movie star. Astaire's almost-quarter-century studio career was a near-continuous labor of screen dance making. The studios' need for new product "set the pace for artistic production and influenced the scope and scale of the entire work of art," which for Astaire I take to be the clip reel itself—the cumulative work of a life in the movies.[83] Asked in 1936, "Is it much of a job to get new dances for your succeeding pictures?" Astaire replied, "It's a terrific job."[84] It was—indeed—a job, analogous in its hours to many less glamorous lines of work. But it was also, undoubtedly, a calling. During one of his most unguarded interviews (with *Interview* magazine in 1973), Astaire allowed of his work, "Well, I don't know . . . it's just—it's a dedication of enthusiasm; I was wildly enthusiastic about doing what I did." *Interview*: "You really loved doing it?" Astaire: "Oh, yes."[85]

Astaire's career breaks down into four periods defined in large part by his relationship to specific work environments (or studios). His career trajectory is, in itself, distinctive among studio-era stars. Astaire's star persona is unconnected to any particular studio. Indeed, Astaire's creative identity—his "self-sufficiency"—comes into focus when his work at different studios and in different decades is compared. Throughout this book, I compare data on Astaire's work by period. As a final preparation before looking at the clip reel and the data, I summarize each period of Astaire's career.

Astaire defined his persona and creative practice at RKO in the 1930s. After the surprise success of his partnership with Ginger Rogers in minor roles in *Flying Down to Rio*, the pair made eight more films at the studio and Astaire made one without Rogers (*A Damsel in Distress* [1937]). After their second film together, *The Gay Divorcee*, Astaire quickly emerged as a very big star. Mark Sandrich, director of *The Gay Divorcee* and five other Astaire films, wrote him just weeks after the film opened: "How do you feel now!!, as I predict at this moment one of the most important names in Motion Pictures. [Critics across the country have] hailed you as a great personality and star."[86] Starting out at RKO gave Astaire a level of artistic license and power over the process unlikely to be found at any of the other four major studios. As scholar Johana E. Rapf has noted, RKO's "house style was shaped less by its producers than by its contracted artists and special effects personnel."[87] Given the unusual nature of musical numbers, especially the postproduction work syncing foot sounds, Astaire qualifies as both artist and special effects creator. Astaire grasped control of the production process on his dances and built relationships with collaborators such as Sandrich and producer Pandro S. Berman that allowed him to write his own creative ticket for a solid stretch of time—provided he work with Rogers. The generally solid box office performance of the Astaire-Rogers team supported Astaire's freedom to make his dances his way. Astaire also solidified his working methods while at

RKO: weeks in the seclusion of a rehearsal hall making dances for himself (and sometimes a partner) with only a pianist and musical assistant (in these years, Hal Borne) and a dance assistant (Hermes Pan, who was more or less around to the end of Astaire's career). The sheer amount of song and dance output of this period (ten films, fifty-two dances, nearly two hours of clip reel content) and the lack of any competing dance-oriented musical film figures turned Astaire-Rogers and Astaire alone into iconic figures—especially Astaire alone as he continued to make film musicals at a consistent rate for nearly twenty more years. Given the demise of the genre in the late 1950s, no one could ever catch up. Astaire's stature is, in part, due to a historical window that was, in effect, only open to him.

Astaire's second period—the seven years from 1940 to 1946—saw him make nine diverse film musicals, from low to big budget, including three in color. After spending the entirety of his first career period at one studio, in this second period Astaire worked all over town. He costarred twice with Bing Crosby at Paramount (working again with Sandrich on one of these [*Holiday Inn*]), twice with emerging star Rita Hayworth at Columbia (the first, *You'll Never Get Rich* [1941], was, in Hayworth's words, a "cheap picture"; the second, *You Were Never Lovelier* [1942], a "big budget picture"[88]), and once with dancing star Eleanor Powell at MGM (*Broadway Melody of 1940*). Astaire made a very cheap independent musical just for the chance to work with swing bandleader Artie Shaw (*Second Chorus* [1941]), returned for one more at a much-reduced RKO (*The Sky's the Limit*), and made two lavish films (his first in color) with the Arthur Freed unit at MGM and director Vincente Minnelli (*Ziegfeld Follies* [made 1944, released 1946] and *Yolanda and the Thief*). Astaire supposedly retired at age forty-seven with the release of Paramount's *Blue Skies*, costarring Crosby, in 1946—a signal year when movie attendance peaked in the United States. Astaire's second period produced nine films, forty-two numbers, and just under two hours of clip reel dancing.

But in 1948, Astaire came back, stepping in for an injured Gene Kelly in the Freed Unit's *Easter Parade* costarring Judy Garland. After this hit, Astaire made six more musicals in the next five years—all but two with Freed, all but one (*Let's Dance*, Paramount) at MGM—before the industry-wide adoption of widescreen formats in 1954. This group of seven color musicals made in the immediate postwar era and in the final years of the Academy aspect ratio (1.37) forms a third period in Astaire's career—one mostly spent at the musical-centric MGM (or, as they called it then, Metro). Between 1948 and

1953, Astaire made seven films and fifty numbers and added just over two hours to his clip reel.

The Hollywood studios converted to widescreen formats for all releases rapidly and decisively in spring 1953. (MGM was about to release *The Band Wagon* and considered trying to project it in the new format, worried it might "not hold up" beside widescreen images and stereophonic sound.[89]) Astaire was not part of the initial burst of widescreen musical production in 1954. His first widescreen effort premiered in 1955 (*Daddy Long Legs*) and two more followed each other closely in 1957 (*Funny Face* and *Silk Stockings*). All three were one-off production deals, albeit with some past collaborators, indicative of the collapse of the production system Astaire had provided with new dances for years. And then, the studio-era film musical genre and production units abruptly ceased to exist. Astaire went to television and made dances for another decade until he finally retired from dancing in 1968. Astaire's three widescreen musicals form a fourth period in his work with fifteen numbers and nearly forty minutes of dancing. And while Astaire's corpus of widescreen dances is comparatively small—yielding limited quantitative data—he made enough dances in widescreen for his strategies in the new format to be understood.[90]

ONE
NUMBERS

6. Film Musical Actions, Bodies, and Numbers

Musical films contain readily recognizable musical actions: singing, dancing, playing an instrument, or any combination of such. Given the Hollywood default toward narrative, musical actions are usually positioned within a story of some sort, although the relationship of musical actions to film musical plots varies greatly and is not of real interest here. Two qualities common to all film musical actions stand out as important for this quantitatively grounded study. First, music—and anything done to music, such as dancing—is a time-based art. On the most basic level, elapsed time (a measurable thing) makes up the raw material of film musical actions. Indeed, film musical actions often greedily burn long stretches of screen time. Some audiences relish basking in the special cinematic glow the genre throws off while singing and/or dancing goes on. Some audiences, of course, do not. The lone preview response card for *The Barkleys of Broadway* (1949) preserved in the Arthur Freed Collection at USC—carefully returned via business reply mail by an individual who self-identified as "Male, 18-30"—dismissed the film this way: "I DO NOT LIKE MUSICALS. I DID NOT ENJOY IT."[1] Put another way, "Male, 18-30" did not enjoy film musical actions. At the *Barkleys* premiere, "Male, 18-30" endured forty-one minutes of singing, dancing, and piano playing (the last of these courtesy of Oscar Levant)—40% of the film's run time. The gender of this respondent—however predictable (perhaps)—is worth noting. Given their quality of extension in time, film musical actions have an identifiable and fixed start and finish. And so, the duration of film musical actions in any film musical can be quantified, analyzed, and compared. For now, let's designate any sustained stretch of time in a film musical that is filled with musical actions as a musical number. (Speaking to the BBC, Astaire used the word *number* to describe what he made.[2]) And as I wrote in *Music Makes Me*, "the film musical" exists to serve "as a commercially viable host genre for musical numbers."[3]

Second, film musical actions involve expressive and excessive use of the body. Indeed, extraordinary uses of the body associated with the cultural category *musical* are, arguably, the central visual topic of the genre. The people—or the bodies—captured on film in film musical numbers are, in the act of screen singing and dancing, transformed into empowered film musical agents different from their nonmusical peers (a group Astaire reportedly referred to as "the dramatic people").[4] Writing in 1976, author James Baldwin wrote of the nonmusical stars John Wayne, Bette Davis, and Humphrey Bogart, "One does not go to see them act, one goes to watch them *be*."[5] Baldwin's turn of phrase doesn't work for musical stars doing musical acts: we go to watch Astaire (or Judy Garland or Gene Kelly) *do*. As film and dance scholar Adrienne L. McLean writes, "Dance cannot be a fictional treatment of itself in performance. To dance, one has to be able to do it, not merely to suggest it (as Albert Johnston puts it, 'The soaring leap is not *indicative* of a soaring leap, it *is* a soaring leap')."[6] Writer Zadie Smith goes further: "A musical is an act of pure chutzpah. You can't do a half-assed musical, with people half singing, half lip-syncing, sort of dancing but sort of not. Good dancing is never shameful—it's awe inspiring. To watch Astaire is to gasp."[7] (Later in this book, Bing Crosby's "sort of dancing" will offer an example to counter Smith's claim—as will select moves by Astaire: in both cases in the interests of masculine self-possession in the act of moving to music.) In a 1941 letter to the jazz and dance band magazine *Down Beat*, a fan of the music identified this difference between musical and nonmusical men on screen: he described the white jazz musicians who were beginning to appear in Hollywood musicals as "guys who can do something" and drew a contrast with leading men, such as Clark Gable, who just *were*. As I demonstrate in *Music Makes Me*, "Astaire's alignment with [jazz] musicians did much to reinforce his image as an unassailably masculine dancer."[8]

Bodies making or responding to music in the film musical enjoy a heightened subjectivity, varied in its intensity and duration by the musical actions they do. Not everyone in a given film musical is afforded the chance to become, by means of their own actions, this special sort of cinematic subject. For example, Alice Faye, a Fox singing star of the late 1930s and early 1940s, appeared in many film musicals opposite leading men who did not sing or dance.[9] Faye enjoyed agency within and beyond the narrative that her nonmusical costars did not. Film scholar Richard Dyer quantified the uneven distribution of musical power in *Meet Me in St. Louis* (1944) such that Tom Drake, who plays Garland's love interest, "only sings twelve notes."[10] By contrast, Astaire's leading ladies are almost always powerful film musical agents—equal to Astaire in their skills in some cases—who sing and dance, though typically dance ability is favored since, given how these films were made, the singing voice of an actor seen on screen could easily be replaced by that of another who is only heard.[11] Partnering female film musical agents who could keep up with him as dancers (to varying degrees) fundamentally shaped Astaire's heterosexual masculinity, giving him the opportunity to put dancing to work toward courtship. The promise of multiple dance numbers featuring a well-matched male-female couple sits at the core of the Astaire corpus.

Any and all agency granted nonwhite musical performers in the film musical relied on the power of the musical number.[12] Astaire and other white stars can be directly compared to Black dancers such as Bill Robinson, the Nicholas Brothers, or John W. Bubbles because the latter were granted some small presence as musical agents in the genre at the highest levels. Film scholar Miriam J. Petty has explored Robinson's career, foregrounding how "Black performers take distinct advantage of the peculiar and fleeting high-relief visibility afforded to them by racial difference. They create performances that are bounded by the strictures of American racism, yet that resonate and Signify in ways that exceed these same boundaries."[13] I make a complementary argument throughout this book: Astaire, a white man working within the same "strictures of American racism," was afforded a capacious and unequal chance to create a body of work that, in its sprawling extent, carves out the boundaries of a specific whiteness. With on-demand access to the corpus of studio-era film, we can juxtapose Astaire and Black artists at will. Audiences of the time had to make these comparisons by way of memory as Astaire never appeared in a film with top-flight nonwhite dancing peer talents. Film scholar Ryan Jay Friedman has explored the inherent tension when Black musical stars (pianist Hazel Scott, singer Lena Horne) and a white musical star (dancer Eleanor Powell) both appear in the same film (*I Dood It* [1943]).[14] Astaire never found himself in (or allowed) a similar situation.[15] And so, a constitutive element of Astaire's whiteness is its structural avoidance of juxtaposition with nonwhite others: by denying nonwhite dancers a presence in his numbers (with the exception that proves the rule in "A Shine on Your Shoes") and by severely limiting nonwhite performers' access to the production machine that made the studio-era screen dance body. Whiteness inheres in the film musical as an expensive, essentially special effects action genre where nonwhite performers are almost never seen or heard. Singing and dancing whiteness is—in itself—a white studio-made thing, as Dyer notes when he refers to the "White so-called integrated musicals."[16] I return to this structural aspect of Astaire's and the Hollywood musical's whiteness later from a quantitative perspective.

Of course, film musical agents—human subjects empowered by the act of song and dance—also function as objects offered up for the viewer's delight and judgment. Film musical bodies make a spectacle of themselves and make of themselves the central spectacle of the genre. Film musical agents, however empowered by their actions, are also exposed and vulnerable. The implications for Astaire—a white man—in offering himself as an object to any and all viewers are considered at length in this book, including the significant moment in *The Sky's the Limit* when Astaire climbs atop a table in a canteen for servicemen during World War II and does a "snake dance" at the demand of Robert Ryan, another (and a conventionally virile) white man. This odd episode—far from the only time Astaire dances for a watching white man—enacts in directly humiliating terms the underlying risk to masculine self-possession involved when any straight man dances while others, especially other men, watch (a situation that obtained for "Male, 18-30" at the *Barkleys* preview as well as any man watching any Astaire film at any time). Astaire's strange (and forgotten) fragmentary dance for Ryan, returned to in section forty-five, finds its context within the normative forcefulness of Astaire's intentionally masculinized screen body. In addition to his use of everyday (rather than "trained") dance gestures and jazz-derived (Black) musical styles, Astaire relied on the power of virtuoso technique, an inner-directed demeanor, and an explicitly aggressive attitude toward others to project his dancing as an act of masculine agency rather than feminized display.[17]

In sum, the commercial feature film genre of the musical offers up a projected world, bounded by time and fixed in content, where select agents—individuals who can sing, dance, etc., and who, the vast majority of the time, are white—execute actions with their bodies understood to be musical. Such actions are distinguished from nonmusical actions by their content (a voice used to sing rather than speak), their form (structured in response to the shape of a popular tune or the beat of a drum), and the technological processes behind their making (filmed to playback). The status of film musical agents begins with access to the capital-intensive industrial plants where musicals were made (a nearly exclusive whites-only zone). Film musicals make a generic contract with their audience promising that select individuals in the film can, may, and will burst forth into musical actions at any moment. Who these subjects are is usually known well in advance; indeed, the chance to see certain individuals doing musical acts is the genre's drawing card. Erin Brannigan describes film musical audiences' "state of sustained expectation."[18] Movie audiences watching a musical wait, full of hope or dread (as "Male, 18-30" at the *Barkleys* preview likely did), for the next musical number to start. Once begun, the reverse obtains: wishing for the dancing to stop, longing for it to go on and on. This oscillation between two sorts of screen time—musical actions (or numbers) done by specific musical agents, nonmusical actions (the default mode for most feature genres) done by anyone on screen—welcomes a quantification of content perhaps unique to the musical among Hollywood genres. Musical time is distinct from nonmusical time in the film musical, just as musical actions (performed with the body and loaded with contradictory meanings for the performer's agency and objectification) stand out from nonmusical actions. Thus, musical numbers, understood as sustained stretches of musical action, can be counted.

7. Counting Numbers Like Hollywood Did

Film musicals were the special effects genre of the studio era—the costliest sort of film to make and the most directly spectacular in their content. Film musical makers understood that counting musical numbers was central to effective production planning and (hopefully) eventual profitability. As Mark Sandrich, director of five Astaire-Rogers pictures, told a reporter in 1937, "Do you realize . . . that we have less time for story development in a picture of this type that we would have in a straight short subject? In the average dramatic feature one hour and forty minutes, or the full running length, can be devoted to story development and character portrayal. In an Astaire-Rogers film we usually have thirty-five minutes of music and dancing—four or five routines. Each of these requires at least four minutes of introduction, so that they fit logically into whatever story we have time left for. You figure it out."[19] Sandrich was a bit over on his stats: the average duration of musical numbers in Sandrich's Astaire-Rogers films is twenty-nine minutes. While planning *Follow the Fleet* (1936), Sandrich drew up a multicolor comparative timeline chart of the first four Astaire-Rogers films that placed every minute of each film into one of six categories: story, titles, music, singing, dancing, and novelty.[20] Sandrich's categories can in turn be sorted: nonmusical actions and screen time (story, titles, music) and musical actions and screen time (singing, dancing, novelty [which for him meant numbers like the title song in *Flying Down to Rio*, which used back projections and giant fans to put dancing girls on the wings of airplanes in flight]).[21] For the nonmusical story portions, the normal approach of estimating a film's length and cost by way of script pages and number of settings worked fine. An estimating script for *Top Hat* (1935) notes, "This estimate covers [dramatic or narrative] action and reaction only as designated in musical numbers. No allowance is made for the musical numbers themselves."[22] Predicting the costs of musical screen time required other methods. Production documents reveal the genre-specific ways the studios counted the quantity, type, and length of musical numbers.

During preproduction for *Blue Skies* (1946), Paramount researched the extent of the music in the 1938 Irving Berlin film *Alexander's Ragtime Band*, a musical, like *Blue Skies*, that featured many old Berlin songs. Paramount's summary of *Alexander's* gave the picture's length (106 minutes) and the number of "vocals" (22) and concluded by dividing all the music in the film into two categories: "Visual-vocal time of music in the picture was *42 minutes*. Including scoring, main title, end, and connecting paraphrase music going from one café to another, the time of music in the picture was *51 minutes*."[23] *Visual-vocal* is one industry term of art for what I am here calling musical numbers. *Visual-instrumental* is the analogous term for dance-only numbers. The other sort of music—"scoring, main title, end, and connecting paraphrase" (which added up to nine minutes of *Alexander's*) is of no interest here: this book is about musical numbers only. By simple math, this document gives 40% of *Alexander's* run time as musical numbers. By my count, only five of Astaire's films reach this percentage: two of those (*Holiday Inn* [1942], *Easter Parade* [1948]) feature old and new Berlin tunes; *Blue Skies* gets close with 38%. (Appendix One column E gives the percentage of total run time taken up by musical numbers in Astaire's films.)

The sum totals for *Alexander's* are followed on the Paramount document by a prose description of the anticipated numbers in *Blue Skies*, with comments (emphasis original) such as: "This is the romantic dance and should not last longer than 3½ choruses. About *3 minutes*"; "Since this is the so-called important prod[uction] number, we can allow *6 to 7 minutes* for it, but certainly not longer"; and "It is difficult to judge the timing on this number before it has been staged, but it certainly shouldn't run more than *5 minutes*." An unaccompanied solo by tap dancer Paul Draper—Astaire replaced Draper shortly after *Blue Skies* started production—is estimated down to the quarter minute. The refrain "shouldn't take longer than . . . " runs across the document: setting the outside possible length of a given number was key for producers managing a film's cost and for the makers of the numbers once their work began. A second count of the musical numbers in *Blue Skies* on this document commits the production team to specific timings—there's a column of figures and a total—and offers further evidence for how numbers were understood as parts of the film. Songs are designated as "[Bing] Crosby solo," "Crosby and [Olga] San Juan," "Draper solo," and "Draper & 8 Girls." Duration, function (romantic duet, "so-called important prod. Number"), and personnel ("8 girls"—no more) are all agreed to in this document, which attempts to nail down on paper the content and extent of film musical actions.

Thinking about the musical actions in a film was also creative and speculative, as seen in a "tentative list of the Numbers that we are contemplating" for "the Astaire-Hutton picture" that would become *Let's Dance* (1950). This undated document from before shooting began has the producers—again at Paramount though a different bunch from *Blues Skies*—balancing the content of a film musical between the studio's star, Betty Hutton, and their one-picture engagement of Astaire. They projected nine numbers. *Let's Dance* has nine numbers, though not all the ones anticipated here. Excerpts from the document follow, with information in square brackets detailing how the plan played out in the finished film.[24]

> "1. Hutton singing; Astaire dancing and singing. This is the USO Unit Show in the interior of a Hangar—runs approximately 3 minutes and is a straight number." [Realized as "Can't Stop Talkin'," a song and partner dance in a quasi-jitterbug style for Hutton and Astaire that opens the film.]
>
> "2. Astaire dancing solo. Instrumental only. This is music around Astaire's piano noodling. Astaire working on this now. In fact, the number is practically all laid out. . . . Incidentally, these are the two numbers which Astaire would very much like to record and photograph ahead of our Production date." [Completed as the "Ad Lib" or "Piano Dance," a tour-de-force solo featuring Astaire playing piano.[25] Astaire always wanted to control when a given number was shot within work on a film. An analogous memo for *The Belle of New York* (1952) notes of Astaire's solo, "I Wanna Be a Dancin' Man," "Mr. Astaire prefers to do this number at the end of the picture. It is partly staged. We have laid it out musically and it runs 4:35."[26]]

"3. This is an Astaire number in which he tells the child a Fairy tale in modern Broadway idioms; except that it is a Fairy tale I cannot tell you any more about it at this time." [The notion of "an Astaire number" is key—it means Astaire is the primary musical agent and that he controls the number's content. In the end, this number became "Jack and the Beanstalk," an Astaire vocal followed by a very short dance—just thirty-five seconds—done in one shot, the last taken on the picture. The extreme brevity of this dance and its abrupt ending—Astaire hits his head on a wall and crawls into bed, apparently knocked out—suggests the desire (and the need) to finally just finish *Let's Dance*.]

"4. This is a cowboy or western number—the first real double number of Astaire and Hutton in the café during a regular performance. There will be no more than 16 girls in the line behind them." ["Oh, Them Dudes" ended up a comic duo song and dance with no chorus girls. Because Hutton danced with Astaire at the film's start, it was effectively their second "double number."]

5.–7. Three proposed vocal numbers for Hutton, one pegged as a comic "novelty"—Hutton's specialty. Hutton's final yield was just one solo vocal: "Why Fight the Feeling," a strange torch song, involving a patio heater, that ends with Hutton jumping into a lake to cool her (literally) smoking rear end.

"8. Is a highly imaginative instrumental only solo by Astaire. This is not worked out at all; this is the culmination and we have referred to it as 'The Thought Dance.' This will be mostly (if it is done) photographic effects and tricks." [Astaire did not make this solo number, although it remained in the plan well into production. He did, however, make a very brief romantic duo dance with Hutton—she's conjured up in Astaire's mind in white chiffon—using photographic effects, such as Hutton appearing and disappearing. This is the only routine in the film that finds no mention in this document.]

"9. The Finale Number must be on full stage with 16 girls, that gives us an opportunity to take our principals off stage and play out the story inside the number. If the Studio makes arrangements with [songwriter Frank] Loesser for a number that he has written which is not a part of the present deal, called 'Tunnel of Love' it will be very easy to set up and I can describe it to you in detail. However, I cannot do this until we have made proper arrangements with Loesser." [Paramount did acquire "Tunnel of Love," so the plan suggested here went forward. Notable is the need for a song that allows Hutton and Astaire to leave a performance in progress that continues in their absence while they go backstage, to resolve the plot in developments unrelated to the ongoing number, and then return for a celebratory bit of song and dance to close the picture. Inclusion of the chorus girls (in the film, girls and boys) was a formal necessity. While the leads are off stage, the number as experienced in the film ceases to claim the viewer's attention—it functionally stops—to "play out the story." An actual tunnel of love, a very elaborate set for the supper club setting, serves to float Astaire and Hutton on and off stage and the film in and out of film musical time.]

This document describes the content of given musical numbers—such as "Astaire dancing solo"—and shows Astaire creatively at work on *Let's Dance* at a specific moment in the filmmaking process. The "Ad Lib Dance," at this point, was ready to go before the camera: this solo, along with "Can't Stop Talking" and "Oh, Them Dudes," was shot as Astaire wished before production officially "opened" (when work on the dialogue scenes involving non-musical performers began).[27] By contrast, the "Thought Dance" was just an idea and eventually adapted into something else. It is crucial to understand all musical numbers in every film as similarly the result of creative and budgetary negotiations and exploration, each impacted by the larger, time-constrained process of making a complex film musical whole. Often studio archives reveal something of these contingencies and a few cut numbers leave a trace there. Yet, for this study I remain focused on the final cut: my quantitative approach deals mostly with what was eventually committed to film and commercially released.

Another type of studio document, this time produced at the other end of the production process, provides a further example of how studios precisely counted musical actions (or numbers). Cue sheets are regularly prepared for legal purposes when a film is ready for release. These documents list every second of music in a film by cue (a continuous piece of music), name the owners for the copyrightable content in each cue (usually the composer or songwriters and the publisher), and categorize the cue by the prominence of its use.[28] Cue sheets document all the music in a film by quantifying the duration of each use (in seconds) and indicating something of the importance of each. (Cue sheets also indicate when a sound is or is not, for legal purposes, properly musical. The cue sheet for *Daddy Long Legs* notes, "Between cue 7 and 8 Jervis [Astaire] throws his drum stick at his cymbal causing musical sound for 3 sec. (unimportant)."[29])

Three binaries typically structure the definition of use on Hollywood cue sheets: background/visual, instrumental/vocal, and partial/entire. Musical numbers are typically categorized as visual (individuals within the film are seen singing, dancing, and/or playing) and entire (the cue has formal integrity, presenting a song whole). Musical numbers listed as visual and partial are best understood as fragments: for instance, the three times in *Easter Parade* when a rehearsal pianist plays while Garland and Astaire awkwardly dance together for the first time, entered on the film's cue sheet as "visual instrumental partial" cues of three, fifty-seven, and twenty seconds in length, respectively.[30] The formal distinction between partial and entire proves an important guide later as we quantify the extent of Astaire's creative labors and sort them into categories. The distinction between instrumental and vocal indicates the absence or presence of singing and, for copyright purposes, the lyrics. The presence on a film's cue sheet of multiple cues categorized as "visual vocal entire" or "visual instrumental entire" indicates that the film is a musical. In this way, cue sheets define the genre of the musical quantitatively as understood by the studios' legal and accounting departments.

Cue sheets account for musical content in units (cues) determined down to the second, an approach at the heart of the studio process of making movies and of this study. Cues as a measurement of musical sound are analogous to numbers as a measurement of musical actions—both measured in seconds. Cue sheets are, however, insufficient for my purposes because they track the use of music rather than the actions of bodies—and, in any event, I have located only five cue sheets among the twenty-nine films in the corpus.[31] My research process involved creating a cue sheet tracking musical actions for every one of Astaire's films. This entailed the quintessential digital humanities task of deciding when, in Astaire's twenty-nine films, any and all musical actions start and stop.

8. 324 Beginnings and 324 Endings

Film musical numbers begin and end at definable moments. Criteria for marking these beginnings and endings are typically clear—the dissatisfied "Male, 18-30" at *Barkleys* could have told us—and often evident simultaneously in several domains.

Endings are often indicated by a decisive harmonic close in the music followed by the silencing of the music and an end to singing and/or danced movement—usually with a pose by the performer that says "all done" or an exit from the scene. Applause from an in-film audience, when present, answers these overdetermined ending actions and, sometimes, precipitates bows from the in-film performers. The combination of decisive musical closure, final pose or exit, and applause occurs some 42% of the time in the Astaire clip reel: it is the most common way his musical numbers end. When an on-screen audience is absent, a pause after the musical close often makes space for applause in the movie theater—the context for which the studios made these films. When watching film musicals alone or at home with a few others—as most of us do now most of the time—the pause after a number designed to accommodate applause from cinema audiences can feel like a lag or a lull. This bit of awkwardness for contemporary viewers registers the loss of the film musical's original social location in theaters, at a time when theaters were the only place to see moving pictures.

Properly timing musical number endings to activate movie theater audience applause was a direct concern for Astaire. In an early draft of his memoir, he wrote, "It is not easy to get applause in a movie but when you get it—it means something. I build for applause climaxes and it comes vociferously at previews and openings and early parts of the runs—but quite often I have caught one of my pictures after awhile and heard not one hand all through the picture." According to Astaire, his desire for movie house applause wasn't driven by nostalgia for live performance. Rather, he was after audible evidence for the intended impact of his cinematic creations. "I found working before the camera much more interesting than theatre appearances. Many people told me, 'Oh you will miss the audience's reaction. You'll miss the applause.' It was not so. I did not miss any of those things. My numbers were built for applause reactions and when they were right they would get them from the movie theatre audiences."[32] After attending a preview of *Carefree* (1938) in Pomona, Astaire wrote to director Mark Sandrich about each number in the film that did not get applause and made suggestions on how to recut the film to ensure the reaction he wanted. The matter was urgent: of his "Golf Solo," Astaire wrote, "That thing has got to get a hand." The fade-out on "The Yam," he thought, was "*too short.*" Lengthening the fade would do the trick. Key to these choices, Astaire wrote, was making sure the audience was "given time to know the number is over."[33] After a preview of *Shall We Dance* (1937), composer George Gershwin similarly weighed in by letter to Sandrich on the transition between Ginger Rogers's vocal chorus of "They All Laughed" and the duo dance that followed. He wrote: "The choruses I thought were excellent, but the recorded applause after her rendition of it somewhat too long and a little too much time was taken up before the announcement of Petrov's [Astaire] dancing with her. I realize that there is a point you are trying to get over, but perhaps in some way this could be shortened as I think it would tighten the number considerably."[34] Without a live audience to help gauge the timing, as performers in live theater do at every performance, film musical makers had to guess the pacing of transitions from musical to nonmusical actions. And by the preview point in the filmmaking process, tweaking the timing after or between musical numbers was just about the only remaining way to adjust creative work done months earlier (perhaps one reason it was the topic of post-preview conversation).

The beginning of a musical number can be a bit harder to pin down but is usually also clear. In general, I understand the beginning of a number as the moment when film musical agents move decisively and definitively toward musical actions—for instance, when a number performed on stage for an in-film audience turns away from any conversation backstage or in the audience and attends directly to the number itself. At such moments, film musical time takes over and a musical number begins. Moments like this might happen after the instrumental introduction to a number has already begun, perhaps in the background behind ongoing dialogue, as in the title number from *Top Hat*. I count the start of "Top Hat, White Tie, and Tails" from the first shot of the theater stage where Astaire performs the number, just after he tells his manager Horace to get him a plane "with wings." Numbers begin when the musical agents in the film set aside anything but musical actions.

The shift to dancing is fraught with peril—especially for men. Early in *West Side Story* (1961), the Jets gang strides menacingly down the street. Then, a member of the gang steps into the street and does a dance step. This shift from nonmusical action (walking) to musical action (dancing) is a deal-breaker for musical-resistant viewers: *West Side Story* is clearly not about tough young men from the streets but about trained dancers who have spent years in the studio and mastered a highly codified dance style. As detailed throughout this book, Astaire's transition into dancing minimizes such disjunctive moments by way of character identity (he plays an entertainer of some kind in three-quarters of his films) and by building his personal dance style on moves that spring from daily life (such as walking) rather than any recognizable dance tradition. The ease with which Astaire slips into "the dance" will be seen to fundamentally support his cis-het masculinity and likely explains much of his equal popularity with male and female audiences during his career.[35]

The shift to singing, however subtle, is always marked. Astaire's singing is, at once, something unusual for a white man to do on screen and something expected for *him*, one of a small fraternity of studio-era singing white men, to do. The beginning of "No Strings (I'm Fancy Free)" (again *Top Hat*) is the most gradual example of this shift in Astaire's output—Astaire only starts singing on the second line of the lyric. But transitions like this are unusual. Typically the shift from speaking to singing is clear, as in the start of Astaire's vocal in "Isn't This a Lovely Day?" (also *Top Hat*).[36] The transition from talking to singing—a shift in the technologies of capturing sound from direct recording on the set to lip-syncing to playback—can be tricky to make in one shot. See, for instance, Garland's vocal entrance on the title song at the close of *Easter Parade*. Standing facing Astaire, she winks at him then runs past him, toward the camera, and quickly turns her back just before she starts singing. This thoroughly unmotivated blocking, likely staged by director Charles Walters, allows Garland to begin lip-syncing to her prerecorded vocal at a moment when her mouth is not visible to the camera. The blocking responds to the musical arrangement, which gives Garland no rhythmic indication for when to come in—she turns her back to the camera for a moment to catch her prerecorded voice. Director Stanley Donen repeated this stratagem with Astaire at the start of "He Loves and She Loves" in *Funny Face*, although Donen's blocking is less contrived: Astaire, realizing his love for Audrey Hepburn, walks in circles and (conveniently) has his back to the camera (and us) when his vocal begins. The lack of aural perspective in prerecorded vocals means his voice is not impacted by the changing position of his body relative to the camera and always sounds as if he's facing us—or, as he in fact is, the microphone. Of such choices is the screen singing body made. The musical arrangement of "Isn't This a Lovely Day?" contains just enough rhythmic information about when the vocal comes in for Astaire to move from speaking to singing in the same shot. Watch the start of the vocal to "Drum Crazy" (*Easter Parade*) for an analogous situation, with less rhythmic information in the arrangement, where Astaire's first lip movements are slightly early. Indeed, shifting from nonmusical to musical actions in the same shot is typically avoided in Astaire's films (data on his practice follows). The normative practice of isolating musical and nonmusical actions in separate shots gives empirical heft to the shot-by-shot accounting for Astaire's screen singing and

44 ASTAIRE BY NUMBERS

dancing in this book. I count numbers as beginning at the start of the first shot done to playback; I count numbers as ending at the end of the last shot done to playback (shots of applause or bows are not included in the total for a number). This approach grounds my data for the duration and count of shots in a number in the industrial practices behind how these films were made.

By this definition and by my count, there are 324 musical numbers in the Astaire corpus. By implication, there are 324 beginnings (when someone in the film initiates unmistakably musical actions) and 324 endings (when the film reverts to nonmusical action and the characters again act like they're in any other genre). Of these 324 musical numbers, 207 (almost precisely two-thirds) begin with or eventually involve Astaire acting as a film musical agent. Break these career numbers down by film and the average Astaire film has eleven numbers, with Astaire in seven—again about two-thirds. Averaging his output as a whole and by film, the chance that Astaire will initiate or join any sort of musical number remains stable—the first of many pieces of evidence for his normative practices and presence in the corpus. There are, however, films that do not fall along this two-thirds average. In three films—*Top Hat*, *Carefree* (1938), and *You'll Never Get Rich* (1941)—Astaire participates in every musical number. He dominates the musical content of these films, at least as measured by our initial count of musical numbers (with all numbers treated as functionally equal). The Astaire film with the fewest Astaire numbers is, unsurprisingly, *Blues Skies*: of the seventeen numbers in this Bing Crosby vehicle, Astaire participates in just four (24%). Granted, Astaire's four prove significant, even signature moments (one is his solo "Puttin' on the Ritz"), but there's an awful lot of the other, more dominant cis-het white male film musical agent (or star)—Crosby—in *Blue Skies*. Crosby even gets the girl. *Blue Skies* is the only time Astaire ends a film without winning a romantic female partner.[37]

9. The Structural Whiteness of the Astaire Corpus and the Studio-Era Film Musical

How quantifiably white are the film musicals Astaire made? Counting the presence of white and non-white performers in each of the 324 numbers in the Astaire corpus provides one answer to this question. As shown in Table 1, 97% of the 324 numbers in Astaire's films include only white performers. For Astaire's 207 numbers, the result is the same—97% white only. Only six

TABLE 1 Numbers in the Astaire corpus by race of performers and racial performance

	Total	White Performers Only	%	With Non-White Performers	%	With White Performers in Blackface, Brownface, or Yellowface	%
All Numbers in Astaire Films	324	313	97%	11	3%	12	4%
Numbers including Astaire	207	201	97%	6	3%	9	4%

FIGURE 9.1

Astaire numbers include nonwhite performers—in all but one case, Black.[38] The nonwhite, not Black exception is Olga San Juan as Astaire's partner in "Heat Wave," a theatrical number. Of Nuyorican (New York–born Puerto Rican) descent, San Juan enjoyed a brief Hollywood career. In a featured role in *Blue Skies*—San Juan and Astaire are not associated romantically in the plot—her pale skin and brown hair present as white (she speaks without an accent), but she performs a range of rather sexy numbers, always in revealing costumes (fig. 9.1). San Juan's ethnic persona is so underdeveloped she is absent from scholarship on Latinas in Hollywood.

Was Rita Hayworth a nonwhite leading lady when she costarred with Astaire in *You'll Never Get Rich* and *You Were Never Lovelier* (1942) early in her career? Hayworth was born Rita Cansino. Her father, a friend of Astaire's from his vaudeville years, was Spanish dancer Eduardo Cansino;

her mother, Volga Hayworth, also a dancer, was of Irish and English descent. Film scholars Adrienne L. McLean and Priscilla Peña Ovalle similarly situate Hayworth's time opposite Astaire as crucial to her definitive emergence as white. McLean traces publicity stories that tracked Hayworth's transition into a "glamour girl" (a white category) by foregrounding her physical transformation—from "jet black" to "russet-haired"—and remaining intentionally ambiguous about her background.[39] Ovalle adds, "Hayworth's racial mobility was facilitated by her partnership with Fred Astaire because he legitimized her dance abilities and helped redefine her sexuality as more American and (slightly) less threatening to the movie-going public."[40] But crucial to Hayworth's whiteness as danced with Astaire was her ability, foregrounded in both films, to dance in a Black idiom that had been absorbed into whiteness as Astaire presented it from the mid-1920s on. Hayworth's whiteness is, in part, made by her knowledge of Black dance and culture. An instance that nudges up against direct admission comes just before the dancing starts in "The Shorty George." As I noted in *Music Makes Me*, Hayworth delivers the last line of the vocal "in a rather heavy black accent. Suddenly they're not just singing about a black character and preparing to do a black dance, but they're indulging in a bit of racial caricature that simultaneously cements their romantic relationship. Only Hayworth does the accent: Astaire never does."[41] As will be shown again and again, holding himself aloof from "the accent" and other racial markers was a basic whiteness strategy for Astaire. Yet both Astaire-Hayworth films also include Latin aspects. *You Were Never Lovelier* is set among the Buenos Aires upper crust—Hayworth and her character's family are nonaccented members— and features Xavier Cugat and his Orchestra, the best-known Latin band in the United States at the time. Astaire does a solo number with Cugat's group—for an audience of one: Adolph Menjou—but when Hayworth crashes a rehearsal and asks to hear a number, Cugat's group, playing "The Shorty George," suddenly sounds like a generic American swing band (in other words, a mix of Black and white). In *You'll Never Get Rich*, Astaire and Hayworth (with the decidedly Anglo-Saxon character name Sheila Winthrop) do a Latin-themed dance (marked by above-the-head arm gestures and Latin motion in Hayworth's hips) to "So Near and Yet So Far," a song with no directly exotic elements in lyrics or music.[42] Of course, as I wrote elsewhere, "It seems self-evident, but it needs to be pointed out that Astaire could never have performed a partner dance, nor sung a romantic or novelty duet, with an African American female partner."[43] Partnering

Hayworth and San Juan—Latinas who themselves crossed over into whiteness—was as close to nonwhite as Astaire went in his female partners.

A second way to measure whiteness in the Astaire corpus tallies up numbers where white performers don blackface, brownface, or yellowface— whether by way of actual makeup or in costuming, scenic, musical, and choreographic content. This sort of racial mimicry—a presumption to perform as a racial other reserved for whites only—occurs slightly more frequently in the Astaire corpus than do numbers with actual nonwhite performers: twelve among the 324 total numbers, nine of Astaire's 207 numbers (4% in both cases). Astaire himself appears in racial drag three times: blackface ("Bojangles of Harlem" [*Swing Time* (1936)]), yellowface ("Limehouse Blues" [*Ziegfeld Follies* (1946)]), and brownface ("Steppin' Out With My Baby" [*Easter Parade*]). The first of these has received much scholarly attention. As author Megan Pugh pointed out, Astaire's blackface routine, together with another by Eleanor Powell, "may have been presented as tributes to Bill Robinson, but they were also ways to demonstrate a mastery of black dance, with Robinson representing that larger whole."[44] Of course, Astaire used Black style pervasively across his work: it is a structural element of his particular brand of whiteness reaching back to his years on Broadway.[45] In a few numbers that do not feature outright racial mimicry, Astaire gets close to admitting the Black roots of his style. As I wrote in *Music Makes Me*, "the overdetermined blackness of 'The Shorty George' suggests a more frank admission of the African American sources of swing than the studio system customarily allowed."[46] "The Yam" (*Carefree*) offers another such example. But outward appearance matters in the making of whiteness out of Blackness—so I do not include numbers like "The Shorty George" or "The Yam" in this count of racial stereotypes in the Astaire corpus.

"Bojangles," "Steppin' Out," and "Limehouse" wear their nonwhiteness literally on their made-up faces. In four Astaire numbers, other white performers put on racial types but Astaire does not. All four are Latin in location: the Caribbean ("Heat Wave" [*Blue Skies*] and "I Left My Hat in Haiti" [*Royal Wedding* (1951)]) and a fictitious Latin American country (the dream ballet and "Coffee Time" in *Yolanda and the Thief* [1945]). In these fantasies of nonwhite otherness, Astaire retains his status as white relative to the exotics around him—even though these exotic subjects are all played by whites (excluding San Juan). While they dress in native or tropical garb, Astaire appears in a light-colored suit or nautical blazer—uniforms of the rich colonial male in the tropics. One of these numbers, "I Left My Hat in

Haiti," toys with white men as sexual tourists and the staging suggests Astaire left his "hat" with many women along his journey. Notably, a monkey returns it to him at the close of the number.

The vague white Hollywood mix of tropical, Middle Eastern, and Spanish motifs in the first version of "Begin the Beguine" (*Broadway Melody of 1940*) finds Astaire nearing the borders of cis-het white masculinity. His specially designed dance costume in this routine—one of just five numbers where he's not wearing everyday men's street clothes or a uniform—serves as a key indicator of Astaire edging toward nonwhite effeminacy.[47] (The budgets and contracts for Astaire's films typically stipulated he would provide his own wardrobe. The continuity of his clothes across the decades remains a constituent element of his masculine persona, even if, as musicologist Oren Vinogradov notes, "there remains little evidence that Astaire's particular [sartorial] style was taken up by any considerable portion of mid-century American men."[48]) Clothes, of course, make—and potentially unmake—the man. In "Begin the Beguine," Astaire wears a quasi-matador costume, resplendent with sequins, cut tightly at the waist, and form-fitting around the hips and buttocks, giving him something of an hourglass figure (fig. 9.2). His bodily dimensions and curves—usually concealed in a man's suit—are instead emphasized. This rare glimpse of the contours of Astaire's body is explained by the vaguely flamenco nature of the dance: he is, in fact, sporting an exotic type toward the white end of the spectrum: Spanish (suggesting that the distance Hayworth and San Juan needed to travel to read as white was not all that far). His partner in the number, Eleanor Powell, tilts much further toward racial caricature in her midriff-exposing harem-style costume, but such bodily display comes as no surprise for the female screen dance body, whether white or not (Powell put on various brown types in her career,

FIGURE 9.2

including two hula numbers, one in taps). The dance content of Astaire and Powell's exotic dance is dealt with in section forty-two.

Counting and comparing the marginal inclusion of nonwhite performers and the slightly larger allowance for whites to perform as nonwhites puts another metric on the overwhelming whiteness of the studio musical. The vast majority of the time, musical numbers in the Astaire corpus feature white performers presenting as white—always with the caveat that whiteness in this popular culture sphere often draws on Black performance tropes. Literary scholar Franco Moretti has explored the notion of accounting for "character-space" in literary works and argues that "measurement matters so much: it makes some concepts 'actual' in the strong sense of the word; it takes character-space, and proves that there is something in the real world (the real world of fictions) that corresponds to it." The musical number space available for nonwhite performers and for white performers presenting nonwhite stereotypes can also be measured. This space—unlike "the real world of fictions"—was, in the moment of production, a concrete expression of Jim Crow popular culture, measured in the career prospects that opened ample room for Astaire but virtually no space for nonwhite others (unless, like San Juan and Hayworth, they could negotiate their own nonwhiteness). As Moretti adds, such measurement is "new because it's precise."[49] Looking rather bluntly at simple presence in film musical numbers, the aforementioned counts of nonwhite performers and caricatures put a precise number on the extent of whiteness in the Astaire corpus (counted by performers in musical numbers): 97% white only, with more allowance for whites to play nonwhites (4%) than for nonwhites to appear on screen (3%). This metric for white dominance can be compared to Richard Jean So's measurement of the prevalence of whites among all authors published by Random House between 1950 and 2000: also 97%.[50]

The fact of the studio system's whiteness—the nature of the studios as fundamentally white studios—must underpin any analysis of the genre. Richard Dyer makes this point with reference to the content of a single film, *Meet Me in St. Louis*.

> The recognition of the role of blacks in creating the wealth that the Smiths [the film's central family] enjoy is absent. Such reference as there is to African-Americans—the coon song, Tootie and Esther's not-quite cakewalk, a statue in the hall—is entirely within the comfortable containment of the black image within entertainment. . . . The perfection of the film may be

based, in other words, on an appalling moral, political, historical suppression.... It is more a case that what made *Meet Me in St. Louis* possible—the confident establishment of the white family—was achieved at the cost of black lives.[51]

Quantitative methods can make a similar point across the corpus of musicals—in this case, those including Astaire, whose interest in Black music and dance might have driven greater engagement with actual Black performers. Not so. As I wrote in *Music Makes Me*, "However, relative to the talents and presence of black performers in the world of show business, Astaire's list of interracial numbers is paltry. Any student of the Hollywood musical feels this lack even when celebrating the careers of black musical stars."[52] Putting a number on this lack is important—as Moretti notes, for the sake of precision—but also as an expression of the degree to which the musical was a white space in a segregated culture. As film scholar Sean Cubitt has noted of classical Hollywood, using Astaire's whiteness grounded on Black style as an example: "Classicism thrives on the displaced dialectic of apartheid America. . . . Astaire's assimilation of African-American vernacular dance for a Europeanized white-tie-and-tails ballet is the type of the fantastic desire to overcome difference, the aspirational utopianism annulled in the spectacular commodity.... This desire is, it scarcely needs repeating, historically specific."[53] Cubitt elsewhere highlights the surface of the classical film: a surface where Astaire's screen dance body finds its home. He continues, "The question of being cannot therefore be posed directly of classical film, nor can it be rephrased as a dialectical or deconstructive reversal between presence and absence. As spectacle, the classical film is literally a surface, a border between presence and absence.... The power of classical cinema to evoke fantasy derives from this ambivalent position. To understand its ramifications, we need to ask: whose fantasy is this?"[54] The short answer is Astaire's and the other white people who made these films and went to see them. Systemic racism explains these statistical measures of racial inequality in the Astaire films. All of the creative choices Astaire made as discussed in the remainder of this book—regarding shot length, how his body was framed, which steps he used where, etc.—were enabled by the access he enjoyed to the almost entirely whites-only commercial system that made these films. The product of his labor—the clip reel—directly expresses this racially segregated space and is itself constitutive of whiteness. As I have noted elsewhere, "The fact [Astaire] was white made it all possible."[55]

The overwhelming whiteness of Astaire's corpus and his personal dominance of the genre across the studio era can also be precisely measured by comparison with other dancers' careers. Table 2 quantifies the film musical careers of thirteen other film musical dancers. For comparative purposes, Astaire's first film, *Dancing Lady* (1933), is included in this count. As the data shows, no one comes close to Astaire's span of activity or number of films. In the 1930s, a decade Petty describes as "an era of normative Jim Crow segregation throughout America," his only male peer was Bill Robinson, who had appeared in five films (two in a supporting role opposite Shirley Temple) when Astaire ostensibly paid him tribute in *Swing Time*.[56] Eleanor Powell emerged as a star when Astaire and Rogers were peaking and faded within the span of a decade. (After costarring with Astaire in *Broadway Melody of 1940*, Powell was cast opposite Red Skelton twice in films that centered on his character more than hers; by the second of these, her last leading role at MGM, the studio was recycling her numbers [the finale of *I Dood It* is a shortened recut of the end of *Born to Dance* (1936) from six years earlier].) In the 1940s, the Nicholas Brothers had a brief presence but never as more than a specialty act and not always at top-flight studios. Gene Kelly's nineteen musical films come into better perspective with the qualification that in five of these he appears in only one number. That said, the ambitious, frequently artistic scale and later high critical reputation of Kelly's films (and

TABLE 2 Astaire and peers, comparative career metrics

	Musical Films	Leading Roles	Featured Roles	Primary Active Years	First Film	Final Film
Fred Astaire	30	29	1	1933–1957	1933	1957
Bill Robinson	11	1	10	1935–1938	1930	1943
Eleanor Powell	13	9	4	1936–1944	1935	1950
Nicholas Brothers	11	0	11	1940–1944	1934	1948
Gene Kelly	19	14	5	1942–1957	1942	1957
Donald O'Connor	26	18	8	1943–1956	1939	1956
Vera-Ellen	11	7	3	1948–1954	1945	1954
Cyd Charisse	15	5	4	1946–1957	1945	1957
Gene Nelson	12	4	8	1950–1955	1947	1955
Marge & Gower Champion	7	6	1	1951–1955	1950	1955
Leslie Caron	4	4	0	1951–1958	1951	1958
Bob Fosse	5	2	3	1953–1955	1953	1958

the MGM Freed unit) has given him an outsized presence in most histories of the genre. Kelly was a creature of MGM and as such presents a star persona framed within a given house style in ways Astaire does not. Donald O'Connor enjoyed a slightly longer career than Kelly. O'Connor began as a teenager in "B" pictures at Universal (a minor studio) then became one of the studio's big stars (in musical and nonmusical films): his musical films for Universal are not generally available. O'Connor made only two musicals at Metro (with *Singin' in the Rain* [1952] easily his best remembered role) and, like Astaire, also worked at Paramount and Twentieth Century-Fox in the 1950s. O'Connor remains unstudied. In the postwar period, the Hollywood film musical abruptly exploded with dancing men. In addition to Kelly and O'Connor, Gene Nelson—working at Warner's, often with Doris Day—created a body of work in the early 1950s that clearly intersects with Astaire's. Nelson, a generically good-looking and quite tall man, often danced with props such as a hat and cane and did a direct, much more athletic answer to Astaire's gymnasium dance, "Sunday Jumps," in *Royal Wedding* (see "Am I in Love" in *She's Working Her Way Through College* [1953]). Among the many other men of the decade—it's hard to imagine a project like *Seven Brides for Seven Brothers* (1954) happening at any other time in the studio era—are two prominent later Broadway choreographers, Gower Champion and Bob Fosse. Both were under contract at MGM when Astaire was there; neither did much of anything with the Freed unit and their films are largely forgotten.

Table 2 also quantifies Astaire's presence as a leading man. He almost always had the leading part, unlike virtually every other dancer in this select corpus. This guaranteed Astaire multiple numbers in each film and grounded his dancing in any given film in his other, time-wise more extensive presence as an actor playing a part. He was never *only* a dancer (as featured performers usually were; the Nicholas Brothers never speak a line of dialogue). Astaire's many nonmusical actions between his numbers—walking, talking, reacting to others—helped situate his dancing as an extension of normal daily life. By this view, the integration of song and dance into narratives is less important than the larger impact of seeing a figure who dances also talk and play a central role within the film within which the dances are situated.

Another way to quantify the overwhelming dominance of Astaire and of white dancers in Hollywood is to count the number of dance routines made by Astaire and his peer group. Chart 2 compares this data, breaking each

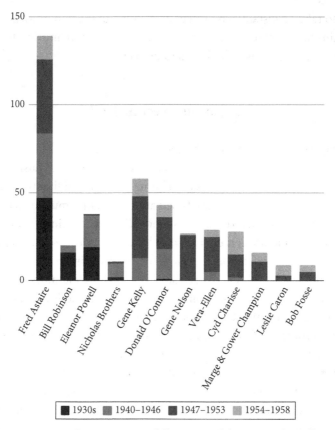

CHART 2 Astaire and peers: count of film musical dance numbers (by Astaire career periods)

performer's career totals down by Astaire's career periods. Every musical number these performers made, whether short or long, provided an opportunity to create a dance and to be seen by movie audiences (originally only when a given film was available, so the window of access for many viewers could be quite small). Astaire's total of 207 numbers is adjusted here to include only those with complete dances—reducing his count to 139. Within this corpus, Astaire's numbers account for a full third of the total. Astaire's output just in the 1930s exceeds the total dances of every other dancer except Kelly. In just three widescreen films, Astaire made more numbers than anyone else in the period except for Cyd Charisse.

The extent of Astaire's corpus—vastly outnumbering any other dancer in studio Hollywood—expands the relevance of this study. To study Astaire in toto is to take a substantial representative chunk of the film musical genre as it pertains to the (male) screen dance body. No other film musical figure can offer this sort of expansive look at the studio era.

10. Corpus "Nesting Dolls"

Counting musical numbers in the above manner affords a blunt measure—but not without utility from a budgetary perspective for film musical makers or as a means to quantify the overwhelming whiteness of the studio musical genre. But what counts in a time-based art like the film musical is how long these numbers last: their duration individually and combined within a film, for the motion picture camera is also a clock. (And the camera as clock had to be accurate. Work stopped on *Barkleys* one morning because of a faulty camera motor. The motor was replaced during lunch and, that afternoon, work on the film resumed both on and in time.[57]) Timecode data for the start and finish of musical actions yields the precise duration of each number. Add the durations of each number to get the total musical number content in a given film (just as the musical-content counters at Paramount did for *Alexander's Ragtime Band*). The durational total of all musical numbers and of those numbers including Astaire function as nesting dolls within the larger duration of the film whole—each a bit smaller (in duration, shorter) than the other.

Consider the musical number corpuses inside the larger Astaire film corpus. It takes forty-nine hours and seven minutes to sit through all twenty-nine films. However, only sixteen hours and ten minutes are needed if you just watch the 324 musical numbers—not so hard to do if the media to hand is the DVD or Blu-ray, with its parsing of a film into skippable chapters. Fast-forwarding in similar fashion through VHS tapes is an inexact and disruptive (also medium-destroying) experience. Watching the films on broadcast TV (as was common from the mid-1950s on) or in a movie theater (as intended by their makers) offers no such shortcuts to the good parts: you must wait for the next musical number and catch it as it goes by (as the original audiences for *Top Hat* at Radio City Music Hall reportedly did repeatedly). If you watch only the 207 numbers Astaire appears in, the time it takes to view his corpus drops to eleven hours and thirty-three minutes—with breaks, a long weekend of all-musical, all-Astaire enjoyment.

The innermost nesting doll corpus is the clip reel, here called, simply and literally, *Astaire dancing*. The *Astaire dancing* corpus—those six hours, thirty-four minutes, and fifty seconds mentioned at the top of the introduction—gathers all the portions of the numbers in his films when Astaire is himself dancing: it is the collective product of years of work in rehearsal halls, recording studios, on the set, and in postproduction. This body of screen dance sits at the center of this book: indeed, I am, in the end, primarily interested in what happens during this 13% of the total duration of Astaire's twenty-nine films.

11. 207 Musical Numbers

Before dissecting the *Astaire dancing* corpus shot by shot, we need to look further at the corpus within which it rests—the 207 numbers that include Astaire. In this section, I sort these bluntly defined spans of musical action into categories by type of musical actions (singing, dancing, playing an instrument) and by formal properties (primarily the relative complexity and/or closure of musical structures). This first sorting of the corpus—shown in chart 3—gives an initial picture of the totality of Astaire's film musical actions and a sense for how these actions unfold in time.

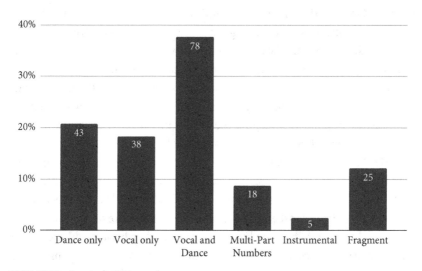

CHART 3 Astaire's 207 numbers

A strong majority of Astaire's numbers—just over three-quarters of the 207—take one song and routine it in one of three ways: vocal only (a song is sung, 18%), dance only (a song is danced, 20%), or vocal and dance (a song is sung then danced, 38%).[58] Within this initial count, if Astaire (or rarely someone else) sings a song, there's a two-in-three chance that a dance to that song will immediately follow. This count attempts to capture the experience of these films and so the direct flow from song to dance is important. If nonmusical actions resume between the singing of a song and a dance to that song (as with "Pick Yourself Up" [*Swing Time*] and "Let Yourself Go" [*Follow the Fleet*], both from 1936), then I count the two routines separately (vocal only and dance only). In such cases, the first-time viewer has no reason to think a dance to the song will follow the singing of the song (as noted, there's about a one-in-three chance it won't). Indeed, that awkward stretch mentioned by Gershwin in *Shall We Dance*, between Rogers singing and the couple dancing "They All Laughed," interrupts the flow of the film sufficiently to count these numbers separately: vocal only (not including Astaire), dance only (Astaire and Rogers).

Nine percent (18) of Astaire's 207 are multipart numbers that unfold unpredictably. Some parts of these numbers do not include Astaire at all. For example, the three name-dance extravaganzas in the Astaire-Rogers cycle—"The Carioca" (*Flying Down to Rio* [1934]), "The Continental" (*The Gay Divorcee* [1934]), and "The Piccolino" (*Top Hat*)—spend considerably more time on dancers other than Astaire and Rogers than they do on the stars of the film. Significantly, Astaire sings in none of these three. Other multipart numbers serve up a medley of short-form vocal-only or vocal-and-dance number types (Astaire and Garland's rise to fame as a vaudeville team by way of four songs sung and/or danced in succession in *Easter Parade*) or place dance-only sections within a stylized montage including nonmusical actions (the Castles' popularity sweeping the nation in *The Story of Vernon & Irene Castle* [1939, hereafter *The Castles*]; the "Girl Hunt" ballet in *The Band Wagon* [1953]). Astaire's two dream ballets—one each in *Yolanda and the Thief* and *Daddy Long Legs* (1955)—also fall into the category of multipart numbers, as do the standalone fantasies "This Heart of Mine" and "Limehouse Blues" in *Ziegfeld Follies*.[59] Most all these multipart numbers are on the long side in terms of duration. While the basic musical number building blocks (vocal only, dance only, vocal and dance) account for most of what happens in multipart numbers, Astaire does some musical actions in his multipart routines that appear nowhere else in his work (such as the use of pantomime in the aforementioned numbers in *Ziegfeld Follies* and the initial section of "Let's Face the Music and Dance" [*Follow the Fleet*]). In such moments, when he is not being his normative film musical self, Astaire enjoys less control over the number. It is generally safe to assume other creative voices are prominent in Astaire's multipart numbers. Archival and anecdotal evidence typically supports this view.

On five occasions, Astaire playing a musical instrument forms the entirety of a musical number. Here, the limitations of this initial sorting into categories come into view. In fact, Astaire plays an instrument on fifteen occasions in his twenty-nine films. The additional ten are dance only or song and dance numbers within which Astaire also plays an instrument. Astaire's ease in shifting between piano playing and tap dancing (as he does in "I've Got My Eye on You" [*Broadway Melody of 1940*] and the "Ad Lib Dance") or incorporating playing the drums into a dance (multiple examples) makes him an especially powerful film musical agent. Indeed, no other major film musical star from the studio era matches Astaire's range of musical actions, in particular his skills at the piano and the drums (hence my comparison of Astaire to jazz musicians such as Buddy Rich in *Music Makes Me*).[60] In isolated cases, Astaire fakes playing an instrument—he did not play the trumpet or harp but appears to be doing so in *Second Chorus* (1942) and *Yolanda,* respectively. Still, in all cases Astaire is visibly convincing in the act of playing. When he plays in the context of a musical routine, his actions are tightly integrated into his singing and dancing—all three basic musical actions can function together in his work (see, in particular, "Drum Crazy").

A final category in this initial sorting of Astaire's 207 numbers—the fragment—is considered in the next section.

12. Twenty-Five Fragments

The fragment—mentioned earlier under the cue sheet designation *partial*—takes up 12% of this initial count of Astaire's 207 musical numbers. Fragments are brief (averaging just 72 seconds) and often interrupted by or simultaneous with dialogue—and yet undeniably musical actions (usually dancing) occur. Fragments offer telling glimpses of musical agents and actions untied to closed forms and set loose in the social world of the films. They tend to lack definitive closure.

Four films, however, do conclude with a fragment that reprises music heard earlier in the film: danced in *Top Hat*, *The Castles*, and *Daddy Long Legs*, sung in *Second Chorus* (just one phrase before a kiss and a jokey exchange of dialogue). The three danced endings feature Astaire with his romantic partner but do not close their relationship off with a complete dance. *Top Hat*, for instance, follows its farcical final scene in Rogers's hotel suite with just a bit of "The Piccolino" on the film's lavish Venice set. Astaire and Rogers, in evening dress and coats, walk in time down a stepped bridge, then move casually into closed ballroom dance position and repeat steps seen earlier in their segment of "The Piccolino." Their relation to the music is not tight, there are no added foot sounds, and the pair spins off to screen right as the film fades to black. The simple notion of Astaire and Rogers dancing off together—whether into a shared life or, as in *The Castles*, in the ghostly memory of Irene, who survives Vernon's wartime death—is considered enough to round out these films. These perfunctory film-ending dances serve as a reminder that many first-run viewers of Astaire's films did not watch them start to finish. The continuous programming exhibition model permitted moviegoers to enter and exit a movie theater at any time. There was little formal need to ballast the form of a film musical with a complete musical number at the close.[61]

One group of fragments involve Astaire rehearsing with the woman who is or will be his romantic interest. All five—two in *The Castles*, one each in *Easter Parade*, *Royal Wedding*, and *Band Wagon*—engage with the show business milieu of their respective plots: none, however, presents anything close to a real rehearsal. The latter three films invest in the fragment as a character- and romance-building device. Garland and Astaire's first rehearsal in *Easter Parade* shows her modest progress and his all-business attitude—he coaches her "closer, closer" into a danced romantic clinch, then abruptly cuts it off with the cry, "lunch." Garland is left, literally, hot (under the collar). This rehearsal fragment nicely sets up their ill-suited "Beautiful Faces" routine, with Garland in a feathered dress, which in turn prepares the vaudeville medley in a shared style that suits them both. In other words, in *Easter Parade* a fragment plays a role in the narrative economy of the film's musical numbers. The rehearsal scene in *Easter Parade* receives the careful treatment given any musical number and caused the standard complications to the filming of a musical number (discussed in section twenty-nine). In short, fragments count expressively and technologically in the film musical. "You and the Night and the Music" in *Band Wagon* puts Astaire and Cyd Charisse in a partner dance of mostly poses amid very big flashpod explosions at a chaotic dress rehearsal for a Broadway show. This fragment serves several functions: a conventional, but not comic, number-gone-awry scenario (pointedly without an audience—the failed version of the show within the film is never seen, only metaphorically represented by a drawing of an egg: after all, what would Astaire and Charisse look like in a genuinely "bad" number?); a moment of bonding for Astaire and Charisse (still finding their way to each other at this point in the plot); and a riff on Astaire's firecracker dance from *Holiday Inn*, where he successfully danced with explosions (thus, an earlier idea in his corpus is repeated as farce). The duo dance fragment in *Royal Wedding* finesses Sarah Churchill's uncomfortable position as the only Astaire love interest who never does a complete dance with him. Astaire and Churchill first encounter each other on the street, both unaware they are headed to the same theater for an audition (Churchill assumes Astaire's following her). At the audition, Churchill does a very brief solo that Astaire cuts short. When he steps in to dance with her, she's chagrined to discover the man from the street is the star of the show. Astaire uses the opportunity to ask her out to dinner. Framed from the waist up and with dialogue ongoing throughout, this fragment deals delicately with Churchill's limited talents and finesses *Royal Wedding*'s unique status as the only Astaire film that never demonstrates Astaire and his romantic partner's love by way of a duo dance.[62]

Show business fragments can also take the form of full-blown numbers occurring in the world of the film that the movie audience doesn't fully see or hear. *Swing Time* ostensibly begins with Astaire leading an all-male vaudeville troupe in the number "It's Not in the Cards." Only two shots from the number made the final cut. Between these fragmentary glimpses, Astaire's sidekick Victor Moore opens the film with an unfunny card trick. It's a frustrating start—especially as we must wait nearly half an hour for *Swing Time*'s first real dance number, "Pick Yourself Up."

Fragments sometimes involve musical actions done outside of formal musical structures. As such, they can reveal aspects of the expressive and production economy of a given film and of the musical as a studio-made thing. In the final reels of *Holiday Inn*, Astaire and Marjorie Reynolds go to Hollywood to make a movie about Holiday Inn, the Connecticut inn at the center of the plot. Instead of seeing the pair in an actual film number, their work is suggested in a montage that splices and fades together four Berlin tunes from the film. Astaire and Reynolds dance in abstract space and, as with the *Top Hat* fragment finale, their relation to the music is unclear (this is not a synchronized dance, one reason it fails to rise above the level of the fragment). Images of the studio system at work and kitschy musical notation appear superimposed over the dancers. The dance content of the Hollywood montage was filmed in a single, five-hour workday (with lunch): February 5, 1942, the last day of the *Holiday Inn* shoot.[63] Astaire and Reynolds danced a "complete routine" against "black velvet" twenty-two times in all (nine takes were printed). The assistant director tried to describe the dance, singling out a "waltz," a "'Boogie' step," "the 'bumps,'" and "the 'lift' step." Five different camera setups captured the routine over the course of the day: one setup used three cameras; others used two cameras for the prism effect seen in the film; yet another setup involved "favoring feet" of the dancers. While the report mentions the song "Easter Parade" (which is heard in the montage), there is no mention of playback on the set: the routine was likely filmed to counts only or just a pianist. Whatever music Astaire and Reynolds danced to during filming, it is not heard in the film: none of their movements sync with the score and no added foot sounds give their bodies weight in the world of the film. The sequence was postscored over a month later, with the prominent piano added as an overdub in a subsequent session.[64] Filmed using special visual effects, the footage gathered that day in February was used by Paramount's editors to concoct a sixty-two-second fragment that abstracts film musical actions for story efficiencies and to introduce the mechanics of Hollywood filmmaking into the narrative. Astaire and Reynolds move in a black space penetrated by other images and filled with music they are not hearing. The components of a film musical number are juxtaposed rather than synchronized. This fragment saves the film's truly self-reflexive film musical moment for Crosby's reprise of "White Christmas"—he bursts out in song and interrupts production on the film within the film—and uses Astaire as little more than a screen dance body marking without fully embodying the genre.

Fragments also function to insert certain kinds of musical actions into a film while simultaneously protecting Astaire from crossing aesthetic lines he was, perhaps, reluctant to transgress. The "Snake Dance" fragment in *The Sky's the Limit* (1942), where Astaire performs at the demand of another white man, is treated at the start of Part Six's discussion of masculine aggression in Astaire's work. The Russian café fragment in *Second Chorus* bears mention here for its flirtation with broad ethnic comedy from which Astaire normally stood well back. In the scene, Charles Butterworth, a bumbling jazz patron, takes Paulette Goddard, a big band manager angling his support for Artie Shaw's group, to a Russian café to hear authentic Russian musicians. "Just think what centuries of Slavic violence have gone into that dance," remarks Butterworth, in one of several clueless lines. Astaire, a trumpeter needing work and working in disguise, is in the band. He does a few "Russian" dance steps, but his clowning never coheres into a routine and instead remains a sequence of stereotypical exotic moves otherwise foreign to his style. The expressive extreme of a genuinely comic or parodic dance seems to lie outside Astaire's comfort zone or sphere of interest, even if he is willing in this scene to affect a thick accent while singing a garbled version of the film's primary love ballad. The Russian café fragment suggests a mode of ethnic performance Astaire would not develop beyond a wink and a nod.

Other fragments distill Astaire's essence to just seconds of film musical action, often also using dialogue. The opening moments of *Holiday Inn* find Astaire on a snowy street where he encounters a trio of white boys dancing for pennies and a Santa seeking donations. (As I have noted elsewhere, the trio was originally scripted to be Black boys.[65]) Astaire's responses to both— a tap break for the boys, some syncopated bell ringing for Santa—instantly insert his rhythmically syncopated (white doing Black) film musical persona into the picture. The Astaire fan's itch for the anticipated "Astaire number" is lightly scratched here with a promise of more to come. *Shall We Dance* also begins with Astaire furiously if fragmentarily tapping, though in this case characteristic action on his part immediately forestalls the entire conceit of the film. *Shall We Dance* asks the viewer to believe that Astaire is a ballet dancer known as "The Great Petrov" (it says so under his portrait). This absurd conceit is demolished in the film's third minute when Edward Everett Horton walks in on "Petrov" tapping away to a "hot" jazz record with taps on his ballet slippers (a footwear fiction workable only in a film musical—a fictive world where it's also the case that shoes without taps magically sprout them, on the soundtrack at least, when a dance begins). Astaire and Horton's conversation leads directly to the theme of the film and destroys it: jazz and ballet don't need to meet and mingle; jazz (Astaire) has already won (if only because there's no authentic representative of ballet in the plot; as Adrienne L. McLean notes, after the first scene, Astaire's connection to ballet is reduced to "a disguise").[66] A subsequent *Shall We Dance* fragment in the same private rehearsal room furthers the hot jazz theme and introduces the film's obsession with technology. Against Horton's wishes, Petrov tap dances to a jazz record on a phonograph (just as Astaire loved to play the drums to jazz records at home). Horton steals the phonograph crank and, inevitably, the machine begins to run down, the record slows, and Astaire stops dancing. This one-minute fragment took all the intention of a full-blown dance number to create. While Astaire's dance steps are comparatively simple, the music presented a particular challenge: it had to be prerecorded to present the auditory illusion of a record running down. The arrangement simulates the slowing down of a phonograph without the unpleasant pitch-level and timbral distortion that would result in the real world. Instead, the recording drops in pitch and slows in tempo incrementally, phrase by phrase, in precise synchronization with Astaire's adjustment of the phonograph, coming to a stop just as Astaire ends up sitting on the floor. The Jimmy Dorsey big band, hired to record the film's dance numbers in violation of union rules, recorded this record that slows down in violation of the laws of recorded sound.[67] This fully realized fragment, just fifty-nine seconds long, shows all the care of a complete dance number, makes its point without the sonic unpleasantness of the reality it falsely represents, and prepares the ground for Astaire to dance with multiple machines in his big solo to follow, "Slap That Bass."

Fragments usefully beg the question of what qualifies as a musical action. Does walking in time to music count? Take, for instance, the two uses of George Gershwin's instrumental "Walking the Dog" in *Shall We Dance*. These unusual sequences—unique to the Astaire corpus and, arguably, the studio-era musical as a whole—feature two musical stars, Astaire and Rogers, simply walking, sometimes in time, sometimes not, to a jaunty little tune that has Gershwin's musical signature all over it. Unfolding with no diegetic sound, these fragments register as a shift to the aesthetics of silent cinema—or, perhaps, they are dance numbers. The brevity, formal open-endedness (each time the music yields to dialogue without regard to musical form), and story function (bringing the couple together) of these charming fragments—the dogs help too—combine to illustrate the utility and expressive and formal efficiency of the fragment as a category of musical number. The promise that Astaire and Rogers will dance together is a precondition of their brand of film musical romance. The "Walking the Dog" fragments begin the process of synchronizing the couple to music but do so without committing them to any directly legible dance movements. They just walk—but in time to Gershwin. The close connection between Astaire's dancing style and everyday movement supports the pleasure of these fragments. The substantive masculinity work done by Astaire's walk, the sole content of "Walking the Dog," is evident in these fragments and treated in greater detail in the midpoint section preceding Part Four.

13. An Alternate Count: 189 Musical Sections

The aforementioned initial sorting of Astaire's 207 musical numbers—bluntly identified by their beginnings and endings—quantifies the normative practices and expectations around musical action as distinguished from nonmusical action in the Astaire films. However, a distinguishing feature of most musical numbers is their evident internal division into discrete sections indicated at the level both of content and of form. Such divisions are implicit in the category *vocal and dance* but also present in the divisions between verse and chorus in vocal-only numbers or the distinct AABA eight-bar phrases of a song as sung or danced. Film musical time is virtually always divided into such formal sections, whether articulated visually by filmmakers (closer shots for singing, full body shots for dancing), performed differently by musical agents (the challenge of lip-syncing ends once dancing begins), or experienced directly by moviegoers (we don't know if "Male, 18-30" disliked singing or dancing more or less but he certainly knew the difference). Let's reconsider Astaire's 207 musical numbers by way of an alternate set of categories that identify formally distinct and discrete sections within extended routines. Astaire's twenty-five fragments fall out of the corpus here due to their brevity, their frequent lack of formal completeness, and the weak way they hail the viewer as musical actions worthy of attention. Astaire's five instrumental-only numbers are set aside as well.

This second count results in 189 sections (see chart 4). The vocal-only, dance-only, and vocal-and-dance numbers from the first count remain in

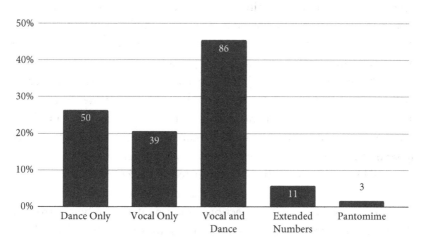

CHART 4 Astaire's 189 musical sections

those categories for now. Seven numbers in the *extended routines* category are here broken open to separately count their formally closed sections. Often these sections use different tunes. For instance, Astaire and Garland's vaudeville journey in *Easter Parade* now counts as four numbers—three combine vocals and dance and move into that category ("I Love a Piano," "Ragtime Violin," "When the Midnight Choo-Choo Leaves for Alabam"); one is sung only and joins that category ("Snooky Ookums"). In similar fashion, the Castles' demonstrations of the polka, tango, and maxixe— dances sprinkled within the lengthy montage profiling the couple's rise to national fame—now count as three separate dance-only sections. Leslie Caron's three imagined versions of her mysterious daddy long legs (the Texas millionaire, the international playboy, the guardian angel) here count as three sections, separated in the film by a cloudy screen and voiceover. Each also uses a different cast: the first, Astaire alone; the second, Astaire with a female chorus; the third, Astaire in a partner dance with Caron. The spring, winter, and summer dances, which follow a vocal by Vera-Ellen (dubbed by Anita Ellis) in "A Bride's Wedding Day" (*The Belle of New York*), here function as three sections and usefully introduce issues of production history. The winter dance is done on ice skates. Astaire requested this number be filmed "at the end of the picture," or after the shooting of dialogue was complete. Metro honored his preference. The skating routine company rehearsed for six days (including a day hiring the skaters)—or one, standard, Monday-to-Saturday studio workweek. After two days off (including the required Sunday) and a four-and-a-half-hour day spent lining up cameras and lights, the ninety-seven-second skating scene was shot in a single seven-and-a-half-hour day. These statistics give an initial glimpse of the efficiency with which Astaire worked within the system: a visually arresting routine with twenty skaters was made in eight workdays, just one of which involved filming (with the associated costs of film stock and crew). Per minute of film seen in the final cut, Astaire required twenty-four-and-a-half hours of rehearsal and nearly six hours of shooting time to produce a number unlike any he had previously made. (Other similar analyses follow in section twenty-seven, where the production efficiency of the skating routine will be put in perspective.) Experienced in *Belle of New York* as part of the extended Currier and Ives sequence, creatively and practically the winter skating routine was a separate section. Counting it as such here introduces the production process and evidence for Astaire's and others' labor into a quantitative view of the Astaire corpus.

Eleven extended routines resist easy division into distinct parts and it makes sense to continue to count them as idiosyncratic spans of unexpected musical action. Among these are the extravaganzas from Astaire's early RKO pictures ("The Carioca" and the title song from *Flying Down to Rio*, "The Continental," and "The Piccolino"), choreographer Robert Alton's unusual "The Wedding Cake Walk" for *You'll Never Get Rich* (interrupted by a marriage ceremony germane to the film's plot), the surreal dream ballet from *Yolanda*, and the formally strange "Girl Hunt." Astaire dances in all these numbers, but a first-time viewer cannot predict when he will do so or for how long. In all eleven, a creative figure other than Astaire is in control much of the time: dance director Dave Gould in the RKO production numbers, Alton in *You'll Never Get Rich*, and director Vincente Minnelli in the *Yolanda* dream and "Girl Hunt."[68]

Astaire had no interest in making dances for others (except a direct partner, often one he was touching), and he had no desire to create extended-form musical routines. His number-making proclivities were straightforward and predictable: sing a song, do a dance, or sing a song then do a dance—always with his own body at the center of it all. By this second counting of Astaire's musical numbers into 189 sections, almost half of the time (46%) Astaire (or rarely someone else) sings then dances to a given song; 26% of the time dance only occurs; 21% of the time singing only occurs. There's a smaller than one-in-ten chance anything else will happen.

To conclude our consideration of the totality of Astaire's musical numbers with an extended metaphor, the formally discrete and generically most significant parts of a film musical (described earlier under the term *musical numbers*) are where the meat of the genre is found. Carving these cuts of musical number meat from the larger carcass of the film by way of timecode analysis and production history offers a quantitative perspective on the content of—and, by analogy, the experience of watching—a given film or films. Consuming film musicals by only watching these choice cuts is a not-uncommon practice: anthology films like *That's Entertainment* (1974) are predicated on the desire for only "the good parts," as is the proliferation of YouTube excerpts that turn classical Hollywood film musical routines into de facto music videos. The aesthetic impact of seeing such Astaire-only compilations on the big screen has been noted. In the case of the Astaire corpus, two-thirds of the film musical meat includes Astaire, and the most typical serving from this portion involves Astaire singing and then dancing to the same song.

14. 159 Dances: The *Astaire Dancing* Corpus

The time has come to move decisively toward a quantitative view of Astaire's films that zeros in on the intersection between his lived body at work making and doing dances and his screen body captured on film dancing. This parsing of the *Astaire dancing* corpus—his clip reel, only "the dancing"—will be central to all that follows.

The *Astaire dancing* corpus directs the viewer to the films with the objectively longest duration of Astaire dancing time. The film with the most total seconds of Astaire dancing is *Royal Wedding* (23 minutes). *The Belle of New York* comes in second at 20¼ minutes. *Royal* and *Belle* were made in succession in the early 1950s. Each has two full-length Astaire solos and multiple lengthy partner dances. In addition, both have multiple numbers I categorize as danced vocals— where Astaire and partner move so much while singing that the vocal portion warrants inclusion in the *Astaire dancing* corpus (more on this topic in section fifteen). More minutes of dancing was no guarantee of success: *Royal* was a hit; *Belle* flopped. *Easter Parade* (20 minutes), *Ziegfeld Follies* (19¾ minutes), and *Blue Skies* (17½ minutes) round out the top five. (Appendix One column D gives the total *Astaire dancing* duration of each film in the corpus.)

The total danced duration statistic illuminates larger trends in Astaire's work when expressed as a percentage under or over his career average for minutes of dance per film (see chart 5). Across his career, Astaire averaged

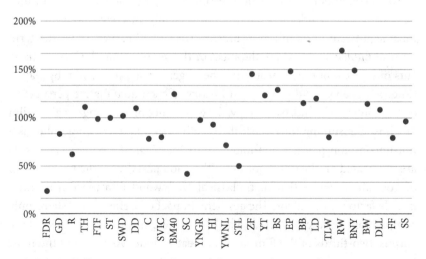

CHART 5 Under/over average for total duration of Astaire dancing content by film

thirteen minutes and thirty-seven seconds of dance per film. Only three films fall substantially (50% or more) below this average: *Flying Down to Rio* (his first, a statistical outlier for several reasons—he wasn't "Astaire" yet) and *Second Chorus* and *The Sky's the Limit* (two low-budget films from his peripatetic 1940s with second-rate production values, although each contains an important Astaire solo). Excepting the four films with the longest dance durations (mentioned earlier), Astaire stays within a 35% range under or over his career per film average.[69] (The median of this data set is 100%; the standard deviation, 33%.) This measure of consistency across three decades of film musical making suggests Astaire had a sense for how much dance could be made within the constraints of the production process (the imperative to finish a picture in a timely manner) and his own creative process (creating, perfecting, and filming his dances). His sense for this apparently didn't change much across his career: the genre as he understood it remained stable in its capacity to host song-and-dance routines. The medium of film set no limit on the duration of musical numbers. A film musical could theoretically include any duration of song and dance. Quantitative measures of the dance content in Astaire's films prove important toward understanding how the economic nature of the studios shaped the content of musical films, literally the extent of musical actions, and how much Astaire thought was enough.

Within the danced duration totals for each film lie the individual durations of each separate dance routine Astaire danced. Averaging these routine-specific durations by career, period, and film provides quantitative answers to the question, how long does Astaire dance once he starts dancing? Unlike the principal recorded audio technology of the time (the 78rpm phonograph record with a limit of roughly three minutes), synchronized sound film put no limits on how long musical actions could go on. And so, the makers of these numbers had to anticipate how long their audience might want to keep watching. In an oral history interview from 1976, Astaire said, "I don't like numbers that go much more than two and a half minutes; I mean, just as a number. A song, you sing a song for a minute or something, then you do a dance afterward; you shouldn't go more than a couple of minutes on the dance."[70] Quantitative methods can test Astaire's remark. I am particularly interested in the length of dance segments. To answer in actual terms the question of how long the average Astaire dance routine lasts, I omit the handful of musical numbers that contain dancing but do not segregate dancing to a formally bounded dance portion. This includes three entirely danced songs, where Astaire and/or his partner sing while dancing throughout the number

("You're Easy to Dance With" [*Holiday Inn*], "Clap Yo' Hands" [*Funny Face*], the first section of "Tunnel of Love"). Also omitted are formally unusual numbers that depart substantially from Astaire's standard approaches (the *Yolanda* dream, the multipart "Heat Wave" and "A Couple of Song and Dance Men" [both *Blue Skies*], "Shoes with Wings On" [*Barkleys*], "Girl Hunt," and all three numbers from *Ziegfeld Follies*). There will be more on these outliers later; for now let's go further toward finding Astaire's norms. There remain some 135 instances of Astaire dancing a formally discrete and complete segment of a musical number. The career average duration of these dance segments is 132 seconds—around two-and-a-quarter minutes. The average for each period varies little.

1930s	137 seconds	3% over career average
1940–1946	135 seconds	2% over career average
1948–1953	121 seconds	9% under career average
1955–1957	139 seconds	6% over career average

Astaire's strikingly consistent normative practice around the overall duration of a dance segment comes into further focus when the duration of dance segments is averaged by film. The musical numbers in a narrative film musical are related to each other in several ways. Each functions within the same narrative frame using the same setting and cast of characters and actors. The relative song-and-dance skills of the cast create opportunities for many (*Broadway Melody of 1940*) or few (*Second Chorus*) dance routines. The need for variety across a film dictates a mix of number types, again shaped by the cast. Astaire might dance two or even three romantic duos as part of the romance plot (typical of the Astaire-Rogers films), but he usually only does one solo—unless his romantic partner in the plot is a weak film musical agent, such as Sarah Churchill in *Royal Wedding*. In that film, Astaire does no plot-driven romantic duos (his only dance with Churchill, as noted, is a fragment) and instead does two big solos and four presentational numbers with Jane Powell (an empowered film musical agent), who plays his sister. The result, as we have seen, was a film with appreciably more dancing than was usual for Astaire. The numbers in a film are also related on the production end by being made at the same time and place (studio house style impacts all of Astaire's work), in black and white or color, and within the same larger budget (two special effects numbers in the same film are unlikely).

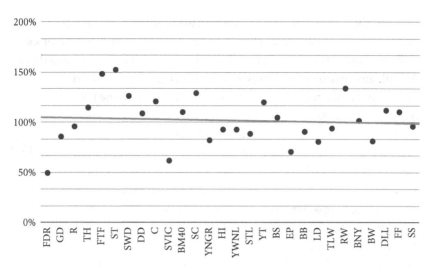

CHART 6 Over/under average duration of 135 dances (by film average) (omitting *Ziegfeld Follies*)

Chart 6 shows the percent under/over his career average (132 seconds) for the average duration of the 135 dance segments by film.[71] The trendline across his career is almost perfectly flat, but the first hint of an important pattern emerges. The extreme brevity of the dance segments in *Flying Down to Rio* again underlines the unique nature of this film: Astaire did not have control over how much he danced at the outset of his career, yet the power of his film musical agency was evident and impactful even in comparatively short dances. After his initial three films established Astaire's fame and control at the studio, the remainder of his RKO output (excluding *The Castles*) sees dance segment durations above his career average, rising to the multiple very long dances in *Follow the Fleet* (on average 48% over) and *Swing Time* (52% over). *The Castles*, Astaire and Rogers's final RKO film, stands out here (falling 38% below average) for its lack of any extended dance segments—perhaps, by this measure, the film is best understood not as a film musical but as a biopic about two performers who did not themselves perform long dances. The qualitative difference of *The Castles* is here accounted for in quantitative terms: the film lacks any substantial dance numbers. Outliers from Astaire's post-RKO periods offer similar insights as well as necessary caveats about this parsing of the data. *Second Chorus* rises 29% above the average in these years but has only two dance numbers—both on the long side. *Easter Parade* (30% under) falls well below the average due to multiple short routines. Of course, this data has nothing to say about the numbers excluded due to their unusual formal characteristics, and films with several or especially long outliers—*Yolanda* and *Blues Skies*—are not well represented here. As with any parsing of numbers and segments, this one is selective and does not tell the whole story, even if it does account for 75% of the total duration of the *Astaire dancing* corpus.

The *Astaire dancing* corpus contains 159 dances (see Appendix Two). I defined these 159 dances based on two criteria: first, by the dancers involved (Astaire alone or various categories of Astaire with others), and second, with reference to Astaire's creative practices and known production histories. For example, the long solo routine "Bojangles of Harlem" is here broken into two segments: in the first, Astaire dances with twenty-five chorus girls; in the second, Astaire dances alone with three enormous shadows of his own figure projected behind him, then concludes with a short solitary section without the shadows after he bests them in a challenge dance. The unusual length of "Bojangles" as a whole (5¾ minutes, the longest dance section after a vocal in the corpus) and the clear division of the dance into two distinct, seemingly unrelated sections also suggest these are, in fact, two separate dances. Archival evidence for the making of the number supports this view.[72] In similar fashion, "Steppin' Out with My Baby" breaks down into two dance segments: one for Astaire with others, one for Astaire alone. As described in an MGM preproduction document, "[Astaire] does 3 specialty dances with 3 different girls.... This is followed by 5 instrumental choruses with Fred Astaire doing a 'solo' dance and a 'slow-motion' dance.... The number finished with an 8-bar instrumental tag."[73] When Gene Kelly broke his ankle on Sunday, October 12, 1947—Astaire was rehearsing in his place by Thursday, October 16—he had already started rehearsing "Steppin' Out" with three female partners: this part of the number was Kelly's idea.[74] Two of Kelly's partners remained in the number: Dee Turnell and Bobbie Priest (first and third to dance with Astaire in the film). Astaire's second partner, Patricia Jackson, replaced Kelly's initial choice, Helen McAllister—perhaps because Astaire chose a bluesy style for this dance.[75] The special effects–driven slow-motion solo was added to "Steppin' Out" by Astaire: it was his idea to tack a trick routine onto Kelly's original conception of the number. And so, it makes sense to understand "Steppin' Out" as composed of two separate dance segments.

Dances internal to extended numbers are isolated in the *Astaire dancing* corpus as a means to keep the focus on Astaire's screen dance body and creative agency as a self-choreographing dancer. In this Astaire-centered corpus, the two occasions during the almost twelve-minute "Carioca" when Astaire and Rogers dance together are all that count, and each counts as a separate segment: the first and second of the 159 dances in the corpus. These two dances (112 and 27 seconds in length, a scant 20% of the entire "Carioca") arguably launched Astaire and Rogers and remain the most aesthetically memorable and analytically salient two minutes and nineteen seconds of *Flying Down to Rio*. Production records reveal as well that Astaire and Rogers's "Carioca" dances were made separately from the rest of the number. Indeed, Astaire finished his work on *Flying Down to Rio* on September 25, 1933, and left town. Over the following two days, the camera crew filmed "56 stock people" and "18 stock people (colored)" in the bulk of the number.[76] These designations document the racial segregation practices of the studio system: Black dancers are designated racially; white "stock people" are as well—as so often, in the case of whiteness, by the omission of a racial marker. These distinctions facilitated the danced content of the "Carioca," which isolates white couples from Black in separate musical sections and separate shots.[77] Other dances carved out of larger numbers in the *Astaire dancing* corpus include the initial and final segments of the lengthy funhouse routine "Stiff Upper Lip" from *A Damsel in Distress* (1937), for which Hermes Pan won a special Academy Award. I am only interested in the sections that include Astaire—the outer two of the three larger chunks into which Pan divided almost nine total minutes of danced screen time. The same goes for the flamenco-esque and swing tap dances to "Begin the Beguine" with Eleanor Powell in *Broadway Melody of 1940*—distinct choreographic moods matched by contrasting costuming and prefaced by stylistically different vocal versions of the song. The lengthy title song production number that concludes *Shall We Dance* is parsed into three chunks, each including different performers: Astaire's ballet-ish dance with Harriet Hoctor and her corps de ballet, Astaire's tap solo with a chorus of Rogers lookalikes in tap shoes, and Astaire and Rogers's concluding victory dance when they finally find each other. Again, it is Astaire's laboring dancing body that is of interest. I do not attempt to understand the work required of others on these films. It should be said—repeatedly—that Astaire's straight white male identity allows him to be the center of this project, just as he occupied the central creative position on almost every dance routine he ever made. This creative agency exercised for so long—over many years making many hours of dance—sets Astaire apart and makes his work literally and meaningfully countable.

15. Sing, Dance, (Spin,) End—but Modestly

Before narrowing the focus to just the dancing, the relationship of singing to dancing in Astaire's work warrants another look. Quantifying the typical order of events in an Astaire number offers some initial insights into how Astaire used the larger form of his musical numbers to embody a precisely calibrated straight white danced masculinity. Within the *Astaire dancing* corpus, I collected data on the order of specific film musical actions, particularly how dancing relates to dialogue and singing and Astaire's normative practices at the close of dance routines. Chart 7 sorts the 159 dances in the *Astaire dancing* corpus into categories reflecting each one's relationship to singing (drawing on the data in Appendix Two column F).

A slight majority of dances—54% (86)—are directly preceded by or simultaneous with singing. Parsing the moment when the singing ends and the dancing begins can be tricky. In fifty-six dances (35%), singing and dancing occupy discrete sections: the singing stops; the dancing begins. In thirty cases (19%), Astaire, while singing, moves his body in a manner that can only be called dancing—I categorize such singing as *danced vocal*. The addition of foot sounds and near-continuous movement during the vocal are the primary indicators here.[78] The vast majority of these—some twenty-seven—have a section of danced vocal followed by a definitive shift to dancing. In

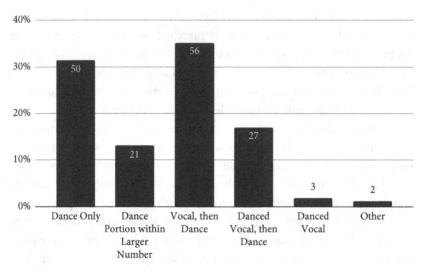

CHART 7 159 dances in *Astaire dancing* corpus

such numbers, the transition from singing to dancing overlaps but is eventually definitive. The earliest such number is "I Can't Be Bothered Now," a short solo made at the end of production on *A Damsel in Distress*. The next such danced vocal into a dance proper comes some five years later in "The Shorty George." The danced vocal appears as a midcareer addition to Astaire's bag of tricks.

There are only three cases where dancing is never definitively separated from singing—a number with an entirely danced vocal. The first of these, "You're Easy to Dance With" in *Holiday Inn*, made in late 1941, marks a genuine novelty in Astaire's work. Astaire displays somewhat superhuman qualities in this number. He sings gently while dancing vigorously and his voice betrays no evidence of physical exertion. Mixed to the front, as prerecorded vocals are, Astaire sings intimately into our ear while executing a physically exuberant partner dance in a rather social style. Anyone with experience swing dancing can register the physical challenge inherent in combining sustained, vigorous dancing with light, romantic singing as Astaire does here with no difficulty. In this exceptional number, the gap between the close-miked, prerecorded voice and the dancing body filmed to playback—a gap hidden in plain sight in the classical musical—proves especially evident.[79] "Clap Yo' Hands," made some sixteen years later, also features continuous singing, some spoken patter, and no separate danced section. In both of these entirely danced vocals, Astaire is not the only singer. "Easy to Dance With" includes a never-seen mixed chorus; Kay Thompson dominates the vocal in "Clap Yo' Hands" and the aesthetic of the number likely reflects her cabaret act. Astaire, at times, becomes a backup to Thompson's over-the-top style—not to discount Astaire's efforts to match her by rolling on the floor. In her nightclub act, Thompson worked with a male quartet—here, Astaire fills in for all four. The third case is the first part of "Tunnel of Love." In this case, as described earlier, the mechanics of the plot insert a gap between the danced vocal and the dance section, which follows the short scene to end the film.

Once introduced in the early 1940s, the danced vocal became a regular presence in Astaire's work (see chart 8). Almost entirely unused at RKO in the 1930s, in his third period a solid majority of routines with vocals feature a partially danced vocal. Most films in this period use the danced vocal more often than not (*Easter Parade, Let's Dance, Royal Wedding, The Band Wagon*).[80] This shift in Astaire's practice of separating song from dance shows a loosening of his aesthetic but does not abandon the strict separation of the

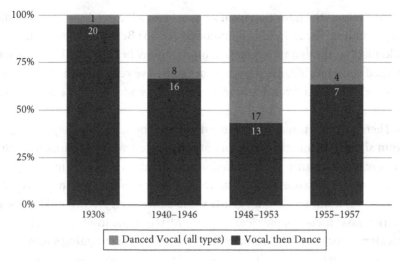

CHART 8 Vocal and dance numbers by type and period

two musical actions. Indeed, danced vocals finesse the transition such that the move to dance is less jarring, more gradual.[81]

The need to pinpoint the moment when the dancing begins can prove tricky, and timecode analysis that requires quantification to the second serves to reveal another aspect of Astaire's normative practices. Astaire makes the transition from singing or danced vocal to just dancing some seventy-six times.[82] In fifty cases (64% of the time), Astaire does not sing and dance in the same shot. Instead, a cut separates these distinct film musical actions from each other. Of the twenty-seven instances (36%) when Astaire does shift from singing to dancing in the same shot, most entail just a few seconds of singing—often just a word or two of the end of the lyric. In short, the task of lip-syncing to a prerecorded vocal is consistently structurally separated from the task of dancing to prerecorded music. Discrete technical challenges central to the job of the screen song-and-dance man are, thus, portioned into separate filmmaking units—into separate shots.

A similar relationship between dialogue and the start of dancing exists. Forty-four percent (71) of the 159 dances are standalone dances that involve no singing: better than two-thirds of these (50) are dance-only numbers, such as Astaire's first solo in the nightclub in *The Gay Divorcee* and "Sunday Jumps" in *Royal Wedding*. Nothing but dance happens in these numbers. Twenty-one are dance segments nestled within extended numbers—such as the two Astaire-Rogers bits in "The Carioca" and "The Continental."[83]

Across the clip reel, dialogue and dancing occur in the same shot on only eight occasions (among 44 possible instances) in dance-only numbers. One of these is the repeated rhythmic chanting "I've just begun to live" that kicks off "Put Me to the Test" (*A Damsel in Distress*): these lines may have been pre-recorded. Four are from Astaire-Rogers pictures and relate to dances being done to prove a point: "Um, kinda hot. Let's try some of that . . . " says Astaire to initiate his and Rogers's second "Carioca" dance; Astaire says "Shall we try it right through? Won't you sit down, Mr. Gordon," just before the start of "Pick Yourself Up." Dialogue in the same shot as dancing creates the problem of recording dialogue while the playback is running. The overlap is only ever minimal except for two notable cases: the first dancing shot of "Let Yourself Go" (Rogers and Astaire get into a little spat about who can keep up with the other) and the nightclub version of "It Only Happens When I Dance with You" in *Easter Parade* (when Ann Miller makes a little speech before coaxing Astaire onto the floor). Only in these two instances does dialogue take up more time than dancing on the transition into the latter; in both a cut occurs shortly after the pair starts dancing, shifting to musical action mode. The start of "Boogie Barcarolle" (*You'll Never Get Rich*) shows another option: include a bit of dialogue in a dancing shot but have the speaker stand with his back to the camera—Astaire shouts, "Music. Now give me some nice straight lines please—go." The practice of segregating dialogue and dancing in different shots reflects the industrial processes that, again, make the musical unlike other genres.

And so, most of the time the shift to dancing, whether from speaking or singing, is marked by a new shot, a situation where the aesthetics of the finished film carry a trace of the production process and mark a separation of film musical actions from each other—a literal and objective separation of song from dance at the level of the shot. This industrial practice supports quantitative analysis since there clearly was, for film musical makers, a distinction between dancing shots and nondancing shots. Thus, the category *vocal and dance* could more precisely be described as *vocal, then dance* or *singing followed by dancing* (most often with a cut between).

And the shift to dancing is normally definitive: only rarely does Astaire sing again after having danced. Of the eighty-three routines in which singing precedes dancing, only seventeen (20%) end with a return to singing. All of these (except "I Wanna Be a Dancin' Man" [*The Belle of New York*] and "How Could You Believe Me . . ." [*Royal Wedding*]) are short, thoroughly modest dances—for instance, "Funny Face" (in the film with that title) and "Triplets"

(*Band Wagon*). In most of these numbers, the vocal after the dance section is a tag—as short as "Stereophonic, adds an extra tonic, Stereophonic Sound" (*Silk Stockings*). The earliest such vocal tag in the corpus comes at the very end of *Shall We Dance*, when Astaire and Rogers reprise a phrase from "They All Laughed." The next vocal tag came some six years later and is more substantial: Astaire bidding goodbye to the bartender whose bar he destroys in "One for My Baby" (*The Sky's the Limit*). "The Babbitt and the Bromide" (*Ziegfeld Follies*) uniquely alternates between singing and dancing—a choice driven by the lyrics and the conceit of aging Astaire and Kelly along the way, an admission of lapses in time between shots.[84]

A more typical way Astaire concluded a number was to start spinning. Thirty-two dances (22% of 143 possible cases) close in this way. Astaire's spins are never technical—such as the displays of sustained fouetté turns in ballet, which often trigger applause. Instead, Astaire's vernacular spins at the close signal a maximum physical engagement in the act of dancing, even a frenzy of movement (see "Slap That Bass"), that can only be followed by an end to all danced movement. His physical engagement with the dance reaches a climax that signals the need to stop, a crescendo of physical activity that marks the end of the dance. Such spinning signals closure of a modest and identifiable sort. He did not turn to dance steps that pointed toward his physical virtuosity or dance training, nor did he deny physical limitations in the real world (such as singing immediately after vigorous dancing). Instead, Astaire increases the speed and size of his dance moves in readily recognizable ways (most any watcher knows the experience of spinning) by way of vernacular rather than technical spinning motions.

To sum up, Astaire's most common practice is to sing, then dance (for an average of about two-and-a-quarter minutes), then end the number (frequently with nontechnical spins). There was no reason to do this. Film musical vocal tracks were recorded several days prior to filming a number. And furthermore, dances were filmed shot by shot usually over several days. The different sorts of breath control needed to do these two musical activities—singing and dancing—are completely separate in the film musical production context. All one need do is watch a stage musical performer attempt to sing after vigorous dancing to understand why the practice is inadvisable in real life: dancing, an aerobic activity, elevates the heart rate and shortens the breath (even for trained performers), making singing difficult. Astaire surely understood the challenge of singing after dancing on the stage. But dancing in the film musical is not an aerobic activity. Indeed, assistant director reports consistently note when Astaire and his colleagues took rest breaks, often while covered with sweat. Astaire's dancing, while sweat-less in film, also seems to signal a lack of real effort in the doing of it.

Astaire's normative practices in making a musical number are decidedly modest. He keeps the dance contained as to length and the relationship of singing to dancing within the bounds of the possible. Of course, not returning to singing also signals the essential modesty of Astaire's singing voice. He was not a belter and was unlikely to sing a big finish. Indeed, many numbers where Astaire sings at the close are shared with belting women, be it Garland (three times in *Easter Parade*), Thompson, Nanette Fabray, or Janis Paige. The lackluster vocal close to *Shall We Dance* is perhaps the best evidence here: George Gershwin thought it needed "a big chorus background as the harmony Fred and Ginger do at the finish seems weak to me."[85] So not singing after dancing was a recognition that his singing was unlikely "to get a hand." This leaves the question of the fundamental modesty of Astaire's dancing, singing, and general performing style. A return to the corpus of his film musical dancing peers sheds light on this aspect.

Astaire's range of motion, carefully modulated in the shift from song to dance and commonly brought to a close with spinning steps, was radically modest in the film musical context. Table 3 lists the physically large and/or technically difficult moves used by the twelve dancers discussed earlier. These exhibitionist steps include flips, splits, high kicks, displays of strength, and extreme stunts. Among women on this list, all had ballet and/or acrobatic training that indicated in no uncertain terms their identities as trained dancers. Several among the men stand out for their consistent use of extreme moves verging towards stunts: Gene Nelson precariously tap dancing on stairway banisters or lifts in a car repair garage; Donald O'Connor manipulating complex environments with many moving objects; the Nicholas Brothers leaping over each other and landing in the splits.[86] The start of a Nelson, O'Connor, or Nicholas Brothers routine promised a particular kind of excitement for moviegoers, different in scale and sheer physical exertion from any Astaire number. Gene Kelly used muscular dance moves as well, with displays of floor work that showed his strength (working in a push-up position or vaulting himself to his feet from a position on his back) and regular climbing and swinging stunts, whether with a ladder (the building site routine in *Living in a Big Way* [1947]) or a silk rope apparently attached to nothing (*Anchors Aweigh* [1945]). Astaire and Bill Robinson alone did not partake of showy steps. They engaged with their environments in everyday

TABLE 3 Astaire and peers' use of physically large and/or technically showy dance moves

	Back Bends	Fouetté Turns	High Kicks	Splits	Flips	Stunts	Slides	Large Leaps	Swinging	Rope Tricks	Solo Displays of Strength	Duo Displays of Strength Partnering Women
Fred Astaire												
Bill Robinson												
Eleanor Powell	x	x										NA
Nicholas Brothers			x	x	x	x		x		x	x	NA
Gene Kelly						x	x		x			
Donald O'Connor					x	x		x	x		x	
Cyd Charisse		x		x			x					NA
Vera-Ellen	x		x	x	x		x	x	x			NA
Gene Nelson			x	x	x	x	x	x	x	x	x	
Marge and Gower Champion						x			x			x
Leslie Caron		x						x				
Bob Fosse					x							

fashion—tapping up steps or climbing on furniture, seemingly fooling around or demonstrating, as Robinson does to Shirley Temple, "a new way to go upstairs." The essential portability of Astaire and Robinson's dancing styles, easily done in street clothes, allows them to slip in and out of dancing just by making noise with their feet while retaining a physical poise and self-possession that seldom makes a show of the body (as flips, splits, and other stunts do).

Astaire engaged in none of the attention-grabbing behavior of other screen dancers. He had no need to initially: his only 1930s competitor was Bill Robinson, a similarly modest dancer visually, also devoted to making rhythm. Astaire's prominence grew as much out of his stature as a leading man and the satisfying nature of the Astaire-Rogers partnership both while dancing and just talking. Astaire could afford to be subtle and, as Part Two shows, his use of select cuts to non-full-figure framings that highlighted his face built character into his dances, enriching his dancing in a way only possible on the big screen. Modesty seems central to his persona, but his aesthetic smallness—his "glorious limitation" (as David Thomson puts it)—is also connected to his access.[87] Would he have danced differently if he only rarely had the chance to do so on film? Would he have bet on small moves if he was only ever in a featured spot?

Also central to Astaire's modesty is his evident mental absorption in his dancing—specifically in rhythm making. Astaire dances for himself: we are free to watch and listen. On records, this absorption often yielded grunts and other vocal responses (listen, for example, to most any track in *The Astaire Story* [1953], a multidisc collection done with jazz musicians). This aspect of his dancing body was not postsynced into film, except on very rare occasions ("Bouncin' the Blues" in *Barkleys*). Uninterested in (and perhaps incapable of) bold physical feats and deeply motivated by rhythm and style, Astaire presents a minimal sort of dancing—as befits a man who is perhaps not, in fact, a dancer but instead just a man dancing.

TWO
SHOTS

> The frame of the screen is a far more moveable thing than the frame of the theatre. . . . This imposes *completely new problems for the choreographer*: it makes his task far more intricate and difficult, gives him new riddles to solve and a wide range of possibilities for his invention.
>
> —George Balanchine (1944)

16. 932 Shots

In studio music departments, the relevant internal parts of a musical number mapped onto the conventional forms of popular song. As noted earlier, a Metro preproduction document for *Easter Parade* (1948) parsed the second section of "Steppin' Out with My Baby" as "5 instrumental choruses with Fred Astaire doing a 'solo' dance and a 'slow-motion' dance."[1] In his letter after the preview of *Shall We Dance* (1937), George Gershwin similarly used the musical unit of the chorus to recommend substantial changes: "I think that 'Slap That Bass' would be greatly improved if one of the two choruses that Fred dances on the floor would be taken out as the number seems about one chorus too long to me."[2] Gershwin recommends a cut that follows musical logic. Indeed, it was difficult not to recut a musical number in relation to musical form: to do otherwise risked musical incoherence. In *Music Makes Me*, I detail the diverse ways Astaire built his dances on the musical forms of popular music: from his varied use of the twelve-bar blues to his choreographed response to the contrasting rhythmic, melodic, and lyrical style of distinct phrases in Berlin's "Cheek to Cheek" (*Top Hat* [1935]).[3]

In this book, however, I do not use musical units to parse Astaire's dances but instead turn toward an objective measure that welcomes uniform counting in seconds across the *Astaire dancing* corpus: our unit of measure—borrowed from studio production practices—will be the shot. As David Bordwell notes, "For Hollywood, the shot is the basic unit of material" and the "basic unit of production." Continuity scripts "made the shot the minimal unit of planning."[4] For musical numbers it was no different, although the relationship of dance to shot was not put down on paper. The 23,690 seconds of the Astaire dancing corpus contains 932 shots—average length, twenty-five seconds; median length, seventeen seconds; longest, 213 seconds; shortest, one second (of which there are ten). Most of these shots take Astaire's dancing body as the primary visual topic: only 9% by shot count (1% by duration) do not. Each of Astaire's 932 shots began as a single continuous piece of film. In classic Hollywood fashion, the making of each began with the cry "action" (in virtually every case preceded or quickly followed by the call "playback" cueing the prerecorded music to which the shot was filmed—there were no microphones on set after *Roberta* [1935]). Each shot ended with the word "cut," often called out in the middle of a dance. Making these pieces of film was Astaire's principal task boiled down to its essential physical element: here is where his lived body meets his screen dance body. Walter Benjamin's description of the film actor's work in his 1935 essay "The Work of Art in the Age of Mechanical Reproduction" applies to Astaire: "His creation is by no means all of a piece; it is composed of many separate performances. . . . [T]here are elementary necessities of equipment that spilt the actor's work into a series of mountable episodes."[5]

Shots are chunks of time within which the dancing body moved (on the day of shooting) and moves (every time we watch it again). Parsing a routine by shot gives direct evidence for how long (at a minimum) Astaire and others were expected to dance during each phase of the routine and for how a dance conceived as continuous in the rehearsal hall was filmed in pieces on the set then put back together in the cutting department. Each shot is a time capsule and routines often combine pieces of time taken from three or four different days, sometimes weeks apart. Shot-based data brings an objective precision to the study of Astaire's dancing. Shots are visibly evident "pieces" of the film, and the length of each can be measured in seconds and in feet (the latter measure of real interest to the cost-conscious studios; feet of film shot per day was a basic metric of on-set productivity and efficiency). Shot-level data can be aggregated at the level of the number, the film, the period, or the entirety of Astaire's career and can also guide the collection of other more descriptive data, such as the content of each shot. The *Astaire dancing* corpus, as a body of 932 shots carved out of the surrounding material in these films, is analyzed in this book along two complementary lines: objective attributes and descriptive categories. This part considers the objective attribute of shot length and the basic descriptive category of how the camera frames the dancing body. Part Three correlates objective shot-level data with studio records such as assistant director reports, linking the actual time Astaire spent at work to the filmed time captured and reassembled in his films (and accessible now).

17. ASL and the Longest Shots

Two objective attributes derived from shot-level analysis allow for a distant, data-driven view of Astaire's creative practice as it unfolded over his quarter century in studio-era Hollywood. The story these attributes tell is one of aesthetic ambition (and even purity), followed by a pragmatic shift toward other approaches that served the same basic end: presentation of the dancing body on film in as ostensibly direct a fashion as possible. In fact, Astaire's dances are far from direct but instead employ the tools of cinema (sometimes in atypical ways) to create a danced continuity that carries its own ideology of the dancing body—implicitly male—in space. The whiteness of this body is a matter of access to the industrial processes that permit the making of high-quality commercial film dances in the first place. Whiteness inheres in the fact that Astaire's highly technical (in the sense of their realization on film) dances exist, and as critic Jack Anderson noted, "Because Mr. Astaire's dances do exist, it is possible to argue over them."[6] The extensive and fixed object of study this book enjoys is, thus, a white thing. The record of Astaire's work permits my entire project, which is—at the core—an inquiry into a motion picture monument to white power. As such, this book admittedly contributes yet more discourse to the already always central cultural figures of white male "genius" such as Astaire. Still, I hope my scholarship also works to de-familiarize Astaire. As musicologist Philip Gentry writes of another icon of Hollywood and American whiteness, "The Doris Day performance belongs to the subtle category of those that are so obvious as to escape attention, aspiring to an almost insidious quality of universality. Presumed unmarked, presumed normal, and yet cloaking a vast operation of labor to maintain those features."[7] This study frames Astaire's labor as always also maintaining his performance of a white male heterosexuality that is specific in its features. The sum of those features is no kind of universal. As author Garth Greenwell notes, "The fallacy of a certain idea of universality is to imagine that any human experience is unmarked by the accidents of geography, history, demographics—to believe that an account of a Congregationalist minister in rural Iowa, say, is somehow larger, more relevant to a shared human story, than an account of sex among gay men. The idea of universality, when used in this way, is nothing more than a maneuver whereby a privileged social position—which is often the position of straightness, whiteness, and maleness—secures its own default status, and therefore its immunity from self-awareness and critique."[8] As social dance historian Maxine Leeds Craig notes, Astaire was not influential; like his model "Vernon Castle before him, Astaire's exceptional popularity as a dancer did not produce a broad reevaluation of the meaning of masculinity."[9] Astaire offers a fantasy of a certain sort of straight white man. His screen dance body is, by definition, a white body. The abundance of evidence for Astaire's body—six-and-a-half hours of dance—also speaks to its whiteness, as comparison with the near-total lack of nonwhite film musical agents in the studio period. Gentry writes, "Whiteness is a system, and one of the rewards of that system is a sense of ownership."[10] White performers and studios owned the film musical by virtue of its expense and its prominent function within the larger Jim Crow system of Hollywood production, distribution, and exhibition—which was racially unequal from start to finish, from the all but entirely all-white studio personnel to the "Colored Only" entrances to Blacks-only balconies in movie theaters across the nation. Astaire's aesthetic choices and the opportunity to make them and change them over time are fundamentally grounded in the white ownership of Hollywood commercial film. (Hollywood whiteness at the highest levels of studio ownership and control developed in dialogue with the history of American Jewishness.[11])

The first objective attribute has a long history in studies of film style. Dividing the total duration of a dance routine (in seconds) by the number of shots in the routine yields the standard film studies measure average shot length (ASL) for each routine. In this study, ASL is not estimated, as scholars have done for feature film wholes, but calculated from a complete accounting of every shot: these are hard numbers capturing all six-plus hours of the *Astaire dancing* corpus. An additional Astaire-specific statistic proves useful: tracking the shot with the longest duration in each routine puts the overall nature of the routine in perspective and clarifies the historical perception that Astaire favored using as few cuts as possible. In fact, he cut all the time, dividing his dances into more and more pieces (or shots) as his career went on. (See Appendix Two columns C and D for the ASL and the lengthiest shot for each of the 159 dance segments in the corpus.) (NB: Throughout this book, the word *long* or *longest* when applied to shots is used in relation to duration in seconds. I do not use *long* to refer to the content of a shot—as in the descriptive term *long shot*, where human figures are relatively small.)

While the average duration of Astaire's dances remained stable across his career (just under 2½ minutes), how that duration was assembled out of individual shots changed markedly. The larger story is this: across Astaire's first six films—through *Swing Time* (1936)—his ASL per number per film shows an upward trend, meaning on average the shots making up each dance segment get longer in duration. From his seventh film, *Shall We Dance*, on, Astaire's ASL consistently declines. Chart 9 illustrates these trends by way of an ASL for each film calculated by averaging the ASL of each number in each film. This approach preserves the shot-length ethos of each dance. Three films—*Roberta*, *Swing Time*, and *Second Chorus* (1941)—stand out for an ASL above seventy-five seconds. Two of the four routines in *Roberta* (ASL 85 seconds) feature a shot exceeding two minutes in length: very long by Astaire's standards—he only ever made fifteen such shots, nine of these at RKO, the two in *Roberta* his first ever. At nearly three minutes, Astaire and Rogers's duo "I'll Be Hard to Handle" (a one-shot dance) is among the longest single shots Astaire ever made. "Hard to Handle"—including Rogers's vocal preceding and separated from the dance by a short dialogue scene—took two days to shoot (December 20–21, 1934). On the first day, the pair rehearsed in the morning. After lunch, the orchestra arrived. "Hard to Handle" was one of the last numbers Astaire shot to live music on set. After rehearsing with the orchestra, the first shot was taken at 3:15pm—it may have been Rogers's

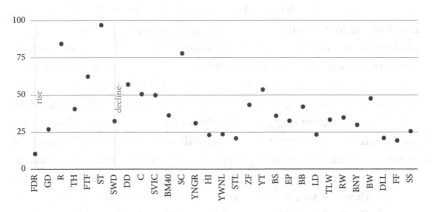

CHART 9 Average shot length (in seconds, averaged by number by film)

vocal; the RKO records are not specific on this account. Day two saw the completion of the number and the somewhat complicated dialogue scene before it, which required conversation between the pair to line up with the band, playing live, so that Astaire could punctuate his points with short tap breaks. This was a very efficiently made number but also a relatively straightforward concept, just Astaire and Rogers dancing in a relaxed manner that welcomed a kind of looseness not typical of their work. The other long shot in *Roberta* is in the pair's languorous dance to "Smoke Gets in Your Eyes" near the film's close. This dance is made of two shots: the first, at two minutes in length, almost completes the routine; the second, a seventeen-second closing shot, facilitates the pair's exit up a set of steps (the first of many such short shots that facilitate closure and/or the negotiation of a physical obstacle). *Second Chorus* (ASL 78 seconds) has only two dance numbers, one of which is a single-shot, 133-second dance with Paulette Goddard to "(I Ain't Hep to that Step but I'll) Dig It," perhaps the easiest romantic duo Astaire ever made (not counting "Things Are Looking Up" with Joan Fontaine in *A Damsel in Distress* [1937] which is hardly a dance). While "Dig It" offered no great dancing challenge, getting a clean (and fun) take of it no doubt did. The lack of archival data for *Second Chorus* prevents gaining any sense for how hard (or easy) it was to film this routine. *Swing Time* registers a career-high ASL of ninety-seven seconds—nearly two-and-a-half times Astaire's career average ASL of forty seconds. A commitment to very long shots in several *Swing Time* routines comes into clearer focus when the Astaire-specific *lengthiest shot* statistic is considered in the next paragraph. Before moving on, it is useful to note that every film after *Swing Time* (except for *Second Chorus* and *A Damsel in Distress*) has a lower ASL than the average ASL through *Swing Time*.[12] Indeed, parsed by period, Astaire's ASL by routine per film drops by more than half—from fifty-one seconds in the 1930s to twenty-two seconds in the widescreen era. His career ASL of forty seconds fails to express this transformation of his practices. Put simply, after *Swing Time* Astaire assembled his dances out of more pieces, literally out of more and shorter shots.[13]

Astaire's move toward generally shorter shots after the mid-1930s is dramatically revealed by a look at the *longest shot* category (again, *longest* refers to relative duration in seconds among all shots in a number or film). Chart 10 shows the longest shot in each film. The 169-second "I'll Be Hard to Handle" shows the dramatic change in approach between *The Gay Divorcee* (1934) and *Roberta* and offers quantitative evidence for Astaire grasping control over how his dances were shot. But there was no follow-up in his next film,

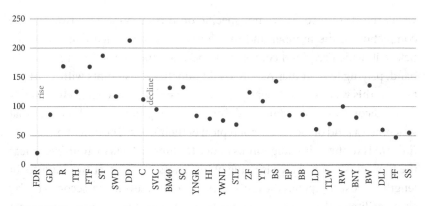

CHART 10 Longest shot (in seconds, by film)

Top Hat, which includes only one shot lasting over two minutes, the single-shot dance in "The Piccolino" (about which more later). However, in their next film, *Follow the Fleet* (1935), Astaire and Rogers execute a one-shot duo dance lasting exactly as long as "Hard to Handle" but in an entirely different mood. "Let's Face the Music and Dance" is a virtuoso display of hitting marks and sustaining dramatic character. The pair negotiates a small step up at the back of the dance area—slightly different levels are a characteristic of RKO sets—and they nail the exit as well, disappearing with one big step behind the edge of the proscenium. There are many moments along the way in "Face the Music" that could easily have scuttled a take: indeed, while executing a turning combination, the beaded sleeves of Rogers's dress hit Astaire smack in the face. But the challenge and intensity of a sustained, moody, even "artistic" dance, preceded by a darkly scored pantomime including two attempted suicides, done in "real" time—no cheating—are what matter here. By contrast, the casual fun of "Hard to Handle" feels like dropping in on a rehearsal—and the scene in the film is one.

Swing Time upped the long shot challenge with three shots each lasting over two-and-a-half minutes, one in each of three major routines. "Waltz in Swing Time" begins with Astaire forcing his rival for Rogers, bandleader Riccardo Romero, to start the music by literally waving the leader's baton arm. Rogers enters and, during a very brief shot, she removes her cloak, Astaire sets it aside, and the pair assume closed ballroom dance position. Because they lack any dance content, I do not count either of the aforementioned actions as part of the dance, which begins on a cut matching the start of the tune. (Several dances have similar preparation shots—for example, "Too Much Mustard" in *The Castles* (1939)—which are not counted in the 932-shot corpus.) The 156-second dance that follows meanders all over an expansive dance floor and ends with an exit behind a translucent wall. "Never Gonna Dance," similar to "Smoke Gets in Your Eyes," unfolds in an almost three-minute shot covering much ground. At the close, the camera follows the couple, via crane, as they singly spin their way up curving staircases to a smaller dance floor. Once there, a twenty-seven-second shot concludes the dance with a spinning sequence and Rogers's exit. As in "Smoke," this cut facilitates a difficult concluding bit: the spinning. The cut may also facilitate a change of camera position. (This cut occasioned some hyperbolic theorizing from critic Robin Wood: "the one flaw in what is perhaps their supreme dance number..., the one cut as they reach the top of the staircase that, in undermining the single-take law of Astaire's choreography, suggests that the god and goddess couldn't quite make it, that they are human after all."[14]) The third very long shot in *Swing Time* is Astaire's solo with female chorus in "Bojangles of Harlem," the first part of this two-part routine. Hermes Pan likely conceived and created this one-shot, three-minute-and-seven-second dance, which uses a crane (a special effect at RKO). With the exception of "Pick Yourself Up," *Swing Time* shows a commitment to lengthy shots that was largely experimental and not indicative of Astaire's career-long practice.

The next group of dances Astaire and Pan created—for *Shall We Dance*—include no very long shots, with only two nearing, but not exceeding, two minutes. The story needs of the film's final production number, requiring many plot-driven cutaways, likely discouraged sustained shots of the dancing figure, as did the gimmicky nature of both Astaire's dance with machines in "Slap That Bass" and the pair's roller skate routine "Let's Call the Whole Thing Off." Astaire and Pan's next project—the Rogers-less *A Damsel in Distress*—similarly worked against making very long shots. The funhouse number "Stiff Upper Lip" explores a varied space from many angles, with many cuts required, and the outdoor walking romantic dance with Fontaine, "Things Are Looking Up," similarly required cuts to negotiate the dancers' movement through the natural environment. But for his film-ending solo, Astaire concocted the longest single shot he ever made: the so-called "Drum Dance," which places Astaire within a semicircular drum set and has him bang and crash away for some 213 seconds—three-and-a-half minutes of hitting drums in a display of absolute synchronization with the prerecorded music. This one-shot number marks an end to Astaire's pushing of the limits of shot length.

Across his second and third periods, Astaire made several memorable long shots. Two from the 1940-to-1946 period reach just under two-and-a-quarter minutes: the swing tap challenge with Powell in "Begin the Beguine" (*Broadway Melody of 1940*) and the easy swing routine with Goddard in *Second Chorus*. It was very rare for Astaire to dance a more than two-minute shot between 1948 and 1953: indeed, there are only two, both in *The Band Wagon* (1953). The first encompasses most of the danced vocal to "A Shine on Your Shoes" and most of the dancing here (as discussed in section forty-four) is done by Black dancer Leroy Daniels. (A similar case occurs in *Blue Skies* [1946]: Astaire and Crosby sing the entirety of "A Couple of Song and Dance Men" and then dance a minute-long double dance, all in one shot. A series of imitations follow, each in its own shot.) The second two-plus-minute shot in *Band Wagon*, from "Dancing in the Dark," raises the question of when a dance begins: Astaire and Charisee spend nearly half a minute of a 136-second shot just walking before taking their first unmistakable dance step—the moment is analogous to the first Jet dance step in *West Side Story*; suddenly they start dancing (although both are, of course, professional dancers).

But these routines stand out as exceptional in Astaire's practice after *Swing Time*. Instead of pushing the limit on shot length or maintaining his practice of building dances around very long shots, he crafted routines that carefully placed cuts within the dance. These cuts divided the dance into more easily made pieces. Difficult tricks, like tossing or catching an object in time to music, could be isolated in a relatively brief shot, increasing the chance of the trick's successful execution and limiting the dance moves before and after the trick that would need to be done each time the trick was attempted—as in "I've Got My Eyes on You" (*Broadway Melody*) and "Let's Kiss and Make Up" (*Funny Face* [1957]). Difficult exits, perhaps up steps, could be finessed as well (see the finale of *You Were Never Lovelier*, in addition to examples already mentioned from *Roberta* and *Swing Time*). Part Four looks closely at the larger implications of Astaire's one-shot and long-shot dances and the way his normative use of cuts works to construct the space within which he moves. For now, it's enough to note that his screen dance body, framed whole at the (literal) center of the frame or splitting center with a partner, remains whether captured in one or many shots. His framing practices, not the avoidance of cuts, are what count. This was clearly what Astaire (and Pan) thought as well.

Chart 11 shows another way to visualize this shift across Astaire's career and also tracks Astaire's gradual abandonment of the one-shot routine. Each

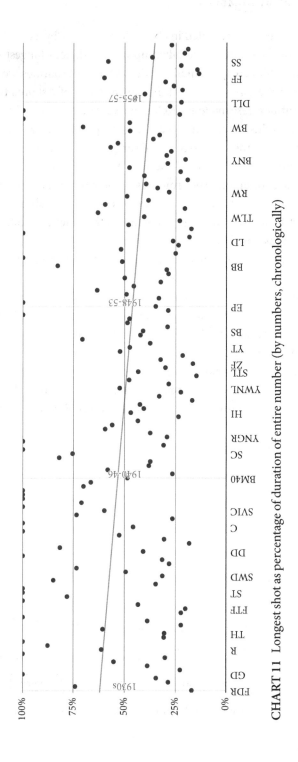

CHART 11 Longest shot as percentage of duration of entire number (by numbers, chronologically)

of his 159 dances is represented in chronological order by a dot showing the percentage of the entire dance taken up by that dance's longest shot. (The dances in each film are given in film order.) One-shot routines score at 100% and appear at the top of the chart. Fourteen (64%) of Astaire's twenty-two one-shot routines were made at RKO; none were made in the widescreen era. Not evident on this chart is the precipitous drop in the duration of the one-shot routines: after the career-record "Drum Dance," all but two—"I Used to Be Color Blind" (*Carefree*) and "Dig It"—come in below the ninety-eight-second average for all one-shot routines. "Color Blind" is projected in slow motion, so the dance as done on the set was appreciably shorter. The trend line in chart 11 shows a career-long decline in the practice of taking a dance in as few shots as possible.

A final way to see this shift toward more and shorter shots involves sorting all 932 shots into categories by length. I have already noted the near-total abandonment of the over 120-second shot after *Swing Time*. Also noteworthy is a decline in shots of more than sixty seconds. Chart 12 sorts all 932 shots into three buckets: under fifteen seconds, between fifteen and fifty-nine seconds, and over one minute. The data is parsed by period and expressed as a percent of total seconds of film in shots of each type. Use of very brief shots—under fifteen seconds—remains consistent but low. The other two categories show a clear trend across Astaire's career. Before the war, shots of

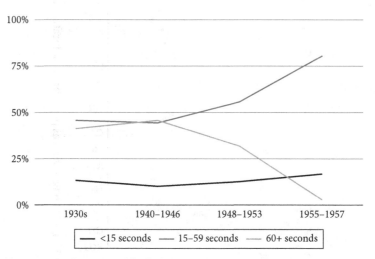

CHART 12 932 shots sorted by length (as percentage of total seconds by period)

over a minute in duration account proportionally for as much screen time as shots lasting from fifteen to fifty-nine seconds. After the war, his practice diverges. The over sixty-second shot all but disappears in his widescreen films—down to just 3%.

This career-long view of Astaire's shot-length practices reveals a changing practical and aesthetic approach. Early on at RKO, a studio where he enjoyed carte blanche, Astaire (and Pan) built dances out of as few shots as possible. This desire inevitably produced lengthy shots. Later, this sort of effort became an exception and the notion of the one-shot dance declined. This shift over time, somewhat matching Astaire's departure from RKO to work across Hollywood, suggests an experimental phase—pushing shot length—followed by arrival at a normative and portable practice, replicated elsewhere with a variety of collaborators. This data puts retrospective comments by both Astaire and Pan into perspective. In 1981, Pan discussed long shots and one-shot numbers with Joseph McBride.

> Yeah, well, at the time, we used to think that it was very important to do a routine in one take, right though, without spoiling the flow or the mood. But after a while, we realized it was to the advantage of the number to do it in sections. Because you can start fresh . . . maybe things were difficult, because to do a routine that's, say three minutes long, is not easy, I mean physically, you get out of breath, you get tired. If you say, "We'll take it up to here and then cut, and then we'll start from a different angle and continue." And we found out after doing it a couple of times it was always much better than doing it straight through.[15]

Remembering the challenge of getting "Let's Face the Music and Dance" in one shot, Pan remarked, "But it wasn't really necessary to go through all that agony."[16] Pan's remarks highlight the production process fact that a single-shot dance is also a single-take dance. Carol Saltus got Astaire to open up about such numbers in 1973, after pressing him on the common notion that he always prioritized one-shot routines. "Well, I did that to a certain extent—you can do that where you think it's useful to do it that way, but it isn't at all necessary. In fact, it's not as good to do it that way. . . . [I]t's very good to use the medium, and go around. . . . I wouldn't—it's a terrifying, tiresome thing to do." Astaire went on, speaking to the practical and aesthetic context specificity of making and watching movies: "You just sweat yourself out, I used to lose ten pounds of something—and you could have done it much easier by cutting in to pieces, and getting an angle and moving in and using the medium.... But you go to a movie, you don't want to see a stage show, you want to see a *movie*. And you can get angles and things that are very attractive."[17] The data in this section supports Astaire and Pan's claims about lengthy shots and one-shot numbers and also expresses in data the shift to more cutting that happened after *Swing Time*. Two reasons—both centered on the dancing body—seem to explain this change in their artistic practice. First, it was less tiring for the dancers. Second, it allowed for the dance to be seen in a medium-specific way. Both of these reasons show Astaire "using the medium."

18. 80 Cutaways and 110 "Inserts"

The previous shot-level analysis of Astaire's dances considers only objective attributes derived from timecode data—the length in seconds of each shot. The decision to make a given shot a given duration was, of course, driven by the content of the dance being filmed and the production context and aesthetic ethos of given periods in Astaire's work. For a few years at RKO, very long shots were a goal. In later periods, shorter and more shots per routine were a normative (indeed, routine) choice. The shift to widescreen seems to have nudged this approach to shot length downward even further. Going beyond these overarching observations requires a data-driven consideration of the content of each shot—initially by quantifying how the dancing body is framed. Gathering such descriptive data takes us closer to the moment when Astaire's real body went before the camera since decisions around how his body was to be framed would have been central to the practical process of making each shot. The distribution by career and period of an initial set of basic shot content categories is given in Table 4. In 1976, Astaire noted, "If you use it the right way the medium can enhance the thing."[18] The "thing" in question here is both a screen dance routine as a whole and the body of the dancer as presented on screen. The use of cinematic tools, such as shots that highlight facial expressions, proves important, as does the establishment of an aesthetic model for framing the dancing body that puts that body at the center as the point of origin for everything around it.

The default content of an *Astaire dancing* shot is Astaire's body framed as a whole—in studio parlance, "full figure." Pan remembered the power of this framing when introduced in *Flying Down to Rio* (1933): "So when Fred and

TABLE 4 Framing categories by shot count and duration in seconds ("full figure" category given as total and in three subcategories: context, Vitruvian, reframed)

Shot Count

	Cutaway		Insert		Full Figure		Full-Figure Subcategories					
							Context		Vitruvian		Reframed	
ALL	80	8%	110	12%	742	80%	82	9%	456	49%	204	22%
1930s	37	14%	24	9%	213	78%	41	15%	155	57%	17	6%
1940–1946	20	7%	45	17%	210	76%	27	9%	143	52%	40	15%
1948–1953	12	5%	30	11%	222	84%	6	2%	115	43%	101	39%
1955–1957	11	9%	11	8%	97	83%	8	8%	43	38%	46	38%

Duration (seconds)

	Cutaway		Insert		Full Figure		Context		Vitruvian		Reframed	
ALL	291	1%	937	4%	22,462	95%	1,343	6%	13,620	57%	7,499	32%
1930s	154	2%	159	2%	6,603	95%	671	10%	5,095	74%	837	12%
1940–1946	58	1%	329	5%	6,756	94%	425	6%	4,276	59%	2,055	30%
1948–1953	42	1%	357	4%	6,917	95%	78	1%	3,430	47%	3,409	47%
1955–1957	37	2%	92	4%	2,186	95%	169	8%	819	36%	1,198	51%

Ginger fested [sic] the charioca [sic] they did a complete routine, it wasn't very long, but still they were in sinc [sic] with full figure with the steps that showed the beauty and effect on the audience was magic. People just went wild. Because they had never seen anything like that before."[19] Seven hundred and forty-two (80%) of the 932 shots are entirely or almost entirely taken up by the full-figure presentation of Astaire's dancing body. Measured in seconds, these 742 shots make up 95% of the duration of Astaire's routines. Before parsing this default "full figure" group, let's consider the 5% of the duration of the corpus that does *not* show Astaire's full figure. This small percentage of non-full-figure framing is divided between cutaways and inserts.

Cutaways are shots within dances that take the camera's (and the viewer's) eye off of Astaire's or anyone else's dancing body. Eighty (8%) of Astaire's 932 shots are cutaways. Cutaways average just 3.6 seconds in length and their incidence declines notably across periods: by shot count from 14% in the 1930s, to 7% between 1940 and 1946, then down to just 5% in the first postwar period. Use of the cutaway increases back to 9% in the widescreen years—mostly because of a single routine in *Silk Stockings* (1957), "All of You," which, during an unusual dialogue-laden transition into the duo dance, cuts between Astaire (dancing alone, trying to convince Cyd Charisse to join him) and Charisse (watching and commenting). In this instance, the relatively smaller corpus of widescreen films distorts comparison by periods.

The purposes cutaways serve in Astaire's dances can be understood quantitatively by categorizing who or what is shown in these shots that do not show dancing bodies. But first, three unique cutaways bear mention. Each offers perspective by way of contrast on Astaire's normative practices. The first is the only one in Astaire's entire corpus that looks entirely away from a dance in progress. "Shooting the Works for Uncle Sam"—among the three dances in *You'll Never Get Rich* (1941) helmed by Robert Alton—is set in Grand Central Station as a group of men, including Astaire, depart their civilian lives for military duty at a camp near the city. Though shot and released before Pearl Harbor, this lone cutaway anticipates how the war would disrupt the norms of the film musical genre. "Shooting the Works" begins as a surprise farewell song and dance addressed to Astaire by the ladies of the Broadway chorus he had been rehearsing—he joins as their leader—and ends with Astaire's tap-dancing feet marching down the station platform. The film transitions to the military camp setting by crossfading on Astaire's marching feet, still making syncopated rhythm, but now among a group of male soldiers (here Astaire's step is out of line). The sole cutaway in "Shooting the Works" introduces a minor character, played by Guinn "Big Boy" Williams, bidding a sad farewell to his mother (she buttons his coat as if he were a child). Neither mother nor son shows any awareness of the colossal sendoff the chorus girls, complete with marching band in tow, are giving Astaire, and in the shot just prior to the cutaway the entire company marches out of the frame. This seven-second disruption of an otherwise brilliantly flexible number—it never quite becomes a solo; the line between the vocal and dance is blurry—registers how the coming war would reshape the content of the film musical. Among the impacts were directly patriotic numbers such as Crosby's "Song of Freedom" (which includes images of President Franklin D. Roosevelt and General Douglas MacArthur) and Astaire's "Firecracker Dance" in *Holiday Inn* (1942)—both were added in the wake of the United States's entrance into the war (the film was in production when Pearl Harbor was attacked).[20] Romance plots left open at the close also became common: at the end of *The Sky's the Limit* (1943), Astaire, playing a fighter pilot returning to active duty, bids an ambiguous farewell to Joan Leslie, the endurance of their love left in the hands of global forces neither can control. The cutaway to a mother and son saying goodbye in a train station during "Shooting the Works" similarly disrupts a musical number that is, itself, about patriotic duty.

The second unique cutaway in Astaire's dances sets the context for a dance filled with physical humor and virtuoso timing. During a transatlantic crossing from New York to London for the royal wedding—in *Royal Wedding* (1951)—Astaire and Jane Powell, playing sibling musical stage stars Tom and Ellen Bowen, agree to perform for the passengers. Warned ahead of time that "rocky" conditions are coming, Astaire assures the ship's captain, "We can handle it." After Powell sings the waltz "Open Your Eyes," the duo's dance begins in an arch, quasi-demonstration manner that works for a brother and sister (the gender coding of ballroom dance as used by Astaire is discussed further in Part Five). The first full dance chorus unfolds with no hint the floor is, literally, floating. After this formally complete first section, the second chorus begins with a three-second cutaway to an exterior shot of the ship in rough seas. The noise of the wind just about drowns out the music: indeed, the film viewer's position during the cutaway is confusing (the music continues even as we pop out for a distant view impossible for any character in the film). Cutting back to Astaire and Powell, the floor begins to tip and tilt precipitously. But the show must go on, and the dance goes on for another minute and a half. The pair's spontaneous negotiation of an antic situation—that seems to only affect them, not the watching passengers—lands Astaire and Powell in a gentleman's lap (Astaire apologizes) and necessitates the dodging of multiple rolling objects, including fruit and a bass drum (pursued by its player). The rough-seas dance after the cutaway demonstrates the absolute professionalism of both the fictional Bowens and Astaire and Powell. Successfully shooting the routine's final sixty-one-second shot, which ends with a loveseat sliding up behind the pair and knocking them to a seated position, required extraordinary control on set masquerading as mayhem on screen, an amazing display of closely planned danced action that appears utterly improvised. The unique cutaway to a larger context—literally, the weather—is essential to the conceit of the entire routine. While Astaire frequently built dances around specific spatial contexts, it was very unusual for the context itself to be dynamic. Only in "Open Your Eyes" does the environment interact dynamically and unpredictably with and shape the content of the dance; Astaire's default approach, by contrast, puts the dance environment under his sovereign command. (Art director Jack Martin Smith described shooting "Open Your Eyes" outdoors on a tilting platform normally used for films set on sailing ships. The set was blacked out with tarps and "hot as the dickens," said Smith, who continued, "It wasn't as pretentious looking on the screen as it was actually being there."[21] Astaire's practice of keeping the focus on the dancing body accounts for much of the unpretentious virtuosity of this number.)

The third unique cutaway pictures Astaire and a few others watching Olga San Juan sing the vocal to "Heat Wave" in *Blue Skies*. This strange number was broadly conceived when Paul Draper was the male lead in the film (as noted, Astaire replaced him after a few days of shooting). "Heat Wave" serves a plot function: the leading man (Draper, then Astaire) goes on stage drunk and falls from a high platform, ending the number and his dancing career. Astaire begins dancing almost from the start: he hears San Juan's voice and slithers over to the bar where she's singing. The camera frames him in full figure, following from behind in a very unusual traveling movement toward the visible San Juan atop the bar. Once he arrives at the bar, Astaire is briefly the subject of a cutaway (fig. 18.1). This unique moment—Astaire framed as an observer of others in an Astaire number—offers a very rare contrast to the overwhelming attention given to Astaire's body across the corpus. Astaire's straight white male dancing body is normally the primary interest—no matter who else is in the number. Cutaways are usually reserved for people watching Astaire, and the shift to musical number mode signals intense focus on Astaire's body.

FIGURE 18.1

A strong majority of the time, cutaways show the almost always amazed faces of people watching Astaire dance. Better than four of five cutaways (83%) present an in-film audience responding to a dance unfolding both in the film and, of course, for anyone watching the movie. Response to the dance modeled by on-screen proxies is the apparent point here, but on a closer look, cutaways often facilitate the needs of a dance in more practical ways. Astaire surely did not rely on enthusiastic onlookers within the diegesis to convince (or even influence) his cinema audience of the quality of his work. Only one among these cutaways shows an anonymous theater crowd: "Ev'ry Night at Seven" (*Royal Wedding*), a number with unusually visible seams, cuts awkwardly to generic onlookers. Most of the time the watchers are a few people or just one, usually characters in the film. Often their reactions signal character or plot developments—for example, when Eleanor Powell watches Astaire sing, dance, and play piano to her image on a sheet music cover in "I've Got My Eye on You." By way of cutaways, Powell repeats the conceit of the song—she has her eye on him—and also learns of Astaire's skill as a dancer (an important plot point). The exchange sets up their first dance together. A single cutaway to Judy Garland during "Steppin' Out with My Baby" seems to repeat the pattern—a female star enjoying Astaire dancing—but actually serves a practical function as a means to exit the slow-motion portion of Astaire's solo. On the cut back to the number, Astaire is back in normal speed. In a similar use, the lone cutaway to Audrey Hepburn watching "Let's Kiss and Make Up" facilitates Astaire unbuttoning his raincoat, setting up his matador-style cape dance. The dance begins with the coat buttoned, likely so it won't be in the way during his umbrella tricks. During the cutaway, Astaire holds his hat high above his head in one hand: there's insufficient time or free hands to unbutton the coat, which simply—magically—is now undone. Still, the wonder of watching Astaire dance is always the keynote to the faces shown in these cutaways. Even the policemen who arrive halfway through Astaire's solo "Music Makes Me" (*Flying Down to Rio*) nod and smile in agreement that he's a good dancer in their five-second cutaway. Only Jimmy McBride (Kelly Brown) in "The Sluefoot" (*Daddy Long Legs*) regards Astaire negatively from a cutaway—and Jimmy does so because Astaire is dancing with Jimmy's girl, Leslie Caron (fig. 18.2). Jimmy's reaction might also reflect his annoyance that an old guy—Jimmy addresses Astaire earlier as "professor"—is so adept at the latest dance (that Astaire remains competitive with young women). Additional cutaways during and shots just after the number round out Jimmy's character. Caron's roommate eyes Jimmy sullenly watching "Sluefoot," and by number's end, the two are pictured together applauding Astaire and Caron's big finish. These few cutaways usher Jimmy politely (and manfully—replacement partner almost on his arm) out of the film, freeing Caron to couple up with Astaire. One such character-building cutaway shows an absent watcher: Rogers, watching from above the tee just before the "Golf Solo" in *Carefree* (1938) begins, is gone from her perch when Astaire looks up to see her reaction to his golfing prowess at the end of the routine. The need to cut away to a viewer is finessed here in a way that keeps Astaire's body central. Rogers is not shown during the dance so that *our* eyes can stay on Astaire's feats of mastery with golf clubs and balls. The cutaway to the absent Rogers at the close comes after Astaire has already hit the last ball and serves as a coda to the dance itself, which remains uninterrupted by any looks away from the film's primary interest, which is always Astaire.

The second most frequent sort of cutaway (14%) shows other, in context decidedly minor, musical subjects responding to or participating in Astaire's

FIGURE 18.2

ongoing musical actions. Other dancers appear in full-figure cutaways as goads to Astaire and Rogers in "Let Yourself Go" from *Follow the Fleet* (1936, Pan recruited Angelenos from local dance halls). The four Black male musicians seen in the last shot of "Since I Kissed My Baby Goodbye" (*You'll Never Get Rich*) are shown twice in Astaire's other guardhouse number, "A-stairable Rag": before the dance begins (so we know who's playing for him) and in a cutaway at the tempo change midway through the routine (a stretch of time when Astaire isn't dancing, used here to remind the viewer again of where and who the music comes from and to break the dance into several shots).

The sounding nature of Astaire's dancing somewhat complicates the aforementioned definition of the cutaway. If Astaire's dancing is almost always both sight and sound, does it matter if the image track cuts away but we can still hear his foot sounds? "No Strings" (*Top Hat*) builds a complicated interaction between four characters across a continuous tap dance, the visual of which is cut away from some eight times. With many cuts back to Astaire dancing, the number has a very low average shot length (ASL) for the RKO years: just ten seconds. Astaire starts to dance, very noisily, and the camera descends—a singular (and simulated) in-camera cutaway—to the room below, where Rogers's sleep is disturbed by Astaire's pounding on the floor (her ceiling). In a series of cutaways, she calls the hotel manager to complain; the manager, in turn, calls Astaire's manager Horace (Edward Everett Horton), whose room Astaire is dancing in, to ask for quiet. The message is misunderstood, causing Horace to leave, passing Rogers in the hall in yet another cutaway. All the while Astaire is dancing up an audible storm—except on the cutaway to the manager's office—and each cut back to Astaire's dancing body is interesting and clever (particularly a shot involving Astaire confronting his reflection in a mirror—see the conclusion). When Rogers walks in on Astaire, now dancing with a statue, his foot sounds are absent, even though he's still moving. The counterpoint of tap solo and meet cute now leans toward the latter. The dance effectively ends—its sound turned off—before Astaire stops moving. "No Strings" demonstrates the varied aesthetic uses of foot sounds—realistic (absent on the cut to the manager's office) and narrative (silenced when Rogers knocks on Astaire's door and enters his room, the moment when the film reverts to nonmusical action, notably with every bit as much subtlety as it slid into musical action at the start of the number).

Nearly half the time (48%), cutaways picture white men watching Astaire—another white man—dance. The men who watch might be interested (Eric Blore as the dancing school manager in "Pick Yourself Up"), indifferent (Griggs in "History of the Beat" [*Daddy Long Legs*]), enthusiastic (Astaire's sailor buddies in "Let Yourself Go"), or holding knives (thugs in "Girl Hunt" [*Band Wagon*]). While the gender dynamics of each of these moments is slightly different, notably, no man in a cutaway (even Jimmy McBride in "Sluefoot") observes Astaire with fundamental distaste. The underlying message, perhaps needed for some, is approval from men for Astaire, a man, dancing. The opportunity to cut away to the watching Black men who share the vocal in "Slap That Bass" (*Shall We Dance*) is not taken but Astaire instead looks toward them throughout the first section of the dance and they are pictured applauding in the routine's final tableau. Multiple situations where Astaire dances for watching men, sometimes structured by way of cutaways, are returned to in Part Six.

The cutaway as a source of character-driven interaction finds its complement in the insert. Insert shots frame only part of the dancing body. By my count, there are 110 insert shots (12% of the total count) in the *Astaire dancing* corpus. The result in most cases is to make the dancers' faces larger. Insert shots allow for affective response by the dancers that is more cinema than dance. As such, insert framings build character during a dance by cinema acting means not accessible to dancers on the stage. Some examples:

- In their first dance together—the first dance segment in "The Carioca" (*Flying Down to Rio*)—Astaire and Rogers delicately lean toward each other to touch foreheads (fig. 18.3). All the rich facial interaction to come between this pair in subsequent films is already present here in

FIGURE 18.3

this moment made larger by means of an insert shot that interrupts the "full figure" framing of their dancing bodies and also emphasizes the unique foreheads-touching "Carioca" step. The tentative way Astaire and Rogers execute the move signals a white American reluctance to use such intimacy to go wild like the brown and Black Brazilians in the number do.

- In the comic duo "I'm Putting All My Eggs in One Basket" (*Follow the Fleet*), Rogers seems to hurt her arm—it dangles from the elbow as if broken. Astaire tries to help her in an insert that enlarges a gag involving both Rogers's arms. When Rogers starts to spar with Astaire, the number cuts back to full figure.
- When Astaire as Petrov dances around the unimpressed Rogers as Linda Keene in the nightclub number "They All Laughed" (*Shall We Dance*), an insert shot permits the pair to whisper back and forth. Rogers: "What am I supposed to do?" Astaire: "Twist." Similar midroutine conversations in insert framing occur between Astaire and Powell in a whispered exchange in "I Concentrate on You" (*Broadway Melody of 1940*) and in casual verbal play with Joan Caulfield signaling Astaire's nonchalant attitude toward performance in "A Pretty Girl Is Like a Melody" (*Blue Skies*).
- An insert in "Please Don't Monkey with Broadway" (*Broadway Melody of 1940*) facilitates a formal exchange of challenges between Astaire and George Murphy—the former slaps the latter across the face with his glove (fig. 18.4); the latter presents the former with his card, which is summarily ripped into pieces. An earlier insert in this male-male duo allows for the repositioning of both men's canes, which are tossed to the floor in annoyance in the previous shot. As with cutaways, inserts serve

FIGURE 18.4

practical functions resetting the physical setup midnumber in ways not possible on stage or in a one-shot routine.

- Two inserts in Astaire and Garland's "Beautiful Faces" (*Easter Parade*) allow for character interaction and whispered dialogue to signal that this routine is not a serious display of talent but instead a mismatch between performing pair and a given style. Garland's failure to perform the extreme femininity of the dance—associated in the film with Ann Miller but also resonant with Rogers in the RKO films—would be evident in any event, but two insert shots drive the point home, in particular the second (where the joke is Astaire's face being caught in Garland's feathered sleeve; fig. 18.5), which is less obvious than the first (where Garland won't release Astaire's hand and nearly chokes him).

Inserts also work best for framing musical actions done while seated, such as playing piano or drums. Indeed, I take the term *insert* from an assistant director report about a shot of this type: "Close insert—Don's [Astaire's] hands playing number on 2nd piano" ("Ad Lib Dance" [*Let's Dance*]).[22]

By enlarging the scale of the dancers' faces, inserts answer a maxim choreographer Kaye Migaki (whom I once worked with) often repeated—"90% of tap dancing is your face." Inserts enlarge faces, giving the screen dance body an expressive power unique to and derived from the cinematic medium. This qualitative difference marks insert shots as especially intense, perhaps as applications of continuity practices from dialogue scenes. Inserts work analogously to and sometimes in concert with cutaways: these two framing types allow for facial interactions between the dancers and/or those watching. Cuts away from full-figure dancing bodies to the smiling faces of Astaire and partner locking eyes occur in "The Continental" (*The*

FIGURE 18.5

Gay Divorcee) and "You're Easy to Dance With" (*Holiday Inn*). A sequence of three quick close-up inserts of the three protagonists in *Broadway Melody of 1940* during their short trio tap finale—together lasting but three seconds in a fifty-four-second dance—leverage the insert as dancer reaction shot to wrap up the film. Several numbers use alternating cutaways and inserts in a shot-countershot effect as in standard continuity editing in the classical style. For example, in the first scene of *The Gay Divorcee*, an angry insert of Astaire glaring at Edward Everett Horton while dancing to pay the bill at a Paris nightclub is answered by cutaways to Horton, who urges Astaire to continue and, at routine's end, holds up his now located wallet. *Holiday Inn*'s "I Can't Tell a Lie" is entirely structured around cutaways to Crosby (playing harpsichord with the band accompanying the dance) and inserts of Astaire and Marjorie Reynolds dancing. Astaire wants to kiss Reynolds; Crosby keeps preventing it by changing the musical style—from quasi-classical to various contemporary popular beats.[23] This conceit explains why "I Can't Tell a Lie" is the dance routine in Astaire's career with the most combined cutaways and inserts (16) and total shots (26) as well the lowest ASL (6 seconds).[24]

The insert category also serves as an analytical bucket for unusual shots that do not picture full-figure dancing bodies. Unconventional framings of groups of dancing bodies, with Astaire among them, occur in two of Alton's numbers in *You'll Never Get Rich* (an extreme side angle on two massed groups in "Boogie Barcarolle," Astaire and Hayworth weaving through a crowd of couples in "Wedding Cake Walk"). The insert as a space for character interaction finds widescreen application when Astaire is literally knocked into "Sluefoot." Standing along the edge of the dance floor in a row of college men—all of whom wear light-colored jackets—the black-suited Astaire looks on at the dance already begun. Caron, in her red dress and partnered by Jimmy, dances by in the shallow widescreen foreground (fig. 18.6.a). A shoving match among some men in the line pushes Astaire into the dance. He moves into the foreground and ends up partnered with Caron (fig. 18.6.b). The camera moves only minimally here—the dance is carefully staged within the widescreen frame—and stays on Astaire (again, his body is the focus). Jimmy's rueful cutaway follows, then a cut to full-figure framing of Astaire and Caron that signals the long-expected partner dance for the stars of the film really has begun.

Inserts aren't necessarily short. Minnelli uses two inserts, together almost a minute in length, to introduce Astaire and Charisse in the "Girl Hunt" bop joint. Astaire enters the club after three previous men. All are framed waist

(a)

(b)

FIGURE 18.6

up only, as is Astaire's entrance and his initial confrontation with a man with a cigar. In a hypermasculine move made large by the framing, Astaire shoves the cigar into the guy's mouth and knocks him to the ground with an elbow to the eye. The cut to Charisse—seated at the bar, she opens her dark green coat to reveal a sexy, sparkly red dress—stays waist up on her as she moves to Astaire. He raises his gun to signal the surrounding thugs, rising from their crouch in the background, to back off, and then returns the gun to his inner coat pocket (fig. 18.7). All of this interaction happens in waist-up insert framing. When Skip Martin's jazzy arrangement drops in loud and strong, the image track cuts with the music to Astaire and Charisse in full figure for their dance. The contrast of the insert shot works here to give the start of this terrific routine a kick. The cut also likely allowed Astaire to film the dance without the prop revolver in his coat.

Inserts and cutaways are specific to cinema. When used as described previously, they make a dance routine more cinematic, more difficult to imagine

FIGURE 18.7

recreated with the same impact on the stage. As noted earlier, cutaways and inserts account for only 20% of all shots by shot count and just 5% of the entire duration of the Astaire dancing corpus—twenty minutes out of six-and-a-half hours of dance. Indeed, in the case of twenty-two single-shot numbers, cutaways and inserts could not, by definition, be used. And beyond this subgroup, a further sixty-two dances never depart from full-body framing (as defined provisionally here). In all, 54% of the dances in the corpus do not use the cinematic device of the reaction shot sorted here into the cutaway and insert categories. This statistical evidence for the overwhelming preponderance of full-body framing of the dancing body leaves open the question of why cutaways and inserts happened at all. The small corpus of dances constructed with greater than 40% cutaway or insert shots (by shot count) helps answer this question. These thirteen dances (8% of the corpus) with statistically high numbers of cutaways or inserts often involve storytelling. "No Strings" and "Sluefoot" are discussed earlier. As noted, the three inserts in the finale of *Broadway Melody of 1940* show use of inserts to set a quick seal on a film's (admittedly thin) plot. Still, the human interaction of the trio speaks to story values over dancing spectacle. Inserts and cutaways form the warp and woof of "I Can't Tell a Lie." The end of Astaire's title-song solo in *Shall We Dance* requires inserts for Astaire to find Rogers hiding in the masked chorus.

Attention to framing types also helps isolate numbers that fail to function as numbers due to an excessive number of cutaways. Too many cutaways—by definition, not including film musical actions—end up compromising the sense that the film is in a stretch of musical action. The "dance" with the most cutaways is the middle section of the extended title song production number that concludes *Shall We Dance*. The sequence begins with a sustained dance: Astaire and Hoctor's roof garden nightclub ballet unfolds for two-and-a-quarter minutes with no inserts or cutaways. This lack, combined with especially distant "full figure" framing, leaves the dance rather cold, with no facial interaction between Astaire and Hoctor to activate any relationship—indeed, this dance feels similar to concert dance viewed from a theater seat. Then Rogers arrives on the scene and her privileged position as the intended audience for the number takes over. Her entrance to the nightclub involves a series of cutaways within cutaways—at the door (three successive cutaways), taking her box seat, whispering with her agent about the content of the number now unfolding more through Rogers's gaze than for the viewer's. Indeed, for thirty-four seconds we hardly see the stage at all and when we do Astaire is absent, yet he returns for a further half minute of dancing, so clearly his part of the routine is still going on, even if his dance here functions as a fragment. The content of the number is communicated mostly by way of Rogers's face and the whispered words of her agent (he explains what's going on both to her and to us—"He said if he couldn't dance with you he'd dance with images of you"). Pan noted of the masked chorus, "That was a situation within the picture. . . . It was a story point rather than a big dance number."[25] When Astaire returns in tux and tap shoes for his solo, the film abruptly jolts back into film musical mode. This limit case stands out for its use of a musical number to tell the film story not by way of the number itself but instead through the eyes of an in-film viewer (Rogers) watching a fragmentary number the movie audience only partially sees.

19. "Full Figure" Framings

Astaire's default "full figure" framing is a nuanced cinematic creation, far from a camera simply recording a dance done in front of it. Astaire reinvented the languages of cinema and dance for purposes specific to screen dance, melding the dance and the camera to each other by way of a hyperawareness of the frame and by building cuts into the dance for both practical and aesthetic purposes. His approach offers sustained visual access to the dancing body, which is presented as a fully disclosed object. There is apparently no mystery here. This strategy intensifies our experience of musical actions and musical time: once into a dance, we stay with his screen dance body until the dance ends.

The "full figure" category contains three types of framing of the dancing body. Each is described and illustrated in separate sections with examples from Astaire's Academy periods, when the aspect ratio of the frame was a square-ish 1.37:1. As Beth Genné notes, Academy ratio "was in many respects ideal for the dancer—it coordinated well with human proportions and indeed emphasized them."[26] A discussion of the ramifications of the shift to widescreen for these "full figure" framing norms follows in a separate section.

20. 456 Vitruvian Shots

The overwhelming framing norm for Astaire's dances puts the entirety of the dancing body—head to toe—in the center of the frame, scaled as large as possible within the need to provide room for (often sudden) danced movement in all directions, including upward. In duo dances, two bodies split center, each occupying one side of the frame. The camera follows the body, making constant minute adjustments side to side, forward and back. The body (or bodies) and the camera are typically positioned face to face—or face to lens—although oblique angles showing the side of the body also occur for variety. The camera's eye is normally at the dancer's eye level. Crane shots are very rare across Astaire's corpus (see section thirty-two) but especially so in this normative sort of shot (only twelve shots of this type [3% by shot count] involve crane movement).

This default full-figure framing is nothing like the view of a dancer on a stage as seen from a good seat in the theater. Two aspects of this way of constructing the screen dance body stand out. First, this view takes the viewer much closer than any audience for conventional concert dance can get. We watch Astaire dance in this framing from *on* the stage, not from across an orchestra pit or proscenium. This positioning of the camera (and the viewer) in a place no in-film audience can go is frequently evident: for instance, when the portico through which Astaire and Rogers are initially seen in "Cheek to Cheek" disappears on a cut to the closer view of their dance (the camera is literally in the place where the pillars were) or when the audience watching Astaire do his solo "I Won't Dance" (*Roberta*)—an audience he interacts with physically at times—literally disappears in the second shot of the dance, which is framed from a new angle (the camera now in the audience's place). In the third and final shot of "I Won't Dance," the audience pops back into place (although they are now well back from the circular edge of the dance floor), offering a further example of how objects change absolute position in the cut. Second, we—the camera—move with the dancing body in a way no fixed theater seat could allow. The space that is visible within the frame is always only the space the dancer needs to do the dance. The implicit relationship of dancer to camera, mediated by the physical nature of the set where the dance is done and also filmed, defines the moves that can be made. Given the imperative to keep the scale of the dancing figure—always seen whole—as large as possible, should the dancer or dancers move too quickly in any direction, the camera will not be able to keep up. Strategies allowing for rapid or large motion are discussed further in Part Four's look at how cuts operate and when they were practically necessary. For now, it is enough to note that this most common full-figure framing implicitly limits the range of motion dancers can use to the speed with which the camera can pan side to side or dolly in any direction without distortion and without calling undue attention to itself. These conditions, as well as the width of the frame, also limit the distance two dancers can be from each other at any given time. Dances with partners, which of necessity already reduce the scale of the figures within the frame when compared to solo dances, are especially limited by this requirement. This rather clinically described normative approach to full-figure framing locks the dynamic dancing body within the frame of the camera and screen, setting limits the camera responds to at all times and which Astaire as dance maker had to anticipate. After all, the dance had to be made so that it was filmable within this rather close full-figure framing aesthetic. The affordances of the camera had to be baked into every dance move. The camera virtually always keeps the dancing body (or bodies) centered, following their motion and often anticipating motion (suggesting the camera knows the dance—which, of course, the camera crew did). As *The Castles* director H. C. Potter explained, "Every time Fred and Ginger moved toward us, the camera had to go back, and every time they moved back, the camera went in. The head grip who was in charge of pushing [the camera dolly] was a joy to watch."[27]

This approach to transforming (and constraining) an actual dancing body into a screen dance body that is whole, centered, and scaled as large as possible is here categorized under the term *Vitruvian*. Leonardo da Vinci's drawing known as Vitruvian man (ca. 1490) provides a reference point for Astaire's normative practice (figs. 20.1 to 20.7). The connection between Leonardo's drawing and Astaire's framing is my own and does not draw on any archival or anecdotal evidence relating to Astaire. I introduce this term for two reasons: First, analogizing film dance to a drawing foregrounds the

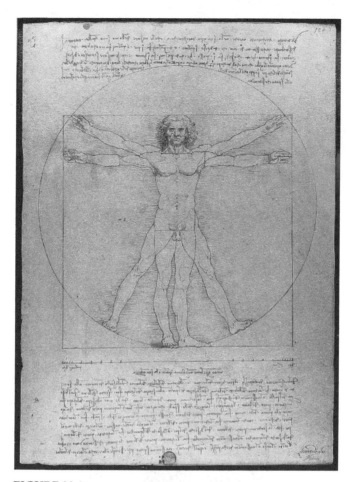

FIGURE 20.1

two-dimensional nature of photography and film as media. Astaire's screen dance body is made of thousands of still images—images similar in that respect to Leonardo's drawing. Second, the status of Leonardo's drawing of a single male figure as representative of an idealized human subject within Western thought lines up with the power of Astaire's screen dance body: drawing and photographed dancer alike stand for a supposed universal that is, in fact, a highly specific type defined by whiteness, Western (Euro-American) origins, and maleness. This type, including both Leonardo and Astaire themselves, is sometimes anointed as genius—another gendered category.

FIGURE 20.2

FIGURE 20.3

FIGURE 20.4

FIGURE 20.5

FIGURE 20.6

FIGURE 20.7

In his Vitruvian man drawing, Leonardo attempted to picture the relationship between the (male) human body and basic geometrical forms as described by the Roman author Vitruvius in the first century BC. I am, however, less interested in what Leonardo intended with the drawing than in its implications for the depiction of the dynamic male form in a two-dimensional medium. Leonardo's drawing pictures an idealized nude man in four possible poses: standing legs together or slightly apart with arms fully extended and perpendicular to the ground or slightly raised. The proportions of the figure are contrived to yield two regular geometric forms: legs together with arms perpendicular to the ground, including the head, match the outline of a square; legs apart (on a curved floor—or perhaps Vitruvian man is jumping) and arms raised a bit fit within the outline of a circle. The dynamism of the figure is implicit—no single pose is definitive. Leonardo has drawn a still image of the male body in motion. The square and circle are not architectural forms in themselves—Vitruvian man is not standing in a massive drain pipe—but instead ideal forms derived from the man himself or inscribed in space by his potential range of motion. These basic shapes are generated by the movement of the man—the square and the circle are implied by his poses and motions. He is the source. In similar fashion, Astaire's screen dance body is dynamic—constantly moving within the regular rectangle of the frame. The camera, with its nearly square aperture and film stock, subjects the body to regular shapes within which the body's movements are inscribed. In Astaire's default full-figure framing—which I group under the category *Vitruvian*—the camera follows the large-scaled dancing body in a manner that suggests the body itself is generating the space within which it is moving, just as the figure in Leonardo's drawing generates the regular shapes that define the space around it. Astaire's screen dance being does not explore space or move through a space constructed by continuity editing. Instead, Astaire creates space as he moves—whether by moving in place (as dancers often do) or while moving in real space across a set designed for dance. (Movement of the dancing body within the real space of a Hollywood set is discussed in Part Four.)

The Vitruvian category of full-figure framing accounts for 49% (456) of all shots and 57% (13,620 seconds) of the duration of the corpus. Shots in this category sustain from start to finish the whole and large, front-and-center approach to framing the body associated with Astaire. Vitruvian shots evidence a hyperawareness of the frame to the dancer's movements—and, it must be emphasized, a reciprocal hyperawareness of the dancer to the frame. The physical task (and technical achievement) of Vitruvian framing must be executed during shooting by the camera operator but must also be built into the dance during the process of its making in the rehearsal hall. The maintenance of Vitruvian figure scale sets significant limits on danced movement that had to be anticipated by Astaire and his collaborators. This spatial play between the dancing body and the camera cuts to the heart of Astaire's screen dance body. The philosophical, racial, and gender implications of Vitruvian framing of the dancing body are considered at length in Part Four. For now, it is crucial to recognize how Vitruvian shots dwell obsessively on the dancing body and subordinate all other priorities to a dynamic, whole, and large dancing human figure.

21. 82 Context Shots

The dancing body seen "full figure" is not always framed and centered in Vitruvian fashion. Sometimes it is put in a social or spatial context that diminishes the agency of the dancer to control space and magnetize the camera's movement. In such framings, categorized here under the term *context*, the dancing body, still presented whole, is scaled at around or less than half the height of the frame and often seen from a slightly elevated angle. The diminished figure scale within the frame is key. Context framing often places dancers in a social and/or story-specific context. Examples include Astaire and Rogers within the crowded world of "The Carioca" (fig. 21.1) or glimpsed through a portico from across a canal in an empty corner of *Top Hat*'s stylized Venice (fig. 21.2). At the close of *The Belle of New York*, Astaire and Vera-Ellen dance into the distant sky on the power of love (fig. 21.3). Context framings might also suggest a balcony seat view of a theatrical

FIGURE 21.1

FIGURE 21.2

FIGURE 21.3

number, including the audience or not, giving a grand scale to the number as a whole, in the process decreasing the agency of the dancers (see "Heat Wave"). This diminishing effect on the power of the dancing body in the normative Vitruvian framing surely accounts for the relative scarcity of context shots, which account for only 9% (82) of all shots and total just 6% of the duration of the corpus.

22. 204 Reframed Shots

In the third "full figure" framing subcategory, our view of the dancing body changes significantly within the shot. The body is reframed within the shot: hence the category name *reframed*, which keeps the analytical focus squarely where it belongs—on the dancing body. It is the camera's (and the cinema audience's) view of that body that is reframed.[28] An important aspect of this category needs stating up front: most of the duration of most reframed shots matches the Vitruvian category described previously. The only difference is a change in the framing of the figure at some point during the shot— as detailed later, typically a shift between insert and Vitruvian framings. This change complicates the regular relationship between body and camera that underpins the Vitruvian category and would have demanded careful and specific coordination between dancers and camera crew to execute successfully on the set (beyond the maintenance of the norm of Vitruvian shots). The 204 shots in the reframed category—22% of the 932 total—play an important role in Astaire's continuity practices.

Reframed shots carry a special relationship to the insert category. Indeed, 84% of all 204 reframed shots involve some sort of insert framing—from ankles up to close-up (face or feet) and every partial framing of the dancing body between. Reframed shots mostly work to finesse a transition into or out of insert framing without making a cut. Moving into and out of Vitruvian framing is by far the norm. Indeed, only 29% of all reframed shots involve context framing of any sort—the remainder never pull back beyond Vitruvian (another way the dancing body sets the limits of the visible).

Reframed shots fall into three subcategories, each of which indicates the important role of camera movement: (1) entirely danced (no camera movement), (2) single camera moves, or (3) multiple camera moves. Thirteen (6%) of the 204 reframed shots involve no camera movement whatsoever, just the dancing body moving in relation to a stationary camera. The earliest of these, from the very end of "Stiff Upper Lip" (*Damsel in Distress*), moves Astaire, George Burns, and Gracie Allen from context framing to seated insert framing in seconds without the three dancers moving themselves (figs. 22.1.a and 22.1.b). In a thirteen-second shot, the trio climbs away from the viewer to the top of a stairway and turns to sit on the top step. Then, the steps in front of them fold flat and all three slide forward into a laughing three-shot of faces and knees. ("Stiff Upper Lip" opens with a similar slide, so Pan is thinking formally by ending this long number in this way.) This reframed shot without camera movement is similar to most reframed shots in that the change in figure scale happens rapidly and at one end of the shot—in this case, at the end. The remaining 191 reframed shots involve either a single camera movement (139 shots, 68% of all reframed) or multiple camera movements (52 shots, 25%). Shots in the latter group mostly occur in numbers where Astaire yielded substantial control, such as the *Yolanda* dream (a veritable study in reframing that tilts strongly toward context framings). The former, much larger group, making up over two-thirds of all reframed shots, is treated here. But it should be emphasized that the shots in both groups similarly effect a significant change in the scale of the dancing body. This transformation of the dancing body from scaled small to scaled large and/or from part to whole within a shot is comparable to the similar cinema effect of cutting between Vitruvian or context and insert framing, only in reframed shots changes in the scale of the dancing body are part of the filmed dance itself. Again, most of the duration of most reframed shots falls into the Vitruvian category—so the reframed shot count is more significant than the total duration in seconds of this category, and the previously stated statistic for the number of seconds spent in Vitruvian framing significantly undercounts the actual amount of time in that default mode.

FIGURE 22.1

Close analysis of reframed shots involving a single camera move reveals rather strict limits on altering the place of the dancing body within the frame. As the subcategory name indicates, all 139 reframe the body only once. The camera movement effecting this reframing goes in only one direction: either pulling back from or pushing forward toward the body. Eighty-eight percent of this subcategory involves camera movement only (the dancers dance in place; all the motion is done by the camera operator). Eighty-six percent make their singular, one-directional move at either end of the shot (at the start, 50% of the time; at the end, 36%). If we combine the single camera move and entirely danced subcategories, a pattern emerges. Within this corpus of 152 shots (75% of the larger reframed category), two-thirds of the time the reframing involves a moving-back, pulling-out motion giving a fuller view of the dancing body—we start close and pull away. Half of the time, this movement occurs at the very beginning of the shot, just after a cut, immediately restoring the Vitruvian norm or, in a few cases, going further to context framing. Some examples demonstrate the ubiquity of this reframing strategy, especially in Astaire's third period at Metro. Each of Astaire's three partner dances in "Steppin' Out with My Baby" is done in a separate shot (three partners, three shots). A cut also marks the start of his solo dance that leads to the slow-motion section. The second and third of these partners/shots and the cut to begin the solo all begin with insert framing that immediately pulls back to Vitruvian (figs. 22.2.a, 22.2.b, 22.3.a, and 22.3.b).[29] As noted earlier, the comically bad feathers dance with Garland in *Easter Parade* cuts between insert and Vitruvian to emphasize various difficulties. The final problem in this dance—Garland turning in circles in place on the opposite side of the stage from Astaire—is shaped to express Astaire's frustration by way of a reframed shot with an initial pull. A cut to a frustrated Astaire framed from

FIGURE 22.2

FIGURE 22.3

FIGURE 22.4

the thighs up follows him and pulls back to Vitruvian as he walks over to Garland and intervenes (figs. 22.4.a through 22.4.c). The role of the reframed shot smoothing the transition between insert and Vitruvian framing is nicely demonstrated here, in a number that also uses cuts to accomplish the same cinematic dancing effect.

The reverse reframing move—pushing in on a dancing body at the end of a shot—also occurs. A singular such shot in *You'll Never Get Rich* offers another unusual moment when the camera takes its eye off of Astaire's body—in this case, in favor of rising star Rita Hayworth. Midway through "Boogie Barcarolle," Astaire and Hayworth are positioned near each other but not side by side: he's alone in front; she's in the chorus line behind him. To single out Hayworth as the film's (and Columbia Pictures' newest) star, the camera reframes the shot to push in on Hayworth, who, ironically but necessarily for the conceit of the shot, does the dance wrong (she looks forward when the rest of the chorus looks back; it works because she has her eye on starting a relationship with Astaire; figs. 22.5.a through 22.5.c). This slow push in on Hayworth is analogous to the famous push in on John Wayne in *Stagecoach* (1939)—a moment when a new screen personality is given a halo of sorts by way of a reframing of the star's body. And even Astaire can't hold the screen for every second of the number under such conditions (especially while working at Hayworth's studio).

One entirely danced reframed shot uniquely sets Astaire's normative framing practices in context by way of contrast: an example of a path almost never taken in Astaire's work. Like the singular cutaway in "Heat Wave" that pictured Astaire as a mere observer in the number, this shot from the "Bachelor Dinner Song" (*The Belle of New York* [1952]) violates the aesthetic

FIGURE 22.5

preeminence given Astaire's body and relegates him to just one part of a larger picture. The number features Astaire with thirteen women. The initial section of the routine has him dance in turn very briefly with just about every woman: Astaire remains center and fully visible throughout; the women come and go, framing him in decorative and varied arrangements when not engaged with him directly. At one point, Astaire climbs atop a dining table. He proceeds to fall back into the women's arms and they boost him forward (this action on a cut to a view from the short end of the table). The entirely danced reframed shot that follows has Astaire jump off the front end of the table, nearest the camera. This cuts him off at the waist (recall *reframed* refers to Astaire's body). He remains there as the women climb up and around the table and all turn toward the camera and strike a shared pose (fig. 22.6). This pictorial moment—which arguably breaks the fourth wall (the women acknowledge the camera by posing for it)—treats the frame as just that, a picture frame within which a symmetrical composition made of many bodies fills the space in an artful manner that draws attention to the composition itself (a motif treated more freely in the number's vocal section). Astaire, in the moment of the pose, becomes just another element of the composition. Earlier in the number, only the women were treated as design elements. Astaire—a male center point—does not pose but keeps moving. When he does hold for the pose, Astaire is in closed ballroom position. This brief held moment subordinates, even erases, him, as the ladies of the ensemble present themselves to the camera. Of course, Astaire is constantly presenting to the camera not as a frozen figure, but rather as a dynamic, space-making (masculine) force. The women in "Bachelor Dinner Song" pose as if aware they are being looked at: Astaire normatively does not (except at the very end of his numbers when, in the midst of a final pose, he often gestures in a way that

FIGURE 22.6

signals he, also, approves of his own work, as if, in the end, only his opinion of his performance really matters—see his solos "I Won't Dance" and "I'd Rather Lead a Band" [*Follow the Fleet*]). After the pose breaks, Astaire returns to the tabletop and back into the Vitruvian framing that prioritizes his body in almost uniform fashion across the clip reel—except for rare moments such as this that suggest an entirely different way of disposing of dancing bodies in the two dimensions of the cinema.

23. Widescreen Adjustments

The transition to widescreen inevitably complicated all three "full figure" framing categories and required new approaches to framing generally. The continued decline in average shot length and longest shot over the three films Astaire made in the mid-1950s suggests a move toward more cutting in the widescreen context. Astaire's limited time in widescreen proved enough to experiment with novel framings of the body typical of widescreen dance generally—such as lying on the floor (as Astaire does in a parodic spirit in both *Funny Face* and *Silk Stockings*)—but the norm of putting the dancing body front and center and making it as large as possible remained. Indeed, the size of the screen in widescreen made the dancing body objectively larger in the movie theater even if it was also surrounded by much empty space to either side.

Astaire remained faithful to the Vitruvian norm of scaling the whole dancing body as large as possible. Doing so required very sensitive camera work not always fully achieved—see "All of You" (*Silk Stockings*) in particular, with feet and the top of heads often cut off. One option to forestall the sense of dancers being lost in the new wider frame was to increase the size of the dance, as Astaire and Janis Paige do to comic effect in "Stereophonic Sound" (also *Silk Stockings*). Within the Vitruvian logic that demands the dance remain frameable, a wider screen allowed for certain kinds of larger motions. Outside Astaire's films this included flips and acrobatics. He never did such moves, likely both because of his age and because of the limits Astaire set on his own dance moves, keeping them as close to everyday movements as possible.

"Too Bad" (again *Silk Stockings*) begs the question of distinguishing context from Vitruvian framing in widescreen given the former category's role of situating dancers in a social setting. "Too Bad" includes seven moving bodies—three Russian Communists on a spree, three women brought in for their pleasure, and Astaire as ringleader of the party. A large round table loaded with champagne and caviar works as a set piece dividing and filling the space. The dance portion is done in two reframed shots. Both pull out quickly from insert framing on a single figure to include full-figure framing of all seven, all of whom move throughout. The first shot begins on a woman in a red dress as she moves toward Astaire. He cha-chas in turn with her, and each of the other two, in an area opened up between the table and a small couch to screen right (about two-thirds of the frame). The round table fills screen left; the women waiting their turn with Astaire pose against it. The three Russians dance singly or with the women Astaire releases behind Astaire's foreground position (their movements reflected in a mirror to screen right add dimension to the whole). Astaire had danced with three partners in turn before in "Steppin' Out with My Baby": his dance with each woman was taken in a separate shot—three partners, three shots. In widescreen, Astaire dances with three women each in turn in a single fifty-second shot—the longest shot in *Silk Stockings*. This triple-partner routine in full figure done in a rich and active context ends with a cut to Peter Lorre, who is dancing Russian-style leg kicks with the support of the table and a chair. Astaire pulls a chair out of the way on the cut, a match on action that effectively puts a further spotlight on Lorre. The second shot of the dance thus begins on an insert framing of Lorre—which makes the knife in his mouth more visible—and quickly opens back up to all seven. The women dance around the table and eventually pull in three of the men for another circling of the table. Lorre goes back to his schtick with the chair. With so much going on, the viewer is left to look wherever they wish. The dance—a mix of choreography (Astaire's dances with each woman) and more casual movement (when the Russians join in)—is folded into much character interaction and multiple points of interest. If watching on a small screen, it's easy to miss the moment when Astaire jabs Jules Munshin in the rear end with a knife two times to the beat of the music. Indeed, there is too much going on in "Too Bad" for a first- or one-time viewer to catch it all. Still, the dance functions exactly as dance had in the Academy musical, and the full-figure framing of Astaire and the women draws the attention of a viewer focused on film musical actions.

Inserts play a new role in widescreen dances suggesting a diminished role for a certain sort of reframed shot. In three widescreen dances, the final pose and chord are marked by an abrupt cut to insert framing at the last beat of the music. This happens first in "History of the Beat" and is repeated in "Something's Gotta Give" (*Daddy Long Legs*) and "All of You." In Academy, Astaire on occasion had the camera push in at the very end of a number, marking the conclusion and final pose with an emphasis on the face—see "I'd Rather Lead a Band," "The Yam" (*Carefree*), "Coffee Time" (*Yolanda and the Thief* [1945]), and "Shoes with Wings On" (*The Barkleys of Broadway* [1949]). Cutting to insert framing on the final beat of a dance, as only happens in widescreen, has a similar effect but does so in rhythm with the music (and as a further confirmation of the close of the number). Pushing in or cutting to insert at the close serves similar functions: both emphasize the dancer's face.

Widescreen demonstrably changed the nature of Astaire and his partners' screen dance bodies. An unusual insert from "He Loves and She Loves" (*Funny Face*) exploits the 3-D effects of widescreen. Near the end, Astaire holds Hepburn in a deep dip. Positioned near the camera, she sweeps from right to left with one arm extended toward the camera (fig. 23.1). The effect on a massive widescreen would have been unusually immersive and intense (viewers at downtown movie palaces would have had to turn their head to follow Hepburn's white-gloved hand). Three similar entirely danced reframed shots in *Daddy Long Legs* similarly exploit the scale and 3-D effects of widescreen. The first two of these come as a matched pair in the middle of the guardian angel dream duo. Caron, with Astaire in the chase, proceeds to run across the lower horizontal of the frame (just past the camera) and, on

FIGURE 23.1

a cut, immediately re-enters across the lower horizontal (again just past the camera). This match on action violates the 180-degree rule that keeps all action on one side of the camera. Crossing the horizontal in this way alters the dancers' bodies—we see them whole, then only partially as they pass over the frame. Later, during their fantasy of a night on the town that sets the couple dancing against images of Times Square, Astaire and Caron twirl into view across the lower horizontal, just as in the dream.[30] Astaire had never made such a move in his previous twenty-six films (and this film is the only time he used it). Fantastic story contexts allowed for such movement, which, in *Daddy Long Legs*, takes Astaire and Caron between or into stylized settings. Again, these entirely danced reframed shots are typical of most in that the moment when the dancers' bodies change the most in relation to the frame—when they cross the lower horizontal—is very brief and comes at one end of the shot.

24. Formal Principles, Expressive Resources, Production Conveniences

The fundamental choices of shot duration and framing discussed in quantitative terms in this part express a variety of creative priorities. Shot duration and framing at once indicate formal principles (Astaire's view of how best to frame the dancing body), serve as expressive resources (adding content to the dance beyond the moving body), and point toward production conveniences (a lengthy one-shot dance poses specific physical challenges not present in a multishot dance). This interplay of aesthetic and practical concerns comes into quantitative focus by parsing Astaire's use of the three full-figure categories by career period and by film.

Context framing was never central to his work, although a career pattern emerges: 15% by shot count at RKO, declining to 9% (1940–1946) and falling to 2% during his third, mostly MGM, period. A modest rebound of the context shot in the widescreen films (8%) is driven mostly by *Funny Face*, which contains four of six context shots in this period. This is the first evidence that specific framing practices might be driven by Astaire's collaborators—in this case, director Stanley Donen (though, again, the small widescreen corpus raises challenges for quantitative analysis). The minimal use of context framing in any period directs our attention to the two competing approaches to "full figure" framing: the Vitruvian norm and the reframed shot.

Chart 13 compares the number of shots (as a percentage of the whole) in Vitruvian and reframed categories for each period. Remember that most of the duration of reframed shots uses Vitruvian framing of the body, so relatively few seconds are given to anything but the normative framing—the change in the shot, which almost always entails camera movement in sensitive relationship to the body, is what's important here. Also important is the technical challenge of the reframed shot, which usually involved camera movement and always involved a substantial change in the relationship between the body and the frame (as opposed to the goal of maintaining a given relationship in Vitruvian). A clear pattern is evident: in the 1930s at RKO, reframed shots were very rare (only 6%). In each successive period, the use of reframed shots increased, until in the widescreen years the two types occur with the same frequency. The most significant change occurs with Astaire's time at MGM after the war: here, for the first time, the reframed shot reaches near parity with Vitruvian.

The distribution of Vitruvian and reframed shots across Astaire's career reflects specific production contexts and collaborators. For example, consider the count of both types (as a percentage of all shots) in six consecutive midcareer films (see chart 14). Films Astaire made at Columbia, RKO, and Paramount use very few or no reframed shots. By contrast, the three films in this group made at MGM turn toward the reframed shot as often as or

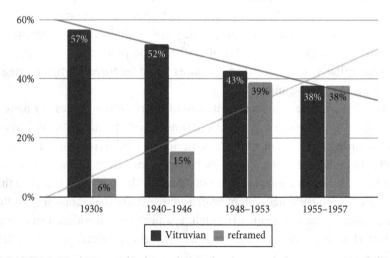

CHART 13 Vitruvian and reframed types by shot count (as percentage of all shots by period)

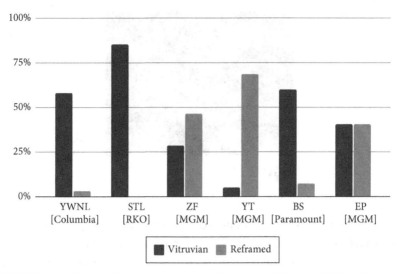

CHART 14 Full and reframed shots in six films from 1943 to 1948 (by shot count as percent of total shots in each film)

much more often than the Vitruvian. The overwhelming use of reframed shots in *Yolanda* reflects the aesthetic proclivities of Vincente Minnelli. The balanced approach between the categories in *Easter Parade* expresses that of director Charles Walters. In this way, we can begin to locate the precise limits of Astaire's agency and track his varying willingness to let others (literally) frame his screen dance body.

Another way to parse how framing types reflect expressive content is to track a common type of reframed shot: an initial pull from insert to Vitruvian discussed previously. Looking at the content of this subcorpus of seventy-three shots, I have isolated thirty-two of a similar type: in a dance already in progress (none are the first shot in a dance), this sort of reframed shot begins on an insert framing that brings extra attention to Astaire's or Astaire and his partners' faces. The effect is strong—we are brought close to human expression that is not primarily danced but rather a matter of facial expression (the essence of film acting). Again, this effect would not be possible outside of film, which affords the choice to isolate and enlarge parts of the body then pull back and restore visual access to the entire body. The first such shot is striking and almost entirely isolated historically. The single cut in "Change Partners" (*Carefree*) suddenly pulls our attention to the longing on Astaire's face (fig. 24.1).[31] The composition of the shot—with Astaire's

FIGURE 24.1

extended arm crossing the frame—only adds to the disruption of normative framing practices (especially in this period of Astaire's work). This extremely intimate moment is enhanced by the closeness of their bodies (essentially full-body contact) coming after a dance when Rogers (under hypnosis) moves under Astaire's nontouching lead. The use of cinematic means to bring the viewer suddenly very close to the dancers is extremely rare in the first two periods of Astaire's career—indeed, it only happens one other time (an oddly disjunctive cut in "The Babbitt and the Bromide" [*Ziegfeld Follies*]).

Then, from *Easter Parade* onward this kind of mid-dance cut to insert framing that emphasizes facial emotion becomes common as to almost be cliché. Fully one-third of all reframed shots in periods three and four are of this type. The aforementioned one from "Beautiful Faces" is not the only one in *Easter Parade*. There's one in "Drum Crazy" that puts the device to comic use: Astaire plays his head like a drum, a dance move enhanced by insert framing (figs. 24.2.a and 24.2.b). Clearly it was possible to use this device in the 1930s—as the single example from the period in "Change Partners" attests. However, it was only at MGM in the late 1940s and after that the practice becomes a regular feature of Astaire's screen dance body (figs. 24.3.a and 24.3.b). And it proved readily adaptable to widescreen (see "Sluefoot" [figs. 24.4.a and 24.4.b] and almost every cut in the duo portion of "All of You"). Significantly, in all these shots the camera marks the beginning or end of the shot, drawing attention to the cut (which interrupts access to the dance) and also, from a production history standpoint, revealing the extent to which the cut was designed into the dance. In these details, the planning of the dance around framing choices, camera movement, and preplanned cuts is especially visible.

FIGURE 24.2

FIGURE 24.3

FIGURE 24.4

The decisions around shot duration and framing type are basic to the making of a musical number. These fundamental choices reflect a range of aesthetic and practical priorities. On one level, shot duration and framing type can indicate the changing formal principles informing Astaire and his collaborators' work. The overwhelming predominance of Vitruvian framing indicates that, for Astaire, only the full dancing body is of real interest. For a time, very long shots were his method for capturing this body on film. After about 1936, he began to build this screen dance body's visibility in shorter shots. Reframed shots, like those of the initial pull variety, became something of a formal principle (and aesthetic tic) in periods three and four, with their repeated use in numbers such as "Steppin' Out" and "All of You." But the initial pull approach was also an expressive resource, bringing the dancer's face into the cine-dance in an abrupt manner. Of course, building a dance out of several shots (instead of one) was also a production convenience, allowing the dancers to parcel out their energy over the course of a shooting day. Reframed shots, which bring the added challenge of adjusting rather than just maintaining the relationship between the camera and the dancing body, may in turn, of course, have created production inconveniences, given that such shots involved multiple moving bodies—dancers and camera. Other basic choices fall into multiple categories: for instance, the common practice of segregating nonmusical and musical actions or singing and dancing into separate shots expresses both a production convenience (easing the transition into or out of lip-syncing) and a formal principle (different shots for different sorts of actions). Part Three looks closely at the production context, seeking to understand in precise terms the way these numbers were made and also the active labor of Astaire and his collaborators' bodies.

Corin Willis has posited the notion of "racial cuts" in classical Hollywood as a general term for "an edit specifically timed to frame and freeze the [Black jazz-making] character in a stereotypical 'racial' pose or gesture."[32] In *Music Makes Me*, I identified such "racial cuts" in the "The Carioca," where light and dark-skinned Brazilians "are all pictured in thrall to the music" by way of rapid cuts and frequently canted insert framing. "Astaire and Rogers are eager to be part of the scene (although their dances are not subjected to the technique of racial cuts)."[33] In retrospect, my conclusion misses the mark: Astaire and Rogers are indeed subjected to racial cuts—specifically those that make up *whiteness*. The notion of racial cuts as defining Blackness must be balanced with the reciprocal (and grossly unequal) power of white normative framing practices in the presentation of white bodies and subjects.

Astaire's aesthetic and technical approach to the construction of a centered screen dance body, often seen in durationally long shots, constitutes its own set of racial practices that make up whiteness. Astaire's framing constitutes a white racial subject: whole, centered, a (male) agent around which space accrues, a unified subject in control of self and the world. The expressive content of insert framing—whether standalone or folded into reframed shots—enhances the interiority of this white dancing subject (who not only dances with their body but also acts with their face), even as Astaire's position as the leading male character in the film plot ties his body in the dance to a character also known in dialogue and narrative (he speaks in addition to singing and dancing). White "racial cuts," in contrast to those defining a stereotypical Blackness, present a unified, almost always literally whole subject with tremendous power over the camera and the space through which it moves—in such consistent choices lies the content of the sovereign racialized white subject.

At the height of nostalgia for classical Hollywood, critic Robin Wood confessed a deep connection to the Astaire-Rogers films dating to his earliest experiences with cinema. Wood writes, "If they contributed so much to my delight, it is clear in retrospect that they also contributed, as 'myth,' to my oppression." Working from one scene and song in *Swing Time*, "The Way You Look Tonight," Wood begins, "First, we must note in passing—though this is secondary and almost incidental—that we have here a cinema shot through with racism and sexism." Wood notes, for instance, the "oily, insincere, and vaguely effeminate foreignness" of Astaire's rival for Rogers's love in *Swing Time* (the aforementioned Riccardo Romero)—a characterization that extends more or less to other films in the cycle—and also how Dorothy Fields's lyric for the song objectifies the female love object as just that, an object to be looked at. Wood continues, "In theory, American democracy means equality for all; on the level of ideology, this translates into 'equality for all white American heterosexual males.' To raise these issues, it is only fair to add, is scarcely to make a specific criticism of *Swing Time*, which simply partakes unreflectingly of general characteristics of its culture. Nonetheless, these characteristics are clearly an aspect of the film's functioning, hence demand notice."[34] Also central to how Astaire musicals function is the creation of the privileged white body—seen whole and continuously—described in this part. And Astaire's access to the means to make this body proves central to its power. It is normative in the sense that it is the default body seen in studio-era film musicals. This male body is the sustained focus of attention.

Its movements control the camera and the space created by the camera. Part Four looks more closely at the mechanics of this relationship as evident in the films themselves. Before that, however, Part Three considers what studio archives reveal about the day-to-day, minute-to-minute process behind the making of Astaire's film musicals and his screen dance body.

THREE
DAYS, HOURS, MINUTES

[Astaire] said, you know, I don't take anything away from the dramatic people. But after all, they do have a script written for them, it's written, and they, in turn, do their own characterization of it. But, he said, you take us dancers. We have to be the bricklayers, the foundation, the painters, the carpenters, well the whole thing. All we've got for inspiration is a piece of song, of music on a piano with a piano player in an empty hall. Now do something great. So we have to think of, practically, you almost, in a way, design the set.
—Eleanor Powell (1981)

Did we practice a lot? Are you kidding? For hours, and hours, and hours, and hours, and hours.
—Audrey Hepburn on *Funny Face* (1988)

Well, we never really thought about it. We just went to work on Monday.
—Astaire's words remembered by Sam Goldwyn Jr. (1988)

25. "It's a Terrific Job"

Astaire loved his work—and he thought of it as work. Multiple journalists attested to this. Gladys Hall, writing for the fan magazine *Modern Screen* in 1937, expressed unabashed awe at Astaire on the set.

> As I sat watching Fred Astaire doing a song and dance, doing it over and over and over, then listening to the play-backs [sic] over and over and over, absorbed, self-critical, obviously nervous and worried and perfecting—as I sat on that sound stage for three mortal hours during which time Mr.

Astaire did not exchange a single word with anyone save for his brief visits to my corner of the set—as I watched, the concentrated, one-tracked passion of the man for the work he does became real to me. No wonder he can't talk about anything but his work, I thought. There isn't anything to compare with it.[1]

While interviewing Astaire in 1935, journalist Dana Burnet seemed to realize that this still-new movie star was, at heart, a highly skilled working man. "'Tell me how you work,' I said. (If you can find out how a man works, and how he regards his work, you'll know more about him than if you took an X-ray of him.)" Astaire replied with a detailed description of his process that began, "Well, I usually start work about five weeks before the beginning of a picture. Start work on my dances, I mean."[2] The notion of dance making as work—and as the work of a man—is the larger focus of this part of the book. Astaire's work was decidedly physical—"a sweat job," he often said of dancing. Burnet continued his line of questioning.

What do you call a day's work? A good day's accomplishment? The Astaire grin grew broader. "My assistant and I say that if we perform two good deeds a day, that's enough. That's a day's work. By two good deeds, I mean two new steps worked out or two new movements invented. If I fall behind in my schedule I work nights. Then, after a routine is in fairly good shape, it may lie idle for two or three weeks while we're making the picture. So I have to rehearse it all over again. I work Sundays and holidays, when I have to. I don't mind that. I enjoy it. I like dancing."[3]

Astaire's seemingly simple statement, "I like dancing"—no surprise from someone who danced professionally for most of his life—is here framed as labor done with enthusiasm, always with a clear goal in view: making, in his words, "my dances."

Astaire was paid a flat fee per picture from *Roberta* (1935) on, with occasional participation in the profits. How much did he make? Extant contracts and documents for the Astaire-Rogers pictures show the rapidly rising per film pay Astaire received, as well as Rogers's much lower and much slower-growing paychecks. Considering just his contracts, Astaire's price went from $20,700 (*Roberta*) to $195,000 (*The Castles* [1939]). On *Top Hat* (1935), *Follow the Fleet* (1936), and *Swing Time* (1936), he enjoyed 2% participation in profits; for *Shall We Dance* (1937), *Carefree* (1938), and *The Castles*, this rose to 7.5% on profits under and 10% on profits over $2 million. Not counting any profit sharing, Astaire's 1930s income at RKO exceeded $640,000 (around $12 million today).[4] Being a dancing white male movie star was very lucrative employment during the depths of the Depression—and Astaire was the only man in the world with the job. Rogers's pay trajectory never came close to matching Astaire's: while the extant documents in her case are less clear, in cumulative terms she seems to have made about half of what Astaire made on their films (this does not include the twelve additional films Rogers appeared in at RKO between her films with Astaire). Of course, Astaire's contracts factored in his creative labor making his own dances. This contribution to the content of the film, unusual for a star performer, surely accounts for his participation in film profits, something Rogers never earned but that Irving Berlin, alone among the RKO songwriters, successfully negotiated. In later periods, Astaire earned a flat fee of between $100,000 and $150,000 for a given span of weeks (usually around twenty-two).[5] But films are unpredictable things to make and more than the contracted time might be needed. As a unit manager on *Holiday Inn* (1942) noted in a memo, "Fred Astaire has given *two weeks* of his time *FREE* as a Xmas present to Paramount."[6] And he went unpaid when retakes were taken at his request: as on the very first few shots of Astaire alone in "Ev'ry Night at Seven" (*Royal Wedding* [1951]).[7]

But Astaire was also an hourly worker. He may not have punched himself in and out, but he was expected to keep regular business hours and be prepared to stay late and show up on off days. A contract memo from 1952 (for two pictures he never made with MGM) stipulates Astaire would not be expected to work past 6pm except for night shots and emergency retakes.[8] Murray Pomerance begins his discussion of Hollywood production methods by highlighting the studios' "obsessive meticulousness about the use of time."[9] The paper trail produced by this obsession opens a close-grained view of Astaire at work. A generous body of archival data—mostly assistant director (AD) reports for Astaire's RKO and MGM films and for Paramount's *Holiday Inn*—allow us to tally up the weeks, days, hours, and even minutes Astaire spent in each phase of the film-musical-making process.[10] This film-level data for nineteen of Astaire's twenty-nine films contains a quantitative picture of Astaire's real body at work making the products of his labors: film musicals and musical numbers. This part of the book uses these sources to get as close to Astaire's laboring body as possible. To repeat, the data presented here reflects only how Astaire spent his time on these films. It is a record of his labor only, not that of others on the film—although anecdotal information about others offers occasional context and texture as well. The studios' obsession with metrics complements my second-by-second account of the clip reel. The archival data on how the clip reel was produced helps locate Astaire's lived body within the traces of his screen dance body. Both rely on measurements of time.

26. "Astaire Was No Doubt Rehearsing Most of the Time"

Like all studio employees, Astaire worked a six-day week. His average workday lasted just over six-and-a-half hours—not counting an hour for lunch and, on very long days, a second hour for dinner.[11] According to the extant archives, Astaire worked past midnight shooting a musical number on only one occasion. On August 6, 1934, Astaire was shooting his "Nightclub Solo" for *The Gay Divorcee* (1934). He rehearsed from 9:00am to 2:30pm (lunch inclusive); then it took until 12:30am (dinner inclusive) to get the number on film. A thirteen-piece jazz band was on the set (providing live music), as well as many extras watching this dance routine that lasts eighty-one seconds in the finished film.[12] Staying late to prepare to shoot the next day was more common, though midnight seems to be the limit. The night before the first day filming on two huge musical numbers—"The Carioca" in *Flying Down to Rio* (1933) and the long finale sequence of *Shall We Dance*—Astaire was at the studio until 11:30pm and 11:50pm, respectively, rehearsing and setting crane movement.[13] But long days like this were exceptional—and in the extant record only happened for Astaire at RKO in the 1930s. There's no hard evidence Astaire and Rogers ever stayed past 8:00pm shooting a dance number.[14] At MGM in the 1940s and '50s, everything usually stopped by 6pm—except on the last day of complicated numbers that just needed to get done, such as the marathon *Yolanda and the Thief* (1945) dream ballet shoot, which ended its eleventh day at 7:20pm, and a scuttled bubble number for *Ziegfeld Follies* (1946), which shot to no avail until 10:45pm (more on this later).[15]

Studio film musical making presented Astaire with five kinds of workdays:

(1) Creating and rehearsing dance routines before shooting began (or before "production" on the film "opened" and the studio started keeping detailed track of progress on the film and the budget)

(2) Creating and rehearsing dance routines *after* production had opened while work on the film was ongoing
(3) Shooting musical numbers
(4) Shooting dialogue scenes
(5) Making sound recordings, whether prerecording for playback or postsyncing body sounds

Time spent doing the last of these—making sound recordings—was comparatively rare and occurred across the entire filmmaking process, seldom taking an entire workday. Recording sessions usually lasted about three hours (in musicians' union terms, one session) or about half a workday. Usually Astaire did other work, most often rehearsing, to round out a day when he had a recording session. (Typically only a handful of days on each film were divided between two sorts of work: most often a combination of rehearsing and something else.) Vocal tracks and dance accompaniments were only prerecorded once a number had been finalized as to choreography—thus, knowing the date a number was prerecorded indicates something of the shift from creating a dance to only rehearsing it. Unfortunately, for most numbers with data it's not clear exactly when rehearsals began. And so, knowledge of when a number was prerecorded mainly offers evidence for how long Astaire spent rehearsing to playback. A corpus of forty-eight numbers with known recording session dates distributed across Astaire's career offers a sense for the span of time between prerecording and filming to playback. On average, recording sessions occurred ten days (counting Sundays) before shooting on a number commenced—seemingly plenty of time for Astaire to rehearse with the recording. However, many times the days between prerecording and shooting a number were much fewer: the mode (most frequently occurring number) of the corpus is three days. The chronological relationship between prerecording and filming a dance was crucial. A memo to the music department on *Yolanda* made a point of this: "it is very urgent that a prerecording should be made for Mr. Astaire's Harp solo which he plays in this set as he will naturally have to have a number of days in which to rehearse to this playback."[16] Sometimes prerecording happened the night before filming— as with "Slap That Bass," which, like most all numbers in *Shall We Dance*, was recorded by the Jimmy Dorsey Orchestra, a popular big band whose recording sessions for RKO were held late into the evenings. The "Slap That Bass" session ended at 12:15am; Astaire was on the set at 9am the next day to start filming the number.[17]

Before the widescreen era, in all but three known cases, recording sessions involved just one number. One of these, for *Easter Parade* (1948), brought together various short components of the medley. The many short musical numbers in that film, again, influenced the production process. Most of the time in the Academy periods, coincident with the studio system norm, musical numbers were made one at a time (a practice that allowed for only the players needed for a given number to be called to that session). Prerecording sessions in the Academy era could happen at any point in the process, whenever a number was ready to be filmed. The normative practice of prerecording each number in a separate session, facilitated by the presence of standing studio orchestras up to the mid-1950s, serves as a reminder that musical numbers were made one at a time—even though each film required a group of numbers, they were each conceived singly.

Prerecording session records for the widescreen films *Funny Face* and *Silk Stockings* (both 1957)—alike somewhat unusual projects in terms of production—show a different practice: all the numbers for both films were recorded early on. All the music for *Funny Face*, including a retake of Astaire's solo "Let's Kiss and Make Up" in a lower key, was recorded in a single eight-day period, before shooting commenced, with several sessions including two numbers. *Silk Stockings* similarly clustered multiple-number prerecording sessions before production opened. Clustering the prerecording of numbers saved money and forced the recording process to be more efficient—and it didn't work out for *Silk Stockings*. After an expensive lost day trying to shoot "Fated to Be Mated" outside on bicycles, the number had to be completely reimagined (by Pan alone; Astaire was now occupied shooting dialogue). The new choreography required a new musical arrangement for the third section. Music department records indicate two different versions of the replacement for the original version: the first scored for "Dance Orchestra" (recorded shortly before filming and used on the set), the second for "Jazz Orchestra" (recorded weeks later likely after the number had been edited together in an instance of postsyncing dance music to an already filmed number). And even this second (really third) version required "sweetener" (extra strings) at yet another recording session.[18]

On his first three films, Astaire sometimes filmed his dances to live music on set. I describe a particular instance of this at the start of *Music Makes Me*. But this was always difficult and was abandoned as a practice during *Roberta*—about half the numbers in that film were filmed to live music on set, the rest to prerecorded tracks. An intermediate practice that tried to hang on to live music on set entailed filming to a piano (and sometimes drums) on set, then adding the orchestra in postproduction. Pan remembered how difficult this was: "At one time, they used to put the music in later, after they'd shoot to a piano track. And which was very, very difficult and would drive everybody crazy. We'd shoot to this piano track... piano and drums and then they'd have to put on earphones and watch the screen and listen to that track and try to get the whole orchestra to fit it, which was very very unsatisfactory and we used to spend hours on the stage trying to get the music to fit the dance."[19] This method was abandoned in 1937, after *Shall We Dance*. From then on, Astaire is always lip-syncing and dancing to prerecorded music. This allowed the days spent shooting to focus solely on the image track.

Astaire, virtually alone among studio actors, still had work to do after production closed. He returned to the lot to monitor the editing of his numbers—Astaire was likely among the only actors ever to visit the cutting department—and he went back into the recording studio to postsync body sounds, primarily tap dancing, for his dances. On such days, Astaire acted as his own "Foley" artist. His female partners, with the exception of Eleanor Powell, did not record their own foot sounds. For instance, Hermes Pan is the sound of Ginger Rogers's feet in all the RKO pictures: Astaire said of Rogers in 1973, "she couldn't tap, and she couldn't do this or that; all the taps were put in by Hermes Pan."[20] Assistant director (AD) reports for a sync taps day on *The Barkleys of Broadway* (1949) states that "six girls danced for Ginger Rogers."[21] The archives for RKO do not account for Astaire's postsync workdays spent recording foot sounds, and so the data presented in this book deals only with the days, hours, and minutes he spent in rehearsal or shooting—the preproduction (for musicals, uniquely extended) and the production (for musicals, uniquely complicated) phases of the process. Chart 15 shows the total number of days (including half days) spent rehearsing and shooting on each film with data.

A new film began for Astaire when he reported for work in a rehearsal hall where his daily task was creating and rehearsing musical numbers before production (or shooting) began. This was private work, for the most part. Astaire normally began rehearsals at 10am and ended at 5pm. He always took a lunch break and, according to him, brought his own lunch (a somewhat antisocial choice). On average Astaire spent forty-one days (just under seven 6-day weeks) creating and rehearsing numbers before any shooting began, a period within which an entire nonmusical film—at some studios even two—could easily have been shot. The average conceals outliers that speak

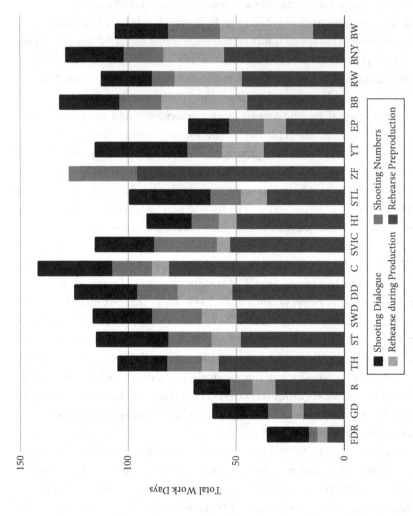

CHART 15 Days Astaire worked on the nineteen films with archival data by type of workday (excluding making sound recordings)

to specific production constraints on individual films and to Astaire's quick learning curve as to how studio production methods might be turned toward his benefit, supporting his creative priorities and process. On *Flying Down to Rio*, Astaire put in just eight days of preproduction rehearsal. By *Top Hat*, his preproduction rehearsal period was up to fifty-eight days, in the range for his subsequent standard approach of spending about seven weeks preparing numbers. A few later films drop well below the average: Astaire spent just twenty-seven days rehearsing *Easter Parade*—a film he joined late after Gene Kelly's injury—before filming started with the numbers "Drum Crazy" and "Steppin' Out with My Baby." Pressure to get the film into production surely influenced this case, but similar demands attended all Astaire's films. He never had unlimited time. The creative work Astaire did during the preproduction period remains somewhat opaque. Studio logs do not generally note which numbers he worked on and for how long he worked on each. AD reports and music department sources do reveal which numbers he filmed first, indicating which numbers were prepared in the initial weeks.

Studio executives knew of Astaire's preproduction methods. In a memo speculating about the number of rehearsal days Astaire might require for the film *White Christmas* (1954, a film he did not do), Paramount production manager Frank Caffey researched previous Astaire films at the studio. For *Holiday Inn*, Caffrey lacked daily data so instead he subtracted the date Astaire started rehearsal (recorded in a memo) from the day shooting began—"This gives an elapsed time of 52 days, exclusive of Sundays, during which time Astaire was no doubt rehearsing most of the time."[22] Several of my estimates of Astaire's rehearsal periods are similarly derived from ancillary evidence, such as pay records for Astaire's dance assistants and rehearsal pianists.

By *Top Hat*, Astaire had learned to front-load musical numbers at the start of the production process. Most every subsequent film began production with several days shooting numbers. Among the Astaire numbers that were the first parts of a given film to be filmed are "No Strings" (*Top Hat*), "Let's Call the Whole Thing Off" (the roller-skating number in *Shall We Dance*), the *Yolanda* dream ballet, "Shoes with Wings On" (*Barkleys*), and "A Shine on Your Shoes" (*The Band Wagon* [1953]). Sometimes a number was ready before its intended film had technically "opened" for production. The short dances in the montage from *The Castles* (tango, polka, maxixe), as well as the special effects sequence with tiny dancing couples on a huge map of the United States, were shot two weeks before production on the film opened. Astaire filmed these numbers, then went back into the rehearsal hall. *Carefree* presents a slightly different process, which Astaire turned into an opportunity to do a dance he had always wanted to do. Producer Pandro S. Berman wrote to director Mark Sandrich on the matter.

> I think the thing to do about the Fred Astaire situation is to definitely get his solo ready now and shoot it while we are waiting for Ginger to become available for the picture. We will have a great deal of lost time if we do not accomplish something in the interval while she is working on *Wonderful Time*, and I think the only thing we can presumably accomplish might be the golf routine or some other solo routine of Fred's. I wish you would pound on this and see if you can work this out successfully and get it in the bag before Ginger is available.[23]

While Rogers finished up her comedic star vehicle *Having Wonderful Time* (1938), Astaire created and shot his "Golf Solo," which was completed before the *Carefree* script was finalized and three weeks before the shooting of dialogue commenced. The "Golf Solo" was a fait accompli the screenwriters had to wedge into the story (it worked easily into the film's country club setting). The preproduction rehearsal period for *Carefree* was inordinately long: eighty-one days. This was surely only tolerated because Astaire was paid a flat fee, not a weekly rate. And he may have taken some days off while waiting for Rogers (the RKO data is incomplete). On average, Astaire spent seventeen days shooting numbers for a film, but this average again conceals variation between films.

Astaire was also an actor and he spent considerable time shooting dialogue. These workdays required Astaire to show up with his lines memorized, to learn his blocking on the set, and to do the expressive labor—the "characterization" required of "the dramatic people." Dialogue scenes were expected to require minimal rehearsal. "10 min. rehearsing" appears regularly at the start of dialogue days on the *Roberta* AD reports in an area listing "Reasons for Delay."[24] Efficiency on dialogue days relied on the script being set and the director effectively managing both actors and crew. *Swing Time*'s AD reported, "Went behind one more day account added dialogue written for Penny's Room."[25] In a similar case on *Yolanda*, Astaire expressed irritation at such rewrites. In the film's first week of shooting dialogue, director Vincente Minnelli changed both the set and the dialogue—the AD was careful to note that the director's decisions slowed progress doing the work to be done: shooting useable takes. Minnelli's changes continued. By the fourth day that week, the AD reported, "Rehearse with Astaire—did not shoot because Mr. Astaire didn't feel that he knew the lines of dialog [sic] which were written and given to Astaire this afternoon well enough to shoot and wanted time to study."[26] During one stressful day a week later, Astaire and costar Frank Morgan "asked that a check be made on how much later it would be and inasmuch as it would take some time [to restart shooting] Company was dismissed and will resume in the morning where we left off."[27] Choreographer Eugene Loring recalled the *Yolanda* shoot: "Fred had to put his foot down about changes on the set. Vince [Minnelli] would get an idea about something pictorial—interesting—but Fred, being such a careful and meticulous worker, it isn't easy for him to change quickly and be comfortable and sure of himself. It wasn't always the happiest situation."[28] On average, Astaire spent twenty-six days shooting dialogue on each film. *Yolanda*'s forty-three days of dialogue quantifies the inefficiency endemic to that film. Astaire's interest in dialogue was negligible according to screenwriter Leonard Gershe: "He was mostly interested in how he looked in the dances. In the few things I worked with him on, never once did he ask for a change in the script. Never once did he ask me to define the character, or what the motivation was."[29]

The preproduction rehearsal period was never sufficient time to prepare all the dances for a film. And so, Astaire also spent some workdays creating and rehearsing numbers while production was "open." These rehearsal days required Astaire to create under pressure with the budget clock ticking. AD forms were designed with nonmusical films in mind. Once an actor who made more than $15 per day had "started" on a film—which usually meant started shooting—their daily status was given as "W" (worked), "H" (hold), or "O" (off). Film musicals required the ad hoc code "R" (rehearsing). I have generally assumed that when Astaire was not engaged in shooting numbers or dialogue, he was rehearsing (in some cases still creating) dances yet to be shot for that film. Direct evidence for this—the designation "R" beside his name when he wasn't required for shooting—is consistent enough to generalize that he did so whenever he could. If he was off the lot, he was listed as "O." Numbers created and rehearsed during production were made under the larger pressure to finish the film, both to free up soundstage space for other films and to get the film to postproduction (and into theaters). The luxury of time to experiment in the rehearsal hall was gone, but the creative and perfecting work still had to be done. Putting off work on really big numbers until all dialogue had been shot was a common approach, often formalized by temporarily closing the production, which somewhat forestalled scrutiny of the budget. Statements on the order of "Picture closed until Dance Number is ready" reflect the unique challenges of the film musical genre.[30] Among the numbers made at the end of the production process are "The Piccolino" (*Top Hat*), "Bojangles of Harlem" and "Never Gonna Dance" (*Swing Time*),

"I Can't Be Bothered Now" (*A Damsel in Distress* [1937], "Hello, Hello, Who's Your Lady Friend?" (*The Castles*), "One for My Baby (and One More for the Road)" (*The Sky's the Limit* [1943]), "Jack and the Beanstalk" (*Let's Dance* [1950]), the skating sequence in *The Belle of New York* (1952), and "Girl Hunt" (*Band Wagon*). These are wildly different numbers. Sometimes Astaire's end-of-production numbers were hugely ambitious ("Bojangles" and "Girl Hunt"); sometimes they were barely imagined, quickly made, and decidedly unmemorable ("Hello, Hello" and "Jack and the Beanstalk"). The perfunctory nature of latter pair was surely influenced by pressure to just get the film done.

AD reports for rehearsal during production are usually a bit more specific about which number was being rehearsed, and in such data the specific pressures of a given film come to light. Astaire wasted three of the nine preproduction rehearsal weeks on *Barkleys of Broadway* rehearsing with Judy Garland (or her dance-in). The rest of this period he worked on the complicated effects number "Shoes with Wings On"—the most cinematically involved routine Astaire himself initiated. Garland was definitively dismissed from *Barkleys* on July 17, 1948 (a Saturday); Rogers joined the film on July 19 (a Monday). Astaire was shooting "Shoes with Wings On" at the time. Rogers started rehearsals that Wednesday. Rehearsals for the duo dance "Bouncin' the Blues" (not planned for the picture when Garland was the costar) must have begun immediately after Astaire finally finished "Shoes," a six-day shoot. Just twenty-three workdays later, on August 20, Astaire and Rogers shot "Bouncin' the Blues" in a single day's work. Besides creating and rehearsing the number, in their first weeks back together they also shot dialogue for a week and filmed the vocal "You'd Be Hard to Replace," which concludes with a fragment of a romantic dance that reads in context as a disappointing tease (reunited after a decade apart and that's all they do?). Much of the initial work with Rogers must have been spent on "Bouncin' the Blues," a mostly side-by-side, two-minute routine that is complicated (in rhythm and tap steps) but straightforward (in the couple's physical relationship to each other, mostly side by side). Only after nearly all the dialogue scenes had been shot were the remainder of the *Barkleys* numbers made, rehearsed, and shot, each in turn. First up was the lyrical duet "They Can't Take That Away from Me" (6½ days rehearsal; 1½ days shooting), then "Manhattan Downbeat" and "My One and Only Highland Fling" (rehearsed together over 15 days, then shot in succession). The complicated, large-cast "Manhattan," with a large dancing chorus, a visible orchestra, and multiple treadmills, took five days to shoot—a big expense of time for a number that feels patched together in the film (the two cutaways to Oscar Levant in a box seat watching the number with multiple women are unusual and suspicious). The comparatively simple "Highland Fling," for just Astaire and Rogers, took only one-and-a-half days—twelve hours and ten minutes—to shoot, making it among the most efficiently shot numbers with rehearsal and shooting data. The intentionally restrained Scottish aesthetic of the stage-bound "Fling," as well as its single-shot dance, surely made the number easy to shoot—although lip-syncing to the wordy vocal was likely a challenge. The balance between the difficult "Manhattan" and the easy "Fling" was part of the calculus behind the making of *Barkleys*— an expensive endeavor with a slow start and major reconception along the way—that finds a reflection in the content of the film. All that remained was the duo dance "Swing Trot." Rehearsed over four days—the first sandwiched between the "Manhattan" and "Fling" shoots—"Swing Trot" (and the dialogue scene after it) was shot in two days, then relegated to a lesser place behind the opening titles of the film, where it can scarcely be seen (another irritation for Astaire-Rogers fans). The ambition and aesthetic success of each of the numbers in *Barkleys* come into new focus when seen relative to its place in the shooting schedule. The AD reports on every film (where available) tell a similar story of fitting the shooting of numbers around shooting dialogue and the need to make and rehearse the numbers themselves.

There was always, of course, the option to work on Sunday. Confronted with twenty-five dancers in "['The Continental'] Hot number not satisfactorily prepared," *Gay Divorcee* director Mark Sandrich "decided to have them rehearse Sunday rather than have entire company standing around Monday while dancers rehearsed," reported the film's AD.[31] In the nineteen films with AD reports, Astaire showed up on the lot on a Sunday only fourteen times. Six were out of his control: he was called in for a full day shooting dialogue. The other eight involved musical numbers. Twice Astaire shot a number on a Sunday: the first day of the *Yolanda* dream ballet and the second of six days on the funhouse routine "Stiff Upper Lip" in *Damsel in Distress*. The former turned out to be the start of a complicated and troubled process (discussed later). The latter was part of a push to finish *Damsel*, which had been closed to prepare two final numbers—"Stiff Upper Lip" and "I Can't Be Bothered Now." "Stiff Upper Lip" is an extravaganza quite unlike anything else in the 1930s. Contained on a single, monstrous set—which includes a 360-degree shot taken from a turntable—Astaire and his costars George Burns and Gracie Allen, together with a crowd of dancers and two minor comic characters, move through a series of obstacles and apparatuses, most of which are themselves moving. This physically challenging number could only have been rehearsed on the set, as it apparently was for nine straight days (including a half-day Sunday rehearsal). Then, over six straight days "Stiff" was shot. The entire package took fifteen continuous days to make. Perhaps the exhaustion of the sustained effort on "Stiff" explains the oddly perfunctory solo "Bothered," which was the last part of *Damsel* to be made. In addition to the half-day Sunday on "Stiff," Astaire rehearsed on his own initiative on five other Sundays, always for about three hours. Except for an hour and twenty minutes during his abbreviated preproduction rehearsals for *Easter Parade*, all of these were at RKO. Astaire's Sunday rehearsals in the 1930s seem aimed at specific challenges or problems, sometimes in the midst of shooting a number. He came in on two Sundays during *Shall We Dance*: between shooting days on both "They All Laughed" (perhaps to revise the dance) and "Slap That Bass" (to rehearse on the engine room set—a complex environment with moving shadows that had to be in sync with the music). Evidence for these RKO rehearsals survives in music department pay records, which show Astaire's rehearsal pianist working on Sunday. The archival traces of Astaire's labors are incomplete and scattered, but those that survive indicate something of the care with which Astaire approached his work. Making "his dances" consumed his time—sometimes even on his day off.

On average for the films with data (again, not counting days spent recording sound), Astaire required 103 workdays to make a film musical: fifty-eight total days rehearsing (56%), sixteen days shooting numbers (17%), twenty-six days shooting dialogue (27%). By this blunt measure, the relationship of days spent rehearsing to shooting numbers—the data that most closely reflects his creative work—is better than three to one, a positive relationship given that time in the rehearsal hall or on set without a camera crew entailed only Astaire and anyone in the number with him. Rehearsing without the camera crew "standing around" was cheaper in both payroll and film costs. On set, work needed to be maximally efficient. The aforementioned proportion of rehearsing to shooting proves remarkably stable across Astaire's career. Rehearsal took marginally more time percentage-wise at MGM (62% of the total) than at RKO (58%), and there was appreciably more rehearsal during the production period at MGM (27% of the time versus only 11% at RKO).

Numbers created, rehearsed, and shot after production had opened follow a pattern. In many cases, Astaire seems to have managed to block out periods of time when he could focus entirely on a given number—create it, rehearse it, prerecord it, and shoot it—and then move on, either to more dialogue or another number. The modular nature of the film-musical-making process is everywhere evident. This approach of preparing then immediately shooting a number finds its most intense expression in *Ziegfeld Follies*, a revue film with no dialogue that is particularly well documented in the Freed collection at USC and not included in any of the previous workday averages. Astaire created, rehearsed, and shot six major numbers for *Ziegfeld Follies* in succession. Each was functionally separate from the others. First, he spent eight weeks creating and perfecting "If Swing Goes I Go Too," a complicated solo with male chorus to a tune with music and lyrics by Astaire himself.[32] He shot "If Swing Goes" in three-and-a-half days, then went the very next day into rehearsals with Gene Kelly for their duet "The Babbitt and the Bromide"—choreographed and rehearsed by the pair over twenty-one workdays and shot over four. (Astaire stepped briefly away from "Babbitt" rehearsals for two days to shoot the film's opening monologue and vocal—"Here Come the Girls." The substantial difference between vocal only and numbers with any amount of dance content is dramatically apparent here.) After a Sunday plus two more days off, Astaire started on "This Heart of Mine" with partner Lucille Bremer and choreographer Robert Alton. Eleven days of rehearsal and the number was ostensibly ready for the cameras. But on the fourth of ten shooting days, the camera crew was dismissed at 10am so that the company could rehearse for the remainder of the day on the set. Given the use of a large turntable and two long treadmills, perhaps the pause in shooting simply indicates a need to rehearse "This Heart of Mine" on the set—a more expensive but sometimes necessary option than the rehearsal hall (since studios only had so many soundstages). After completing "This Heart of Mine," Astaire had a light workweek, with just two rehearsal days and a day postsyncing taps (by this time his solo and the duo with Kelly had been edited). The major labor of "Limehouse Blues" followed. This thirteen-plus-minute "dramatic pantomime" was filmed in two large chunks: the Chinatown framing narrative (eight days rehearsing, four days shooting) and the dance with Bremer in a fantasyland of exotic Chinoiserie (nine days rehearsing, five days shooting). Finally, Astaire and Bremer made a duo dance involving bubbles (and many bubble machines) intended as the big finale for *Ziegfeld Follies*. Rehearsed over eight days, the four-day shoot was interrupted on day three by an entire morning spent "rehearsing end . . . of dance routine" and "building drains." Attempts to complete the thing stretched to 10:45pm that night (extremely late for Metro). After a further five hours of shooting the next day, with an early afternoon start, the bubble number was declared a washout. An alternate version without Astaire and Bremer was filmed months later. In the end, "If Swing Goes," the product of nine weeks' work, was also cut after the August 1945 Boston preview. In sum, the twenty-six-week *Ziegfeld Follies* project—all of it spent making, rehearsing, and shooting musical numbers—yielded thirty-six minutes of Astaire numbers and nearly twenty minutes of Astaire dancing in the release print.

The conclusion of production on *Ziegfeld Follies* occasioned a letter about Astaire preserved in the Freed Collection at USC.

> 31, Aug, 1944
>
> LA, Ca
>
> TO WHOM IT MAY CONCERN
>
> We, the undersigned, devote this page to the expression of our gratitude to those who made it possible for us to be associated for a while with FRED ASTAIRE, a man endowed with qualities so innumerable that all the superlatives we could find would still fail to adequately describe his genuine greatness.
>
> Never have we seen a man, whose name has been star-calibre for so long and whose talent is outstanding, give out with as much hard work for the many months of most difficult and tiresome routines, and yet maintain through it all such a fine spirit of tolerance, consideration and cooperation with respect to every one around him.—It was a pleasure and a great privilege at all times to serve such a man.
>
> The indomitable spirit shown by Mr. Astaire while working under high tension shall remain an inspiration to every one of us, even long after the picture has been forgotten.
>
> All of us who worked on the picture.[33]

This testimonial hints at, without pinning down, the nature of the *Ziegfeld Follies* shoot: does "tiresome" mean tiring or something else? Mention of "high tension" is less ambiguous. "A fine spirit of tolerance" may point toward personality clashes avoided or neutralized. Astaire was clearly neither temperamental genius nor sensitive divo. Astaire's masculine authority—projected in contexts where he was at once performing and creating—comes through in the triple iteration of the word *man*. A figure of stature and authority of "star-calibre," Astaire was also a good working companion, especially in the eyes of the less exalted figures on the film who—pointedly—signed the letter as a group (not giving their names). The theme of "hard work" done to exacting standards in a spirit of respect and "consideration" emerges around the figure of Astaire. The notion as well that the people "who worked on the picture" were serving Astaire indicates something of the cooperation required to make a film musical and the centrality of Astaire's body. As subsequent evidence from the AD reports suggests, Astaire was devoted to his work and did it in a spirit of diligence and self-criticism. The highly professional working environment of the studios suited him and the default to masculine authority present among producers, directors, and technical crews surely also supported Astaire's long tenure and considerable stature as a dancing man and self-choreographing dance maker.

27. "NG"

Assistant director (AD) reports in the studio era were preprinted forms submitted daily during production. The forms differed a bit from studio to studio and over time. Astaire worked all over town, so the AD reports for his films offer slightly different, but mostly comparable, data. Much of the data is quantitative and the unit of measure for all time-related matters is the minute.

At RKO in the 1930s, AD reports were typed in triplicate on onionskin. These one-sided documents quantified progress on a film by several metrics: call time, time started, and time finished for the company and each individual cast member—these reports function as timecards—as well as the number of camera setups and the specific shots (or "scenes") filmed. Scenes were numbered in the shooting script and referenced as such by the AD. This method didn't work for musical numbers, which were not planned out by the writing department but crafted elsewhere. The music department generated musical scores, but these fulfilled their function during prerecording sessions. On set, the music was just a recording—a phonograph record before the postwar advent of magnetic tape. Staging and choreography were worked out in the rehearsal hall or during practice days on set—here, as well, no textual trace was needed during the shoot as everyone in the number would have known their steps. Still, the AD had to keep track of progress shooting a number, which often took several days. Standard practice across the studios was to refer to individual shots within a musical number by letter: thus, the three-day "Top Hat, White Tie, and Tails" shoot completed shots "A," "B," and "C" on day one; "D," "E," and "F" on day two; and "G" through "K" on day three.[34] Separate boxes on the RKO AD report form record the feet of film used for sound (dialogue recorded on set on film stock) and image (the negative) as well as an estimate of "time" (minutes of final cut film content) made that day. All of these numerical measures of progress on the film were then tallied from the day production "opened" and compared to the budget or shooting schedule. At the top of the RKO AD report, two cumulative measures provided a box score of sorts for the film. On the left, under the heading "ORIGINAL SCHEDULE," days of rehearsal and photography and the estimated finish date (for production only—none of these reports include the postproduction work of editing, adding sound effects, etc.) were entered. On the right, the AD had to declare the film "On Time" or enter a specific number of "Days Behind." Half days behind was a common measure. The number of days "Idle" was also tallied. Three AD reports from *Carefree* tersely note, "Company idle on account of [director] Mr. Sandrich being ill."[35] Nothing happened on these days—except on the third Astaire and Rogers rehearsed. A separate document in the *Carefree* file calculated the total loss (or cost) of Sandrich's absence at $7,128.50.[36] The studio collected an insurance payout of $50,000 for the interruption in production on the film.[37] The RKO AD reports focus obsessively on the metrics of the filmmaking process—all measured more or less in units of time. After 1935, an added "Reasons for Delay" box gave ADs at the studio the chance to contextualize work on the set with a bit more detail and freedom. They were, however, a generally laconic bunch.

At Paramount, AD reports detailed each day's work on a shot-to-shot level and provided information directed toward the cutting department as much as the producer's office. Timecard information for individual actors is lacking, as is any running tally of progress on the film as a whole. Instead, a series of columns record progress on each camera setup, including "Takes Made" and "Slates Printed"—an important measure of productivity, the number of takes ideally as low as possible to get the needed one or two printed slates. Further columns record "Time First Take" and "Time Scene Completed." Thus, Paramount tracked how time was spent on the set in greater detail than RKO. A column taking up about half the page invited the AD to give a "Description of Angles, Action and Dialogue." Entries here reduce the content of a shot to abbreviated prose, again mostly useful to the cutters. There's little room for side comments on the Paramount form, although anxiety about how time was spent is evident when an AD notes "REHEARSING" or "SAME SETUP" (indicating the cameras and lights were not repositioned between shots).

Neither RKO nor Paramount AD reports delve into the personalities on the set or the special challenges of filming musical numbers—specifically the difficulties inherent in dealing with dancing bodies. At MGM, however, AD reports were two-sided documents that made ample room for a more descriptive record of film musical agents doing their bodily work. The front side (similar to the forms at RKO) kept track of the actors' arrivals, lunch breaks, and departures. The back of each MGM AD report was a blank page where the AD typed a free-form "LOG" of how time was spent on the set. Organized by shot number, the progression from "Line & Lite" (positioning the cameras and lights) to "action" to "print"—as arranged prescriptively in the columns on the Paramount form—was detailed minute by minute in abbreviation-heavy, grammar-lite prose. MGM ADs accounted for every take and sometimes also noted which were printed. Takes that were "NG" (or no good) received quick explanation, such as "ng dia" (actor's mistake in the dialogue), "ng sound" (bad dialogue recording reported by sound crew), "ng sound noise" (violations of the "quiet on the set" rule), or "NGA" (action).[38] Musical numbers occasioned their own set of "NG" annotations: "NG sync" (a lip-syncing mistake) and "NG dance action" (a missed step).[39] An interruption of any kind to the work of taking shots was noted, such as a ten-minute wait on the first day of "Shoes with Wings On"—5:30pm to 5:40pm on July 19, 1948—because of "Mr. Astaire changing shirts." The MGM AD logs are filled with similar data tracking the bodies of the actors doing the singing and dancing at the heart of the film musical.

A log note about an unexpected delay during "The Ritz Roll & Rock" (*Silk Stockings*) shoot provides a sense for how ADs (and the studios) thought about time: "NOTE—in time space 10:46 to 11:23 inc[lusive]—It was found impossible to keep from shooting over set in mirror reflections [sic], it was decided to hang additional drapes during lunch to correct this."[40] The AD reports yield much significant "time space" data on individual numbers that opens a comparative perspective on efficiency at the level of the number and the dance routine in Astaire's work. Seventy-eight of Astaire's musical numbers are represented with sufficient data in the surviving AD reports to determine how long it took to shoot them. The distribution of these numbers across Astaire's career periods is less than ideal: half from the Freed unit at Metro, one-third from RKO in the 1930s. Dividing the time it took to film each number—measured in both workdays and minutes—by the length of the number in the finished film (which in most all cases matches the prerecorded music track) results in two productivity statistics that can be compared across this archive-driven subcorpus:

(1) Hours and minutes of shooting time required to produce one minute of filmed song and dance in the finished film
(2) Duration in seconds of musical number footage completed on average in a day of shooting

Table 5 breaks down these numbers by studio and size of the cast. On average, for the seventy-eight numbers in this corpus it took just over five hours (5:06) of shooting to produce one minute of final cut musical number footage. A lower number is better here from the studio's perspective, indicating fewer minutes of shooting to seconds of useable film. By this data, MGM was a more efficient studio (6% under average) than RKO (8% over). Among the most efficiently shot numbers by this measure are "How Could You Believe Me . . ." (1:42), "My One and Only Highland Fling" (2:05), and the "Drum Dance" (2:08). These are all fairly straightforward numbers—only the "Drum Dance" is choreographically complicated—with simple sets for Astaire alone or with a partner. None have complicated camera movements or crane shots. All could be conceivably reproduced on stage. Surprisingly, even seemingly difficult numbers appear on the most efficient list—such as "Open Your Eyes" (1:52) and "You're All the World to Me" (2:10), both done on complicated

TABLE 5 Shooting efficiency for seventy-eight numbers with archival data

	Average Hours of Shooting to One Minute of Final Cut Film	% Under/ Over Corpus Average	Seconds of Final Cut Film Taken Per Day	% Under/ Over Corpus Average	# of Numbers in this Subcorpus
ALL	5:06		109		78
RKO	5:30	+8%	105	−4%	29
MGM Freed Unit	4:48	−6%	113	+4%	39
Solitary Solos	4:35	−10%	99	−10%	16
Duos	4:58	−3%	122	+11%	38
Numbers with More than Two Performers	5:28	+7%	92	-15%	24

moving sets. Here, efficiency during shooting remained high due to lengthy rehearsal on the set. Very inefficient numbers tell a different story. "I Used to Be Color Blind" (8:52) was perhaps complicated by the need to film a one-shot dance in slow motion so that it would sync up with a recording at normal speed. It seems to have taken several days to get the plan to work. "Manhattan Downbeat" (10:16) appears similar to other late-in-the-production-process numbers discussed later, where a less than fully rehearsed routine is moved to the shooting stage before it's properly rehearsed. Astaire's two partner dances with Joan Leslie in *The Sky's the Limit* took a relatively very long time to film and have very high shooting time-to-minute of final cut material stats: "My Shining Hour" (6:54) and "We've Got a Lot in Common" (8:45). The AD reports don't reveal why, but clearly getting both on film was a comparatively inefficient process. Leslie was not an experienced dancer and both routines are intricate, with much side-by-side unison dancing of the sort that required both partners to independently get every step right.

The number of performers involved in a number seems to have impacted efficiency in shooting. Variance under and over the average presents significant differences when the corpus is sorted by the number of dancers involved. Astaire all alone—his solitary solos—come in below the average (−10%), while dances involving more than two dancers, including solos with chorus, are over (+7%). The duo dances—with men or women—sit just below the average (−3%). These statistics confirm a common-sense notion that when Astaire worked all alone, as he did about a quarter of the time, he worked more efficiently, and that numbers with a chorus took more time. Planning for a film surely kept this in mind.

Turning to the second efficiency measure in the seventy-eight-number corpus considered here, the average shooting day produced 109 seconds of final cut musical number. Here, a higher number is better, indicating more feet and seconds of film in the can at day's end. As this statistic largely tracks the first, departure from the average is, again, minimal (RKO 4% under the corpus average; MGM 4% over). Variance under/over the average is, again, significant when the corpus is sorted by the number of dancing bodies on the set. Routines with more than two performers, almost all including a chorus, drop 15% below the average. Surprisingly, solitary solos also sit well below the average (−10%), while routines for Astaire with a partner rise 11% above the average, signaling a more efficient process on the latter. This data suggests the importance of the work day as a unit measurement informing studio production methods and practices.

A final way to parse both of these efficiency measures reveals significant productivity variance from number to number and day to day. Here, the corpus of seventy-eight is divided into groups by the number of total days it took to shoot the number. As Chart 16 shows, numbers completed over one or two days of shooting were significantly more efficient, falling well under the average of just over five hours needed to produce a minute of film. Numbers shot in one day spent just 4:57 (3% under corpus average) to make a minute of final cut material and produced 127 seconds (over two minutes) of footage per day. Two-day shoots, including numbers that took one-and-a-half days, were appreciably more efficient, needing 4:26 (13% below the average) to film one minute of final cut material and producing on average 123 seconds of footage per day. Shoots lasting three or more days were dramatically less efficient by both measures, as were shoots dragging on to five or more days. The common-sense caveat here, of course, is that one- and two-day shooting numbers tend to be shorter in overall duration and less complicated in execution than numbers shot over three days or more. Still, and again, plans for the numbers in a given film needed to balance the complexity and forces used to ensure timely completion.

These efficiency statistics, tilted toward MGM as they are, provide a context for understanding the AD reports that any studio executive would readily appreciate—and surely relish (even in retrospect). Just looking at the

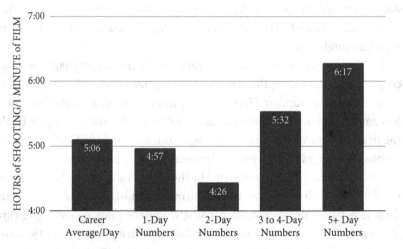

CHART 16 Hours of shooting to produce one minute of final cut musical number footage averaged by workdays spent shooting number (for 78 numbers with archival data)

daily reports, one might conclude that a number like "This Heart of Mine" (8½-day shoot) was especially expensive in terms of shooting time per minute of final cut film. In fact, the twelve-minute number, admittedly an ambitious undertaking, was relatively efficient when it was before the cameras (just 9% above the shooting-to-final cut footage average). The same cannot be said for the similarly long, twelve-minute *Yolanda* dream ballet, which took eleven-and-a-half days to shoot (42% above shooting-to-footage average). Two of those eleven days on *Yolanda* resulted in no prints: not a single useable take, a disastrous report; cameras were rolling but there was nothing in the can at 6pm. Producer Arthur Freed was on set during both of these objectively unproductive days. On the first lost day, Freed fussed with details ("Mr. Freed did not like star ornament on Miss Bremer's forehead—took it off—had to fix makeup—put it back on"). On the second, the penultimate day of the shoot, Freed pulled rank and called it a wrap ("Note: Mr. Freed ordered shooting stopped because everyone was very tired from rehearsing all day").[41] In the end, producers had the power to extend (or curtail) shooting. The AD reports existed to give quantitative evidence for how the film was progressing and name any offenders who slowed the process (including the producer).

Some seemingly slight numbers show up in the AD reports as taking a relatively long amount of time to make. "By the Light of the Silvery Moon" (9:44 shooting per one minute of footage) and "Hello, Hello, Who's Your Lady Friend?" (8:02), both from *The Castles*, were fantastically inefficient in the making. The first of these, a two-day shoot, involved retakes of restaged material on the second day. Astaire stayed late on day one to rehearse with Sonny Lamont, the hapless portly man he dances rings around, and on day two shots "B" and "C" were redone. Such rethinking indicates Astaire making creative changes on the set, but the freedom to do so was always limited and taking such license proves exceedingly rare in the archive. "Silvery Moon" was typical of the inefficient *Castles* shoot.

The primary task on shooting days was getting printable takes. A subset of ten Astaire solos from the Freed unit films, *Holiday Inn*, and *Let's Dance* offer a glimpse of how many takes it took to get the needed printable slates.[42] This corpus contains 111 shots, with the number of takes for each recorded by the AD. These are shots taken on the set and do not necessarily correlate to shots in the film (see the discussion of cutting in the next part). For eighty (72%) of these shots, the reports also note how many takes were printed. The MGM ADs, working without a form to fill in, didn't always keep track of slates printed (though someone on the camera crew certainly was). On average, Astaire took 6.5 takes of each shot. Among the shots with the data, on average two takes were printed. Combining these stats, Astaire's earns a career batting average of .320 (not bad for baseball or, apparently, studio-era musicals). Still, the averages conceal difficult droughts when Astaire tried and failed to get the one necessary printable take. Again and again, a particular shot in each routine proved tough to get, racking up sixteen, eighteen, twenty-one, twenty-two, even twenty-three tries. In the case of thirty-four shots (43% of those with data), shooting moved forward on the basis of just one printable take. This data suggests just how delicate Astaire's art was at its point of origin—the dancing body before the camera. Some of the things he does on film he was only ever able to do once with the camera rolling. His screen dance body performs feats of dance action otherwise not available to his real body on command. Astaire the screen dancer acts perfectly—if identically—time after time forever (or as long as moving pictures endure).

As noted previously, the AD reports provide many explanations for why given takes were "NG," or no good. "NG action" or "NG synch" were something the dancers would have known. Mistakes in the dance would have required a new take. Astaire's love of throwing and catching objects could also run up the number of takes. The cut number "If Swing Goes I Go Too" was apparently filled with the throwing of drumsticks. One shot, described as "side angle for throwing drum sticks," required nineteen takes, only four of which were complete. The trick failed 80% of the time. Another shot described as "Astaire throwing drum sticks to dancers" failed across fourteen takes and the company gave up. After a night's sleep, the company returned to the shot for eight more takes.[43] A hat-tossing bit in "Seeing's Believing" racked up a "total 21 takes (5 takes NG account of pigeons—15 takes NG Mr Astair's [sic] hat throwing action NG)"—the extra NGs in this note speak to frustration.[44] A hat trick in "I Wanna Be a Dancin' Man" (*Belle of New York*) led to a literal measurement of the expenditure: "Note: Mr. Astaire doing difficult gag in which he kicks hat from ploor [sic] and catches—it caused so many takes to be shot—average lenth [sic] of incomplete takes approx. 17 ft."[45] Some explanations for high take counts are cumulative, as if the AD gave up on writing a minute-by-minute account and instead summarized a welter of events after the fact. A seventy-minute "time space" describing a shot in "Shoes with Wings On" that involved shoes flying out of the set on wires was translated into AD speak this way: "Shoot 16 takes NOTE: Time out between takes for reloading camera twice, trimming lamps 3 times and

Mr. Astaire changing clothes once."[46] The workday ended at 6:50pm (late for Metro) with the shot completed.

A final measure of efficiency brings rehearsal time into the story. For seventeen numbers, data on time spent rehearsing is also recorded in the AD reports. With three different durational measures in hand for these numbers—hours of rehearsal, hours of shooting, minutes of musical number in the final cut—we can understand the efficiencies of the studio system and Astaire's place in it from yet another quantitative angle. All seventeen were created and rehearsed, then immediately shot, largely without the distraction of other work on the film, an approach discussed earlier typical of numbers made late in the production period and of the revue film *Ziegfeld Follies* generally. And so, this subcorpus represents a particular kind of number made under certain constraints, although the four *Ziegfeld Follies* numbers in this subcorpus were not done under the pressure of completing a narrative film. Four general scenarios for the time required to both rehearse and shoot a musical number emerge in this data: (1) much rehearsal and a long shoot, (2) much rehearsal and an efficient shoot, (3) little rehearsal and a long shoot, and (4) high efficiency in both rehearsing and shooting. Table 6 groups the seventeen numbers by these four scenarios, with data for each number that suggests the diversity within each scenario. Columns A and B give each number's under/over percentage for the average hours and minutes of rehearsal and shooting needed to yield one minute in the final film (similar to the efficiency measure hours of shooting to one minute of film given in Table 5 by studio and number type). In this smaller subcorpus of seventeen numbers, the average amount of time needed to create and rehearse one minute of musical number in the finished film is thirteen hours and twenty-five minutes. The average shooting time for one minute in the film is four hours and fifty-three minutes (13 minutes under the average for the 78-number subcorpus detailed previously). Column C in Table 6 assigns each number a rating that reflects the proportional relationship between time spent rehearsing (off or on the set) and time spent shooting. A higher rating indicates relatively greater time in rehearsal and, per completed minutes of film, higher efficiency before the cameras. The average across the subcorpus is 2.75 (quite near the 3:1 ratio given earlier of days rehearsing to days shooting numbers). A combined rating near one indicates near- or close-to-equal amounts of time spent in rehearsal and shooting—a seemingly less efficient process, since shooting involved a sizeable array of studio crews and rehearsing required only the performers involved in a given

TABLE 6 Rehearsal and shooting efficiency for seventeen numbers with archival data

NUMBER	A Under/Over Average: Hours Rehearsal to One Minute in Film	B Under/Over Average: Hours Shooting to One Minute in Film	C Efficiency Rating: Column A/Column B (higher = more time in rehearsal hall, greater efficiency on set; below 1 = more time on set than in rehearsal hall)
AVERAGE	13:25	4:53	2.75
MUCH REHEARSAL, LONG SHOOT			
"If Swing Goes, I Go Too" [ZF]	+201%	+3%	7.65
Currier and Ives: Winter Skating [BNY]	+82%	+17%	4.10
Yolanda and the Thief dream ballet	+21%	+42%	2.25
MUCH REHEARSAL, EFFICIENT SHOOT			
"The Ritz Roll and Rock" [SS]	+43%	−19%	4.65
"I Left My Hat in Haiti" [RW]	+57%	−7%	4.45
"One for My Baby (and One More for the Road)" [STL]	+43%	−8%	4.09
"The Babbitt and the Bromide" [ZF]	+19%	−9%	3.46
LITTLE REHEARSAL, LONG SHOOT			
Shall We Dance finale [all sections]	−39%	+23%	1.30
"Stiff Upper Lip" [DD]	−49%	+15%	1.17
"This Heart of Mine" [ZF]	−65%	+9%	0.86
VERY EFFICIENT			
"You're All the World to Me" [RW]	+2%	−57%	6.31
"Coffee Time" [YT]	−22%	−14%	2.40
"Girl Hunt" [entire sequence, BW]	−33%	−19%	2.18
"Bojangles of Harlem" [ST]	−43%	−5%	1.59
"Limehouse Blues" [ZF]	−62%	−1%	1.00
"Fated to Be Mated" [SS]	−70%	−3%	0.81
"Never Gonna Dance" [ST]	−87%	−39%	0.56

number. When the combined rating drops below one, shooting time exceeds rehearsal time, likely indicating that much of the number was worked out or simply rehearsed (even learned or created) on the set with camera and lighting crews, in Sandrich's phrase, "standing around." Success making musical numbers demanded an efficient path from creation to rehearsal to printable takes needed to edit the whole thing together. This data gives a glimpse of select journeys along this path—each specific to each number, some measurably more efficient than others, and some producing the needed footage by way of a seemingly risky path.

By bean-counting producers' standards, the best scenario for the making of a musical number combined relatively little rehearsal with a shoot that took as little time as possible. The opposite—relatively much rehearsal and a protracted shoot—combined the worst of both necessary tasks. The *Yolanda* dream ballet was just such a number. This very long sequence required 21% more time in rehearsal and 42% more time shooting than the average. In addition, its ratio of rehearsal to shooting is a below-corpus average 2.25— indicating limited efficiency in rehearsal or extra difficulties on the set (the many reframed shots probably contributed to the many hours in front of the ballet's nearly always moving camera). The dream ballet was the first part of *Yolanda* to be made and the rest of it took a long time as well (as noted with regard to shooting dialogue). And then the film bombed badly. Costing $2.4 million to make, *Yolanda* resulted in a $1.6 million loss.[47] If it had turned a big (or even modest) profit, of course, no one would have cared how much it cost to make and the many hours spent on the dream ballet would have seemed worth it.

Every musical ran such risks—although the general weirdness of *Yolanda* wagered on the tastes of the Hollywood audience considerably. (Astaire said of the film thirty years after making it: "Beautiful, but not very good."[48]) Still, the hazards inherent in the genre had to be moderated somehow. Hiring Astaire was one way to reduce risk—he was enduringly popular with audiences and he knew how to efficiently produce the genre's main attraction: musical numbers. But even Astaire could be inefficient. The number in Table 6 with the worst efficiency rating is "If Swing Goes, I Go Too," the cut solo from *Ziegfeld Follies*. Astaire spent more rehearsal time on this number than any known other and the shoot ran over the average on efficiency as well. (My estimate of 4 weeks spent rehearsing before the first known data point [the day the number was prerecorded] may be on the long side, but it's hard to imagine Astaire making "If Swing Goes," which included a large male chorus, in any less time.) The problem here is the astounding 7.65 relationship between time rehearsing and shooting. The ice-skating section of *Belle of New York* also racked up rather low-efficiency stats—substantially over average for both rehearsal and shooting—but it was a contained and entirely novel (for Astaire) sequence. *Belle* was a long and difficult shoot: a whole week on this short musical sequence—not even a minute-and-a-half of the film—surely contributed but might not otherwise show up as especially inefficient time spent.

The balance between rehearsal and shooting was influenced by factors other than the number itself. Pressure to finish a number so as to finish a film was important. Several approaches were used for numbers made late in the production process. The results varied, as shown by four production numbers that each involve comparable use of a dancing chorus. "I Left My Hat in Haiti" rehearsed 57% more than average and enjoyed a slightly more efficient than average shoot; "Bojangles of Harlem" rehearsed 43% less than average and also enjoyed a near-average shoot. The "Bojangles" chorus is notably ragged in their dancing unison, especially before Astaire enters (watch the first shot with vocals): is this sloppiness the product of insufficient rehearsal and/or a that's-good-enough attitude toward the rushes (when Astaire wasn't on screen)? The shadow effects in the second part are technically brilliant if, at times, oddly framed and edited. The many short shots pasted together to make this special effects dance may hint at a cobbling together in post-production from takes that were not useable in longer chunks. The complicated "Shall We Dance" sequence, with two female choruses (one ballet, one tap) rehearsed a third less than usual, then shot about a quarter more than usual. A very low rating of 1.30 hints at pressure to get the number before the cameras, perhaps leading to the relatively long shoot. Piecemeal use of the number in the film adds to the suspicion that it never quite added up. "The Ritz Roll and Rock" rehearsed 43% more than average and enjoyed a notably efficient shoot (19% under average). On-set problems may have necessitated substantial revision to the choreography (descriptions in the AD reports don't quite fit the number as danced in the film). In any event, "Ritz" is a relatively unambitious routine, filled with gimmicky tricks and sliding to the floor. Here, the extra amount of rehearsal raises serious questions about a lack of inspiration and a falling back on silliness.

Numbers in this subcorpus with substantially less-than-average rehearsal time (negative numbers in column A) suggest a calculated risk that it was time to go before the cameras. Routines that involved a danced relationship to an involved set, often with elements in motion, such as "Stiff Upper Lip" and "This Heart of Mine," likely involved much experimentation with both the set and the cameras. Both shifted to shooting after relatively truncated rehearsal periods. And then there are the numbers with almost no rehearsal, when most of the work had to have been done on the set—a situation where the performers simply lacked the normal level of preparation. "Never Gonna Dance," the last portion of *Swing Time* to be made, started filming after just five hours of rehearsal. After over eighteen hours shooting, the number was completed with a very high shooting efficiency (39% below normal). "Never Gonna Dance" is regularly celebrated as one of the great Astaire-Rogers routines: dance critic Arlene Croce called it "the supreme dramatic event of the series."[49] It is, upon examination, remarkably simple. Much of the opening is just walking and posing. One stretch of dancing and music is borrowed from "Waltz in Swing Time," and the spinning conclusion, including the parallel moves up twin curved staircases, is, in terms of sheer dance steps, relatively simple (in content if not necessarily execution). And the number includes no foot sounds—unusual for an Astaire-Rogers duo—which means no complicated tap rhythms to work out during the creation phase. Given the data on how long it took to make it, "Never Gonna Dance" emerges as intentionally simple—perhaps one reason it has such "dramatic" impact.

The single most efficient number in the subcorpus is "You're All the World to Me," Astaire's dance on the walls and ceiling. The straightforward concept of the number likely made this a relatively easy project. Astaire worked alone on one of the smallest dance floors (!) he ever used—a small, furnished room built within a mechanism that allowed it to turn (the film's art director called it a "squirrel cage").[50] There was no way to rehearse this number anywhere but on the set, since almost every move relates to the set and mastery of the turning room was central to discovering what dance moves were even possible. Astaire would have quickly discovered all the possible ways to relate to the setting in his characteristically noisy manner (he had lots of experience dancing on and with furniture). When the shooting day arrived, the single camera (and cameraman) was locked into place, ready to rotate with the drum and the room. There was no way for Astaire to leave the frame as the set effectively contained his movements; most problems of the moving camera sustaining Vitruvian framing were solved by default. "All the World to Me" was a fantastically efficient shoot, but not without its frustrations (details of the day and a half spent on the number follow in the next section).

160 ASTAIRE BY NUMBERS

The simplicity of getting this dance on film was likely repeated in many of his similarly straightforward solitary solos.

28. "NO TIME LOST"

Unlike the unceasingly positive puffery of fan magazine profiles or the gauzy, unspecific memories of later-life interviews, assistant director (AD) reports contain concrete information about the filmmaking process recorded in the moment and submitted daily as a film progressed. The notes in these AD reports—especially at MGM, which allowed for more freedom in reporting—were preemptive ammunition for any subsequent blame games. As such, they offer mundane but revealing access to the set, from near-complete chronicles to passing glimpses of Astaire and company singing and dancing (and sweating). The theme of time spent—and lost—runs across the AD report archive. The tracking of performing bodies is also central to AD discourse. Time and the body emerge as key themes in the following account of how film musical numbers were filmed.

On November 18, 1941, the first day of the *Holiday Inn* shoot, Astaire, Bing Crosby, and Virginia Dale filmed "I'll Capture Your Heart," the opening number in the film. They prerecorded the vocal three days earlier and the AD report indicates "PLAYBACK ON ALL TAKES."[51] It was a seven-hour-and-twenty-minute day of lip-syncing. The first shot, taken at 10am on the dot—the performers' call was 9am—is described by the AD as a "long shot, master" from the top of the number through the "middle of 1st chorus" (six takes, the second and the last printed). An "EXTREME L.S. [long shot]" of the same followed (one take, printed). Then the approach changed. Two cameras simultaneously took "FULL FIGURE SHOTS" of the "Complete number" (ten takes, the seventh and the last printed). After a late lunch starting at 1:30pm, the company returned and spent an hour and a half on a "CLOSE SHOT—complete number" (five takes, three printed). "CLOSE" here means from the thighs up—defined earlier as an insert shot that only shows part of the performing body. It was now almost 4pm and "I'll Capture Your Heart" was more or less in the can. With two hours left in the workday, director Mark Sandrich tried a few other setups and stagings and filled in shots he still needed to successfully edit this vocal number with a few dance breaks into a musical scene. First, Sandrich took a "LONG SHOT" (or full figure) from the middle of the second chorus to what the AD called a "comedy exit" (one take, printed).

Next, picking up at the point when Crosby "sings HOT LICK" through to the end, Sandrich used the same camera setup with a change to the action—the AD noted "NO TIME LOST... different exit" (two takes, both printed—one of these ended up in the film).[52] Then Sandrich returned to the top of the number for two short shots involving Dale's entrance (she crosses downstage while the men watch and sing from upstage). At 5:52pm, the workday was over and three-and-a-half minutes (about 3%) of *Holiday Inn*'s one-hour-and-forty-minute run time was ready for editing (and postsyncing of taps).

With several master shots, as well as close shots and special angles, the editors could go to work pasting together the number—which, in the film, contains thirteen shots. Sandrich's approach on the set might be understood as shooting coverage (a master shot and various closer angles). A more apt comparison would be methods used in live television about a decade later: multiple cameras simultaneously capture the performers doing an entire number framed in severals ways—long shot, full figure, thighs up—to be cut between for variety and emphasis. While live television was edited on the fly, filming to playback permitted multiple takes that could all be edited together, since each was built on the same prerecorded audio foundation. And so, the finished "I'll Capture Your Heart" is a collage of cuts from the fifteen printed takes made on November 18. The seams show a bit during the second half of the number: watch how the bouquet and box of candy Crosby and Astaire throw behind the bench change position on the floor, indicating shots selected from different takes. (Note as well that the candy box makes no sound when it hits the floor.) The single candy wrapper Astaire tosses to the front of the bench remains in place throughout: the crewmember in charge of continuity did their job. Sandrich approached "I'll Capture Your Heart"— a vocal number with some dance breaks—as he might a dialogue scene: a master shot, then closer framings, then special angles. Still, the edit shows a bias toward continuous action in relatively few shots—after all, Sandrich was there when Astaire developed his approach to "full figure" framing at RKO. The rhythmic back and forth of the song and the need to see Astaire dance and Crosby make some dance-like motions required full-figure or thighs-up framing throughout. Cutting between close-ups—as might have happened in a dialogue version of the song's conceit—would have resulted in a choppy edit and have sacrificed the interaction among the performers, whose faces, on the big screen, would have been visible in a manner no stage performance could ever allow (and that can get lost today if the viewer's screen is small). This was an atypical day shooting musical numbers for Astaire. First, "I'll

Capture Your Heart" is a vocal number, so while Astaire certainly staged it, choreographed his dance breaks, and rehearsed with Crosby, the number did not come to the soundstage with specific shots built in (as Astaire's dance routines did). This allowed Sandrich to capture the number in the way he did. Second, during filming, Astaire, with Crosby and Dale, did the entire number several times over. AD reports suggest Astaire generally worked methodically, shot by shot, usually in order, completing a routine in sections. This includes the vocal segments preceding dance segments.

Occasionally, a number was shot out of sequence, usually for practical reasons that reveal something of the strategies behind a typical day shooting dance on an Astaire picture. The three sections of "Fated to Be Mated" (*Silk Stockings*)—each done on a different set—were shot first, third, and second relative to their film order. The exigencies of soundstage access perhaps played a part in this decision. A tricky shot was sometimes saved for the end of the day. For instance, the subway platform dance in "Girl Hunt" was completed in a single day (January 14, 1953). The first three hours were spent on a sixteen-second shot featuring "acrobatic dancers" that opens the scene (six takes). Next, two hours were consumed by Astaire and the blonde Cyd Charisse's single-shot, seventy-six-second dance, with thugs turning flips and shooting each other in the background (six takes). This most important shot for the two dancing stars was done when they were maximally rested. After lunch, it took nearly two-and-a-half hours to make the twelve-second shot just after the dance, with its "powder flash effect" and push in on Astaire looking into the subway tracks ("That bullet was meant for me," he says in voiceover). It was now 3:30pm and time to make the shot *before* Astaire and Charisse's dance, a five-second shot of Charisse running in and sliding perfectly in time into an embrace of Astaire's leg. This complicated bit of physics required half an hour of preparation with Charisse's stand-in and nine takes with Charisse, all but the last rejected as "NG sliding action—re-wax & dust sliding surface between takes."[53] Thus, the four shots in the subway sequence were filmed in one, three, four, two order. Integrating Charisse's slide into the seventy-six-second one-shot dance that follows it would have been theoretically possible—we can imagine the possible reframed shot—but, from a production perspective, risky and time consuming. And so, the cut can be explained in part by the efficiencies of shooting. But the day wasn't over: it was only 4:24pm and the company moved to another set to rehearse another part of "Girl Hunt," prepping (but not shooting) the next day's first setup. Notably, the first section of "Girl Hunt" to go before the cameras—during the two days prior to the subway scene—was the "bop joint" sequence, which follows the subway scene in the film. This makes sense given the fragmentary nature of "Girl Hunt" and is another argument for isolating dance routines or segments as I have in the *Astaire dancing* corpus.

Actor Sir John Gielgud visited *The Band Wagon* during the "Shine on Your Shoes" shoot. He recalled, "I was staggered—because I'd never seen a musical film being made—at the way he could begin in the middle of the dance."[54] Gielgud's reaction measures, again, the distance between nonmusical and musical performers. Filming a number shot by shot meant sometimes starting in the middle. It also meant that numbers shot over multiple days conceal one or more night's sleep for the dancers in their cuts. Judy Garland and Astaire had a night's rest just before the dance break in "A Couple of Swells" (*Easter Parade*).[55] Astaire's special effects dance with two pairs of disembodied shoes in "Shoes with Wings On" combines shots taken at the end of one day (the matte shot of the shoes) and the start of the next (Astaire).[56] For most of the "Shoes with Wings On" shoot, Astaire did his part first, and then the set was blacked out and the dancers seen only as shoes did theirs. In this case, knowing there wasn't time for both versions of the setup, the "shoes" dancers went first, effectively ending Astaire's day a bit early and letting him shoot his portion the next morning, when he was rested. Just before the "Shine on Your Shoes" vocal begins—just after the cut on Astaire tripping over shoeshine man Leroy Daniels's leg—everyone in the number has been refreshed by a night's sleep. On this, the third and final day shooting the number, most all of the vocal and dance portions of "Shine on Your Shoes" were filmed. The day climaxed and concluded with the bursting forth of what the AD calls the "Caliope [sic] monster" (production lingo for the mystery box in the arcade that explodes with flags and lights). The final shot of "A Shine on Your Shoes"—when Astaire pays Daniels and exits the arcade—had already been taken on the first day's work on the number, so that particular cut jumps back in time two full days.[57]

Two multiday solos were almost complete at the end of a workday. But instead of pushing through and finishing that day, fatigue on Astaire's part argued for putting off the final shot until the next morning. These cases are instructive as to the visible calm of Astaire's screen body in insert framing, even after a long stretch of vigorous dancing. "Shoes with Wings On" was assembled in order over a marathon five-and-a-half-day shoot. At 3:35pm on day five, all but one shot had been taken, the final eight seconds of the number when shoes fall from above and knock a jumping and spinning

Astaire to the floor. It took two hours and twenty minutes to get the camera into position and check the rigging on the falling shoes. At 5:55pm, the company took the first of three takes, each requiring "Time out . . . to re-rig falling shoes." At 6:20pm the company was dismissed with the number unfinished. The AD explained, "NOTE: Mr. Astaire said he was too tired after his day's work—that his makeup was shot—that he did not feel he could get the shot satisfactorily tonight—so he went home at 6:20pm."[58] The next morning, with everything lined up already, the crew was on hand at 8:30am to "Pick up with Take 4." Astaire showed up fifteen minutes early (and freshly made up) to his 9am call. After a little rehearsal, take four was shot at 9:30am. Then someone, perhaps director Charles Walters, wanted to try a "diff[erent] boom movement—Diff[erent] version of ending." Three takes and it was only 9:50am. "At the request of Mr. Astaire," three more takes of the "1st version" of the shot were taken and at 10:20am, "Shoes with Wings On" was finally done. The final shot from "Shoes with Wings On" shows a rested Astaire at the end of a long dance routine. Surely part of the reason he wanted a night's sleep was his knowledge that the final shot framed him in a medium shot. This strategic approach to insert framing also occurred during the "Firecracker" shoot. The inserts when Astaire pulls firecrackers out of his pockets and lights them were done at the start of the second day shooting the number; the Vitruvian shots of him reacting to these firecrackers had already been taken the previous day.[59] So, these cuts toggle back and forth between Vitruvian and insert framings and the afternoon of January 29 and the morning of January 30, 1942.

Astaire filmed his numbers without knowing what each take looked like. Video-assist technology, which gave instant access to a shot just filmed, came along shortly after Astaire's studio career ended and there's no evidence of any such technology on his sets. Astaire dreaded seeing rushes or dailies (first looks at unedited footage). Pan recalled in 1981, "He used to have me go see the rushes first. He'd say, 'I won't go see them. I just can't stand to watch it.' . . . Then he would go and see them alone. Maybe with me. But he would never go with the director as a rule. . . . After the first day, we would have maybe half the number shot and he would look at that."[60] It was essential for Astaire to assess the rushes, which must have been stranger still for being shot-length chunks of dance projected silently (Astaire had to line up the prerecorded music track in his head while watching). The on-set stakes for deciding to print a given take and/or move on to the next setup and shot were, thus, very high and made blindly. Rushes were the first chance to assess the rightness (or wrongness) of the basic decision to print select takes made over and over on days spent shooting numbers.

The evidence for retakes of musical routines is surprisingly slim. The most notable is "I Wanna Be a Dancin' Man," which was completely reshot with a new set, costume, and camera movement. Survival of the original version, which was only rejected after it had been edited to the audio track (which both versions share), allows for comparison—a rare glimpse of Astaire doing the same routine twice. ("Dancin' Man" is discussed several times in subsequent sections when our attention turns toward framing and settings.) The troublesome outdoor numbers "Things Are Looking Up" and "A Foggy Day (in London Town)" in *A Damsel in Distress* not only took up five shooting days initially—with time lost for "RAIN & DARKNESS"—but also had to be reshot (likely only partially) on a single day ten days later. The perils of exterior shooting were normally avoided on the musical, which was expensive enough already. Astaire and Bremer did a half day of retakes on the *Yolanda* dream ballet—extending the longest known shoot of Astaire's career. Substantial retakes near the end of production on three numbers in *Let's Dance* signal the problems of that film and the cobbled-together quality of the truncated romantic routine with Betty Hutton. A day of retakes for various nondancing bits of "Girl Hunt" some three weeks after Astaire's work on *Band Wagon* ended suggests that the complicated piecing together of that sequence was less planned out than anticipated during the four weeks of its rehearsal and shooting during production.[61] A day and a half of retakes two weeks after the very long *Belle of New York* production closed were spent on the treadmill shots in "Oops"—where Astaire and Vera-Ellen dance on a horse's back in front of less-than-convincing back-projections. Here, the technical challenge of one section of a very long routine simply had to be solved, given the "time space" of the dance on the prerecorded audio track for the number to which the company had committed itself four months earlier. "Oops" is among the Astaire numbers it took the longest to make in terms of the sheer number of days from start of rehearsal to completion of shooting.

Twice at RKO Astaire did substantial retakes of solo routines. Astaire shot "A Needle in a Haystack," his first solo set in a domestic space, with live musical accompaniment on set on July 19, 1934. The seven-hour day meant the orchestra players qualified for compensation for two recording sessions. Then, on the evening of July 21, Astaire and actor Charles Coleman, who plays Astaire's valet and assists him in getting dressed in the dance portion, returned to the living room set from 7pm to 9:35pm to reshoot the one-shot, eighty-six-second dance. This unusual evening shoot—on a Saturday night, no less—was necessitated by the film's crew being occupied all day with dialogue scenes not including Astaire. The live recording from two days earlier must have been used as a prerecorded track. Astaire likely saw the rushes for the dance and decided it needed redoing. Similar evening retakes happened on the title song from *Top Hat*. Five days after the number's three-day shoot, Astaire returned to retake shot "E" at least five times. This seems to be the central, solitary section of the routine, when the men's chorus is absent from the stage and Astaire does both a cane-centered routine and a series of dramatic poses that suggest a confrontation with invisible adversaries.[62] Astaire worked for almost four hours on this section of the routine, ending the added session—he had shot dialogue that morning—at 11:45pm. He had the next day off.

29. "Wet with Persperation [sic]"

A primary task for the assistant director (AD) was to monitor the front-of-camera talent—their physical presence (or absence) and, since musicals involve the strenuous act of dancing, their visible freshness or fatigue. The monitoring of bodily fluids was key. As Astaire recalled in 1973, "It was blood and sweat.... It was tears too. The tears came from the girls. If they cried at rehearsal, I was sure we had a hit."[63]

Attendance was taken. Astaire showed up on time almost all the time. He often showed up early on the complicated "Shoes with Wings On" shoot.[64] Ginger Rogers was often late to the set at RKO, especially as the 1930s wore on. A "Reason for Delay" one morning on *The Castles* captures the intimacy with which actor bodies were tracked: "Miss Rogers checked in studio 7:56a.m.—had hair washed—reported on set 10:30a.m."[65] When Judy Garland was five minutes late to shoot the completion of "A Couple of Swells," the AD noted it.[66] The next day, Garland was late again (9:17am) for her "ready to shoot" call of 9am. At 9:50am, she left the set to seek medical care, first with the studio doctor, then off the lot at her private doctor. Gone all morning, Garland called the AD at 12:15pm saying she would be back on set by 1:15pm. The AD declared her "ready to work" at 1:44pm.[67] Such notes, which track unfolding developments over the day, can be understood in Garland's case as Metro building the case for her dismissal from the studio—which occurred during her brief time as Astaire's costar in *Royal Wedding*.

Still, on this day when shooting finally got going at 1:44pm, the *Easter Parade* company managed to get the vocal number "Snooky Ookums" and the onstage portion of "I Love a Piano" on film.

Another case of Garland showing up very late during *Easter Parade* affords a glimpse of Astaire at work making a fragment. At 1:30am on December 9, 1947, Garland called Wally Worsley, an MGM production manager, to say she couldn't make it in until after lunch. (In his memoir, Worsley notes this happened all the time and that he learned "never to answer the telephone after midnight." Still, he continues, "I would arrive at the studio in the morning to find that she had called someone else."[68]) Garland's call necessitated changing the plan for the day—she was to shoot the song "Michigan." Instead, the company did the rehearsal hall scene. Astaire showed up five minutes early to his 10am call that day and must have learned then that Garland would be very late. So, he spent two hours with director Charles Walters, "reh[earsing] while waiting for Miss Garland." Then, they broke for lunch. Garland showed up after lunch and the day unfolded with the normal delays: more rehearsal, now with Garland (36 minutes), changing into wardrobe (28 minutes), rehearsing some more (9 minutes), waiting for new drapes for the set (32 minutes, used for more rehearsing), adding lighting (2 minutes), and finally, at 2:47pm, Walters could call "action."[69] Finishing the four-minute rehearsal hall scene took the rest of the afternoon and the morning of the next day, when the company arrived at the dance fragment proper (Astaire and Garland dancing to piano accompaniment).

The rehearsal hall scene combines nonmusical and musical actions and shooting methods in revealing ways. The very short dance fragments for Astaire and Garland (discussed in section twelve) occur within a dialogue scene and were supervised on set by the director, not the dance director. (Musical numbers were typically under the direction of the dance director, whose name was listed at the top of the AD report on days when a number was shot—thus, for *Easter Parade*, "ALTON (WALTERS).") Unlike a day spent shooting numbers, sound was recorded live on set in the rehearsal hall scene. Four minutes were spent "Add[ing] li[gh]ting to eliminate mike shadow."[70] Freedom from worry about mike shadows likely liberated camera movement substantially in musical numbers and an entire crew usually on set—the soundmen recording dialogue—was absent. In their place, of course, was a sound crew responsible for the playback machine. Filming the dance bits in the rehearsal hall scene slowed production to a crawl: "Reh[earsing] dance routine, Miss Garland & Mr. Astaire" (48 minutes), then "action for camera" had to be rehearsed (6 minutes), then more rehearsal for dancers and camera (a total of 36 more minutes) before four total takes of the first dance shot. This was done to live sound—there was no playback on set and three minutes were spent reloading sound—so Astaire's verbal counting of the beats in the scene was there in part for postsyncing of the piano. Actor Wilson Wood in the role of Marty the piano player makes a fairly creditable pianist but it's clear he's never actually playing and at times his motions are markedly off the music (which was added later so would have been impossible for Wood to match anyway). And even though the music in the film was not heard on the set, clearly Astaire had worked out the exact number of measures needed to complete the melody of Berlin's tune "Beautiful Faces." The timing of the fragmentary dance is built on a song tune just as in any full-blown number. The complications of filming musical numbers is also evident in three minutes spent by "Director & cutter discuss[ing] setup." When Astaire's character abruptly calls out "lunch" at the end of the rehearsal hall scene, the company did, indeed, break for lunch—after which Garland finally shot "Michigan."

Attendance was also taken on the return from lunch and reasons for lateness were noted. Two of the "principal [female] dancers" in "Too Bad" (*Silk Stockings*) were blamed by name for a twenty-five-minute "delay" on the second day shooting the number. This egregious wait was, however, passed off on someone else: "The reason they were late was due to the fact that Mr. Pan took them to see rushes at the beginning of the lunch."[71] Pan was perhaps taking the fall for young dancers new to film (one was Barrie Chase, Astaire's partner in his television years). As noted, Astaire hated seeing rushes and he usually sent Pan to see them first—lunchtime was likely the earliest chance to view the previous day's work. Studio heads had the power to extend lunch breaks and when they did so, their names appear in AD reports. The *Swing Time* AD reported, "30 min. lost at noon waiting for Mr. Astaire who was having lunch with [president of the studio] Mr. [Leo] Spitz."[72] Garland and Astaire were presumably excused for being twenty-eight minutes late back to the set of *Easter Parade* while being "detained at Mr. Mayer's party."[73] The head of the studio, L. B. Mayer, could interrupt production at will. After his return from the party, the AD notes a further ten-minute delay as "Continue waiting for Mr. Astaire"—an interesting lack of information that perhaps speaks to Astaire's normally solitary lunches in his dressing room, where he could remain focused on the work at hand.

If the shooting of a musical number was completed at midday, rehearsal for the next number was expected to proceed immediately. Shooting dialogue after finishing a number generally did not occur: both kinds of shooting required too much planning and were too contingent on how the shooting of either went to safely schedule other activities. They remained separate—except of course for bits of dialogue on either side of a number, which seem to have been mostly done before the number itself was shot. Astaire and Garland finished "A Couple of Swells" (a 2-day shoot) at noon, then took a slightly longer lunch (1¼ hour) and rehearsed until 4:35pm on the vaudeville medley routines (shot over the following 2 days).[74] Astaire concluded the difficult four-day "Seeing's Believing" (*Belle of New York*) shoot at 11:58am and, before going to lunch, rehearsed the "Boardwalk" tap dance (next before the cameras) for half an hour. A four-hour rehearsal of the "Boardwalk" routine after lunch rounded out the workday.[75]

The studios kept business hours and work was to continue until closing time—at least until after 5pm, if not all the way to 6pm. If a given shot was completed late in the day, it was standard practice to set up—or "L&L" (line and light)—the first shot for the next day. But Astaire could, and frequently did, call a halt to work based on his physical condition, as he did on the first day of "Fated to Be Mated," when the AD noted at 5:42pm, "Company dismissed due to Mr. Astaire being too tired to go on."[76] The end-of-the-day calculus was delicate and, in some cases, perhaps just a waiting game. On the first day of the initial two-day "I Wanna Be a Dancin' Man" shoot, the AD noted at 4:31pm, "Mr. Astaire was exhausted from strenous [sic] dancing & unable to continue." At 4:50pm, the director called it a "Wrap."[77]

ADs kept track of how much rehearsal was needed and by whom. Astaire was frequently given time to rehearse, as on the morning of the difficult fourth day of the "Shoes with Wings On" shoot, when thirty minutes were spent "Waiting for Mr. Astaire, Reh[earsing] to playback."[78] On the fifth day of that number, when shots of Astaire breaking a large plate-glass window were to be taken, Astaire spent an hour just after lunch "Reh[earsing] to playback—Perfecting dance routine." The AD added, perhaps to show the crew was busy as well, "check camera setup."[79] Of course, the reverse situation obtained more often. Much time was always spent adjusting the lighting; rehearsal during this necessary work was also noted: for instance, twenty multitask minutes during "Coffee Time" spent "Lighting—(Astaire rehearse on side)."[80]

Practical delays and equipment adjustment or repair constantly caused delays: four minutes to "Fix hat securely on pole" ("Seeing's Believing"); nine minutes to "Fix flickering arc [lamp]" ("Shoes with Wings On"); seven minutes to "Change from RO #3 to #9 Boom to get more height" ("Girl Hunt" subway dance); eighteen minutes salvaged on the set of *Easter Parade* as "Principals reh[earse] while flat tire on boom is repaired"; five minutes "Placing horn as per Mr. Astaires [sic] request" so he could hear the playback music ("Coffee Time").[81] Problems with the equipment could destroy everyone's work and had to be dealt with expeditiously so as not to delay progress. Late one morning while shooting "Shoes with Wings On," twenty-two minutes and one take were lost due to a slow camera motor. The AD noted: "Lunch (Changing motors during lunch hour)."[82] The first shooting day on *Swing Time* began behind schedule with "60 minutes lost a/c sound trouble."[83] Problems continued the second day but the first shot was—somewhat—on time: "Vibrator in sound blew out—lost 25 minutes replacing it. 1st ok take at 10 a.m."[84] It was all a wash in the end: the first three days on *Swing Time* were spent filming an Astaire solo with male chorus, "It's All in the Cards," that would appear as a two-shot fragment with the incredibly high (and bad) efficiency measure of eighty-four hours of shooting time to one minute of film in the final print. Daily progress could be illusory and for all the attempts to monitor it, filmmaking was an unpredictable process. In the moment, on the day, all that could be measured was whether or not shots were being taken and who on the set was slowing the process of doing so.

Beyond technical adjustments and squeezed in moments of rehearsal, there was the simple need to rest—easily the most common AD explanation for nontechnical delays on set. The AD report for day two of "Couple of Swells" shows repeated breaks for "Miss Garland & Mr Astaire resting" between the nine takes of shot 132G (a 42-second dance portion).[85] Dealing with sweat is paired with "resting" and the need to change into fresh wardrobe throughout the AD reports. Indeed, perspiration was an index of the need to stop work. The sweat labor of dancing—mentioned often by Astaire—worked on the set to authorize a pause in work that was monitored minute to minute.

- The AD on "I Wanna Be a Dancin' Man" made the same spelling error three times in the same report: "Mr. Astaire resting after strenous [sic] dancing" (6 minutes); ten minutes later, "Mr. Astaire changing wardrobe (Wet from strenous [sic] dancing)" (8 minutes); at day's end "Mr. Astaire was exhausted from strenous [sic] dancing & unable to continue."[86]
- "Steppin' Out with My Baby": Astaire changed clothes "as he perspired too profusely during rehearsal" (25 minutes).[87]

- "Fated to Be Mated": "NOTE: between takes Mr. Astaire & Miss Charisse had to change clothes due to perspiration."[88]
- "A Shine on Your Shoes": "Mr. Astaire chg [sic] to dry and pressed wardrobe" (9 minutes).[89]
- The "Girl Hunt" "bop joint" was especially hot. The AD logged thirty-one minutes of camera and lighting crews setting up a new shot with dance-ins, adding, "meanwhile Miss Charisse having hair recurled due to perspiration [sic], changing hose with run and getting into dry wardrobe (1st outfit wet with perspiration [sic])." The same day everything stopped for eighteen minutes to "Wait for Mr Astaire—drying out wardrobe (stage temperature high during shooting due to shutting off ventilators to keep fog smoke effect at constant density)."[90] The AD shields Astaire and Charisse from blame by noting a change in normal conditions due to the unique nature of the number.
- "Bouncin' the Blues" (a 3-shot dance) was filmed in one day. During that day, the AD recorded waits of thirty-five, twelve, twelve, fifteen, and twenty minutes described variously as "Waiting for cast to rest and dry out" or "change to dry clothes" from being "wet with perspiration." Time was also spent recombing Rogers's hair. The longest of these breaks carefully parsed what was going on and which of the two stars needed more rest than the other: "10:50–11:25 Waiting for Miss Rogers to change clothes and have hair fixed, curl coming out, due to perspiration. Also waitinf [sic] for both to rest. Mr. Astaire ready 11:10am."[91]

In a 2017 talk titled "'A Nice Easy Dance': Managing the Musical's Working Bodies," Adrienne L. McLean addressed the gender question raised by sweat in the classical film musical. Focusing on "Leslie Caron's profusely sweating body" in "Sluefoot" (*Daddy Long Legs* [1957]), McLean argued that "the Caron example shows that in fact film form itself cannot always 'conceal the body'—or more to the point, the effects of labor on women's bodies, especially. Certainly Fred Astaire is sweating here too; one can discern the glint of beads on his face from time to time. But he simply doesn't have enough skin showing to make it the issue it is for Caron; instead, he can discreetly perspire into a silk union suit or the Kleinert's dress shields the costumers had undoubtedly thoughtfully placed into his jacket." McLean's goes on, "For the male performers, it is not so much that their perspiration was edited out, but rather that it actually was on an essential level invisible."[92] Astaire's sweat—dried out between takes on the set and so wiped away in the cuts of the final edit—was indeed invisible: and so, arguably, was Astaire's body. He is a figure in clothes (usually his own)—unlike Gene Kelly and Gene Nelson, who showed some skin—and so Astaire could present as a super cooled man (physically and affectually, even preternaturally). This too was a strategy to maintain his cis-het masculinity (of a certain refined type) and, as McLean notes, only open to Astaire because he was a man.[93]

Remarkably, the available reports chronicle only one injury. On the fourth day of "Shoes with Wings On," production stopped for thirty minutes: "Waiting for nurse to come to stage, Mr. Astaire's hurting his right knee during last take. Nurse to stage at 11:25am examined knee, and suggested ½ hour rest but Mr. Astaire kept exercising same and wanted to try another take before lunch." He shot two takes and spent a suspiciously long twelve minutes "fixing his shirt"—perhaps buying some time regarding his knee. After shooting two more takes, ten minutes were spent deciding to print two of these four takes and break for lunch because, after all, "Mr. Astaire's knee hurting." The next shot, described as "gun business," was not strenuous, and after a night's rest, Astaire had no reported difficulties the next day.[94] The only other physical impediment to Astaire shooting delayed *A Damsel in Distress* for several days: the AD reported Astaire "could not work because boil on chin."[95] He no doubt spent the time rehearsing.

A common explanation for additional takes tersely indicated Astaire's power on the set: "Mr [sic] Astaire wanted another."[96] The shot in question here was the third in "You're All the World to Me." Having done five takes—and agreed "take 3 good"—Astaire asked for another. His request was granted and, along with "take 3," printed. One of these two shots is in the film—indeed, as discussed in the next part, both might be through the use of an invisible cut. In one case, producer Arthur Freed himself came to the set to convince Astaire to be happy with shots taken, to stop shooting more takes, and to move on. The first shooting day on "Sunday Jumps" had been productive—just one shot remained in the routine on day two. A long AD notation from the start of the second day's report tells the story.

> 9:16 – 9:25 Discussion between director (Stanley Donen) and producer (Arthur Freed) re: advisability of making more takes on 2nd cut of dance routine – (Sc. Slated 15X1B) – which 19 takes were made yesterday – 7/6/50 – Mr. Astaire wanted to make more takes, as he felt doubtful as to whether company had a good take – This cut involved the part of the dance routine in which Mr. Astaire danced with hat rack – After discussion Mr.

Freed informed unit manager, who had called Mr. Freed to stage – that he had decided no more takes were necessary.[97]

"Sunday Jumps"—a relatively efficient number (2:38 spent shooting per minute in the final cut)—was completed by noon that day and Astaire went into rehearsal for "Ev'ry Night at Seven." That number too caused Astaire concerns. After completing it and seeing the edited final product, he requested and himself paid for a two-hour retake of part of the number some six weeks after production closed and over five months after the number was originally shot. Whatever the cause, the AD reports suggest persistent dissatisfaction on Astaire's part with his work on *Royal Wedding*. The retakes for "Ev'ry Night at Seven" suggest this feeling lasted into postproduction.

Showing emotion or refusing to continue got in the way of efficient work and appears very rarely in the archives. Pianist Jean Sablon, part of an on-set band in *The Castles*, refused to lip-sync to the heavily accented vocal for "Darktown Strutters Ball." After holding up the production for an hour and twenty minutes, Louis Mercier replaced him.[98] Among the only evidence for Astaire getting upset is an AD note from the full day during which Astaire shot the gravity-defying "You're All the World to Me": "Mr Astaire not too happy," noted the AD during the two-and-a-half hours spent filming the danced vocal (done in one 100-second shot).[99] It took ten takes in all: the first five all described as "Unf[inished] for dance action" (Astaire's fault); the next two were "NG for camera—boom movement bad" (cameraman's fault); the next and eighth was judged "good hold." At this juncture, Astaire is described as "not too happy." He had rehearsed this difficult routine on set for seven days and just getting a useable take of the vocal portion, before the set even begins to turn, was proving tough. The shot is, for a danced vocal, quite complex—holding Astaire in insert framing most of the time as he moves about. Perhaps this easy part had been under-rehearsed. Quickly before lunch, they filmed the "tag" of the number (after the walls and ceiling dance when Astaire settles into an easy chair for a final pose). Then, after lunch, it was time to shoot the two-shot dance with the revolving set. The camera operator was strapped into his harness. Astaire got the first part—a 100-second dance riding the revolving set—in two takes shot over forty minutes. It could have been tighter but between takes the camera operator asked to be unharnessed so his harness could be rerigged. Both takes were good enough to print. The second shot—intended to be almost as long at ninety seconds—followed but was not so simply made. Five takes—three with "unf[inished] dance routine"—yielded but one good take (printed). Inevitably, "Mr. Astaire wanted another." A sixth was shot and printed. It was now 4:26pm. The AD reported there remained "one shot to do in the revolving set tomorrow morning" but "Astaire being very tired" didn't want to try it.[100] Instead, they put off finishing the number—or quitting for the day (evidently not a possibility at that time in the afternoon)—and the company moved to an adjacent set and took a brief shot of Astaire crossing through a hotel corridor just before the number in the finished film. They all returned to the revolving set the next morning and spent just under two hours filming some more. Astaire was rehearsing "I Left My Hat in Haiti" by 11am.

Who controlled the shooting of a number? Ostensibly the director, but clearly many other agents on the set had some influence. Giving or withholding the labor of their performing body was one way to exert some agency over the workflow on a shooting day. Astaire, as we have seen, had several reasons to hand for calling a wait. He seldom just declared the need for a break. On the one-day "Bouncin' the Blues" shoot, Ginger Rogers arrived ten minutes past call, then took fifteen minutes "limbering up" and ten more "to get dressed and have hair combed." After lunch, Rogers spent another ten minutes for hair combing and fifteen "reh[earsing] to playback."[101] Rogers had only been on *Barkleys* for four weeks. It was her first musical (and only second film) at Metro.[102] This was not her shop. Fully aware that she had saved the picture by taking over on short notice for Garland—who reportedly did a pass through the set after being fired and insulted Rogers—these pauses can be understood as Rogers marking this new ground as her territory. She didn't stop the work substantially and she was always prepared. But she did mold the workflow of the day to her needs—and the AD kept track of every minute.

Waiting for sweat to dry or hair to be combed offers a bodily excuse for a hold in the process. An unexplained note in the "Shine on Your Shoes" AD reports signals just how much we cannot know about the encounter of performing bodies with the complex yet very human process that turned them into screen bodies. On September 25, 1952, from 2:47pm to 2:56pm, the entire *Band Wagon* company, including forty-three extras, halted work on this complicated number to "Wait for Leroy Daniel[s]," the Black man brought into the number to do a dance with Astaire.[103] It was Daniels's third day ever on a Hollywood set. No explanation was given by the *Band Wagon* AD for why the only Black man Astaire ever danced with put the entire MGM moviemaking machine on pause for nine full minutes.

MIDPOINT

"I Just / Won't / [Don't?] Dance"

>Astaire makes an art form of slouching.
>
>—Beth Genné (2018)

In 1959, Astaire's long-time dance assistant Hermes Pan suggested one way Astaire's dancing might impact the viewer: "Fred can dance a very intricate routine, and he makes it look so simple and easy. It gives the audience a sense of self-identification and a feeling that they, too, can do it."[1] Pan picked up this theme in an oral history interview more than twenty years later: "That's the art—to make it look like nothing, so everybody has the feeling, 'Oh, I could do that, if I could just dance a little.' They don't realize how much sweat it took to perfect something that looks like walking."[2] One problem with a dance made "to look like nothing" is its ambiguous relationship to dance as a larger category. If we accept Pan's view, the historical and technical content of Astaire's dancing as it relates to the category of dance remains decidedly opaque. Pan's comments similarly withhold any concrete sense for the intended inclusiveness of "everybody" in the "audience"—men? women? moviegoers? social dancers? musical movie fans?—and offers little as to the content of how Astaire moved his body in the dance, except for the notion of dancing as walking.

This idea is, of course, open to reversal—perhaps, instead, Astaire makes walking look like dancing. Indeed, a veritable refrain across the Astaire discourse celebrates his walk. *Newsweek* (1953): "The very walk of Fred Astaire is a light, syncopated sidle which can set a scene atremble."[3] Eleanor Powell (1973) spoke of Astaire's "jaunty little walk"; Betty Comden (1988) reached for the same adjective: "He had that jaunty stride that nobody else has."[4] Nancy Reagan (1988): "I loved to just sit and just watch him walk across the screen."[5] MGM producer Roger Edens about a book number (1958): Astaire sings "and then *bursts* into that wonderful walk of his."[6] Leslie Caron (1988): "the way he walked was already like dancing."[7] Hermes Pan (1973): "He walks with sort of a bounce and a rhythm, sort of a loose rhythmic saunter that looks as if it's, in a way, dancing. I remember Gershwin wrote music especially for that.... It was just a walking back and forth on a ship ['Walking the Dog' in *Shall We Dance* (1937)] but it sort of took on a dimension of importance and you've often heard people say they just liked to see Fred walk down the street. Well I think that had a lot to do with it—the style with which he walked around."[8] Even Astaire, speaking in 1973, singled out walking as a category of motion he assessed in himself: "I can think of a lot of faults in everything that I did and occasionally I would see something that I liked and it would be something that was simply the most unimportant thing—it may be the way I walked across the scene to get from one place to another." Later in the same interview, Astaire lamented, "Dancing is so difficult."[9] David Thomson zeroes in on a moment of walking in *Silk Stockings* (1957) "before the dancing begins." In the scene prior to "Fated to Be Mated," Astaire, "muttering 'Hallo, hallo . . . ,' hobbles over to meet [Cyd Charisse]. That movement... was exquisite, original, and Astaire. The emotion of the moment—of lovers reunited—hardly seems to strike him. But ask him to move from A to B and he is aroused. This touches on a vital principle: that it is often preferable to have a movie actor who moves well than one who 'understands' the part. . . . [V]ery few men and women can move well in front of a camera. . . . With Astaire this effect is far more concentrated, because it is his single asset."[10] A dancing man celebrated as a walking man occupies a peculiar position vis-à-vis the categories *dancing* and *man*. The aforementioned comments all locate Astaire's walk as a kind of danced action that falls below the strict designation *dancing*. Caron and Pan carefully separate the two: for Caron, Astaire's walk was "like dancing" (but wasn't strictly so); Pan finesses the comparison with stacked-up qualifiers that try to separate being from perception—Astaire's walk "looks as if it's, in a way, dancing" (but clearly isn't quite). In Astaire's *New York Times* obituary, Richard F. Shepard made a similar point without direct reference to walking or any other content: "It was the kind of dancing that caught the imagination, even of those who disdained the very thought of witnessing any dancing at all."[11] Walking this line (pardon the pun) *while dancing* gets to the heart of Astaire's straight white male persona. As cultural critic Marcelle Clements wrote in a nostalgia-drenched piece from 1980, "The Astaire genius consists in never dancing over the line . . . good cheer without doltism, warmth without mawkishness, elegance without archness, nonchalance without indifference, and excellence devoid of arrogance." Searching for a real (as in actual) man matched to Astaire's measure, Clements goes on, "Is his persona a total fiction? . . . Most guys I know won't even dance cheek-to-cheek except as a joke, and it's usually with each other."[12] Clements's joke about men dancing together raises the "good sexuality" question and she comes close to admitting the Astaire of the silver screen isn't real (as, of course, he isn't).

Pan's discourse of "simple and easy," "look like nothing"-style likely didn't sit all that well with Astaire himself. The dialogue cues into both "The Babbitt and the Bromide" (*Ziegfeld Follies* [1946]) and a television duo with Barrie Chase from twenty years later alike undercut notions that the dance to follow is being cooked up in the moment: in the latter, Astaire introduces their routine as a "studied improvisation," to which Chase wryly adds, "with plenty of rehearsal."[13] Speaking to a reporter in 1957, Astaire said, "My routines may look easy, but they are nothing you throw away while shaving. It's always murder to get that easy effect. I don't try to make things look easy. I'd like them to look hard so people would know what work went into them."[14] (Note Astaire's comparison between shaving and dancing—both, presumably, manly activities.) Again, Astaire masculinizes his dancing as work. John O'Hara echoed the theme in a 1962 profile of Astaire: "All his professional life he has maintained this same kind of integrity: he takes a job, he works and works and works on it until he is ready, and then he delivers. And then he goes home."[15] O'Hara casts Astaire as a working man toting a lunch bucket and returning to his tract house: of course, Astaire did usually take a lunch and he did tend to stay home in the evenings (rather than hitting the Hollywood social scene). Again, masculine action of a type—hard work—stands in here for any description of how Astaire actually danced, perhaps not something O'Hara felt all that comfortable putting into words. Anxiety about dancing as a job lingers behind all this talk about how hard Astaire worked. An exchange between Astaire and Cyd Charisse in *Silk Stockings* makes the argument in a Cold War context. Charisse, playing a Soviet official, dismisses dancing as no sort of real labor: "Dancing is a waste of time," she says, adding, "You go go go but you don't get anywhere." Astaire's bemused response—"You're telling me"—ducks Charisse's critique of dancing by folding it into his romantic efforts with her (which shortly after succeed in getting her dancing as well). Such deflection proves a recurring strategy for Astaire whenever he was presented with questions about the content or meaning of his (work) dancing.

Another common line on Astaire's dancing that also lacks concrete content as to how he moved praises his apparent perfection. Charisse framed the theme as hackneyed even as she repeated it in her 1976 memoir: "It has become a cliché to say that Fred Astaire is a perfectionist, but it must be said, because it is his essential quality."[16] The notion of Astaire as perfectionist goes back to his years on the Broadway stage. His sister Adele dubbed him "moaning minnie" for his constant rehearsing to get everything just right. This curiously emasculating nickname—from a teasing older sister, after all—takes the negative view and founds the discourse of Astaire as a solitary genius who didn't like to party and was single-mindedly focused on his work. Astaire's Hollywood peers expressed the same thought in laudatory terms. Bob Fosse combined notions of perfection and ease when interviewed in 1973, noting in Astaire "this overwhelming desire for perfection. And yet whenever I saw it on the screen it always looked as if he had just made it up. It had a tremendous improvisational look to it."[17] Improvisation and ease are alike disavowals of intentional content—just fooling around suggests a sort of dancing not made of *dance* as defined elsewhere. Astaire is not in the tradition—he is alone, a solitary and perfect figure. Bing Crosby, quoted by John O'Hara in 1967, linked Astaire's perfectionism to character.

> There never was a greater perfectionist, there never was, or never will be, a better dancer, and I never knew anybody more kind, more considerate, or so completely a gentleman. I made a couple of pictures with him, and if my work in these pictures was any good, it was because some of his class rubbed off on me. I—notoriously a sloppy, slovenly workman—I love Fred, John, and I admire and respect him. I guess it's because he's so many things I'd like to be, and am not.[18]

Crosby presents Astaire as an ideal of manhood—and, notably once again, as a man of work—grounded in the integrity that flows from craftsmanship, from doing a complicated task well. Quoted in 1959, just after he directed Astaire in *Silk Stockings*, Rouben Mamoulian granted Astaire some unsettled edges while also folding him into the white male category of genius: "Fred is a terribly complex fellow, not unlike the Michelangelos and Da Vincis [sic] of the Renaissance period. He's a supreme artist, but he is constantly filled with doubts and self-anger about his work—and that's what makes him so good. He's a perfectionist who is never sure he is attaining perfection."[19] The problem with perfection—same as "look like nothing"—is the lack of content, as if Astaire's dancing is all execution rather than a mix of execution and actual movements that situate Astaire, as a straight white male dancer, within a history of human beings—specifically men (not all straight or white)—moving their bodies to music in a manner understood to be dancing.

Astaire himself regularly dodged the content question by avoiding any description of his work that used the vocabulary of an established dance tradition. "I just dance," he insisted in the last sentence of his 1959 autobiography *Steps in Time*. It was a line he repeated to a journalist in 1959 ("What has Astaire to say about his genius? 'Rubbish. I just put my feet in the air and move them around!'"[20]) and again in 1973 ("The years just went by. I really don't know how the dance started and I don't give a damn where it's going. I don't think about art. All I know is that there were musical comedies with people dancing. So that's what I did. I just danced."[21]). At least in the latter instance Astaire situated his work in a specific milieu—musical comedy, which, as he noted in *Steps in Time*, was a realm where "there should be no limitations" on how the dancing body moved. But disavowal of artistic intention was just avoidance, as another journalist noted in 1976: "He frequently has said, with specious modesty, 'I'm just a hoofer.' Now, he said to me, 'I just move where my feet take me.' This is piffle."[22] Piffle, indeed. In a 1976 oral history interview with Ronald Davis, Astaire phrased his refusal a bit differently and in masculine and class-based terms: "I just think I'm a guy who ... I guess I don't think that *deeply* about it [dancing]. Maybe I'm not well educated enough to think that deeply about it. Maybe I'm lucky that I'm not!"[23] Astaire—after defining himself as "a guy"—says the question just doesn't interest him, then suggests he lacks the knowledge to answer, then posits his lack as an advantage. The most he would ever admit to as to why he danced was the profit motive, another content-empty category—"I was trying to make a buck.... I just did it for entertainment. I had no idea about saying anything.... I'm a rat if you want to get to know me."[24] Astaire's avoidance of questions of intention, expression, or, for that matter, manifest content in how he moved his body while dancing demand examination as themselves expressions of his straight white male identity. Not having to call what he did anything in particular was his privilege—it was just something he did. That he did it in a mass media space where he bestrode the scene—because he was first on the scene and also because he made movie dances for so long—only added to this privilege. He was, from very early on, something close to a fact of nature. In fact, of course, Astaire's dancing on film was a product of a commercial culture industry that systematically limited opportunities for white women (who aged out early), everyone of color (barred from leading roles), and effeminate men (limited to coded comic sidekicks).

In this context, it's more than a bit ironic that the one descriptor Astaire did apply to his dancing style was the word *outlaw*. Here's the relevant passage from the final page of *Steps in Time*: "I wanted to do all my dancing my own way, in a sort of outlaw style. I always resented being told that I couldn't point my toe *in*, or some other such rule."[25] The word *outlaw* seems to imply dancing that sits decidedly outside any traditional or historical rules governing a given style—here, specifically, ballet (which mandates a turned-out position). Ballet and any form of artistic pretension—anything not done "to make a buck"—remained, for Astaire, something to be avoided. He repeatedly shucks off ballet positions with visible distaste throughout "Slap That Bass" in *Shall We Dance*, a number from a film where he (absurdly and unconvincingly) plays a famous ballet dancer. If anything, Astaire skewed the other direction—toward low or simply popular dance content. In the BBC radio documentary he said, "I didn't like ballet too much, it was too cut and dried and it wasn't my racket. I just couldn't do and didn't want to do it. I went into the more popular and remunerative type of entertainment."[26] Choreographer Eugene Loring noted Astaire's aversion to any verbal suggestion in the rehearsal room that he was doing or had knowledge of ballet: "If you say arabesque, he doesn't want to do it. Ballet to him is sissy. I'd always have to say, 'When you stick your leg out in back.' I had to be very careful not to use ballet terms with him."[27] Astaire apparently resisted terminology that might render the moves he did anything less than conventionally masculine (or not "sissy," slang for gay). Notecards intended to guide Astaire's closing remarks at the American Film Institute (AFI) tribute—derived from his autobiography—include the following prompts (which he did not use on the night): "But I didn't do anything that I *didn't* like, such as inventing 'up' to the arty or 'down' to the corny. I happen to relish a certain type of corn. What I think is the really dangerous approach is the 'let's be artistic' approach. I know that artistry just happens. Believe it or not, there is even an artistic way to pick up a garbage can."[28] Interviewed for the same event, Pan said, "He hates to be arty" and added, "He says what, can't be worse than a serious dancer. Can you imagine anything worse that a, what do they mean by a serious dancer. And I know exactly what he means, cause I feel the same way."[29] These negative remarks about ballet resonate symptomatically as anti-elitist—as Astaire remaining aloof from any self-defined "artistic" group or tradition. When Astaire mentions the possibility that a typically masculine chore like "picking up a garbage can" (which he does in *The Belle of New York* [1952]) might be done artistically, he empties the category of all meaning—and casts his own preoccupations back to the manly realm of work.

The one dance tradition to which a good amount of Astaire's dances can be directly tied is social dancing as done by male-female pairs in the ballroom dance style. In 1946, cine-dance scholar Mary Jane Hungerford understood ballroom style as "the real secret to the success" of the Astaire and Rogers pictures: "Everyone wants to glide gracefully over the dance floor with a skill that never threatens his or her faultless grooming, in the arms of a partner whose expression shows that the experience is undiluted bliss." Hungerford noted of the Astaire-Rogers dances, "There are always some movements so simple that audiences feel able to imitate them," and added of the style's purchase when applied to film, "only exhibition ballroom dances lend themselves to this sort of *mass exploitation*."[30] Astaire—who hated and resisted any casual social dancing (despite women always wanting to dance with him)—exploited this connection to create a chain of social dancing schools in the mid-1940s. Astaire's incorporation of social dance moves in his screen dances gave concrete content to his heterosexuality and supported Pan's notion of viewers—probably men—thinking, "Oh, I could do that, if I could just dance a little." Social dance content turns up often in his duo dances, as discussed in Part Five, and analysis of these moves helps tie his work to specific gender roles.

The other dance style obviously evident in Astaire's dancing is tap. Tap dancers and historians have situated Astaire at the edge of the tradition. Marshall and Jean Stearns (1968): "Fred Astaire developed a style of dancing, which although it did not employ the best tapping in the world, made good use of it in combination with other movements."[31] Constance Valis Hill (2010): Astaire "never intended to be a straight exhibition of tap dance expertise. Instead, Astaire makes stories out of the dynamic variety of tap dancing."[32] Brian Seibert (2015): "Here, as elsewhere, Astaire was the white exception, built like an eccentric but graceful as a leading man, his rhythm-boy feet guided by theatrical ideas."[33] Seibert never strays too far from the race question: "As with Gershwin and Balanchine, the question of what [Astaire] took [from Black dancers] is worth notice because of what he made of it."[34] Bob Fosse went straight to the race question as well: "And again, there is no tap dancer like him. At least, certainly, no white tap dancer. There are black [*sic*] tap dancers I think are very good. I don't know of a white dancer that has that sense of rhythm he has."[35] Astaire used tap all the time but rarely exclusively—so that tap becomes a tool for his presentation of a certain kind of masculinity, specifically a noisy one, and also one that is singular to him from his position as a leading man in film. Black tapper Charles "Honi" Coles (1960s): "Astaire sells body motion, not tap."[36] Astaire would seem to have agreed, telling Bob Thomas in the 1980s, "When I'm called 'a tap dancer,' it makes me laugh. Because I *am* in a way, but that is *one* of the kinds of dancing I do.... I had a little different treatment of how to *apply* it. I didn't just set out and hop into the 'buck.' I'd move around and do things."[37] As Part Six will show, tap dance provided Astaire an excuse to make noise, to use his dancing to disrupt or dominate the scene in an assertive, even threatening manner. Tap, understood rather broadly as syncopated dancing concerned primarily with the making of sounds on the floor with one's feet, afforded Astaire the chance to play the bad boy. Astaire's tap dancing undeniably expressed a Black dance and musical style, which Astaire did while dressing like the most elite of white men (English aristocrats) and inhabiting a light entertainment, nearly all-white genre that created, in the words of a line from *The Barkleys of Broadway* (1949), a world of "fun set to music." This appropriation of Black style in the making of a white persona marks most of mainstream (white) American popular culture and, as I have written elsewhere, Astaire is a foundational figure in this regard reaching back to mid-1920s Broadway.[38] Megan Pugh agrees, noting of the Astaire-Rogers films that, apart from "Slap That Bass" and "Bojangles of Harlem" (*Swing Time* [1936]), "race isn't an explicit theme, and tap stands for a more general form of power and freedom, a form that denotes not blackness, but Americanness."[39] Pugh's invocation of "Americanness" deserves qualification as American whiteness.

Who gets to be an outlaw? Better yet, who gets to be an icon of powerful normative categories like white, straight, and male—which Astaire was and is *while dancing*—and claim outlaw status with a straight face that others take at face value? The answer, of course, is Fred Astaire, a singularly powerful straight white man. (Similar moves by male establishment figures to claim outsider status include Senator John McCain's media identity as a "maverick" and President Barack Obama and musician Bruce Springsteen's shared 2021 claim to be "renegades."[40]) The remainder of this book seeks to understand the substantive content of Astaire's self-described "outlaw" screen dance style as an instance of a straight white male establishment figure of the middle twentieth century, supported by tremendous cultural and actual capital investments, constructing a highly individual, essentially nontransferable (therefore inimitable) screen dance embodiment of a straight white male body. Part Four returns to Astaire's default Vitruvian framing for a close examination of the ensemble of aesthetic and practical choices that made this approach to the screen dance body possible. I consider how Astaire used the tools of moviemaking—framing, staging, and cutting—to present his body as the center and origin of everything around it, in effect, as the maker of the visible world. The relationship between his dancing body and the moviemaking machine that captured and repackaged it is central. His approach, again detailed by way of quantitative analytical methods, reduces the human form to a two-dimensional figure of fantasy that signaled a stable identity and minimized fleshliness. On close examination, Astaire's screen dance body is, itself, a special effect, hardly real at all. Parts Five and Six move into a closer consideration of the danced movements Astaire did—the content of his movements separate from their cinematic presentation. Again, quantitative methods offer a new perspective. Part Five quantifies physical contact and relationships between Astaire and his partners in the two-thirds of his dances that are duos. The gender coding of ballroom dance proves central to this inquiry, as does the residual egalitarian resonance of vaudeville double acts. Part Six counts the recurrence of select moves Astaire used repeatedly to declare a noisy masculinity: some steps original to him; some drawn from the most generic tap vocabulary; some not, properly speaking, dance steps at all.

Before moving to these specific inquiries, I want to return to Astaire's deflecting line, "I just dance." These words, intended to shut down any discourse of meaning or intent, can also be read as a disavowal of dance as a capacious category that demands *some* adjectival qualification. Astaire's claim to "outlaw" status and his resistance to "arty" dancing or any sort of prescriptive dance tradition recalls the title of a song he sang and danced to in *Roberta* (1935)—"I Won't Dance." This title might be taken out of context as a refinement of Astaire's "I just dance" claim, in which he refuses to admit the word *dance* carries any content or history or denies said dance histories have anything to say about him. In this reading, "I won't dance" captures his refusal to submit to any pre-existing definition of what *dancing* is—and yet he moves. Claiming "I just dance" and, by implication, insisting "I won't dance" in any set style set the stage for a further disavowal: I don't dance; I'm simply putting on my hat or taking out the garbage or merely walking. Of course, Astaire might also add that doing all three (and actually dancing) is, in the end, a "sweat job."

FOUR
FRAMES, SETS, CUTS

The dancer's basic tool is the space through which he moves; it is his business to create, out of emptiness, the ordered patterns of art. Astaire's special virtue, as an artist, has been to dominate any space he chooses, with consummate ease. One does not imagine him struggling for this dominance, and the spectator for the most part fails to remember that such ease can result only from the most intense off-stage efforts.

The seams of his work never show, and neither does the intensity of the man who creates it. In fact, nothing shows but what Astaire wants to show, which is casualness, coolness, a state for relaxed elegance, a shy humor, a modesty which seems to hold his art very lightly—as an unprecious achievement.

—Richard Schickel (1962)

30. Shadows on the Wall

Astaire's RKO films abound with shadows and silhouettes: the title cards for *The Gay Divorce* (1934) and *Swing Time* (1936) similarly render moments from both films' dances as silhouettes (fig. 30.1). A back-positioned spotlight throughout "Waltz in Swing Time" doubles Astaire and Rogers on the floor in front of them in a circle of light that follows them as the camera does (fig. 30.2). Shadow selves turn behind Astaire as he rounds a corner while spinning near the close of "Slap That Bass" in *Shall We Dance* (1937, fig. 30.3). And, of course, the second portion of "Bojangles of Harlem" in *Swing Time* separates Astaire from his shadow in a competitive Peter Pan encounter that, contrary to Barrie's narrative, has the real boy (Astaire) send his shadow selves packing (rather than seeking rapprochement in reattachment; fig. 30.4). Beyond the RKO years, "I Wanna Be a Dancin' Man" (*The Belle of New York* [1952]) and "The Ritz Roll and Rock" (*Silk Stockings* [1957]) both open with Astaire in silhouette. In the latter, top hat and cane reveal their

FRAMES, SETS, CUTS 185

FIGURE 30.1

FIGURE 30.2

FIGURE 30.3

potency as body-altering objects that instantly identify Astaire's particular masculine figure (fig. 30.5). Shadows and silhouettes admit and celebrate the flatness of the medium. Astaire noted this in a 1959 interview, saying, "The flat surface of the screen robs [the dancer's body] of three-dimensional quality."[1]

FIGURE 30.4

FIGURE 30.5

In 1936, Graham Greene famously described Astaire as

> the nearest approach we are ever likely to have to a human Mickey Mouse; he might have been drawn by Mr. Walt Disney, with his quick physical wit, his incredible agility. He belongs to a fantasy world almost as free as Mickey's from the law of Gravity [*sic*], but unfortunately he has to act with human beings and not even Miss Ginger Rogers can match his freedom, lightness and happiness.... It needs an effort of mind to remember that Mr. Fred Astaire was not invented by a film director and drawn by a film draughtsman. He is the nearest we are ever likely to get to a human Mickey, near enough for many critics to have noted the resemblance. If one needs to assign human qualities to this light quick, humorous cartoon, they are the same as the early Mickey's: a touch of pathos, the sense of a courageous and impromptu intelligence, a capacity for getting into awkward situations.[2]

Both Mickey and Astaire are fully realized when pictured as flat figures composed of dynamic, high-contrast, unshaded lines and areas. And, if we limit Astaire to his screen dance body, both Mickey and Astaire are fundamentally creatures of two dimensions.

In his book-length meditation on sex and cinema, *Sleeping with Strangers: How the Movies Shaped Desire*, David Thomson wrote of Astaire: "Astaire (real name Austerlitz) was not gay, and on film he rose above notions of intercourse. I enjoy Astaire, because he is not entirely or merely human. He is made of light, music, and the sound of his heels on hard floors. Sometimes he feels more animated than carnal."[3] Thomson uses this view of Astaire to argue for a peculiar sort of sexuality: "That's where Astaire comes into consideration as one of the first great asexual models in film. Buster Keaton was another.... I'm not calling those men homosexuals: but I'm convinced their meaning was, if not gay, then a step toward neutrality or the notion that being seen is the sexy thing in the movies. So gay can refer to a style—just like feminine or masculine or childish."[4] Thomson's idiosyncratic argument indicates a restless search to understand the impact of Astaire's screen dance body as somehow not fleshly, as not implicated in the world of sexual relations between bodies. And, indeed, it literally is not. Comparing Astaire to animated figures and finding his sensuality in acts of sustained visibility—"being seen is the sexy thing"—points toward the otherworldly nature of his screen body.

Novelist Zadie Smith returns to Astaire often. Her 2016 novel *Swing Time* borrows its title from one of his films. In the essay "Dance Lessons for Writers," Smith cuts to the heart of Astaire's screen dance body: "Astaire is clearly not an experimental dancer like [Twyla] Tharp or [Pina] Bausch but he is surreal in the sense of surpassing the real. He is transcendent. When he dances a question proposes itself: what if a body moved like *this* through the world? But it is only a rhetorical, fantastical question, for no bodies move like Astaire, no, we only move like him in our dreams."[5] This part of the book gathers evidence for the concrete choices behind Astaire's "surpassing the real" dances. I offer an empirical answer to Smith's "rhetorical, fantastical" question, grounded in the moment of encounter between dancer and camera, when Astaire's real body did move "like *this* through the world" but only for the span of a shot and for the purposes of the film footage that captured his motions. In the process, we can understand the ontological claims Astaire's screen dance body makes in the dream world he constructs by way of his movements in time and space on film. Astaire's screen dance body was made in the frame, on the set, and in the cuts. Attending to each of these spaces helps define the formal qualities and aesthetic and practical parameters of Astaire's dancing. The strategies he used to dance "like *this*" also come into view when the spatial coordinates inherent in his frames, sets, and cuts are examined. *Pace* Smith, the screen dance body Astaire aspired to—and mostly achieved—is not transcendent. It is specific to a time and place and access to creative tools that were, themselves, fantastically expensive, unbelievably rare, and historically transitory. This fact of history codes Astaire's screen dance body as white by virtue of nonwhites' lack of access to the studio musical-making machine. As Shannon Sullivan writes, "There exist a co-constitutive relationship between the racing of bodies by means of space and the racing of space by means of bodies. Each reinforces and makes possible the other such that the casual relationship between them is circular, not linear."[6] Whatever transcendence Astaire's dancing might engender in the viewer is an epiphenomenon of the absolute control he displays. Astaire's control operates in both the content of his dancing and the context where he danced "like *this*" such that his dancing still "exists . . . to argue over." I return to this fantasy of the empowered (white) individual at the close of this part, after detailing in physical terms the stuff of which Astaire's screen dance body is made.

Astaire aspired to a screen dance body that was perfected. This old news is worth reiteration on the way to a substantive detailing of Astaire's approach to making the dancing figure in the frame. As the assistant director (AD) reports considered in Part Three attest, across Astaire's career, perfection sometimes required many, many takes. The dancers made mistakes, and the camera operators did too. Some of the multiple takes were required to get the camera movement just right, especially when considering that Astaire shot his numbers blind, without the immediate input of video-assist technologies that only appeared in the 1960s. He had to wait until the dreaded rushes to see the results of the shoot. Director Vincente Minnelli told the BBC: "Astaire always works hard but he's very shy and requires a lot of reassurance, you know. He never thinks he's good. The more you try and convince that he's fabulous the more he thinks he could do better. He wouldn't see his rushes. He'd stay in the alley and pace up and down until you came out and then keep for a half an hour asking you questions about certain things. It'd be much easier if he'd actually seen the rushes but he couldn't bear to."[7] Only after viewing the rushes could Astaire know if the dance had been executed and filmed to his satisfaction. It is extraordinary, therefore, to see so little evidence for retakes of musical numbers. Astaire's approach to making dance numbers for film was so tightly focused and consistent (and done in a context of utter technical professionalism), it appears he and his collaborators were able to determine on the set, in the moment of making shots yet unseen, if they had successfully created the image track materials from which an acceptable finished screen dance could be made.

Thus, Astaire's dance-making process must have always kept the camera in mind. Looking at his own body in the mirror while dance making, he must have also been conceptualizing how his and his partner's bodies would be framed. The frame (and the camera that defined it) was an understood presence in the rehearsal studio where the dance was made before the dancers arrived on the set. Framing, camera movement, and anticipated cuts shaped his choreography long before any actual camera was to hand. Looking at Astaire's work from this angle—attending to the frame as part of the creative process, as a real physical thing (if always invisible to the dancers) that had to be negotiated correctly vis-à-vis the dancing body and the camera during shooting—suggests Astaire practiced a kind of choreographing in the camera. The perfected screen dance body required a certain kind of perfect framing that served a specific approach to editing (and continuity), which in turn shaped fundamentally the ontology of Astaire's screen dance body. Informing this relationship at every step (literally) was the set where the dance was done for the camera. The importance of the dance setting as a place for particular actions again distinguishes the musical from other Hollywood genres. Production records and interviews attest to Astaire's deep concern that the floors on which he danced be just right—as to both their springiness and their speed. Beyond just the floor, Astaire's frequent engagement with specific spaces (steps or levels) and objects (from furniture to props) made dance settings even more important to his process. All these elements are considered in this part of the book.

In a 1937 interview for *Theatre Arts*, Astaire articulated his aesthetic goals for filming dance numbers: "I have always tried to run a dance straight in the movies, keeping the full figure of the dancer, or dancers, in view and retaining the flow of the movement intact.... I think that the audience can get a bigger reaction watching a dance on the screen than behind a fixed proscenium arch—probably because they get a larger, clearer and better-focused view, and so derive a larger emotional response."[8] Astaire's practical strategies for achieving this "larger, clearer and better-focused view" are expressed as follows as underlying principles of his screen dance body. These principles are interdependent—each helps define the other—and could be stated in any order.

- This body is **flat**. There is little to no attempt to bring out the roundedness of the human figure.
- This body is **whole**. All parts—from head to toes to fingertips—are visible almost all the time.
- This body is scaled as **large** as the frame allows. The content of the dance facilitates achieving this principle.
- This body is seen from a **level view** matching the dancer's eye to the camera's lens. Use of cranes to move up or over the body is limited and often an indication Astaire is not in full control.
- Our view of this body is **sustained**. Cuts away from the dancing body are unusual and serve a clear purpose (as with the limited use of cutaways and inserts discussed earlier).
- This body remains **centered** in the frame. When the dancer or dancers move, the frame (and the camera) moves with them.
- This body is **exact and accurate** in its motions—no mistakes are evident—and in its negotiation of physical space and any objects to hand.
- This body is perfectly **synchronized** to the music on the soundtrack, and all body sounds, especially foot sounds, match the motions of the dancers exactly and credibly.

These principles result in a cinematic illusion where Astaire's screen dance body, acting like a magnet for the frame, seems to produce the very screen space through which it moves. Astaire does not explore space; instead, the space around him comes into being as he moves, as the frame (and the camera) obsessively follows his and his partners' dancing figures. Susan Sontag's notion of "camera-looking" as evoked by Douglas Rosenberg expresses this priority: "*Camera-looking* is an active performance that frames an event and elevates it while 'screening out' all other information. It is an act that implies a reverence for that which is framed and eschews all that is outside the frame."[9] That said, Astaire dances (and generates space) in a way that remains comfortably within the limitations dictated on his dancing body by the affordances of the frame and camera. Astaire's art can be understood as "classical" in this sense: he does not struggle against expressive constraints (such as the inherent two-dimensionality of screen space) but moves comfortably within them; they determine his freedom to move and he is content to remain within the bounds they dictate. For this reason, a quantitative consideration of Astaire's dancing body as it moves through the space of the set and as it is framed by the camera makes sense. Quantitative analysis captures Astaire's normative aesthetic principles in practice and also identifies unique or rare moments when the principles are violated.

Realizing the aforementioned dance body on film in practical terms required Astaire and his collaborators to work like land surveyors, who use optical tools to understand the location of objects in space relative to each other and to the surveyor. These principles required knowledge at all times by the dance makers, dancers, and filmmakers of

(1) the location of all four edges of the frame relative to the dancing body,
(2) the relationship between the set on which the dance is done and the edges of the frame implicit in the camera's position, and
(3) the division of the dance as continuous action into separate shots, the taking of which predetermined cuts that would be stitched back together during editing.

The first two of these entail the necessary knowledge of limits—an understanding of where the borders and the edges lay. The third proved a source of tremendous opportunity to remake the "real" world into an artificial space where the equally artificial screen dance body moves with absolute freedom and perfect agency. The aforementioned aesthetic principles and points of knowledge are considered later, with special attention to how framing and cutting choices generate Astaire's screen dance being and the space within which he moves. Often, but seldom visibly, this space and the objects in it defy physical reality. Astaire's corpus works a very practical kind of magic—exceeding any mere sleight of hand—that serves a relentless prioritizing of our supposed direct access to the dancer. This magic is visible, now, due to our complete access to these films. Only close, repeat, at-the-viewer's-command analysis of Astaire's work is likely to yield the perspective on his work given here. These are details and small choices a viewer in the movie theater or on broadcast television is unlikely to catch. Astaire and his collaborators surely knew his film dance numbers in exactly the way described here. They scrutinized these dances frame by frame at every step of the process. Indeed, discussions about the location of the frame, camera positions, the dancers' relation to the dance setting, and the division of a dance into shots (building cuts into the final edited number) surely formed the substance of much conversation in the rehearsal hall and on set. The AD reports do not capture the substance of this talk, but it certainly went on—as the AD on "Ritz Roll and Rock" noted: "Dir[ector] & cameraman discuss the shot in relation to cutting picture."[10]

This part of the book looks closely and quantitatively at the relationship between the dancing body, the frame (as synecdoche for the camera), and the dance setting where body and camera meet. The goal is to understand the practical decisions that produced Astaire's flat, whole, large, level-viewed, sustained, centered, perfect, synchronized screen dance body. The strategies used to create this cinematic fiction limited and freed Astaire's screen dance being. His ontological status is made of these choices—as is his whiteness and maleness, which are constituted here in his decades-long access to the tools that made his larger project possible.

31. Frame Awareness

The screen dance bodies in Astaire's numbers are whole and sustained entities framed at a level view as large as possible and as continuously as possible. "Cheek to Cheek" (*Top Hat* [1935]) embodies these combined principles almost perfectly. Only three times in this almost four-minute dance does any part of Astaire's or Rogers's body venture beyond the frame—in all three cases an extended arm, the body at its widest point, as Leonardo's Vitruvian man demonstrates (figs. 31.1 and 31.2). The third such transgression of the frame comes with an apparent dance modification: at a pose of maximum extension during a very active moment late in the dance, Rogers crooks her free arm

FIGURE 31.1

FIGURE 31.2

FIGURE 31.3

(fig. 31.3). Doing so prevents her arm from being cut off by the frame edge on the pose (even if getting to this point entails some brushing across the screen-right frame edge). On this pose, Astaire's free arm is fully extended—in short, the couple does not match. Rogers's pose acknowledges the frame and keeps her body whole. It took a few films for Astaire, working with Pan, to develop this high sensitivity to the frame. While making a dance, Astaire and Pan needed to avoid moves that were too big or too quick to keep within the frame. On duo dances, they also had to remain vigilant about the distance between the partners: keeping both bodies in the frame at the desired scale limited the ways they could explore space and how far apart the two dancers could venture. The frame acted as a tether of sorts between the pair.

Astaire and Rogers's earliest routines do not follow these guidelines and feature cuts of a sort that were strictly avoided in later dances. In their first dance in "The Carioca" (*Flying Down to Rio* [1933]), Astaire and Rogers bonk heads—with a nice hollow sound effect—and separate as if from the force of their collision. Rogers wanders outside the frame, necessitating a cut to a context shot from above to keep both dancers in view (figs. 31.4.a, 31.4.b, and 31.5). The pair's reaction to their heads-only collision could easily have been staged to keep both in the shot: evidently they were not yet that sensitive to how couples' dancing in Vitruvian framing worked (this was their very first shoot). This moment also offers evidence for camera bias toward Astaire's body during duo dances in a slight shift toward Astaire as they part, a move that keeps him centered as Rogers moves off screen right. This bias toward his body—the male in the pair—occurs elsewhere in his work (see, for instance, "Things Are Looking Up" in *A Damsel in Distress* [1937] danced with Joan Fontaine, perhaps his least able partner, which follows Astaire when the couple parts; she is left to rejoin him further along the way). Astaire's dancing body is—always and from the beginning—the center of attention: perhaps an unlikely place for the man in a romantic dancing couple to be.

A moment from late in "Night and Day" (*Gay Divorcee*) which features choreography taken from the Broadway stage and not designed with the

FIGURE 31.4

FIGURE 31.5

camera in mind, further shows how large and rapid movements could necessitate a cut. Midway through the dance, Rogers tries to exit and, when Astaire stops her, she palms him away on the chin in slow motion. He goes skittering across the dance floor and a prominent cut to context framing captures his movement (figs. 31.6 and 31.7). Without the cut, he would have exited the frame in Vitruvian framing. We are aware, in this cut, of the shift in the scale of the dancers' bodies. Clearly, rapid and large movements and significant distance between the couple were welcome on the musical stage—where all dancers are only ever seen in the context of the entire stage—but difficult to capture on film within Astaire's emerging aesthetic of the whole and sustained dancing body. Such moves did not recur.

The dances in *Roberta* (1935) suggest a parallel struggle to locate a middle ground where the body could be large, whole, and sustained over a lengthy shot. "I'll Be Hard to Handle" is filmed as one shot, and there are many moments when Astaire and Rogers's feet are lost at the bottom of the frame—which means, of course, that either they moved across the line of the frame

FIGURE 31.6

FIGURE 31.7

(invisible to them while dancing) or the camera operator failed to dolly back enough to keep them completely within the frame (fig. 31.8). The pair's other up-tempo tap number from *Roberta*, the finale dance to "I Won't Dance," also includes moments when the exuberance of the dance brings Astaire and Rogers to a position where the bottom of the frame cuts off their feet. By contrast, their slow dance in this film to "Smoke Gets in Your Eyes," a dance with minimal tap sounds on a floor with grid lines, unfolds with the couple framed just a bit smaller and with no breaches of the frame.

By the time of "Cheek to Cheek," Astaire and Pan understood what could (and could not) be filmed within the rules they had set for themselves. They and the camera crews at RKO were experienced and skilled at their reciprocal tasks: following the dancers with a maximum of responsiveness and making dances that were easy for the camera to follow. There are no awkward moments when feet are cut off in "Cheek to Cheek." The figures are scaled just a bit smaller than in "Night and Day" or "I'll Be Hard to Handle"—a trade-off of figure scale in the frame for wholeness that locates a sustainable point of balance between the two. The dance is effectively shaped to the camera and the camera shaped to the dance. For instance, the final cut in "Cheek to Cheek" anticipates a large and fast dance combination traveling forward toward the camera. The move is so perfectly framed and they hit their marks with such precision that Astaire seems to momentarily step on the edge of the frame itself (fig. 31.9). There are several other such moments in this and other later dances—see the cut just before a traveling step forward in "Isn't This a Lovely Day?" (also *Top Hat*).

Once established, Astaire's awareness of the frame edges remained acute. This aspect of his screen dance body was, of course, reliant on the quality of the men who moved the camera. Multiple times in the first draft of his

FIGURE 31.8

FIGURE 31.9

memoir, Astaire made a note reminding himself "must credit camera men."[11] Working on an independent film like *Second Chorus* (1941), Astaire's crew was less skilled. Twice in the "Concert Solo" the frame is noticeably jerked into position to get Astaire's foot back into the frame. These moves are small but, in the realm of perfection Astaire sought to create, can be seen as an effort to save a take. Projection on the big screen amplifies such corrective camera motion substantially. The crew at RKO who worked with Astaire and Rogers in the 1930s seems to have been largely gone when he returned to the studio in 1943 to make *The Sky's the Limit* (1943). His duo dances with Joan Leslie combine a somewhat larger figure scale than normal and a lot of hands cut off by the frame edge. Finding the sweet spot for duo dances between as large as possible and an allowance for dancing was evidently difficult on this production (perhaps another reason these dances took so long to film). By contrast, the single dancing body of "One for My Baby (and One More for the Road)" in the same film is perfectly framed in every shot. Of course, it wasn't always possible to move the camera just a bit to keep Astaire's body whole. The composite nature of the special effects in "Shoes with Wings On" (*The Barkleys of Broadway* [1949]), which entailed taking every shot twice then combining in postproduction, meant that the camera could not move—and so adjustments when Astaire stepped out of the frame could not be made (fig. 31.10). Such moments capture a compromise in framing necessary to meet a different goal driven by special effects. The shift to widescreen made head-to-toe framing newly difficult and several numbers in *Silk Stockings* cut off feet and/or heads (see "All of You" and "Fated to Be Mated"; fig. 31.11). This was, in effect, a return of the problem solved in *Roberta* of scaling the body as large as possible while keeping it whole from top to bottom. Astaire didn't work in widescreen quite long enough to definitively solve this challenge.

FIGURE 31.10

FIGURE 31.11

Thus, the frame acted as a third partner in all duo dances. To keep both dancers in the frame, they had to remain within a set distance from each other—with said distance set by the desired figure scale and the camera and always subtly changing. Of such triangulations is Astaire's screen dancing made. The duo "So Near Yet So Far" in *You'll Never Get Rich* (1941) between Astaire and Hayworth seems especially uncontained. Two cuts with no appreciable change of angle seem to be working simply to keep the couple within the shot as their moves grow larger. But even this was insufficient. At one point, they get so far apart that their outside arms are both cut off (fig. 31.12). This only ever happens here.

A similar moment in the extraordinarily perfect "This Heart of Mine" (*Ziegfeld Follies* [1946]) flirts with the frame edges. Moving in turn between two contrary motion treadmills, Astaire and Lucille Bremer reach toward each other and switch treadmills at the last moment, just before they would

FIGURE 31.12

FIGURE 31.13

have been carried off screen (figs. 31.13.a and 31.13.b). This virtuoso dancing within and with the frame shows how the goal of a whole figure made camera movement and danced movement both a game of continuous full disclosure. This imperative to keep the dancing body fully in view marks another difference between the musical number and narrative conventions in Hollywood. In his study of camera movement and narrative in classical Hollywood, film scholar Patrick Keating writes, "Storytelling inevitably involves the play of information. Bound by a frame, the cinema discloses some details but not others.... When the frame moves forward, a part of the storyworld becomes more visible, and another part of the world disappears. To watch a dolly shot is to see the cinema's selectivity in action."[12] This is decidedly not how the camera works for Astaire. Astaire's ubiquitous dolly shots work to sustain full disclosure of the dancing body: the body is the principal subject and continuous access to said body remains always the primary aesthetic imperative. This genre- and artist-specific approach to the use of filmmaking tools in turn created a cinematic technique that forced camera crews to also dance. A 1936 profile of RKO cinematographer David Abel in *American Cinematographer* claimed as much, describing the scene on the set for an Astaire number as an occasion where the camera crew moves to the music—in short, dances—right along with Astaire:

> As Astaire does his dance maneuvers, so does Abel rehearse his camera crew. . . . As rehearsals proceed, the crew learn the song music and take words from the lyrics as cues to the star's immediate destination. In this way, they can anticipate camera mobility.
> The Operative Cinematographer, eye glued to view-finder, keeps the star in frame with thought for correct composition. The Assistant is alert for changing focus. Others man the crane or ambulator [the dolly]. . . .
> When Astaire is satisfied as to the perfection of his effort, Abel is ready for the "take." Then, as he puts it, "When the camera starts, it's every man for himself." As an instance of co-ordinated team-work, it is a superb sight.
> A madly whirling, dancing photographic target, with Abel lighting and lensing it with all the uniformity of a stationary subject! Even so, a minute slip in the timing of the camera's manipulation and all-important flying feet are cut off, or vital expressions go out of sharp focus. It is a formidable undertaking. It calls for fathomless alertness, patience, perseverance. No tricks are used. What Astaire does on the screen, he does before Abel's camera—and Abel captures it.[13]

The upper edge of the frame also required attending to—since Astaire liked to jump. (When dancing for records in the early 1950s, he commented of his tap style: "I get off the floor a great deal."[14]) Four jumps reveal attention to this edge. In "Bouncin' the Blues" (*Barkleys*) Astaire and Rogers leap in the air and just touch the upper horizontal of the frame, bending their arms just right (fig. 31.14). The camera stays level with their position on the floor, so the dancers are responsible for holding the line—not leaping too high (to take their heads out of frame) and not raising their hands too high as well. Astaire and Rogers had done this before. At the leaping exit from "Pick Yourself Up" (*Swing Time*), their hands brush but do not cross the upper horizontal of the frame (fig. 33.15). This exuberant negotiation of an obstacle—the small railing around the dance floor—communicates tremendous joy (and skill) in the dance while also remaining neatly within the frame. With even less headroom in widescreen, Astaire's "Texas Millionaire" solo in *Daddy Long Legs* (1955) ends on a freeze frame of him in midair (fig. 31.16). During the preceding series of jumps, he manages not to alter the absolute position of

FIGURE 31.14

FIGURE 31.15

FIGURE 31.16

his head: in short, Astaire jumps from the waist down only. A fourth jump demonstrates the narrow tolerances of Vitruvian framing and the bias toward Astaire's body. In "Ev'ry Night at Seven" (*Royal Wedding* [1951]), Jane Powell tickles Astaire under the chin. After grabbing his crown, Astaire leaps up and the camera follows his action with a swift tilt up then down, nearly cutting Powell off at the ankles (fig. 31.17). (A similar but less successful

FIGURE 31.17

FIGURE 31.18

move in "I Can't Tell a Lie" from *Holiday Inn* [1942] just after the abortive conga beat, again favors Astaire, who is, again, the only one jumping.)

Once set, an aesthetic principle such as frame awareness in Vitruvian framing could be violated for expressive emphasis. An especially affecting example from the 1930s comes in the quickly made "Never Gonna Dance" (*Swing Time*). At a moment of maximum romantic despair, Rogers moves away from Astaire. The camera follows her—keeping her in Vitruvian framing—and, in the process, leaves Astaire cut off at the ankles (fig. 31.18). His move to follow her takes him back into the frame and into physical wholeness, intensifying the expressively insistent gestures that follow. Two principles are violated here: wholeness of the body (not cutting off the legs) and the priority of Astaire's body.

32. A Level View

"One for My Baby (and One More for the Road)" famously featured Astaire dancing on a bar. The number took a relatively long time to rehearse, and part of the challenge was designing the bar to facilitate dancing. Overage reports in the RKO production file document additional costs to "Extend bar and back bar to length of 33 feet. This is required by Mr. Astaire's dance on the bar top. Provide safety platform between front bar and back bar as requested. Development of dance on bar has made this necessary."[15] Astaire also requested a "new press wood dance floor in bar and lobby," likely so he wouldn't hurt himself jumping between the bar and the floor. These memos document Astaire's creative work as both making a dance and shaping the setting for the dance (here actually designing the set).

The danger of this dance on a narrow elevated platform was played up for the press but not emphasized in the way the dance was shot. The sizeable difference between the level of the floor and the level of the bar was not heightened by camera angles but instead perceptually eliminated by way of multiple cuts. Each time Astaire moves between the floor and the bar—four transitions in all—a cut resets the camera so as to preserve a level view of his body (figs. 32.1 and 32.2). When he's dancing on the bar, the camera (and the viewer) is effectively suspended in the air opposite him. There's little attempt

FIGURE 32.1

FIGURE 32.2

to emphasize the purported danger of the bar by shooting him from the floor. This approach to the setting and the principle of the level view resulted in an average shot length (ASL) of thirteen seconds for "One for My Baby"—quite low for a solo of this type in this period. Similar strategies are evident in "The Carioca" (seen mostly from a position no one in the film enjoys) and "Slap That Bass" (when Astaire climbs onto an elevated walkway to dance with machines, the camera pops up on a cut). In all these numbers, the camera and audience are floating in space so that a level view of Astaire's body might be maintained.

One way to moderate the two-dimensionality of the dancing body is to use a crane to move over, above, and/or around the body, turning the human form into a sort of sculpture being explored by the camera. Director Busby Berkeley had done this quasi-abstractly in his early 1930s explorations of female flesh. But Astaire eschewed using the crane to move around the shape of the body. Only fifty-two (6%) of the 932 shots involve crane movement.[16] These rare shots appear almost entirely within a set period and work environment. Nearly four of five occur in films made at MGM or with MGM-associated directors between 1944 and 1953, plus a handful in *Funny Face* from 1957 (the six crane shots in *Funny Face* make up all but two in Astaire's widescreen films). Vincente Minnelli accounts for nearly one-third of all Astaire's crane shots, Stanley Donen for a further 17%. Robert Alton uses three in *You'll Never Get Rich*. There are only four crane shots at RKO: two in "Bojangles" and two in "No Strings" (*Top Hat*, this pair serve the narrative by moving through the floor to Rogers's hotel room). The first Minnelli crane shot typifies a standard approach at MGM that violates Astaire's level view. In "This Heart of Mine," at the very end of an eighty-four-second, strictly Vitruvian shot of Astaire and Lucille Bremer dancing, the camera suddenly rises up and over the pair to peer down at them in a dramatic held dip (a reframed shot ending in an insert framing; fig. 32.3). A cut back to Vitruvian follows immediately. This up-and-in-at-the-end crane shot, like the majority of reframed shots, only disturbs Vitruvian framing for a few seconds, offering a briefly sculptural view of the couple. Nine of the fifty-two crane shots—five in numbers directed by Minnelli—follow this single-move pattern: up and in on the dancers, usually resulting in insert framing. (A reciprocal type of crane shot, used about as frequently as the up-and-in-at-the-end shot, cuts to a high angle then immediately normalizes the view back to level Vitruvian. See similar moments in the heaven portion of "The Babbitt and the Bromide" [*Ziegfeld Follies*] and "Bouncin' the Blues.")

FIGURE 32.3

A more frequently used crane movement up at the end of a shot responds directly to the choreography while sustaining full-figure framing. In eighteen cases, the camera cranes up and pulls back to either give a grand view of a large group of dancers or make space in the frame for two dancers to execute a dance combination that travels quickly and covers much ground, almost always following the trajectory of a large circle. The former sort uses context framing for a full stage effect (see the similar full company views in "The Wedding Cake Walk" and at the close of "Boogie Barcarolle," both by Alton in *You'll Never Get Rich*). The latter sustains a closer view of the pair but lends their movement a dynamism, often matched by the orchestration, which also rises in volume and harmonic or timbral richness—see examples in "Babbitt," "He Loves and She Loves" (*Funny Face*), "Boardwalk Waltz" (*Belle of New York*), the "Guardian Angel" dream (*Daddy Long Legs*), and "Coffee Time" (*Yolanda and the Thief* [1945]). As with the up-and-in-at-the-end approach, crane shots of couples in large-scale motion briefly lend their bodies a three-dimensionality not evident from the default level view. We catch glimpses of the tops of heads and shoulders that grant a roundedness to their bodies absent from a frontal, level view. None of these shots are normative for Astaire. Indeed, he seems to have been uninspired by what cranes could do. Pan articulated this bias to the BBC: the camera, he said, needs to be "straight on"; otherwise, the body is distorted if the camera strays "up too high."[17]

One unique crane shot captures Astaire's commitment to the centered framing of the dancing figure scaled as large as possible. The vocal portion of "Seeing's Believing" (*Belle of New York*) is staged on the side of the Washington Square arch. Astaire's first task in the dance is to climb a ladder up to the top (fig. 32.4). He ascends in time to the music, pausing a bit on

FIGURE 32.4

each rung. With each step up the ladder, the camera, positioned below and to the side, ratchets up as well, methodically maintaining Astaire's centered position, holding when he holds and moving when he moves just exactly as much as he moves. Astaire moves through space up the ladder but his place in the hierarchy of the frame remains constant: he is always dominant and center.

Two Astaire solos make substantial use of cranes. The first, the initial chorus section of "Bojangles of Harlem," was likely Pan's idea and the choreography almost certainly Pan's as well. Within their push toward ever longer shot durations that peaked in *Swing Time*, Pan created an extraordinary three-minute shot that begins with Astaire seated (he's revealed by the chorus's removal of a racist caricature of a Black body). Astaire rises and proceeds to dance (the chorus forms lines around and then behind him). To conclude this portion, Astaire travels forward and, in violation of standard practice, crosses the bottom edge of the frame, striking a pose that reaches forward and gestures up. As if in response, the camera begins a crane motion back and up—note how Astaire gestures a few more times as if to encourage the movement—to a position looking down on the expansive floor and company of twenty-six dancers (figs. 32.5.a and 32.5.b). A section of the routine marked by patterns made by the entire company follows. This was the first substantial crane movement Pan and Astaire had ever used in a dance. A similarly dramatic crane move follows Astaire and Rogers up the curving stairs and back together at the top in "Never Gonna Dance," the routine made just after "Bojangles."

Only one routine that was firmly under Astaire's control consistently uses crane shots, this time of a very subtle nature: Astaire's solo "I Wanna Be a Dancin' Man," which was reshot in its entirety against a new background.

FIGURE 32.5

Comparison of the two versions reveals large and small changes. The original set is drab with a curtain at back that shapes the dance floor into a rectangle. The final version, while still within a proscenium, suggests an abstract space, curved at the back and seemingly suspended in luminescent blue—a disc that, with the circular spotlight and resulting shadow, proves a throwback to the highly formal dance floors of RKO. Astaire's body is central and is all. A slight rake to the dance floor contributes a subtle complication that, together with the added crane movement, gives Astaire's body a sculptural quality otherwise absent in his solos.

The original version (danced vocal followed by dance with vocal tag) uses nine shots in all; the final only uses five. The cutting of the dance portion in both is the same, providing evidence that Astaire built cuts into his dance, even in a very straightforward routine on a flat floor such as this one. The only cut that's really required is the final one that places his straw hat—cast away when the tempo changed—in place for him to pick it up. The other cut during the dance serves no apparent purpose but, by 1952, it would have been very unusual for Astaire to do a 124-second shot that would result if the two long shots in "Dancin' Man" were combined into one. The major change in cutting happens during the danced vocal. The first version chops up the vocal by way of three cuts between insert and Vitruvian framing. In the final version, a sustained eighty-one-second varied camera movement reframed shot contains the entire vocal and moves smoothly and repeatedly between insert and Vitruvian framing. Also new in the final version vocal are very subtle crane motions up and down executed without pushing in. Astaire's white-suited figure against the abstract blue background comes off as slightly less flat than usual, especially given some slight low-angle camera positions. The rake of the floor may be doing this work but on the whole the vocal for the revised "Dancin' Man" gives Astaire's body a distinctive sculptural dimension not seen elsewhere in the clip reel. Subtle crane movement on his full figure continues in the dance and again distinguishes the revised from the original version. The latter is level throughout except for two slight elevations (both at the end of a shot, respectively for a grand circle combination and set of larger and faster moves). Neither camera move is repeated in the final version. Instead, the camera moves freely if very subtly between slightly elevated and lowered angles. The raked floor, again, complicates our perception of this movement, but comparison of framing between the original and final versions confirms a significant difference. The revised version sacrifices a bit of figure scale for the gain of a sculptural effect on Astaire's body. Worth emphasizing is simply how utterly unusual this was and how subtle this isolated example is. The vast majority of the time Astaire's body is pictured straight on (figs. 32.6 through 32.9).

Astaire's minimal or nonuse of the crane contrasts with the very different approach of Gene Kelly. Following Astaire, Kelly generally keeps the body

FIGURE 32.6

FIGURE 32.7

FIGURE 32.8

FIGURE 32.9

whole, but Kelly differs from Astaire in his repeated attempts to express the three-dimensional reality of the human dancing body. Kelly's filmed dancing celebrates the body as a rounded and dynamic form, almost always in rich color with expressive force, as a muscular sculpture around which the camera moves. This effortful body also appears in radically large and small scales, contexts that are monumental and romantic, epic and artsy. Crane shots are essential to Kelly's ontology of the dancing figure, as when he used the up-and-in-at-the-end crane shot to push in on his face (for instance, in "Singin' in the Rain").

In Kelly's work, the filmed dancing body extends and reaches with muscular force into utopian dream worlds, expressing a political philosophy that puts expansion and exploration and destiny—perhaps of the manifest variety—within reach. This contrasts strongly with Astaire's more modest, street-level ontology of the filmed dancing body. There is a sober reserve and a lack of dimension—a dryness or flatness (no pun intended)—to Astaire, one reason I think he sometimes fails to impress contemporary audiences unfamiliar with his work and distant from the discursive tradition celebrating him. My students generally just don't understand or are frankly unimpressed by Astaire but can go on and on about Berkeley or Kelly after watching one number. Astaire's implicit ontology of the human being in the world of the frame presents a modest political statement: mediated bodies are but shadows; they are not "real"—but in the rarified and perfected space of the frame, the dancing human figure can be presented as whole in a sustained manner that posits a sense of order and balance and moderates any sense of risk or danger. Containment and control are, again, a keynote to this larger aesthetic.

33. Dance Settings

In dialogue scenes, actors followed chalk marks on the floor indicating where a given bit of movement should end. Such marks ensured the actor arrived at a point of maximal lighting and sound and also assumed that the floor where they stood was not visible. Full-figure framing in most genres is quite unusual—indeed, the so-called *plan américain* (a shot from around the knees up) skirts head-to-toe framing with a convention that frames about three-quarters of the body and leaves the floor unseen. But, for Astaire, dancing bodies needed to be seen whole, and musicals, as Astaire made them, presented a problem for the hitting of marks (and the loss of efficiencies gained thereby). Full-figure framing necessitates a full view of the floor—and any marks thereon. Indeed, assistant director (AD) reports document appreciable time spent cleaning the floor between takes. And so, dancers needed to know their relation to the camera, the frame, and the set without the conventional approach used in the studios—yet another practical distinction to the musical genre within classical Hollywood. The most visible way for dancers to register their relationship to the camera was for both dancers and camera to find common fixed points of reference on the set, whether actual objects and structures or decorative patterns on the floor. Marks on the floor that were out of camera range, perhaps beside or behind the camera (analogous to the numbered marks, invisible to the audience, at the front edge of proscenium theater stages that allow performers to find their position) are possible aids to placement as well. One advantage enjoyed by film musicals was the lack of microphones recording dialogue during shooting to playback. This likely allowed for an unimpeded coordination between dancers and the camera—although the position of the playback equipment was important (as noted in Part Three).

One way to understand dance settings as significant to the dancer-camera relationship is to consider the potential portability of a given routine outside the context where it was captured on film. Can the dance be done anywhere, or is the execution of a dance specific to a given configuration of spatial elements, such as platforms, steps, or furniture? Astaire was sensitive to this when he toured the European Theatre during World War II performing for soldiers. He created a routine he could do anywhere, at the drop of a hat, with or without music. But this kind of maximally portable dance was not the norm in Astaire's films. Just under half the dances in the clip reel use a flat floor. The reciprocal just-over half wed the dance to a specific setting that requires levels and/or various apparatuses. These percentages for dances on flat floors and those using specific settings are stable across Astaire's career.

The shape of Astaire's flat dance floors proves a significant design element—both for the dances done on them and for the effect of the dance as a piece of screen art. Circular dance floors and patterns appear again and again in the RKO films, framing the reach of the dancing body, indicating scale and proportion, giving the viewer a sense for how far the dancers on screen are traveling in space—with the body of the dancer serving as a measure of how large the circle is. The analogy with Leonardo's Vitruvian man-as-the-measure resonates in these circles. Astaire and Rogers enjoy sole access to an elevated round platform, ostensibly supported by seven pianos, in "The Carioca." Astaire does his first solo in *The Gay Divorcee* on a more modest round platform in a Paris nightclub. The round dance floor in *Roberta*'s Café Russe looks to be appreciably larger than both of the previous two—as befits the more extended routines done there. The difference in size between these circles indicates something of the new importance of Astaire and Rogers at RKO: their dance floors literally expand. Elaborate silver patterns painted on the floor frame from below both "The Continental" (*Gay Divorcee*) and "The Piccolino" (*Top Hat*, fig. 33.1) and serve similarly as reference points for the dancers (more on this follows). Such circular settings limit the range of each dance but do not limit the camera's movement (the camera frames only the dancers, not the shapes within the setting).

By contrast, the sand dance portion of "No Strings" is done within a circle of sand framed precisely by the frame edges. Astaire defines the limits of the dance by casting a circle in sand onto the floor (although sand is already visible; the dance floor has already been prepared). While dancing he

FIGURE 33.1

FIGURE 33.2

stays strictly within the circle, which he must to execute sliding sand dance steps. The camera remains in place throughout: it does not follow him, and when he goes to the edges of the circle, Astaire slightly crosses the vertical frame edges (fig. 33.2). The steadiness of the frame situates the circle of sand within a rectangle without reference to Astaire's moving figure. In this dance, Astaire uniquely dances not as a Vitruvian man—his movements do not generate the space within which he dances. At the end of the sand dance, Astaire moves—the camera now following him—to a low chair, where he stretches out in a near-perfect diagonal dividing of the frame. The resulting final image for the routine is a compositional accomplishment of the RKO camera crew (fig. 33.3).

The routines that cannot be done on an empty flat floor include twenty that incorporate levels or steps of some sort. In these dances, movement between levels provides both useful points of reference and genuine challenges to shot length. These dance settings include the following subtypes.

FIGURE 33.3

- Short sets of steps adjacent to a flat dance floor, variably positioned at center back ("Night and Day"), to one side ("The Piccolino"; the garden niche in the final pose of *You Were Never Lovelier* [1942]), a symmetrically arranged pair at the back (the duo dances that close *Roberta*), and even to the front (steps revealed late in the dance as a means of exiting *The Band Wagon*'s "Dancing in the Dark" [1953]).
- Long flights of stairs adjacent to a flat dance floor. In their second routine in "The Continental," Astaire and Rogers waltz down then sprint up a wide array of steps. In "Never Gonna Dance," each twirls up their own curving staircase to rejoin at the top. Very tall stairways take Astaire and partner to a high elevated platform in "I Concentrate on You" (*Broadway Melody of 1940*), "Heat Wave" (*Blue Skies* [1946], and "Clap Yo' Hands" (*Funny Face*, where the final ascent is part of the plot; Astaire and Kay Thompson do the dance to "get to the second floor").
- Low platforms that articulate the dance setting horizontally. Very slight levels occur in three important duo routines in the Astaire-Rogers cycle: "Isn't This a Lovely Day?," "Let's Face the Music and Dance" (*Follow the Fleet* [1936]), and "Change Partners" (*Carefree* [1938]). Just a few inches in height—less than a sidewalk curb—these platforms subtly break up the dance setting and might be seen as hazards, easily causing the dancers to trip. While adding dimension to the space, they also function as reference points. In the most involved set of such platforms— "Isn't This a Lovely Day?" danced in a park gazebo with three levels (plus a larger drop to the ground)—Astaire and Rogers measure the distance between the levels in a traveling combination that shows both their mastery of the space (they land together just within the front and lowermost level) and the scale of the space as built for their bodies (they

are in a world constructed to fit their bodies doing a dance designed to fit the space). The dimensions of the gazebo and Astaire and Rogers's bodies enjoy a veritably Vitruvian relationship that, in turn, facilitates the number's strict Vitruvian framing. In an analogous moment late in "Change Partners," Rogers spins toward the camera, away from Astaire, and comes to a stop perfectly astride a very low platform stepdown. A similar low platform divides the space where Astaire dances both parts of "Steppin' Out with My Baby" (*Easter Parade* [1948]). Here, the horizontal line created by the step serves the special effects: it marks the border between Astaire's slow-motion dance and the regular-speed motion of the chorus. All the dances using these low platforms are filmed from a frontal position throughout; an oblique angle would draw attention to the edge, causing a diagonal line to disrupt the frame.

The remaining sixty-three routines are highly specific as to setting. A flat floor area or various combinations of platforms, ramps, and/or steps are combined with large objects, such as chairs, couches, or pianos. This persistent aspect of Astaire's dances—his repeated interaction with spatially complex dance settings—was not enjoyed by all his fans. A male respondent at the *Band Wagon* preview wrote, "Astaire is an excellent dancer. Why not let him dance? And not on the furniture."[18] But it proves to be a key component to his conceit of "just" dancing or, perhaps, *not* dancing but instead just fooling around. Astaire's urge to dance "on the furniture" goes back at least to his last stage show *Gay Divorce*, which included the partner dance up and over a small table reproduced at the end of *The Gay Divorcee*. (An even earlier point of origin: Astaire's first vaudeville act with sister Adele involved the pair dancing on platforms shaped like tiered wedding cakes embellished with bells and electric lights.[19]) His desire to dance in relation to large immovable objects works to naturalize Astaire's dancing as engagement with the specifics of the environment he encounters and not as dancing per se. It also serves the conceit of his "outlaw" style, since moves done in relation to objects are rare in most dancing styles. (Notably, Astaire's purported tribute to Bill "Bojangles" Robinson is done on a flat floor; Robinson's signature dance routine on a short set of steps is never referenced, here or elsewhere in Astaire's work. By contrast, Eleanor Powell's blackface tribute to Robinson in *Honolulu* [1939] is all about steps.) Astaire's danced negotiation of furniture is both playful and relatable for the viewer (particularly, perhaps, children). Dancing in this way recasts dancing as an everyday action, not an action rooted in any particular movement tradition or history. When Astaire and Charisse enter the third dance setting in "Fated to Be Mated" (*Silk Stockings*), they look around at the array of apparatuses—most with a nautical theme—and seem to reflect for a moment on their luck at finding a room full of crates, barrels, and poles to climb on and swing from. In this dance, created by Pan and designed around the apparatuses that he certainly arranged, Astaire's default pleasure in exploring a complex environment becomes a shared pleasure for a romantic couple.

Large objects also offered Astaire multiple surfaces to hit. Like a child, he treats every surface he encounters like a drum and, of course, he danced with drum sets multiple times. The too-tight semicircle of the "Drum Dance" (*Damsel in Distress*) is the most restrictive of the apparatus dances. "Drum Crazy" (*Easter Parade*) distributes drums around a toy shop, allowing for a dance of continual surprising engagements with resonant surfaces—each of which was carefully placed to accommodate Astaire's movements; Astaire's movements also were surely inspired by each object's placement. Similarly, the curving built-in cabinet in "No Strings," which Astaire measures in turns and hand slaps, is scaled exactly to his body. The serendipity of such engagements with a complex environment reaches a high point in "I've Got My Eye on You" (*Broadway Melody*). This long vocal and dance solo, which includes a piano solo, finds Astaire moving through a backstage area littered with apparently random objects and structures—from an upright piano to a wishing well to scattered upholstered chairs to a small sidewalk café set with a long awning and a street curb. Everything is there for him to spontaneously use, but, of course, everything is also preset because his dance required precise planning. The camera follows him in Vitruvian framing throughout, never showing the larger set but only Astaire in a given place within it (he's ostensibly on a theater stage but the camera's relation to the proscenium remains unknown; there is no context or establishing shot of the space). Indeed, the priority given Astaire's body trumped any spectacle of the set—even when Astaire's sets were especially spectacular. Home movies by Ira Gershwin on the set of "Slap That Bass" communicate the incredible scale of the engine room set in ways the dance in the film never does.[20] The only spectacle allowed is Astaire's dancing body. The comparatively modest "Audition Dance" (*You Were Never Lovelier*), like "I've Got My Eyes on You," involves Astaire stepping up to and down from bench-height levels not high enough to necessitate the cuts described earlier in "One for My Baby" and "Slap That Bass." The frame (and camera) instead follows him up and down from these medium-height levels by way of a tilt: the MGM crew on "I've Got My Eye on You" matches Astaire's repeated moves up and back off a bench with maximum accuracy. As with the crane shot in "Seeing's Believing," Astaire remains perfectly centered.

34. Danced Continuity

Perhaps the ultimate expression of the flat, whole, sustained, perfect, level-viewed, centered, space-making, two-dimensional screen dance body is the one-shot routine. Astaire made twenty-two. Two-thirds of these date to his RKO years. The duration of these twenty-two one-shot dances generally maps onto the pattern of a rise in shot length through *Swing Time* followed by a drop off and slow decline in shot lengths after: the three-plus-minute "Drum Dance" shows a lingering interest in the practice. Most significant among the one-shot routines for this discussion is the duo with Rogers in "The Piccolino." This dance captures Astaire's obsession with a continuous view of the dancing body while also fetishizing the feet (an aspect of Astaire's screen dance body that stretches from *Flying Down to Rio* to the opening moments of *Silk Stockings*). The 125-second one-shot dance that closes the long "Piccolino" production number begins on Astaire and Rogers's feet as they dance from their table, down two steps, and to the exact center of the circle pattern painted on the floor. The compass rose-like pattern acts as an elaborate mark and they hit it perfectly, at which point the camera dollies back to Vitruvian framing for the remainder of the dance and shot (this is a reframed shot). The intricate dance they do remains almost entirely within the inner two of the four concentric rings painted on the floor and they repeatedly return to the innermost ring at the ends of phrases. In the middle of a vast dance floor, Astaire and Rogers remain intimately connected and all the grand patterns of the previous chorus potion of the dance are forgotten in this restoration of Astaire's screen dance values. At the end, Astaire and Rogers dance back to their table. While covering the distance, their differing step size complicates negotiation of those two steps. Astaire steps up before Rogers: for a moment, their previously perfect synchronization is interrupted (fig. 34.1). This slight imperfection in their negotiation of the dance setting was the product of the commitment to taking this dance in one shot. Most of the time a cut was made just before such an obstacle was approached, allowing for an adjustment of the dancers' relationship to the dance setting

FIGURE 34.1

and permitting them to move through real space with a perfection that was not attainable in "The Piccolino." An exactly analogous case from *Roberta* of the pair concluding a number by ascending a short flight of steps, only this time using a cut to adjust their position in real space, is discussed later.

No dance expresses the limitations of the one-shot routine like the "Drum Dance"—the longest single shot Astaire made (apparently—see section thirty-seven). Trapped within a small semicircle of drums, the only possible direction is forward. The camera dollying back just before Astaire begins to move forward telegraphs each of the three such moves. The routine proves monotonous. Another limitation of one-shot routines is expressed by a lack in the "Drum Dance." Astaire dances with drumsticks in his hands for well over three minutes and only once (near the start of the dance) does he boldly toss and catch a stick (elsewhere in the number he twirls a stick through his fingers twice and very cautiously flips a stick only once; otherwise, his hold on the drumsticks is continuous). The challenge of multiple tossing and catching tricks was likely a physical feat too far for so lengthy a routine that already involved countless points of synchronization between danced motions and the music. As discussed in the next section, Astaire tosses or catches hand-held objects in over one-third of his dances. The one-shot dances are very poorly represented among the throwing or catching routines: only two involve objects in motion—the "Drum Dance" and "A Needle in a Haystack" (*Gay Divorcee*, which has Astaire pause to catch his hat and umbrella, carefully tossed to him by his valet, on his way out the door). A negative correlation between two sorts of Astaire routines is evident: one-shot dances and dances with objects do not overlap and Astaire's clear preference was for the latter.

Given the limitations of the one-shot routine, cuts proved essential. Indeed, Astaire's screen dance body is normatively made by way of cuts. His use of cutaways and inserts with narrative functions has already been discussed, as have reframed shots, mostly used to transition between insert and full-figure framing types (as with the up-and-in-at-the-end type of crane shot favored by Minnelli). This leaves the cuts between Vitruvian shots, those between context and Vitruvian shots, and those involving reframed shots that begin or end in Vitruvian and relate across a cut to another Vitruvian framing. (My classification of Astaire's 778 cuts identifies the framing at the beginning and end of each reframed shot.) For the purposes of this discussion, all such cuts will be understood as made between full-figure framings. Crucially, this kind of cut freed Astaire to control time and space—both in the finished film and on the set—while maintaining full-figure framings. With cuts as a practical and expressive tool, he could create ambitious routines not filmable in one shot and unlikely to be doable in person. The collaged wholeness of the Astaire-style screen dance body comes into sharp focus when these cuts are analyzed both for how they operate aesthetically and for clues as to how they permitted a nonrealistic negotiation of the real space of the dance settings where real dancing bodies moved for the camera.

There are 314 cuts connecting full-figure framings of the dancing body—one-third of all cuts. Their distribution over Astaire's career periods shows a marked trend (see the line in chart 17). Cuts between full-figure framings account for 40% and 38% of cuts in his first two periods, respectively—through 1946. In his third period, their frequency drops to 29%, and in the widescreen years, down to 21%. To better understand this decline and its impact on the status of Astaire's screen dance body, it is useful to sort cuts between full-figure framings into two groups based on the use of context framing. There are 106 such cuts that involve context framing (context to Vitruvian or context to context). As shown in the dark gray columns in chart 17, the decline in this type of cut matches the decline in the larger category. This sort of cut radically rescales the dancing figure—82% of these cut between context and Vitruvian framing. More significant for this discussion are the 208 Vitruvian-to-Vitruvian cuts in the corpus—22% of all cuts. This count combines cuts between Vitruvian shots with cuts from Vitruvian to reframed shots that begin in Vitruvian and the reverse (reframed shots ending in Vitruvian that cut to Vitruvian). The distribution of these cuts across periods shows significant variance and is different in contour from the overall category and the context-framing subcategory just described. As shown by the light gray columns in chart 17, these sorts of cuts account for around one of four cuts in Astaire' first three periods, with a bump between 1940 and

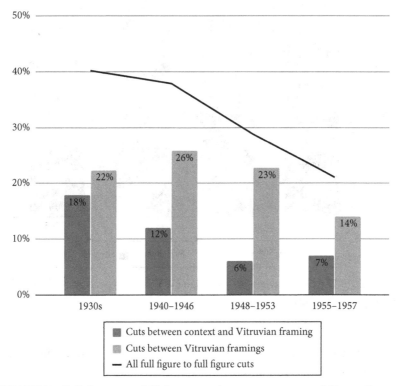

CHART 17 Full-figure–to–full-figure cuts by type as percent of all cuts (by period)

1946. A significant drop-off occurs in the widescreen films. The cuts between Vitruvian framings are the most fraught in terms of sustaining the continuity of the dancing body. Cuts using context framing involve appreciable changes in scale, similar in their cinematic effect to the use of inserts and cutaways—our view of the dancing body is significantly altered. Cutting from Vitruvian-to-Vitruvian framing raises the issue of why the cut happened at all, since the aesthetic priority of sustaining a large, whole dancing body is undercut by the disruption of a cut. On close examination, the reasons for such Vitruvian-to-Vitruvian (hereafter V-V) cuts are often evident and serve various purposes.

One way to understand the distribution of V-V cuts calculates the percent of such cuts in each number. Chart 18 sorts this data into three groups: numbers with no V-V cuts, numbers that are 1% to 50% V-V cuts, and numbers with 51% to 100% V-V cuts. The results are then grouped by period. As the data show, half of the numbers Astaire made at RKO in the 1930s did not

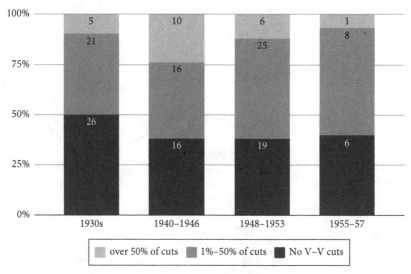

CHART 18 Use of Vitruvian-to-Vitruvian (V-V) cuts as percent of all cuts (by numbers and periods)

use even one V-V cut (the preponderance of one-shot numbers in this period proves significant here), and numbers made of more than 50% such cuts were quite rare (just 10%). This distribution changes markedly in the later periods, with increased use of the V-V cut registered both in percentage-wise fewer numbers with no such cuts and a dramatic increase in Astaire's second period in the percentage of routines using more than 50% V-V cuts. This data offers further quantitative evidence for a shift in Astaire's approach to piecing together shots to make a number in the 1940s. Almost half of his numbers composed of over 50% V-V cuts were made in this period, including four that are built almost entirely of such cuts: part two of the *Yolanda* dream ballet and "Be Careful, It's My Heart" in *Holiday Inn* (both using only V-V cuts) and "Puttin' on the Ritz" in *Blue Skies* and "One for My Baby" (both using 80% V-V cuts). Three of these numbers were firmly in Astaire's control: he chose to make these cuts, doing so (often) toward quite practical ends.

Sorting V-V cuts by their function shows how the choice to make this sort of cut shapes the status of Astaire's screen dance body and the claim this body makes on the world as represented on screen. My sorting of these 208 cuts accounts for multiple variables. I balance evident aesthetic explanations driven by Astaire's commitment to Vitruvian framing with more practical explanations (such as when a cut facilitates the filming of a hat trick or a repositioning of the dancing body in real space). My categorization foregrounds practical explanations when possible since these often offer direct evidence for choices made in the rehearsal hall and on set. Such cuts reveal the practical magic (or deception) behind Astaire's normative screen dance body. Chart 19 summarizes this data, again by percent of use in each period, putting all 208 cuts into one of three larger categories: direct, cheated continuity, and other (a category that combines five subtypes, each of which accounts for under 5% of the total).

By far the most common across Astaire's career (65%) are direct V-V cuts that adjust the framing of the dancing body only slightly. Those that introduce a new angle (43%) occur almost twice as often as cuts that slightly rescale the dancing body while remaining within the Vitruvian standard (22%). Some of these shots, of course, offer both a new angle and a rescaling: these are counted in the rarer rescaling category. The new angle might be a subtle side view ("I Won't Dance" [*Roberta*]) or a ninety-degree change ("Golf Dance" [*Carefree*]). Rescaling cuts often occur just before large and fast dance combinations, which require more space, such as the final cut in "Cheek to Cheek" discussed earlier. Similar cuts occur in "Isn't This a Lovely Day," in the heaven section of "The Babbitt and the Bromide," and twice in "So Near and Yet So Far." V-V cuts that change angle can be understood in practical terms as well. They might facilitate a change of camera position that allows

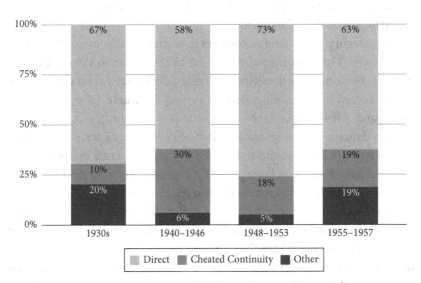

CHART 19 Vitruvian-to-Vitruvian (V-V) cuts by type (by period)

us to follow the dancers into a new area, as in "Thinking of You" (*Three Little Words* [1950]), where Vera-Ellen and Astaire move through a spacious ocean liner lounge. The first cut in "Dancing in the Dark" (*Band Wagon*) does similar work: Charisse and Astaire have danced away from the camera; a cut allows the camera to quickly catch up to them. As already noted, V-V cuts also allow for a maintenance of the level view—as in "One for My Baby" and "Slap That Bass." None of these numbers are seen from anything like a seat in the theater. We are, in fact, suspended in air or popping back and forth, all so that the Vitruvian straight-on, whole figure might always be seen that way. As Alan M. Kreigsman noted in 1973, "There are no seats and no house from which one could see Astaire's dancing with the same clarity and wholeness as in his film musicals. . . . He put us in idealized, moveable seats. . . . [H]e set before us a dreamer's vision of the dance."[21] And yet, this "dreamer's vision" is almost always anchored to a narrative set in the "real" world. V-V cuts reflect the production advantage of chopping a dance into chunks but also, inevitably, raise the possibility of not doing so and filming an entire dance in one shot. Cuts to a new angle also afford variety. As Pan noted in the BBC radio documentary: "Certain steps you have to arrange for the camera. In other words you say, well, this looks great from this side but it's nothing from here. Like coming forward, you don't really see the effect—as if you maybe get a little off, it changes the idea of motion and speed by the placement of your camera. And you always have to keep in mind where the camera's going to be for every step you do, otherwise something that might look great to the eye would look terrible in the camera."[22]

The category *other* brings together five statistically unusual ways to cut between Vitruvian framed shots that call attention to the cut in some manner. These are cuts involving crossfades, dance actions on the beat that are reinforced by the editing, dancers exiting the frame, practical musical needs, and a few unique cases. On just four occasions, the cut is a crossfade on dancing bodies in motion. Two of these effect a transition from a private space (a living room) to a theatrical stage. "I Love a Piano" kicks off the vaudeville medley in *Easter Parade*. The song begins in Astaire's apartment and transitions via crossfade cut to Astaire and Garland on stage. The cut happens during a turning lift, and the match between the shots is absolutely perfect. Astaire repeated this crossfade transition in his next film in "Manhattan Downbeat" (*Barkleys*) with an almost identical turning step, this time with Rogers (whom he did not lift). Cuts on dance action that reinforce a musical beat are very rare. I find just two at either end of Astaire's career: the last cut in "Top Hat, White Tie, and Tails" and a drop to his knees in "History of the Beat" (*Daddy Long Legs*). Both cut on a strong musical arrival to Astaire with his arms fully extended to the sides, a gesture—found in Leonardo's "Vitruvian Man"—that makes the body as wide as possible. The latter number is similar to the widescreen-era practice of cutting to insert framing on the final chord (as happens in "History of the Beat," "Something's Gotta Give" [also *Daddy Long Legs*, just before the vocal tag], and "All of You"). The rarity of a cut responding to the music in this way brings into focus Astaire's normative practice of *not* involving the cut in the musical and rhythmic structure of the dance. The dancing is done by his body; the camera records this body; the cuts do not relate rhythmically to the music, which instead provides a continuous whole to which the shots are attached. While the camera was always in mind in the rehearsal hall, using the cut as a kind of second-order "move" or "step" in the dance as edited was not at all common. In other words, Astaire's principles work within the Classical aesthetic of continuity. The frame edge was always available as an exit, but movement across the vertical is quite unusual—found in only nine cuts, six of which are in the RKO dances, all of which are in dances involving one or two others besides Astaire. Astaire never leaves the frame during a solo. On several occasions, a V-V cut coincides with the end of an unaccompanied tap break and the restart of the prerecorded music track. Such cuts likely facilitated coordination of the dancers with the playback, which was played on a phonograph on set. This happens in "I'd Rather Lead a Band" (*Follow the Fleet*, twice), "Slap That Bass," and "Begin the Beguine" (*Broadway Melody*).[23] The problem of getting back into playback from an unaccompanied tap break midshot seems to have been solved by *Three Little Words* (see "Mr. and Mrs. Hoofer at Home"). In short, V-V cuts on the restart of playback in RKO films were necessitated by technical constraints. Changes in film technology across the quarter century Astaire worked in Hollywood were also a factor in the practical and aesthetic options on offer and choices made.

Cuts explained by the practicalities of filming a screen dance form the larger category *cheated continuity*. This sizeable group (50 cuts, 24% of all V-V cuts) puts the cut to work toward the making of dance actions and physical adjustments in real space that would be prohibitively difficult or impossible to film without making a cut. The incidence of this sort of cut increases dramatically after Astaire's time at RKO. There are three subtypes: cuts that isolate difficult dance moves (Astaire's manipulation of hand-held objects proves important in this subtype), space-making cuts (which allow for subtle or substantial changes to the dancers' position on the set or to an entirely different set), and invisible cuts (which join two takes of what is manifestly the same setup in an effort to edit the available printed takes into a more perfect whole). There is some overlap here, as several cuts prepare difficult moves by adjusting Astaire's physical position in the real space of the set. Each of these subcategories is treated in a separate section.

35. Object Impermanence

Leslie Caron recalled Astaire during breaks on *Daddy Long Legs*: "But Fred would start playing with a chair, or with a cane, or a coat that was there—*he* would doodle. I remember going out for air, and as I came back into the rehearsal room, he was dancing a number with a coat hanger."[24] Astaire often dances with a prop. Doing so was central to his persona, such that on his 1958 television special he did "a prop dance without props, instead miming a series of objects he had danced with in his films, including a piano. Drummer Alvin Stoller provided the sound of these invisible props from off camera, showing how important the element of sound was in Astaire's prop-centered routines."[25] Indeed, fifty-seven (36%) of the 159 *Astaire dancing* numbers (plus "If Swing Goes I Go Too" [cut from *Ziegfeld Follies*] and "I'll Capture Your Heart" [*Holiday Inn*]) include the use of a hand-held item that is handled by Astaire in some way. Props, similar to furniture and other structures, provide something to dance about or with and also introduce an added element of difficulty to the dance. They also indicate a playful, boyish nature: Astaire can't just hold anything; everything potentially becomes part of his dancing. Astaire handles fifty-four different objects—most only once, including (in alphabetical order) ashtrays, a bowling pin, coins, fans, gloves, guns, matches, scarves, toast, trumpets, and a violin. By far Astaire's most frequent prop was the cane (used in 14 numbers) and an umbrella used as a cane (a further 2 numbers). The cane as a tool of masculine display and aggression is saved for section forty-seven.

An important subset within these object-using numbers are those where Astaire engages in acts of tossing, catching, hitting (golf balls), and firing (shooting a gun, striking a match). In these thirty-five dances (22%), objects are turned into independent physical entities to be interacted with in time to the music, which acts as a regular pattern against which the object is used. Astaire's acts of throwing, catching, and firing combine to display his mastery of both space and time. Bob Fosse noted how tricks with props contributed to the sense that "Always [Astaire] seems to be doing risky things and things that could fail."[26] Fosse added in another context, "There was always a sense of a little dangerousness when he was dancing. I mean, it could be with a prop or something he *might* drop, that *might* fall."[27] Of course, there was no risk given such tricks were captured on film. The real risk only obtained during shooting. Hat and cane tricks were difficult to shoot: as shown in Part Three, they often required many tries yielding only one printable take. The shot containing such a trick shows mastery of just that trick in just that moment on the crucible of a soundstage; Astaire was sometimes only able to successfully execute a throwing or catching trick one time. Astaire recalled for the BBC how often the partner moves up and over a dining table failed on stage in *Gay Divorce*, leaving him and Claire Luce on the floor. Luce recounted she was injured, hospitalized, and her dancing career cut short.[28] Remarkably, Astaire would stop the show, restart the orchestra, and keep trying until the dangerous move was accomplished.[29] Doing the same move in the film *The Gay Divorcee* allowed him and his partner (now Rogers) to take as many tries as needed, and of course, done successfully once for the camera such a feat is endlessly repeated by Astaire's screen dance body. Several throwing and catching tricks are contained in their own shot. In "I've Got My Eye on You," a reframed shot opens out to track the distance between Astaire and the tiny compact he tosses onto an awning then catches in his hat exactly on the beat (figs. 35.1.a through 35.1.d). His toss and catch of a bowling pin in "Sunday Jumps" (*Royal Wedding*) is a similar reframed shot, this time incorporating crane movement, which nonsensically pulls back and up to reveal that the ocean liner gymnasium where he's working out has an improbably high ceiling. Shots like this demonstrate a mastery of objects in time and space to music—but such mastery is contained in a separate shot. In both cases, an otherwise unnecessary cut isolates the trick in its own shot.

The practice of putting object tricks in their own, relatively short shots can be found across Astaire's post–*Swing Time* films. The urge to capture entire dances in one shot—generally set aside after *Swing Time*—seems to have yielded to a construction of dances around shorter shots that add up to a dance unlikely to ever have been done in one take due to the specific physical challenges involved. Indeed, the "Golf Solo"—the very next solo Astaire made after his longest-ever shot, the one-shot "Drum Dance"—is constructed on a sequence of Vitruvian-to-Vitruvian (V-V) cuts that isolate discrete physical challenges in separate shots.

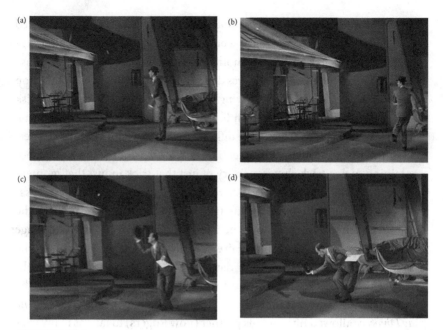

FIGURE 35.1

- Shot one: four balls hit with an iron using a medium swing from a patio surface.
- Shot two: one ball hit with an iron using a full swing, followed by one ball hit with a wood using a full swing (both balls preset on tees in the grass; Astaire switches clubs in a tossed exchange with his caddy). He also knocks five balls off their tees with his foot.
- Shot three: five tee shots in a row, each a drive down the fairway with a wood.

The V-V cuts separating these acts of golfing skill—perhaps the most complicated of Astaire's object dances given the addition of an element (club hitting ball)—also shift the angle ninety degrees: shots one and three look down the fairway where the quality of Astaire's golfing can be assessed (surely some in the audience directed their gaze at the golf balls). This group of three shots is preceded by a seventy-six-second shot/dance that does not involve the manipulation of objects and ends with several spins. It is impossible to imagine the golf number performed in real time. Cuts—in this case, of the V-V variety—make Astaire's display of skill on the golf course possible. Other dances that rely conceptually and practically on a recourse to trick-oriented cuts (including some V-V) are the "Firecracker Dance" in *Holiday Inn* and "Seeing's Believing" in *Belle of New York*. Similar tosses of a cane or umbrella into a nearby stand are isolated in short shots in the "Audition Dance" and "Let's Kiss and Make Up."

These dances involve visible acts of skill manipulating objects. Less visible cuts related to and facilitating the use of objects often entail the repositioning of objects and offer our first examples of how cuts were used to create a screen world that defies material reality (even as Astaire's aesthetic sought to suggest a given dance was directly represented—done in real space and time). Attention to moments when Astaire drops things or picks them up proves instructive. In the final scene of *The Gay Divorcee*, Astaire enters Rogers's hotel room, tips the four bellboys in attendance, then romantically tosses his hat and coat aside to take Rogers in his arms and begin their dance that travels over the couch and up and across the table. On a cut just six seconds after Astaire casts his hat and coat aside, the rightmost bellboy is now holding the discarded hat and coat (the latter neatly folded over his arm). This sets up Astaire's swaggering exit from the film with the bellboy's top hat (already Astaire's signature). The messiness of reality—the need for the bellboy to pick up and fold the coat Astaire tosses aside—is elided entirely by way of a cut. Objects come and go like this across Astaire's films. The canes Astaire and George Murphy drop early on in "Please Don't Monkey with Broadway" (*Broadway Melody*) are placed exactly where they need to be when the time comes to pick them up: an insert shot of the two men grimacing at each other facilitates repositioning these props. The hat Astaire tosses aside at the end of the vocal in "I Wanna Be a Dancin' Man" reappears on the floor—where it could not have been during the dance—for the number's vocal tag. The stool where he puts his metronome and the hat stand he dances with like a partner (his largest prop) in "Sunday Jumps" and the chair he briefly partners in "All of You" are all only in the dance setting when needed and when there these objects are always exactly where they need to be. The tree with the monkey on it reappears on the final cut in "I Left My Hat in Haiti" just in time for the monkey to jump into Astaire's arms (likely an even tougher shot to get than those involving "pigeon action" in "Seeing's Believing"). The world of objects is always to Astaire's hand. Only in the highly stylized "The Babbitt and the Bromide" does the reality-defying aspect of Astaire's use of props come in for some (gentle) spoofing. In the third section, set in heaven, Astaire and Kelly grandly throw away their harps, which never audibly land. At number's end, in a virtuoso instance of hitting their marks on an unmarked expansive flat floor, the harps drop from above to be caught by both dancers. It's a great trick but in practical terms Astaire nearly always relates to objects as if he were in the heaven of "Babbitt."

Several dances are substantially conceived around the opportunity cuts provide to reposition objects. Chief among these is the first section of "Puttin' on the Ritz," where Astaire drops and kicks a cane as well as catches canes that leap up from the floor of their own accord into his waiting hand. Careful analysis of the number reveals how strategic V-V cuts made this possible. The dance begins with a seventy-nine-second shot during which Astaire fixates on his cane, establishing an oppositional and even violent relationship with the object—several times he knocks it angrily against the floor. Two V-V cuts isolate the following tricks in one shot:

(1) Astaire throws the cane to the floor.
(2) He kicks the cane off screen left at a sharp angle with a back-footed move.
(3) He travels forward on a nearly straight-on angle to find a cane (purportedly the one he kicked) laying on the floor. The cane's presence is revealed as the frame follows him forward.
(4) On arrival at the cane, this (preset) object leaps into the air. Astaire catches it. The mechanism that makes the cane jump is briefly visible.
(5) Astaire then dances back to where he was when the shot began.
(6) He, again, throws the cane to the floor.
(7) He dances to screen right, just enough that, as the frame follows him, our view of the cane on the floor is cut off.
(8) He dances back to the cane, which has been visibly adjusted from where it formerly was.
(9) The cane again leaps into his hand and Astaire catches it.

This action fills twenty-two seconds of screen time, involved at least two canes, and would be impossible to reproduce on stage (since how the tricks were accomplished would be visible). The pattern in the shiny parquet floor surely acted as marks for Astaire to hit. The initial cut allows for the preset of the first leaping cane. During step seven, while the camera follows Astaire's body, someone crept onto the set to position the cane onto the mechanism that would make it leap, a necessary action that had to have been done very quickly and with a precise sense for the changing position of the frame around Astaire—the reverse sense needed by dancers to stay within the frame. (A similar complete removal of an object midshot outside the moving frame happens early in "Shoes with Wings On." The customer with the white tap shoes leaves his brown street shoes on the floor and exits in his socks; the brown shoes are struck from the set by someone who crept onto the set but remained out of frame while Astaire escorts the customer out the door.) The use of V-V cuts to preset leaping canes occurs again in the second half of "Puttin' on the Ritz," when Astaire dances with a special effects chorus of himself.

"Puttin' on the Ritz" involved a single prop: a cane. "Let's Kiss and Make Up" ups the ante to three props—an umbrella, a hat, and a raincoat *cum* matador's cape—used in a manner that required the props to be in a precise relationship to each other within a rectangular setting articulated on its long side by several wide arches. And while most of the cuts in "Let's Kiss" are not of the V-V variety, the relationship of Astaire's body to the props from shot to shot is always evident. A near V-V cut is, however, instructive. The first of these successive shots begins with Astaire swinging the umbrella like a baseball bat (an object he never uses). Cane moves seen in "Puttin' on the Ritz" (knocking the cane on the ground) and a golf swing follow. The challenging content in this shot is a sequence of tossing and catching tricks with the umbrella that require him to knock the object into the air—first with his knee, then with his foot—and catch it. The cut comes on a short pose seen on both sides of the cut: shot to shot his position relative to the cape is markedly different; the camera has changed position and so has Astaire (figs. 35.2 and 35.3). The second shot begins with a high cane toss—reminiscent of the big cane toss that concludes "Top Hat, White Tie and Tails" (as if working with an object requires its own crescendo)—then moves to the collecting of the hat and coat, both on the ground. The repositioning of the camera and of Astaire in the real space of the dance setting facilitates this action with three props in one shot.

36. On-Set "Jump" Cuts

The aforementioned cut from "Let's Kiss and Make Up" is, in effect, a jump cut—Astaire's absolute position in space on the set abruptly changes on a cut that announces, if quietly in the midst of much music and dance, that the represented screen reality is not possible in the "real" world. Of course,

FIGURE 35.2

FIGURE 35.3

the original viewers of *Funny Face* would scarcely have had time to register these details (and if they did they were watching with odd intentions). Astaire relies across his work on his audiences not having the kind of pause-and-rewind or freeze-frame access to his dances enjoyed in the age of the VHS, DVD, and YouTube. His aesthetic choices depend on our not seeing the seams as it were but instead buying a number as whole cloth—as, in effect, a one-shot number made of multiple shots. For this reason, the term *jump cut* is apt if, admittedly, not used here within the strict meaning of the term (which implies the visually evident, usually quite blunt, removal of part of a continuous shot).

In this section, I examine nine "jump" cuts from nine numbers, each of which noticeably reconfigures physical reality. All nine are cuts between full-figure framings. All but two numbers are ostensibly occurring in the real world, where space and bodies are expected to be stable and obey the laws of physics. Five of the numbers are in-film performances for in-film audiences that project conceits of liveness. These cuts express further exploitations of cutting to make film musical dances that, while projecting a fictional conceit of continuity, in fact could only be performed by the fictive construct of the screen dance body.

Adding bodies: "The Ritz Roll and Rock"

Like many widescreen numbers, the final two shots in Astaire's last studio-film solo, "The Ritz Roll and Rock," are filled with bodies on the floor. In the first of this pair, three groups of backup dancers take turns doing a short combination that travels rapidly and boldly across the set and ends with the dancers lying full out on the floor. The first group—four women—travel forward as the camera dollies back. The second and third groups—each with three men—travel laterally across the widescreen frame. Astaire cavorts in the middle throughout and, once everyone else has hit the deck, he too slides to the floor. At the end of the shot, eleven bodies total are on the set (fig. 36.1). After the cut, each of the two groups of three men have been augmented by a fourth man (fig. 36.2). Throughout the routine,

FIGURE 36.1

FIGURE 36.2

Astaire is backed up by eight male dancers. Only in the running and sliding shot is the group reduced to six total, likely because there was insufficient room for groups of four to do the running and sliding combination. The limited space of the set required a reduction of the chorus during one short part—one shot—of the dance. On the cut, the chorus is restored to its normative size for the number, likely to fill space and restore parity with the four women.

Instantly reversing momentum: "Audition Dance"

Astaire's screen dance body defies Newton's laws of motion by way of a cut in the "Audition Dance" in *You Were Never Lovelier*. In an especially surprising moment in a dance almost entirely engaged with a furnished environment and props, Astaire rides an armchair backward to a crashing stop—exactly on the beat—in a corner. After a cut on this seated position, Astaire rises to continue the number. This cut would seem to be unnecessary but was, in fact, important to keeping his screen dance body in motion even as his real body could not make the transition. At the end of the slide, Astaire is still in thrall to the physical forces of his arrival in the corner—his body forced back against the back of the chair, his legs not on the floor (fig. 36.3). At the start of the second shot, which includes a very slight repositioning of the camera, Astaire is leaning forward in the chair, his arms lifting him up and out in time to keep on dancing (fig. 36.4). It's likely the routine could not have been rehearsed as a continuous dance to the prerecorded audio.

FRAMES, SETS, CUTS   233

FIGURE 36.3

FIGURE 36.4

Changing dancers' location in real space on a pose to facilitate exiting up steps: "Smoke Gets in Your Eyes" and "Dancing in the Dark"

The lyrical dance to "Smoke Gets in Your Eyes" could have been done, like two other numbers in *Roberta*, in one shot. The grid pattern on the floor and attention to the levels of the dance setting show why a single cut—just seventeen seconds before the dance's end—was made. Astaire and Rogers's exit required a unison leaping move up a small flight of steps (a tricky move likely much more difficult for Rogers, who did it in heels). The couple's position relative to the steps just before the leap was crucial to a successful (and safe) negotiation of this move. Attention to the grid pattern on the floor reveals a slight adjustment closer to the steps on the cut (figs. 36.5 and 36.6). The perils of the one-shot routine are evident here. To do this dance in one shot, the pair would have had to end up—after two minutes of lyrical dancing—at exactly the right spot to enable the bold leap up the steps for the exit. Doing so must

FIGURE 36.5

FIGURE 36.6

have proved impossible on set. And so, on a brief pose, facing each other, the routine's sole cut moves Astaire and Rogers to the perfect position for their stunning negotiation of the steps.

The end of "Dancing in the Dark," made nearly twenty years later, employs an identical strategy. The second of only two cuts in this number allows for a repositioning of Astaire and Charisse in the real space of the set just before they dance up a flight of steps to board a waiting carriage. As in "Smoke Gets in Your Eyes," the cut occurs on a brief pose: the couple is still. Lacking gridlines to register their position on the set, the "jump" in the cut to a substantially different location on the set can be triangulated using the fixed position of the lamppost and bench and the edge between the grass and the cement promenade that serves as the dance floor (figs. 36.7 and 36.8).

In addition to adjusting the dancers' position in real space, this cut also facilitates a fundamental remaking of the dance setting. The new angle after the cut, unbeknownst to the viewer initially, is from atop a short flight of steps. Subtle crane movement follows the pair up the steps, then restores the Vitruvian, level-view default of the entire number for the close. The dance

FIGURE 36.7

FIGURE 36.8

setting, viewed camera to dancer's eye level throughout, is revealed in retrospect to have been at the bottom of an unseen hill the dancers must climb out of, via the steps, to make their exit. In the cut that repositions their place in space, this unseen hill has been introduced to the set. The bulk of "Dancing in the Dark" assumes a camera position effectively inside this hill. When Astaire and Charisse move forward up the steps and into the elevated space where the carriage awaits, one edge of the rock formation that looks down on their dance floor is revealed. Once seated in the carriage—the dance now done—a cut to a back-projection shot just before the carriage starts moving obviates the need for the carriage seen in the dance shot to move.

Changing dancers' location in real space while moving: "I'm Old-Fashioned"

Cutting shortly before the end of a number to facilitate an exit occurs in yet a third duo dance, "I'm Old-Fashioned" from *You Were Never Lovelier* danced by Astaire and Rita Hayworth. Here, the cut occurs with the couple in motion, specifically while spinning. Cuts on spinning near the end of a number are a not uncommon choice, but this particular cut stands out for two reasons: on the cut the dancing couple's position in real space is altered, and their direction of travel also changes.

The second half of "I'm Old-Fashioned" is done on a rectangular area framed from its long side—a patio in Hayworth's home with carefully arranged outdoor furniture and two double doors into the house to either side. This symmetrical setting recalls many RKO dances; indeed, *You Were Never Lovelier* comes the closest of any non-RKO film to recreating the stylized glamour of the dance settings in the Astaire-Rogers pictures. The cut in question precedes Astaire and Hayworth's cute exit out the rightmost doors on the patio. They approach the doors in a closed position spin. When begun, the spin has the couple traveling parallel to the front edge of the rectangular patio (fig. 36.9). They are not, at this point, traveling toward but rather past the doors through which they will exit. After the cut, Astaire and Hayworth are suddenly traveling directly toward the door from a position to the far-screen-right end of the patio (fig. 36.10). The unchanging position of the

FIGURE 36.9

FIGURE 36.10

furniture allows for a precise mapping of their position in the space of the set. Across the cut, Astaire and Hayworth travel toward or past themselves, traversing the same real space in a dance that could only be done on screen.

Cuts that are not to be believed (or noticed): "Swing Trot" and "Limehouse Blues"

Some cuts between full-figure framings are simply not to be believed. Such cuts violate the continuity of matter so fundamentally that the effect can only be understood as a direct admission that the screen body is not real or a confidence the viewer will not notice or care. These cuts come from unusual sequences that emerge as outliers that cross aesthetic lines otherwise closely guarded.

The Barkleys of Broadway opens unlike any other Astaire film, with a dance number, "Swing Trot," done behind the opening titles, which are themselves framed by a gold picture frame. Eighty-two seconds into this ninety-nine-second routine (on the last of the group title cards), a singular crossfade (unlike any in Astaire's corpus) admits to an editing together of two unrelated takes: the two shots joined here contain completely different dance steps; any conceit of continuity to the routine is compromised. The final two title cards (for Arthur Freed and Charles Walters) follow and the gold frame border fades out. Then, a final cut moves Astaire and Rogers (still dancing but in a pose) from the stylized dance setting of the number to a position two steps below the dance setting, which is now revealed to be on a platform (figs. 36.11 and 36.12). The scale of their Vitruvian framing matches nearly exactly, though their relation to the set behind, of course, changes as they are now farther away from it.

FIGURE 36.11

FIGURE 36.12

Minnelli's "Limehouse Blues" in *Ziegfeld Follies* contrasts two sorts of Asian exoticism: the Chinatown setting of the framing narrative and the Chinoiserie dreamscape Astaire's character enters after being shot. While the Orientalist content of both settings is examined in Part Six, here I consider the dreamscape's persistent reliance on "jump" cuts to reposition dancing bodies in space. This purely formal element of the "Limehouse" dance section shows Astaire, with partner Lucille Bremer, (literally, physically) being moved from place to place in a dance setting by way of cuts in a manner unlike any of the numbers over which he had control.

The big reveal in the "Limehouse" dreamscape comes when the lights suddenly come up on a huge set composed of blue set pieces populated by thirty gray-blue figures arrayed against a yellow background—easily the grandest of the up-and-back-for-a-big-view crane shots. Astaire and Bremer stand out in bright red. Every cut from this point on in the number involves substantial changes of position, whether for the camera or for the dancers within the space. The first cut moves the camera only: a piece of the set, formerly to screen left, is now screen right. The viewer's relation to this massive set made of many large elements is immediately rendered ambiguous. At the end of this shot, Astaire and Bremer walk toward the semicircular "moon" bridge. On a cut that matches a dramatic cymbal crash in the score, the pair are teleported to the opposite side of this same bridge, which they proceed to cross (traveling toward their former position; figs. 36.13 and 36.14). The lengthy, three-and-a-quarter-minute routine for Astaire and Bremer that follows contains two cuts (each preceded by the up-and-in-at-the-end crane movement Minnelli favored), both of which move the pair to a different absolute position in the flat-floored clearing in the set where they dance. The reason for these "jumps" is unclear and their shifts in absolute position are, surely, not to be noticed.

FRAMES, SETS, CUTS   239

FIGURE 36.13

FIGURE 36.14

The wormhole in *Holiday Inn*

One constraint on musical numbers in *Holiday Inn* is the need to do so many *at* the inn itself—a relatively cramped venue that the film holds within rather realistic bounds, perhaps to underline the conceit that it is a "real" space. The space of the inn is variously configured for each holiday and holiday-themed number: a nightclub setup with tables around a dance floor for New Year's Eve ("Let's Start the New Year Right"); a small stage serving as a bandstand for Lincoln's birthday ("Abraham"); a rectangular dance floor surrounded by long tables with the band at one narrow end for Washington's birthday ("I Can't Tell a Lie"). The two patriotic numbers added after Pearl Harbor are staged on a large outdoor proscenium stage with a front curtain (the scale of the film expanded in response to America's entrance into the war). The only holiday number not done for an in-film audience is "Be Careful, It's My Heart." The dance setting for this number, ostensibly done in the same room where the other indoor numbers happen, defies any sense of continuous space in the most noncontinuous Vitruvian-to-Vitruvian (V-V) shots in the corpus.

Astaire and partner Marjorie Reynolds dance an entire vocal chorus of the song—sung by Crosby, supposedly unaware they are dancing behind him—against a raised area with a banister (seen in several previous numbers). Just at the start of an instrumental dance chorus, a cut reverses the couple's position, moves several tables set for dinner at the inn off the dance floor into an adjacent area, and—more significantly—enlarges the dance area considerably (figs. 36.15 and 36.16). The couple's orientation toward a large heart reverses: initially they face it; on the cut, it's to their backs. In the space previously containing just one table next to the large heart, there are now two tables positioned well behind the heart. This space will be important to the dance that follows as the heart is used to make a silhouette and the couple burst through it to climax their dance.

When the dance is over, restoring Astaire and Reynolds to the "real" space of the inn occurs efficiently but, again, nonsensically from a continuity perspective by way of two cuts. At the end of the number, Astaire and Reynolds strike a pose against the heart (fig. 36.17). A cutaway to Crosby establishes an eyeline match but elides the couple's actual position (fig. 36.18). The next shot neatly

FIGURE 36.15

FIGURE 36.16

FIGURE 36.17 ...

FIGURE 36.18

FIGURE 36.19

inserts Astaire and Reynolds back into the inn but gets their position entirely wrong: they now seem to be facing the heart they burst through, except, of course, that heart couldn't have been in this room in the first place (fig. 36.19). Subsequent dialogue scenes in this setting confirm that two different walls with the big heart were constructed: one smaller (with the tables on the dance floor), the other expansive with windows on falling snow (for the dance).[30]

37. Invisible Match on Action

Cutting on the dancing figure always entails an answer to the question: what dance actions will be constituted by the cut? Airborne motion crosses a clever cut in "A Shine on Your Shoes" (*Band Wagon*): Astaire tosses a baseball to a booth attendant, who catches the ball (in rhythm) in the next shot, facilitating a change in camera position and substantial rearrangement of the arcade machines (as noted on assistant director [AD] reports). Astaire also applied this approach to cuts on dancing bodies in midair: jumping at the end of one shot, landing in the next (see Astaire and Vera-Ellen's leap off a small platform in "Baby Doll" [*Belle of New York*]). Perhaps the cut comes on a pose?—as happens five times in succession in "All of You," during each of which the dance action seems to freeze. Or will the cut be on dancers in motion? And if so, what sort of motion works best to minimize the disruption of the cut? Cuts on spinning seem to be a favored choice, often at the end of a number (as discussed in "I'm Old-Fashioned" and "Shoes with Wings On"). Other numbers that cut on spins at the close include "Slap That Bass," "Night and Day" (where the cut seems to set up Astaire placing Rogers on a nearby round couch at the close), and "The Last Waltz" (*The Castles* [1939]). Perhaps the most famous cut in Astaire's work occurs just before the spinning combination that ends "Never Gonna Dance." This over-three-minute dance has but one cut, twenty-seven seconds before the end. Made very quickly at the end of production on *Swing Time*, "Never Gonna Dance" includes an elaborate crane shot analogous to that used in the chorus girl section of "Bojangles of Harlem" (as noted earlier, made immediately before "Never Gonna Dance"). This shot follows Astaire and Rogers back and forth across the expansive Silver Sandal nightclub floor, up a pair of curving staircases, and returns them to Vitruvian framing on a triangular platform at the top. The cut occurs just before a series of spins within spins—the couple spins, then Rogers only, etc. (see section forty-one)—and ushers Rogers out, leaving Astaire behind to strike a forlorn pose. All these cuts on spinning come at the peak of their respective numbers and can easily be missed or mistaken for a blink—none entail major changes in angle or figure scale; they are so subtle as to be near invisible.

Indeed, these shots on spinning action point toward genuinely invisible cuts that demonstrate Astaire's well-rehearsed ability to do the same moves in exactly the same way in exactly the same place on a set in take after take.

The virtuoso match-on-action cutting done to a prerecorded musical foundation is also evident here: the cutters behind Astaire's dances represent a pinnacle of filmmaking craft. Four nearly invisible cuts (described first) are informed by a small handful of others (treated subsequently) that fail, surely because of the fixed content of the printed takes to hand. I do not count these four genuinely invisible cuts among the total count of 932 shots and 778 cuts in the *Astaire dancing* corpus. Each was a very late discovery in my analysis of the clip reel.[31]

The dance to "You're All the World to Me" seems to be done in two shots, each taking up three choruses of the song. The invisible cut in this routine comes at the start of the fifth instrumental chorus (just after Astaire, on the screen-right wall, rolls onto his back and shakes his bent arms and legs with glee; figs. 37.1.a and 37.1.b). Slight differences in the lighting, in Astaire's shadow (sharply cast throughout the routine), and in the developing of the original film make this invisible cut discernible (if only after repeated viewing). The touchiness of color in this period helps reveal this editing together of two takes from the same angle.

Seeing invisible cuts in black and white relies on both attention to changes in the lighting and evidence from AD reports. The "Firecracker Dance" includes an invisible cut seventeen seconds after the return to full-figure framing after the insert shot where Astaire lights a long string of fireworks. A very slight change in lighting on Astaire's face—an artifact of the developing process—reveals this invisible cut (figs. 37.2.a and 37.2.b). AD reports confirm this cut by omission. If we disregard the invisible cut and attend to the AD's descriptions of shot content, no single shot containing all the dance content of this part of the "Firecracker Dance" was taken. This apparently

FIGURE 37.1

FIGURE 37.2

continuous shot is made of two shots seamlessly and perfectly joined. And it comes as no surprise that Astaire could do this in this routine. The floor of the "Firecracker Dance," while a mess of expended flash pods, was a precisely marked space: Astaire had to know where all the pods were. Here, he had to hit his marks perfectly.

A third invisible cut is evident thirty-seven seconds before the end of the "Drum Dance." On a move with his back to the camera, the position of the drapes behind him visibly shifts, indicating a different shot (figs. 37.3.a and 37.3.b). And so, the "Drum Dance" turns out not to be the longest shot Astaire successfully took after all—it's just his longest single-shot number, a record salvaged in the cutting room and by Astaire's fantastic consistency on the set. Indeed, the conceit of the number as a single shot likely necessitated finding a spot where two takes could be spliced together as nondisruptively as possible, signaling Astaire was not completely happy with any single printed take.

The fourth invisible cut, unlike the others, involves a partner. In the *Gay Divorcee* "Table Dance," a stutter in the image but not the soundtrack just before Astaire and Rogers do a lift over an ottoman indicates the join of two takes in this difficult dance with many obstacles.

There are several failed or nearly invisible cuts that a viewer might miss if they blink at the right time or, if watching a physical print of a film, might dismiss as flaws in a given copy of the film rather than the film negative itself. Several of these come on spinning combinations—see the final cuts of "Slap That Bass," the "Jukebox Dance" (*Broadway Melody*), and the "Concert Solo" (*Second Chorus*). Particularly messy final failed invisible cuts not on spinning action occur in "My Shining Hour" (*The Sky's the Limit*), "I Concentrate on

You" (*Broadway Melody*), and "Nevertheless" (*Three Little Words*). The last of these is especially bad: Astaire and Vera-Ellen's relationship to the piano bench changes in the cut, revealing their completely new position on the otherwise flat and unmarked dance setting (figs. 37.4 and 37.5). A fixed point

FIGURE 37.3

FIGURE 37.4

FIGURE 37.5

of reference here betrays a move in real space during a rather simple duo dance. The change in scale is also jarring. None of these failed invisible cuts are flaws in the prints, since the prerecorded music track holding the edit together unfolds without interruption. These failed invisible cuts reveal some limits to Astaire's perfection.

The cuts detailed in this section touch on the very essence of Astaire's art—the making of full-figure shots that are subsequently edited together with utmost precision. Astaire effectively pushes film editing to and (in the failed invisible cuts) beyond its limits—with the limits being located in the meeting of the dancing body and the camera on the set, an encounter anticipated in the rehearsal hall.

38. "To Project Intelligence"

The combination of strategies and conceits brought together in Astaire's default Vitruvian framing make up more than just a dance captured on film. It is a dance and dancing body otherwise impossible outside of film. It is an assemblage of danced moments—contained in shots that capture time itself—reassembled into a new sort of whole that's a collage of more than just moments in time but also positions in space. And yet, almost everything Astaire did—and still does—resides within the realm of the possible: it's indexical (shot by shot) and arguably made of rather quotidian elements (he doesn't do fantastic leaps or spins or splits, like others do; much of his dancing is built on motions one might use to—well—take a walk or put out the garbage). Hungerford's "fundamental test of a cinedance" that "it could not have been done on any theatre stage, nor could it effectively be transferred to one" qualifies for many of Astaire's routines, but only if we look closely and against the illusion of wholeness Astaire worked to produce.[32]

The screen dance body of Astaire's normative practice is contained in the space of the frame—the limited field of contact between the body on the set and the camera—and limited to motions that work there, in that precise and technological context. This is a modest and rather small realm, easily contained in a furnished private room, especially if the body in that frame is going to be as large as possible, which limits the size of dance moves, etc., around and around. For this reason, the limits the frame imposes prove more constrictive to duo dances than solos. Still, the space of the frame finds substantial liberation in the time-shifting power of the cut—which frees Astaire to separate certain tricks out from the rest of a dance or to take an ideal position in the dance setting relative to some part of the dance or to splice together movements in contrary motion as if they were one and to literally, if sequentially, meet himself coming and going. The aesthetic pose (or fiction) that each of his dances is a continuous action—the stylistic assurance that every cut matches—and, for those aware of it, the common and repeated line that Astaire favored lengthy shots work to turn what is a collage of moments into a continuity of gestures that add up to a whole and suppress awareness of the parts. This was particularly so for Astaire's intended viewers—unlike us today—who couldn't stop his dancing, freeze his figure, press rewind, etc.

The real space of the set, designed as it was for dancing for the camera, is constantly renegotiable within a visual regime that privileges the body by employing a framing practice that follows the body. The body moves, and all else falls in place around it. This Vitruvian-framed body enjoys the dignity of wholeness, an integrity and self-sufficiency that prevents any single part of that body from being fixated upon. Only Astaire's feet are ever fetishized—a choice that feeds his noisy masculinity (see Part Six).

Choreographer Herbert Ross, who worked on Astaire's final television special, said of him, "Many dancers are merely physical or exotic. Astaire manages to project intelligence."[33] I suggest the intelligence Ross sees in Astaire is an effect of the fundamental choices Astaire made (and could make) in the crafting of his screen dance body. Ross contrasts Astaire's "intelligence" with the "merely physical or exotic"—both qualities he dismisses as "merely" are raced nonwhite and gendered female. Following this move, we can understand Astaire's "intelligence" as implicitly white, straight, and male, derived from the tight control Astaire exercised over his dance movements (minimal and contained [including within the frame]) and the presentation of his body on screen (seemingly direct—but, as this part has shown, collaged together on many levels). This control was entirely predicated on the power he enjoyed as a straight white male movie star who could—for close to a quarter century—walk on to any Hollywood lot and set the aesthetic agenda and production tempo for about thirteen minutes of any movie he was in. His sustained access to the studio machine enables the very notion of his style: he dances so much that general principles about his work can be established qualitatively and quantitatively. If he had only made eleven numbers, as the Nicholas Brothers did, it would be harder to suggest a consistent cinematic style. The generous length of Astaire's clip reel matters for the securing of his aesthetics as straight, white, and male—and, of course, for the very premise of this quantitative study of his work (yet another textual monument to his "genius"). Repetition of the same aesthetic strategies over many films builds his identity as both creator and screen dance body and reinforces his whiteness and maleness—only a white man could do this across the full decades of Astaire's career.

What Astaire did with the fantastic filmmaking machine at his disposal was unrelentingly and decidedly modest. As Ross also noted, "And he never did more than he could do. He had refined what he could do to a high art, and he never tried to exceed it."[34] Ballet critic Alexander Bland pointed toward Astaire's limits as well and detailed what he saw as the contents of Astaire's dancing.

> Devising almost all his own choreography, he clearly relied on what he did best and most easily: a marvelously fluent, fast, twinkling kind of movement linked with great musicality to decorative taps and swinging romantic curves and pauses, with much use of plastic épaulement and wide arms (unusual in jazz dancing), and always in lively contact with his partner.... Unlike Gene Kelly, he rarely ventured into ballet movement, and his range was restricted: passion, eroticism, earthy humor, grandeur or savagery were outside his scope. Like a pianist playing with the right hand only, he drew his music from the light end of the scale—the sentimental, touching, charming, unashamedly prettified world of musical comedy. His real achievement was the distillation of that well-worn art form into something pure and stimulating. Balanchine called him "the most interesting, inventive and elegant dancer of our time." Like an angel dancing on the point of a needle, Astaire at his best produced the frisson of a fragile feat perfectly executed.[35]

Bland locates Astaire "on the point of a needle." My analysis of the complicated mechanics behind Astaire's flat, whole, large, level-viewed, sustained, centered, perfect, synchronized screen dance body describes the minute calculations required to keep his balance on so small and sharp a foundation.

To sum up, Astaire's screen dances consistently present a dancing human figure expressed in the abstraction of shadow and silhouette in two dimensions, as an outline more than a rounded form, as an idealized and stylized shape lacking fleshly presence, as a Platonic or Renaissance humanist ideal—an aspiration to perfected human form—that carries with it a politics of withdrawal from the messiness of real life and an elision of the fact of flesh, muscle, and space. (His aversion to visible sweat falls into this as well.) This approach necessitates framing the body to preserve the entire figure—keeping at bay the power of any single part to distract attention—and from a mostly frontal position, for it is in the entire figure that his notion of expressive integrity resides. Astaire presents a peculiar ontology of wholeness—flat and dynamic, perhaps as insubstantial as the shadows of which it is made. These many small but defining aesthetic choices constitute a politics scaled to the human and expressed in individual mastery of an environment defined by the dancing body—not a body confronted by space but a body that makes the world in its own narrow orbit. This body, crafted in the medium of film, is raced as white.

Within this view of Astaire, a trick shot from "Night and Day" can be seen to capture something of the essence of the "point of a needle" on which Astaire danced. In this seven-second shot, Astaire and Rogers face each other and move rapidly along the depth axis, up and down a small set of steps, toward and away from the camera, which is positioned to see them through a table that repeats Vitruvian man's basic forms—a square and a circle (fig. 38.1). Part of the set (the table) in this case is physically distant from Astaire and Rogers's bodies—but they are still dancing in relation to it and the camera and doing so with incredible accuracy, as if the dance is being done in the viewfinder of a surveyor's theodolite—or, and in fact, in the viewfinder of a movie camera that marks in physical reality the edges of the frame. For a factory-made piece of machinery, Astaire's dances in Hollywood

FIGURE 38.1

film musicals routinely display the incredible machined tolerances evident in this shot. The surveyor's problem inside every shot Astaire made is expressed here in a metaphor that is, of course, also an actual photo of a physical setup in a real place (on Gower Street in Los Angeles) on a particular day (either July 3 or 5, 1934).

FIVE

PARTNERS

I have more leeway if I am working alone. When I work with a partner I have two people to think about instead of one.
—Fred Astaire (1959)

39. The Adele Question

The partner question haunted Astaire's entire career. While on the stage, he did only one show without his sister Adele. For a quarter century they were inseparable in the public and critical imagination. Astaire's initial success in Hollywood was, again, in a team—this time a romantic pairing with Ginger Rogers. At the end of the 1930s, when he left RKO, there was no knowing if Astaire could continue to hold the audience without her. He did, of course, but always by dancing with yet more partners, each of whom was compared to the others (and especially Rogers) by reviewers. Every media profile rehearsed his list of partners; every interviewer asked him, indelicately given Astaire's façade of politeness, to name his favorite.

How often did Astaire dance with a partner versus by himself or with more than one other person? Chart 20 parses the 159 dances of the *Astaire dancing* corpus by participants (using data from Appendix Two column E). Astaire dances by himself—with no one else involved—some thirty-five times (22% of the corpus). Across his career, when Astaire starts dancing and executes a complete routine, there's a nearly one-in-four chance he will be the only dancer on screen. These solitary dances for a straight white male dancer form a significant body of screen dance lasting nearly one-and-a-half hours in all and distributed with regularity across Astaire's twenty-four years before Hollywood cameras. By comparison, Gene Kelly made fifteen solitary solos, Gene Nelson only seven.

The remaining 124 routines (78%) feature Astaire dancing with others—an implicitly social context that requires him to respond to other dancing bodies (and persons). Ten solo routines (6% of all routines) include a

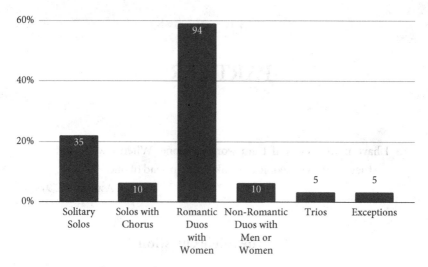

CHART 20 159 dances in the *Astaire dancing* corpus by participants

chorus: five times, all female; three times, all male; twice, mixed male and female. All but two of these solos with chorus are theatrical performances for in-film audiences using the conventions of a star backed by a chorus (a format Astaire used several times on Broadway). The two nontheatrical solos with chorus—"Bachelor Dinner Song" from *The Belle of New York* (1952) and the international playboy segment from *Daddy Long Legs* (1955)—alike feature Astaire interacting with a group of adoring females who respond to him by excessively buttressing his masculine prowess. In both of these insistently heterosexual numbers, the chorus women are presented as individuals who swoon in the very presence of Astaire—in *Daddy Long Legs*, in typical widescreen fashion, they literally fall to the floor. In such ways do the social implications of Astaire's dancing solos done in company with a chorus speak directly to his cis-het male identity. The two instances of Astaire dancing with multiple representations of himself complicate the solo-with-chorus category. The three huge shadows in "Bojangles of Harlem" (*Swing Time* [1936]) and the row of Astaire doubles in "Puttin' on the Ritz" (*Blue Skies* [1946]) alike recall his antagonistic relationship with the similarly attired men behind him in solos with male chorus such as "Top Hat, White Tie, and Tails" (*Top Hat* [1935]; he pantomimes killing them all) and the sailors in "I'd Rather Lead a Band" (*Follow the Fleet* [1936]; he tries to act the drill sergeant, they kick him in the rear). Three of these numbers present Astaire in direct conflict with other men—whether actual others or multiple projections of himself. ("Ritz" is the outlier; there's no tension between Astaire and his doubles.) The difference in "Bojangles" and "Ritz" is the evident fracturing of Astaire's extraordinary solitary self by way of special effects—and so I count these two as solitary solos. The ways in which Astaire attacks other men in groups is considered in Part Six.

A decided majority of Astaire's dances with others—ninety-four numbers (59% of this corpus)—involve a duo routine with a romantic female partner. In nearly two-thirds of his routines, Astaire dances as the male partner in a heterosexual couple. This normative relationship between two bodies of different genders in Astaire's dances finds contrast and context in his five (3%) trio dances, each done with one man and one woman, and his ten (6%) nonromantic duo dances with a male or female partner. Three of the nonromantic duos put Astaire's female partner in drag: "A Couple of Swells" (*Easter Parade* [1948]), "Oh, Them Dudes" (*Let's Dance* [1950]), and "Where Did You Get That Girl?" (*Three Little Words* [1950]) complicate the male-male duo category. One duo with a man stands out as utterly exceptional: "A Shine on Your Shoes" (*The Band Wagon* [1953]) pairs Astaire with a Black shoeshine man danced by nonprofessional dancer (and actual shoeshine man) Leroy Daniels. It is crucial to understand this number not as a solo but as a duo. The final section of this part analyzes "Shine on Your Shoes" against the norms of Astaire's dances with white male and white female partners.

Five remaining dances (3%) fit none of the above categories and are grouped together as exceptions: three large-cast routines in *You'll Never Get Rich* (1941) by Robert Alton (Astaire is never quite the soloist in any) and the outer sections of the dream ballet in *Yolanda and the Thief* (1945) by Eugene Loring (in his dances with the washerwomen and the bad crowd at the racetrack, Astaire is oddly, sometimes literally, displaced from the center or absent from the screen). Astaire yielded substantial creative control to Alton and Loring in these routines and these exceptional segments are more theirs than his. Indeed, some twelve years after *Yolanda*, Astaire remained aloof from Loring on the only other film they both worked on. A title card for *Silk Stockings* (1957)—the only one of its kind in all twenty-nine Astaire films—distinguishes choreography for Astaire's dances (by Pan) from "all other dances" (credited to Loring).

All of Astaire's relationships with partners were shaped by his original partner—his sister Adele. Being siblings, Fred and Adele did not present as a romantic couple. Their first vaudeville act was a bride-and-groom routine but they were so young it played as dress-up. Subsequent vaudeville routines were built around kids stuck indoors on a rainy day and, when they were a bit older, a topical medley called "New Songs and Smart Dances." As the Astaires' biographer Kathleen Riley describes these acts, in addition to their shared specialty dances Fred always did a dance solo, usually to a tune with a title referencing Black music and rhythm.[1] Adele did not tap and, as I write elsewhere, she apparently never absorbed Black syncopated style into her singing as Fred did around the crucial year 1924 (when the Astaires starred in *Lady, Be Good!*, a Broadway musical by the Gershwin brothers that opened a few months before the premiere of George Gershwin's jazz-for-the-concert-hall instrumental piece, *Rhapsody in Blue*).[2] The Gershwins' and Astaires' "similar career breakthroughs in 1924 mark the mainstreaming within white establishment culture of Black-infused syncopated musical performance by young white talents who enjoyed access to the concert hall and Broadway stage their black peers and models did not."[3] Fred and Adele always played siblings in their Broadway book shows, where each had a romantic partner with whom they typically did not dance. Partner dancing in an Astaire show meant Fred and Adele having fun together. Their numbers tended to be novelty routines ("Little Swiss Miss"), silly dress-up ("Hoops," "The Babbitt and the Bromide"), rhythm tunes ("Fascinating Rhythm," "White Heat"), and songs of family loyalty ("Hang On to Me"). Their crowd-pleasing signature closer—the "run around" ("shoulder to shoulder, Fred and Adele would jog, or rather lope, around the stage in a widening circle, with their arms extended as though they were grasping the handlebars of a bicycle—all the while looking purposeful in their imaginary journey and accompanied by an incessant 'oom-pah, oom-pah' beat. As the music quickened, so would the pace of their revolutions."[4])—communicated the pair's "nutty" quality and tilted toward Adele (her funny face sold the schtick). In his stage career, Astaire was accustomed to working with a partner but not a love interest. He had almost no experience making duo dances of romantic seduction when he created "Night and Day" for *Gay Divorce* (largely reproduced in the film adaptation). This de-emphasis on romance arguably set the foundation for Astaire's career as a romantic lead. As much of this part will show, Astaire's relationship to his female romantic partners often shades toward a parity that can be read alternately as a view of heterosexual partners as equals or as the woman in the couple acting as a man might. Adele—a very strong personality with whom Astaire could not play romance—likely lingers on whenever Astaire relates to his romantic female partners in a spirit of parity. The other foundational partner unseen in the films is Hermes Pan, a gay man with whom Astaire, in close and long collaboration, crafted his conception of heterosexual romance as a danced relationship (section forty-three considers Pan and Astaire).

40. "Two Equally Matched Individuals"

As noted in the introduction, critic Gregg Kilday argued in 1981 that Astaire successfully turned the European dandy type "straight." Tacitly assuming a robustly heterosexual national consciousness, Kilday continued, "To the American mind, of course, dandies were always slightly suspect, slightly sissy. If not actually homosexual (Oscar Wilde's sin), they were adolescently narcissistic." Successfully avoiding the charge of narcissism—tough to do when performing as a dancer for a mass audience—serves here as an index for Astaire's "straight" not "sissy" persona. In exchange, writes Kilday, "Astaire takes the dandy's self-obsession and turns it inside out, offering himself to his dancing partner as if two equally matched individuals is not just possible, but inevitable.... It hardly ever happens that way in real life, of course." In the classic Astaire-Rogers dances, Kilday says, "the attitude is never anything-you-can-do-I-can-do-better. Instead, each half of the couple ends up performing for the other's delight."[5]

In any dance, "two equally matched individuals" need to be appropriately matched in height. In romantic dances, a good match typically means the man is taller than the woman, although the difference between the pair matters much—it shouldn't be too great—and always shapes the choreographic possibilities. Book writer Betty Comden once noted that Astaire "always was unhappy about his dancing partners, always said they were too tall for him."[6] Eleanor Powell loved to retell the story of Astaire soberly assessing her height before agreeing to dance with her in *Broadway Melody of 1940*.[7] Easily quantified, height entails absolute and relative measures. Astaire was five foot nine. Full body framing in musicals prevented him from fudging his height as other male movie stars did and do. As a dancer, he was stuck with his given stature, which, he knew, would be instantly evident relative to his dancing partner and anyone near him on screen. Astaire danced duo routines with twenty-seven partners who received billing and one who did not (Leroy Daniels): twenty-two women, six men.[8] The average height of Astaire's partners—male and female—was five foot five; the average for only the women was five foot four.[9] Among the four white men he danced with, Bing Crosby and Gene Kelly were both two inches shorter than Astaire. George Murphy (five foot eleven) and Jack Buchanan (six foot two) were taller: Astaire dances with both in tails and top hats. In this very small group of five representative white Hollywood men, Astaire was of medium height. He was, though, considerably slighter than any. (In a 1953 profile, Astaire reported his weight as 138 pounds when not on a picture and 133 pounds when working on a film, adding, "On me those extra pounds are noticeable."[10]) The majority of Astaire's female partners were between five foot four and five foot seven. Those on the upper end—Cyd Charisse, Ann Miller, and Audrey Hepburn—tend to wear flats when dancing with Astaire, regardless of the dance style. Charisse wears low heels in the "Girl Hunt" bop joint—her red-sequined dress would seem to demand something other than flats. It's one of a handful of duo dances with a female partner where Astaire wears a hat the whole time—a choice surely baked into the choreography.[11] Hours staring at himself and Charisse in the rehearsal hall mirror would have constantly reminded Astaire of the height relationship between the pair (moderated in the bop joint via his hat; fig. 40.1). Women on the lower end of the height range could afford to wear heels when dancing with Astaire. Ginger Rogers (five foot four) always does. This decision not only makes her (faked) tap dancing more credible—unlike Vera-Ellen and Miller, who tap in ballet slippers—but also sets the expressive foundation for her style: Rogers moves like she does in part because she's in heels. Rogers's heels bring her to near-equal height with Astaire. Given the dynamic nature of their dancing bodies on screen, simply walking beside Rogers might make Astaire appear at or even under her height (fig. 40.2). The slightness of Astaire's frame and the consistent closeness in height with his female partners influences every duo dance he made. He could not cut the figure of a he-man. He does not frame

FIGURE 40.1

FIGURE 40.2

his female partners as a larger object around them but instead balances beside them. As noted, this balance opened the way toward an especially reciprocal sort of partner dancing that allowed for slippage of the heterosexual couple toward a kind of parity suggesting sibling comity or, depending on the dance moves, a fraternal relationship (one between two equal men). The content of his dances with women easily tilts toward content suitable for two men—this literally happens in his three partner routines with women in drag; indeed, those dances often include a sort of performed male-male relationship absent in Astaire's dances with male partners.

Astaire was constantly asked to compare his partners and he had a ready deflective quip to hand. As a *Los Angeles Times* reporter wrote in 1978: "He has ducked the question of his favorite partner or partners for decades—usually stopping the questioner cold with a dead-panned 'Gene Kelly' or 'Bob Hope' or 'Bing Crosby.' "[12] This stock retort from a very bad interview subject cleverly dodges professing a preference for any one woman—after all, a gentleman doesn't tell—but also tacitly buttresses Astaire's heterosexuality. No one, the joke assumes, would dream of misinterpreting Astaire's naming of male partners as evidence of gay desire or identity—even if he does waltz in closed ballroom position with Gene Kelly three times in their dance in *Ziegfeld Follies*. The allowances for men to dance with each other in the mid-twentieth century United States, especially in theatrical contexts, should be factored into any reading of these moments. Still, the comic "men's dancing class" for sailors, which Astaire leads in *Follow the Fleet*, attracted the attention of the US Navy, who communicated a desire for the scene to be cut through the Production Code office. Producer Pandro S. Berman replied directly to the Navy, assuring them the scene "as now written has all suggestive or effeminate dialogue or action removed."[13]

The remainder of this part explores in quantitative terms how Astaire's duo dances present "two equally matched individuals." Central to my method is a parsing of the relationship between Astaire's dancing body and that of his partner. The presenting gender of that partner is, of course, abidingly significant but also surprisingly fungible. The relative nearness in height between Astaire and his female partners—the woman typically only a few inches shorter than him—establishes the basis for a reciprocity that leans toward danced unisons, where both partners do the same steps. This is not, however, a gender-neutral dancing. Instead, Astaire and partner's characteristic tilt toward unison brings his female partners into a danced relationship with Astaire's straight manhood that casts *them* as surrogate straight men. A fair portion of the choreography he dances with women Astaire could have danced with men without compromising his presentation as straight. In a very few cases, Astaire does a double dance that could be done by two women—his infrequent edging toward an always also feminized exoticism is the key to these outliers. The distinction between couples (understood here as a heterosexual pair) and doubles (used here in vaudeville parlance for two performers of the same gender) is blurred in Astaire's duo dances. Slippage between these two categories of duo dance is constant across Astaire's output. (I use couples and doubles in this sense throughout.)

Two comparative metrics support my claims. First, I count the seconds of physical touching, including contact of any kind, between partners in each of ninety-six partner dances.[14] Expressed as a percentage of the total duration of the dance, this metric registers how Astaire and his partners' bodies interact within the gendered codes of Astaire's style—which is, itself, substantially made of borrowed moves from social dance and the vaudeville stage. Second, I analyze the content of each dance along a spectrum of six types of physical relationships between the partners—from supported partnering (such as lifts or dips) to contrasting movements (where each does different moves). Quantifying the amount of physical contact and types of relationship between partners' bodies allows for an understanding of Astaire's duo dances that does not rely on technical terms from any one dance tradition—not helpful in Astaire's case—but instead measures the visibly evident relationship between the partners. Both of these quantitative measures—the first objective, the second descriptive—turn on the question of leading, a matter that goes to the heart of traditional heterosexuality. Astaire was a leading man whose primary work, in duo dances with women, might be construed as actually, physically *leading*—as the man in partner-based Western social dancing did from the mid-nineteenth century to the mid-twentieth century. Astaire's status as a leading man who had to literally lead proves especially salient toward an understanding of gender roles and sexual identities in his work.

In a *Frank and Ernest* comic strip from 1982, cartoonist Bob Thaves famously offered a reading of Astaire through his most famous partner. Standing in front of the poster for a "Fred Astaire Film Festival," the eponymous title characters are told by a woman, "Sure he was great, but don't forget that Ginger Rogers did everything *he* did backwards and in high heels." This line—recycled by many as a comment on gender generally—misconstrues the specifics of Astaire's work on several levels. First, Astaire was responsible for creating dances; Rogers was not (although she reportedly contributed once she joined rehearsals with Astaire and Pan, a point when the dance was usually largely made). The differences in Astaire's and Rogers's respective pay and work time on a film (his preproduction weeks in rehearsal) reflected this difference in responsibility. Second, partner dancing in ballroom dancing style—a primary reference point for Astaire and Rogers—is centripetal, not directional. And while the male partner may start out stepping forward, soon enough he's stepping backward. Both partners cover the same ground in terms of forward and backward motion, their relationship more a matter of opposite and reciprocal motion. Third, Rogers's taps were dubbed by Pan. Her competence as a tapper is unknowable. She manifestly did not do "everything *he* did." Finally, a further substantive difference between Astaire and Rogers—beyond their footwear (and Rogers could wear heels only because she was five inches shorter than Astaire)—is that one leads while the other follows. However, this last generalization turns out to be not very helpful in describing the dances Astaire and Rogers—indeed, Astaire and any partner—did. The truth is more complicated and often neither partner is leading, a situation that throws into relief the complicated gender and sexual dynamics of Astaire's duo dances. Given that Astaire created his duo dances, his was generally the leading presence—he determined the moves (an understanding any informed viewer assumes to some extent). Astaire's creative voice behind his dances means an analysis of these dances can reveal the concrete content of *his* understanding of the relationship between two people—at least within the codes of a dance for two in a Hollywood musical film. And so, a pertinent question would be the relative frequency with which Rogers or any of Astaire's partners (male and female) are directly led by Astaire, are given the chance to take the lead themselves, or dance with him in a way that makes any sense of a leader moot.

Direct touching contact between partners takes many forms: from a full embrace to the formality of closed ballroom position to linking arms to holding hands. Averaged across the subcorpus of ninety-six duo dances, Astaire and partner are in direct physical contact with each other in some way 52% of the time. This number alone signals the significant extent—nearly half of the time—to which danced leads or relationships do not rely on physical contact. Breaking these numbers down by the performed gender of his partners reveals predictable and unexpected results. In the ten dances with men, with women dressed as men, or with female partners in nonromantic scenarios, Astaire and partner make physical contact just 13% of the time.[15] In the eighty-six romantic dances with women—where romance is part of the plot or tropes of romance are being performed within a theatrical number—Astaire touches his partner only 56% of the time. This surprisingly low percentage is a first indication of the extent to which Astaire's romantic duo dances project a kind of parity between partners belied by the partnering conventions of ballroom-style social dancing.

Touching while dancing was a mainstay of social dancing from the midnineteenth century on. Indeed, concerns about men and women touching cut to the heart of the controversies social dance periodically caused (at least until the 1960s). *The Story of Vernon and Irene Castle* (1939) dramatized this history without calling much attention to it—although the dances Astaire and Rogers did in that film are among the most conventional in their presentation of heterosexuality as defined by a man leading a woman. In 1965, Astaire was asked about the new social dances that did not call for any touching, such as the Twist. He remarked, "When two people are on a dance floor and they don't touch each other and are sometimes oblivious of each other, and when they walk around looking in opposite directions and are more concerned about themselves than with whom they are dancing—those dances aren't vulgar. I just think they're nuts."[16] Key to Astaire's critique is both the lack of touching as a constitutive aspect of a social dance and situations where dancing partners are apparently "oblivious of each other." In Astaire's duo dances, the partners are always aware of each other, even when not touching and even on the rare occasions when they are not doing coordinated movements. In short, an implicit agreement to dance together in a coordinated and reciprocal manner is implicit across Astaire's duo dances. This agreement is enacted in a variety of ways, each of which signals the nature and depth of the pair's relationship. By my analysis, Astaire employs six basic ways of physically relating to a partner. These six ways can be arranged along a spectrum from the most connected (supported partnering and closed ballroom position) to the least (double-act unison and contrasting movements) and perhaps understood to move from most to least stereotypically heterosexual. In fact, even the nonromantic dances include sections of closed ballroom position, and a slight majority of the romantic duos include sections of double-act dancing (where the partners face front, as on a stage, and do identical moves without touching). And while nonromantic duos involve less touching, the range of ways the partners touch is identical to that of romantic duos, if differently manifest. In other words, one set of descriptive categories is sufficient for all of Astaire's duos: couples and doubles alike employ all six types. No category is exclusive to the romantic or the nonromantic dances, suggesting that Astaire's representation of romantic love shades rather strongly into more equitable partnerships such as might obtain between two men (or two women). In a chapter on heterosexuality and dance in film musicals, Richard Dyer posits four sorts of physical relationships: "side by side, mirroring, mutually holding[,] or in relations of dependency." Working casually with these categories, Dyer qualifies somewhat any implications in the notion of leading: "As one watches a dance, it may be a bit heavy to insist too much on such gender differences, though there are occasions when his leading pressure can be quite marked."[17] My six categories are at once more specific than Dyer's and consistently point toward the importance of gender differences such as those coded in ballroom dancing, a style that is directly visible in Astaire's corpus. I also apply my categories to a corpus of nearly all of Astaire's duo dances in a consistent manner, lending this analysis a measure of precision.

In the next section, I describe each of the six types, with representative examples from across the Astaire corpus. After considering the six ways Astaire and his partners relate to each other, I further delineate Astaire's performance of masculinity and straightness by considering several groups of numbers that use similar partnering types or strategies—for instance, his dances with women that could have been done with men. Informing all these categories is the underlying gender ideology of compulsory heterosexuality—which proscribes a restrained but confident leading role to men and a decorative and submissive following role to women. Astaire's duo dances regularly subvert this ideology even if, of course, they also reinscribe it again and again—particularly in the sensuous contrast between a man in a conventional and impersonal all-black tuxedo or tails and a woman in an elaborate, highly individual (cut to her frame), physically revealing evening gown. Indeed, costuming is a powerful initial indicator of a given dance's gender ideology: when the woman wears pants (as happens on seven occasions: the three drag numbers and four with Rogers sporting trousers, a fashion-forward trend in the 1930s), the dance tends toward parity—with the caveat that any implications of equality occur on male, or androcentric, terms.

41. Six Positions for Doubles and Couples

Supported partnering

Supported partnering locks the couple into a single physical unit. Their weight is shared and the moves they do are unimaginable without each other. The whole that is the pair becomes an inseparable sum of its parts. In supported partnering moves, Astaire usually works as ballast or gives a supportive boost. Ballroom moves such as deep dips and brief turning lifts or kicks, common in Astaire's dances, require a complete transfer of the woman's weight to the man, even if only for a moment. By contrast, ballet moves such as a supported arabesque by the woman or framed turns are exceedingly rare (see "Something's Gotta Give" in *Daddy Long Legs* for an instance of the former).

Supported partnering occurs in only 42% of romantic partner routines. In more than a few of these, the type manifests in a single deep dip (*The Castles'* "Tango" and "They Can't Take That Away" in *The Barkleys of Broadway* [1949]) or a few modest turning lifts ("My One and Only Highland Fling" [*Barkleys*] and "Sluefoot" [*Daddy Long Legs*]). There are only two lifts where Astaire holds his partner in the air for a sustained amount of time, both from the late 1930s: the first in the slow-motion "I Used to Be Color Blind" (*Carefree* [1938], fig. 41.1), the second at the close of "The Last Waltz" (*The Castles*). More normative is a simple leaning pose or assists that cast the partner briefly into the air, as in the eight identical lifts at the climax of "The Yam" (*Carefree*, fig. 41.2), where Astaire rests one leg on a table and launches Rogers over it (he reprised the move with Vera-Ellen in "Mr. and Mrs. Hoofer at Home" [*Three Little Words*]). A rarity for Astaire and mostly the work of choreographer Michael Kidd, the subway dance in "Girl Hunt" (*Band Wagon*) unfolds as a sequence of supported, often quite sexy poses,

FIGURE 41.1

FIGURE 41.2

moved through in sensual slow motion with violent interjections by the gangsters flipping, shooting, and falling dead in the background (fig. 41.3). Charisse as partner in "Girl Hunt"—and the hard-boiled mise en scène of the larger routine—makes the difference. A short passage in the bad crowd section of the *Yolanda* dream ballet has Astaire supporting Lucille Bremer in an analogous series of poses, none of which could be called sexy. Indeed, in practice each of the six partnering types is inflected by the expressive possibilities a given partner brings to Astaire's rather fixed, typically solicitous and attentive persona.

Only one example of supportive partnering occurs in the nonromantic dances. In "Oh, Them Dudes" (*Let's Dance*), Betty Hutton and Astaire, playing cowboys in a saloon, get progressively drunker. Well into the dance, Astaire collapses face down on the floor. Hutton tries to no avail to hoist him up by his belt. And so, she crawls under him and raises him into the air on her back (fig. 41.4). She spins and Astaire goes crashing to the floor. This truly weird and potentially injurious moment—Astaire lands hard on one arm—typifies both

FIGURE 41.3

FIGURE 41.4

the violence of many of Astaire's dances with men and the special license for extreme acts provided by a dance for Astaire and a woman dressed as a man.

Closed ballroom position

Closed ballroom position has the partners face each other with the man's right arm around the woman's back (resting somewhere between her shoulder blade and waist) and her left hand resting on his shoulder. The man's left and the woman's right arms are held up and to the side with hands clasped. This position, with the frame of the arms more or less rigid, visually signals social dances such as the waltz and fox trot. Both terms—*closed* and *ballroom*—are important. The latter connects this relationship with Western European social dancing and the upper- and middle-class etiquette of the ballroom or cotillion. This highly formal pose, conceived with stiff but cushioned arms that keep the couple safely separate if dangerously proximate, was adapted in later less respectable and more flexible styles, such as swing, but remains a visual referent to an entire regime of gender relations built on a patriarchal and heterosexual base. The word *closed* indicates how this physical relationship locks the couple into a unit that moves as one, with a shared center of gravity and momentum. The moves that can be done in closed ballroom position require closely coordinated motion together as a four-legged unit.

Closed ballroom position occurs in four out of five romantic dances. However, only one dance—*The Castles*' thirty-six-second demonstration of the polka—uses it exclusively. Otherwise, closed ballroom position is used with other types. Several dances are primarily in closed ballroom position. "You're Easy to Dance With" (*Holiday Inn* [1942]) remains mostly in closed ballroom position, perhaps because Astaire's partner, Virginia Dale, was not that skilled or, alternately, due to the novel choice to have Astaire sing while dancing throughout the number (fig. 41.5). The effect is one of constraint and constant illustration of Berlin's lyric—this relatively easy dance routine retains for much of its length a stereotypical dance position, with dance here meaning social dance as done by adults (not the more explosive and athletic swing style of youth of the early 1940s—a different, more difficult routine that relates to the lyric ironically can be imagined). Other numbers with sustained use of closed ballroom position point toward the challenges and advantages of this type. "I Used to Be Color Blind" in *Carefree* reveals, in slow motion, the delicate coordination between partners the position demands. Astaire and Rogers's respective calculations of each other and the space they move through are evident in their faces and the minute adjustments and hesitations of their bodies. The title number in "Funny Face" (1957) is danced almost entirely in closed ballroom position, a choice that fits the very tight space in the darkroom set—likely the smallest dance setting Astaire faced. Nearly half of "Open Your Eyes" in *Royal Wedding* (1951) is danced in closed ballroom position, a choice that keeps Astaire and Jane Powell, playing brother and sister, at an appropriately

FIGURE 41.5

formal distance where they can enact utterly conventional gender roles. Then, when high seas begin to tilt the dance floor, the pair can hang on to each other. Closed position, an inherently conservative relationship, can be activated by the music. Astaire and Rogers pop into closed ballroom position when a waltz begins in "I'm Putting All My Eggs in One Basket" (*Follow the Fleet*)—the only time they touch in this combative number. Astaire and Gene Kelly behave similarly in "The Babbitt and the Bromide" (*Ziegfeld Follies* [1946], fig. 41.6). Three times the waltz sends them into each other's arms—Astaire takes the female (following) position all three times; each passage in closed ballroom hold is brief, often because the music changes, shifting out of triple meter. (By contrast, in "A Couple of Song and Dance Men" (*Blue Skies*) Astaire and Crosby do not fall into closed ballroom position when the music goes into triple meter. Instead, Astaire awkwardly takes hold of Crosby from behind by an arm and a leg [fig. 41.7]. More on Crosby's not quite dancing in section forty-five.)

FIGURE 41.6

FIGURE 41.7

Flexible holds

Closed ballroom position, as the name would suggest, locks the dancers into ballroom dance moves and motion. It was far too restrictive to support Astaire's flexible approach to duo dancing. And while Fred and Adele likely took up closed ballroom position on occasion, it could not have been the mainstay for a sibling duo oriented toward humor, intricate steps, and novelty effects. And so, a range of other holds, freer and more open to variation but still involving physical touching and leading, must have marked the Astaires' dancing. This flexible approach proves the center point of Astaire's duo dance style, especially in the romantic dances. Most flexible holds involve one point of contact, instead of the closed ballroom position's two, allowing for more dynamic, less linked movement but keeping the pair within arm's length at least (a boon to keeping them within the Vitruvian frame). Hand holds with the same hands (bodies facing) or opposite hands (bodies facing or side by side; fig. 41.8 from "Babbitt") increase the distance between partners and permit larger gestures and steps. Swing dancing, which came to prominence during Astaire and Rogers's heyday, reveled in such moves, although relatively few of Astaire's dances are in the elastic swing style (see, especially, "Can't Stop Talkin'" [*Let's Dance*]). Side by side with one arm around each other's backs or waists recurs often and makes for a tight unit that permits facial interaction that's visible to the camera, open as this position is to one side (fig. 41.9 from the finale to *You Were Never Lovelier*). Releasing either side of closed ballroom position easily transitions to most of these flexible holds. Dance scholar Beth Genné describes these holds: "Astaire used many creative variants of the unclasped-locket hold ... keeping the couple from being locked into a face-to-face position."[18]

FIGURE 41.8

FIGURE 41.9

Another flexible hold option incorporates moments of not touching understood to be part of a larger touching combination. I use the term *touch and release* for such passages. Here the dynamism of the couple in any of the aforementioned closed or open holds is increased by an occasional separation that leads toward a return to touching. The clapping pattern in "Coffee Time" (*Yolanda*) forces Astaire and Bremer to constantly release and then find each other again. The climax of "Never Gonna Dance" (*Swing Time*) uses an especially brilliant spinning touch-and-release combination. Making a larger circle, Astaire spins with Rogers in closed ballroom position—taking advantage of the centripetal force such movement creates—and then he lets her go (she keeps spinning) and catches her some steps later, repeating the combination several times (figs. 41.10.a through 41.10.f). Touch and release speaks to a very high order of coordination between the dancers. Letting his partner go, Astaire must be there to meet her: she must also be at the appointed spot, ready to reconnect.

Two lyrical dances from Astaire's third period are composed almost solely of flexible hold combinations. "They Can't Take That Away from Me" is a lyrical study in flexible holds—one dip and a brief moment of closed ballroom position are all that interrupt the flow of touch and go. This, of course, matches the moment in *Barkleys* quite well, with Josh and Dinah not quite ready to reconcile. The dance is situated narratively as a routine for which the Barkleys are famous. The frisson of the performance in the film's plot comes from their reperformance of married lovers' passion during a still-unresolved marital crisis. Constant touch and release and all kinds of open holds speak to both the virtuosity of their union and the fragility of this moment in their marriage. "Dancing in the Dark" (*Band Wagon*) presents another study in flexible holds. After some individual exploratory moves,

FIGURE 41.10

Astaire and Charisse face each other and, for the first twenty-six seconds after the beat begins, mirror each other without touching (a type discussed next). Once first contact is made—Astaire's hand on Charisse's waist—the remainder of the dance flows in and out of side-by-side and facing positions with the partners lightly touching and only ever briefly releasing each other. Two meaningful interruptions to the freely unfolding, almost always physically led partnership occur. They do not touch for several seconds just before Astaire, in the third and largest of such moves, pulls Charisse up to a fully extended position atop a park bench. This visual climax, matched in the swelling music, is enhanced by the in-context lengthy separation between the dancers' bodies before it.[19] The other interruption in the dance's string of flexible holds comes just after the cut that positions the pair to move up the steps to the waiting carriage. They dance up the steps separately, the only such unison dancing in "Dancing in the Dark."

One form of flexible hold is common in male-male dances: walking or dancing arm in arm. Kelly and Astaire do so during some of the biggest dancing moves in "Babbitt," as do Garland and Astaire in *Easter Parade*'s "When the Midnight Choo-Choo"—a number that could easily be done by two men (figs. 41.11 and 41.12). In a potentially more subversive example from *Band Wagon*, Astaire and Jack Buchanan, after alike failing to stick a hat trick and tossing away their canes, stroll arm in arm out of "I Guess I'll Have to Change My Plan" (fig. 41.13). A queer reading of the lyric—is the change in the plan a decision for these two men to choose each other?—finds support in Buchanan's ambivalent sexuality. He has no love interest in the film beyond his extravagant passion for the theater. Review cards from the *Band Wagon* preview

FIGURE 41.11

FIGURE 41.12

point toward several ways to read him in relation to Astaire. Policing the latent sexual content of the film and fingering his portrayal as gay, one woman wrote, "BUCHANAN IS OBVIOUSLY EFFEMINATE." A man, who praised the film as "PEPPY AND ENTERTAINING," commented, "ESPECIALLY ENJOYED THE DIFFERENT TWIST WITH MR. BUCHANAN. FRED ASTAIRE HAS FINALLY FOUND A SUITABLE PARTNER!"[20] Strolling off arm in arm with Buchanan—who was five inches taller than him—surely frames the pair, for some moviegoers, as a couple. Astaire was normally surrounded by obviously queer supporting male characters who, by comparison, enhanced his normative masculinity (casting Astaire as the most "normal" in the group). Buchanan, the only such figure Astaire dances with, plays that role but, in this double act, he and Astaire also do identical steps. The potentially subversive nature of men touching while dancing together comes to the fore here. But it's all about context and facial expression. "My One and Only Highland Fling" (*Barkleys*), with almost entirely side-by-side unison dancing, is situated as romance by having Rogers eagerly take Astaire's arm for much of the dance in a spirit of adoration (fig. 41.14). She looks toward him with ardor throughout

FIGURE 41.13

FIGURE 41.14

and even kisses him on the cheek to cap a phrase: evidence for the strong if humorously tamped-down heterosexual current flowing through this dance.

Mirroring

If Astaire and partner are touching on average 52% of the time, what of the 48% when they are not? Three partnering types that involve no touching account for this time space. One of these types—contrasting movements—is self-explanatory. The other two are crucial to Astaire's duo dances: both involve finely coordinated movements and no evident leading by anyone. How can this relationship between two partners be explained? Some such moments are obviously rehearsed and part of a performance. We expect professionals to set and practice their steps and to work together with precision—this is the essence of the vaudeville double act, when two performers do the same steps in unison while facing forward (the type discussed next). But if the two members of a double act face each other, the narrative changes—especially in routines that are not diegetic rehearsals or performances. When two people who are not both dancers by trade (the case in 28% of Astaire's duos) manage to anticipate each other's movements perfectly, something quasi-mystical is being claimed about their relationship. The subtext is, of course, perfect and/or spontaneous compatibility. But it also suggests parity: no one is leading, both are following, or, perhaps, both are intuiting the other's movements or the pair is suddenly greater than the sum of its two parts *without* those parts being in any way connected (as supported partnering and closed ballroom position require).

The first such moment of romantic telepathy comes in "Night and Day" (*The Gay Divorcee* [1934]), a dance adapted from the stage. Most of the number unfolds with Astaire literally pulling Rogers into the dance, grabbing her hand, holding her in closed ballroom position, and spinning her out and in. But for a curious twenty-seven seconds, Rogers and Astaire detach. She doesn't run away and the pair dance the same steps facing each other (fig. 41.15). Astaire looks intently at Rogers, but she just looks down, lost in her own romantic reverie. This moment is fleeting but crucial: in a dance about resistance—she tries to leave multiple times—Rogers engages with Astaire without being held. And the steps they do together speak of a deep coordination of desires and body knowledge. They even move up and down the semicircular steps to the back, a moment framed in the novelty

FIGURE 41.15

FIGURE 41.16

shot from under a table discussed in the previous part. One way to read this moment in "Night and Day" is as Astaire exerting a kind of Svengali effect: his lead is so potent it can be sustained in the absence of touch. But the parity of their stances suggests otherwise. Indeed, Astaire as touchless mesmerizing lead is made explicit in only two numbers—as the keynote to "Change Partners" in *Carefree* (fig. 41.16) and briefly during the "Guardian Angel" dream sequence in *Daddy Long Legs*. In the former, Astaire, in the role of a psychiatrist, has literally hypnotized Rogers. He moves her about the patio space and directs her completely. Throughout the dance, Rogers's normally expressive face is completely shut down—one reason this dance comes off as cold and, within current gender politics, positively disturbing. But Astaire as Svengali proves a rare pose. It is altogether more common for Astaire and a female partner to face each other and dance the same steps, mirroring each other without touching, positing a unity of mind and body, a perfect reciprocity. It need not be romantic and appears in over half of the nonromantic duos.

Double act

Of course, the most common explanation for unison nontouch dancing is professional: performers offer polished performances in perfect synchronization with each other. The standard stance for such presentational dances is side by side (about one arm's length apart) facing front—an ideal arrangement for Vitruvian framing in Academy. Astaire and Hayworth's one-shot "Rehearsal Dance" at the start of *You'll Never Get Rich* (fig. 41.17)—framed as Astaire checking to see if Hayworth knows the steps—remains entirely in this stance. This type—here called *double act*—builds directly on vaudeville. Curiously, it does not seem to be typical of Fred and Adele's act: she did not tap.

Double acts are all about unison, and so pronounced differences in double-act dancing can offer insight into the individuals in the pair. In "Can't Stop Talking"—their first dance together in *Let's Dance* and the first to be filmed—Astaire and Betty Hutton express their arms very differently: Hutton, very large and extended; Astaire, small and casual (fig. 41.18). "Can't Stop

FIGURE 41.17

FIGURE 41.18

Talking" is the most athletic and extreme swing-style routine Astaire did. Hutton, a mainstay of Second World War swing culture—recreated here for a scene set in the recent past—expresses the style with maximum verve, while Astaire adopts a less extroverted energy. By the next duo number made and in the film, "Oh, Them Dudes," Astaire proves able to match Hutton's physical abandon, albeit in a hypermasculine drunk cowboy role (which lets him let his hair down). Attention to double-act relationships can reveal palpable similarities as well. Partners who could "match" Astaire—taking his style and skills as a kind of standard—often excel in double-act routines. "Where Did You Get That Girl?" with Vera-Ellen, both in tuxes, proves a study in closely matched style, with just the smallest added expression in Vera-Ellen's shoulders and head (fig. 41.19). This dance for two dancers in tails could go several ways: two men, two women dressed as men (the queer potential of the lyric is ripe), or as done by Astaire and Vera-Ellen. And double-act numbers come in several expressive varieties: the driving tap of "Please Don't Monkey with Broadway" (*Broadway Melody*, fig. 41.20) or the relaxed quasi-soft shoe of "I Guess I Have to Change My Plan"—each done in white tie

FIGURE 41.19

FIGURE 41.20

and tails with a different male partner: the frenetic George Murphy and delicate Jack Buchanan, respectively. Astaire dials up or down to match both. Notable is Astaire's commitment to unison in all these dances. By contrast, the Nicholas Brothers, an actual double act, take solo turns in most all their dances—always in a spirit of pride in the other's skills. Astaire's double-act routines remain locked in continuous shared motion, except for the development of nondanced aggression (see "Please Don't Monkey with Broadway" and "Babbitt" as discussed in section forty-seven).

A recurring sort of double-act dancing adapts the unison side-by-side position to highly romantic contexts. It happens first in "Cheek to Cheek" (*Top Hat*). On the first time through the song's "B" phrase—"Oh, I love to climb a mountain..."—Astaire and Rogers do some easy double-act tap to a considerable lightening of the texture (foot sounds are added). The moment is potentially confusing—are they performing and for whom?—but can be read as evidence for an ability to speak on equal terms established in their earlier duo dance, "Isn't This a Lovely Day?" And, in any event, on the repeat of the "B" phrase they fall back into closed ballroom position. When the extravagant "C" phrase—beginning with the lyric "Dance with me"—bursts forth, Astaire and Rogers, now without foot sounds, perform a unison side-by-side combination of very large moves, covering much ground with full arm and leg extensions. Such bravura bursts of nontap, traveling, and extended double-act relations also occur in "Never Gonna Dance" (fig. 41.21), "They Can't Take That Away from Me," "Let's Face the Music and Dance" (*Follow the Fleet*), "Smoke Gets in Your Eyes" (*Roberta* [1935]), "My Shining Hour" (*The Sky's the Limit* [1943], and Astaire's duo with Harriet Hoctor in *Shall We Dance* (1937, fig. 41.22). All these dances are of a quasi-serious romantic nature, with the woman in an elaborate gown and a tone of high stylization.

FIGURE 41.21

FIGURE 41.22

FIGURE 41.23

These couples achieve a kind of virtuoso lovemaking while dancing by briefly separating so as to execute elaborate double-act unison steps. The standout feature of "Cheek to Cheek" is the dance's easy transition between the casual camaraderie of egalitarian double-act tap and the high romance of bravura side-by-side display.

Double-act relationships, whatever the style, invariably set constraints on the dance. Ostensibly, a double-act routine might be done by one dancer—a single—but double-act routines tend to be limited by the relatively less room in the frame to move around, often yielding a kind of in-place dancing that privileges tap. For this reason, mostly in-place double-act tap is a great fit for Academy aperture. The position works less well in widescreen where each dancer needs to be as large in their movements as possible. "Stereophonic Sound" (*Silk Stockings*) is a catalog of crazy attempts to fill the excess space even a double act can't easily use—including laying full out on the floor (fig. 41.23). Of note with double-act relations is the dancers doing the same routine on the same foot. Their moves are identical in this way as well. This is *not* the case when Astaire and Caron do their featured sections in double-act positions in "Sluefoot," one small indication that this number is always conceived as a couple's dance. Indeed, they slip in and out of one-touch holds throughout.

Contrasting moves

Only fifteen dances in the duo dance corpus include moments when the partners do radically different and uncoordinated moves. This was a rare choice. Four of these involve the woman in the couple resisting Astaire's desire to dance with her ("Night and Day," "Never Gonna Dance," "All of You" [*Silk Stockings*], "It Only Happens When I Dance with You" in Ann Miller's apartment [*Easter Parade*]). Such moments, always fleeting, cast Astaire as the insistent male seeking physical contact with a woman. In "It Only Happens When I Dance with You," the need for the female to cooperate with the male's touching lead is emphasized repeatedly: Miller stops dancing the moment Astaire stops touching her. The cooperation required for partner dancing is just not there without physical leading. In these moments, Astaire and partner enact standard narratives of men wanting sex and women resisting.

The nonromantic duo "Clap Yo' Hands" (*Funny Face*) for Astaire and Kay Thompson features consistently different moves for both. Only in the soft shoe patter section—a double-act reference to vaudeville complete with corny jokes—do they do the same thing for a sustained stretch of time. Instead, Thompson holds forth (and sings) throughout while Astaire, dancing with a guitar, frenetically serves as a sort of backup dancer. "Clap Yo' Hands" is a deeply strange number explicable in part by the huge contrast in style between the two performers. A similar mismatch informs the vocal duet for Astaire and belter Ethel Merman on a 1966 episode of the television variety show *The Hollywood Palace*. In both of these, Astaire's default modesty—the subtlety of his overall aesthetic—comes in for kidding due to his unusual pairing with a very strong woman with an over-the-top style.

Brief passages of a lack of coordination between partners frequently serve as a source of comedy. Astaire has two frenetic fits in "How Could You Believe Me..." (*Royal Wedding*) activated by violent collisions with Jane Powell, who stops his leaping about by embracing him in a spirit of just wanting to stop the craziness. In similar moments of release, Astaire makes several comic mistakes and does a crazy solo in "Sluefoot"—indications of a youthful spirit in this fifty-something man crashing a college dance. Lack of coordination can also signal incompetence (Garland's many failures to follow or release in "Beautiful Faces" [*Easter Parade*]), concern over marital fidelity (in "Mr. and Mrs. Hoofer at Home," Astaire takes a phone call while seated and taps along to the exotic rhythm in the musical score—perhaps suggesting another woman on the line; Vera-Ellen looks on with concern and executes contrasting poses), or dogged persistence on the part of only one of the pair (Astaire ends "I Can't Tell a Lie" [*Holiday Inn*] doing deep trenches while Marjorie Reynolds, in an eighteenth-century gown, looks on in dismay).

One number uses uncoordinated moves as a persistent theme. "I'm Putting All My Eggs in One Basket" is the exception that proves the rule. Astaire and Rogers are out of sync more often than not in this number—Pan called it "a comedy routine"—which poses the question of what happens when a double act breaks down: the apparent answer is that fighting ensues.[21] In an always uncomfortable moment, Astaire releases Rogers during a flexible hold and lets her fall painfully to the floor. He keeps on dancing; Rogers remains sitting, in an amazingly unfeminine position, and stares forward (fig. 41.24). In a similar moment in "Babbitt," Astaire and Kelly are holding hands in a swing-style move when Astaire lets Kelly fall to the floor (fig. 41.25). An

FIGURE 41.24

FIGURE 41.25

underlying hint of rudeness in Astaire's persona is evident in both numbers: the first of which could be done by two men, the second of which uses several touching holds that might be thought only appropriate for a male-female couple. The continuity of Astaire's identity when doing a double or a couple dance is evident here in his willingness to let any partner fall.

42. Change Partners?

Hyper-heterosexual dances

Duos with no double-act-type dancing remain committed throughout to a heterosexual hierarchy even if they incorporate no-touch mirroring, which works in this context as a signal of romantic compatibility. *Top Hat*'s "The Piccolino" (61% touching) offers an especially normalized version of heterosexual romance. Astaire and Rogers begin at their table to the edge of the dance floor—they are a couple there as well. They move in closed position to the center of the concentric circles painted on the dance floor. The one-shot dance that follows moves easily along the spectrum from closed ballroom position to no-touch mirroring. The couple is always turned toward each other, the dance's centripetal construction echoed by the circles on the floor. With no supported partnering moves and near-constant motion, "The Piccolino" presents a fantasy of compatible modern straight love without the drama of dips and lifts or the outward-facing equality of double-act presentation. Astaire and Rogers remain absorbed in each other throughout and even dance together back to their table, where the perfect reciprocity of their love can be assumed to continue. This comparatively modest routine, in particular among the thirty-five Astaire and Rogers did together, posits the pair as a somewhat reasonable model for straight dancing couples in real life. *Swing Time*'s "Waltz in Swing Time" (71% touching) and *You Were Never Lovelier*'s "I'm Old-Fashioned" (73% touching) remain within a similarly limited spectrum of types, although the former is clearly also a virtuoso display of sheer skill.

"Something's Gotta Give" explores the power of a touching lead as a means for a man to claim a woman's body. This dance presents a hyperfeminine young woman being seduced by an ultra-dapper and very rich man a generation or two her elder. Astaire and Caron move through straightforward ballroom dance moves that a relatively skilled couple might easily copy that feature Caron more than Astaire. Early on, Astaire releases his touching lead at the end of a phrase. The pair face each other and Astaire reaches out with intention to reclaim Caron's hand, a move registered across both dancers' bodies—at this moment, Astaire's much older leading man effectively claims Caron's coed ingénue (fig. 42.1). For all his style and later-life bachelorhood—perhaps indications of a not-so-straight figure—this guy wants this girl (one reason my undergraduate students usually find *Daddy Long Legs* creepy). The dance that follows plays with the pair getting very close then suddenly pulling away from each other only to be pulled back, by way of no-touch mirroring steps, into touching proximity (often a tight ballroom hold). Widescreen allows for repeated expression of this tension in spatial terms not possible in Academy (they can get objectively farther away from each other in the wider format and still remain in Vitruvian framing; fig. 42.2). In the similar May-December narrative of *Funny Face*, Astaire directs Audrey Hepburn by hand through almost every second of "He Loves

FIGURE 42.1

FIGURE 42.2

and She Loves." The romantic fantasy of the number, expressed in the combination of location shooting by a French castle and nonrealistic cutting of the space, is further buttressed by the extravagance of the couple's touch-and-release combinations and selected supported partnering moves, including (as noted earlier) deep dips that exploit widescreen.

All of these hyper-romantic dances lack the equality inherent in double-act positions and foreground the heterosexual codes inherent in both the social signals of closed ballroom position and the more specific expressive interplay of desire felt between a man and a woman allowed for by flexible holds. Touch—and the frisson of release that leads to more touching—remains constant throughout.

Almost-no-touch dances

On the opposite end of the spectrum, dances with female partners that involve little to no touching open the possibility of Astaire doing the routine with a man instead of a woman. The lack of heterosexual hierarchy or romantic scripts attached to specific holds, such as closed ballroom, suggests parity and possible gender reassignment. Table 7 lists the twenty duo dances with 20% or less touching.[22] The two nonromantic numbers with female partners—"Stereophonic Sound" and "Clap Yo' Hands"—and four duos with a male partner make this list, although it's noteworthy that "The Babbitt and the Bromide" (20% touching) just barely makes the cut. ("A Shine on Your Shoes" has a lot of touching—Daniels literally shines Astaire's shoes; the two are in constant if deeply hierarchal contact.) Two of the three dances with women in drag appear here as well. "Oh, Them Dudes" is, again, an outlier with a degree of contact that's quite unusual, suggesting that Astaire could do things with women dressed as men he didn't do with male partners.

This leaves twelve duos with women that do not involve substantial or *any* touching contact. Some of these have already been considered: the "Guardian Angel" dream with Caron (Astaire as Svengali), the "Rehearsal Duet" with Hayworth (a double-act test), and "I'm Putting All My Eggs in One Basket" (a comedy of contrasting movements). The latter two of these could easily be done with a male partner. Most of the remainder are also candidates for male-male pairings. "Ragtime Violin" offers a precursor to the similar vaudeville routine "Fit as a Fiddle" in *Singin' in the Rain*, danced by Gene Kelly and Donald O'Connor, with friendly male contact such as one riding piggyback

TABLE 7 Dances with 20% or less touching between partners (as % of total dance duration)

Number	Partner	Touching (as % of Total Duration)
"Begin the Beguine" (swing version, *BM40*)	E. Powell	0%
"Ragtime Violin" (*EP*)	Garland	0%
"A Lot in Common with You" (*STL*)	Leslie	0%
"Rehearsal Duet" (*YNGR*)	Hayworth	0%
"Clap Yo' Hands" (*FF*)	Thompson	0%
"Where Did You Get That Girl?" (*TLW*)	Vera-Ellen	4%
"I Guess I'll Have to Change My Plan" (*BW*)	Buchanan	5%
Guardian Angel Dream Ballet (*DLL*)	Caron	6%
"A Couple of Swells" (*EP*)	Garland	6%
"How Could You Believe Me…" (*RW*)	J. Powell	6%
"A Couple of Song and Dance Men" (*BS*)	Crosby	7%
"Stereophonic Sound" (*SS*)	Paige	7%
"I Won't Dance" (duo version, *R*)	Rogers	8%
"I'm Putting All My Eggs in One Basket" (*FTF*)	Rogers	8%
"Isn't This a Lovely Day?" (*TH*)	Rogers	11%
"I Left My Hat in Haiti" (duo section, *RW*)	J. Powell	13%
"Please Don't Monkey with Broadway" (*BM40*)	Murphy	14%
"They All Laughed" (*SWD*)	Rogers	17%
"When the Midnight Choo-Choo Leaves for Alabam" (*EP*)	Garland	18%
"The Babbitt and the Bromide" (*ZF*)	Kelly	20%

on the other. The soldier's canteen number, "A Lot in Common with You," for Astaire and Joan Leslie has no gendered content. Indeed, a jump Leslie does over Astaire is repeated verbatim with Astaire leaping over Leslie. The theme here is not shared romance but an absolute similarity of sensibility, a common-ness expressed in exuberant double-act tap. Two other diegetic numbers with women repeat this approach: "When the Midnight Choo-Choo" (with Garland) and the swing tap section of "Begin the Beguine" (with Eleanor Powell). In the former, touching contact between partners is in masculine modes—arm in arm and arms on shoulders from behind (for a train effect). In the latter, Astaire and Powell match each other step for step and never touch.

Insights from the aforementioned two numbers can be expanded to locate Judy Garland and Eleanor Powell within a subset of Astaire's female partners more generally. Table 8 shows the average percent of touching per number, ranked lowest to highest, for the eight women with whom Astaire danced four or more routines. Garland and Eleanor Powell, both of whom made only one film with Astaire, rank extremely low in absolute and relative terms. What about these two partners discouraged dances that involved touching? Garland's failure at touching leads is shown for comic and character effect in "Beautiful Faces," her first vaudeville routine with Astaire in which he has coached her to be like his former partner, the hyperfeminine Ann Miller. Of course, the real presence informing "Beautiful Faces" is Rogers—the feathers on Garland's unattractive gown, which end up strewn all over the floor, reference an oft-told anecdote about Rogers's dress for "Cheek to Cheek." The joke in "Beautiful Faces" is Garland's serial inability to manage any sort of touching type of partner dancing. Her failure at touch and release is particularly acute: she neither releases nor reconnects as needed. But such partnering is not Garland's natural skill—as she tells Astaire, with an edge in her voice, "You told me to move like that." Instead, she's better at double-act styles, especially as seen to great success in "A Couple of Swells," an iconic number Garland recreated step for step on television (without Astaire) in 1964. The key transition toward equitable double-act partnering in *Easter Parade* kicks off the vaudeville medley, which ends with the decidedly male-male

TABLE 8 Partners dancing four or more routines with Astaire (in increasing order of average touching contact per routine)

	Average % Touching Contact / Routine	# Routines	# Films	Total Duration of Dances with Astaire (Hours: Minutes: Seconds)
Eleanor Powell	26%	4	1	0:11:13
Judy Garland	28%	5	1	0:08:30
Jane Powell	46%	4	1	0:10:51
Lucille Bremer	50%	4	2	0:22:13
Rita Hayworth	51%	5	2	0:11:17
Cyd Charisse	54%	6	2	0:14:33
Vera-Ellen	57%	9	2	0:21:29
Ginger Rogers	60%	35	10	1:13:45

"When the Midnight Choo-Choo" discussed previously. The medley begins in Astaire's apartment with "I Love a Piano," a rhythm tune Garland belts out to Astaire's great pleasure. When the dance begins, they stand side by side—double-act style—and start a unison routine while holding hands. The love plot of the film, expressed in their performed relationship, is cemented here—and in the spinning hug that transitions so beautifully into their first on-stage number. Holding hands in double-act position—something two straight men wouldn't do—subtly marks the dance and the Astaire-Garland couple as sufficiently romantic, even though none of the dances that follow in the film will take their danced romance any further. There's just enough touching in the double-act-style "I Love a Piano" to secure *her* femininity relative to Astaire, since she never does a successful conventionally feminine dance.

Astaire's partnership with Eleanor Powell proves completely different—even though, as with Garland, Powell and Astaire touch each other very little in their dances. Powell and Astaire's partnership was understood as something of a summit of the greatest Hollywood dancers of the moment: this distinction, alone, signals the whiteness of their teaming—the promo line should more accurately be the top two white tap dancers. As Astaire said of Powell in 1973, "She dances like a man, anyway she did then, suppose she still does."[23] In *Steps in Time*, Astaire was a bit more specific in how Powell danced "like a man," and in the process connected noisiness to masculinity: "She put 'em down like a man, no ricky-ticky-sissy stuff with Ellie."[24] Powell herself repeated the line to Joseph McBride in 1981, with a caveat: "I dance so close to the floor, that I'm really very masculine, masculine in my work.... I'm feminine really, but my dancing is so strong."[25] So it should come as no surprise that foot sounds are heard for almost the entirety of their over eleven minutes of dancing together in *Broadway Melody of 1940*. The content of Astaire and Powell's dances, which average a very low 26% touching but very high 88% foot sounds, captures something of the inability this pair had in coming up with any way to dance together other than a modified double-act relationship that relentlessly signals agreement (no turn taking here either). In reflections from 1974, Powell recalled their working relationship as a crisis of authority: "We had no choreographer at all. What made it so difficult was that nobody could do what I was doing but me. Up to the time Fred worked with me, he had always had a young lady that he could teach.... But me being my own choreographer and Fred being his own on *Broadway Melody*, who was going to tell who what to do?"[26] As noted, the swing tap portion of "Begin the Beguine" involves no touching whatsoever. It does, however, include facial interactions, none of which signal romance. Instead, their looks at and reactions to each other speak to peevish competition—see Powell's reaction to Astaire at the start (fig. 42.3) and during the unaccompanied tap break. The energy between them reads as that of siblings, not lovers. The harlequin number "I Concentrate on You" is one of the oddest duo routines Astaire ever made. He hated his costume and, in the midst of production, penned a long-hand note to producer Jack Cummings: "Dear Jack: I made a test last night in the most *god awful and* ill-fitting Harlequin outfit and am ashamed to have it go through the laboratory baths. That coupled with the fact that Powell may be an inch or so taller than I am in the number and that 'my' hair is so different to Murph's [George Murphy] makes me a little ill in fact it gives me a pain where I should have pleasure. Would you kindly come and discuss the blasted situation with me? Your loving son—Fred A."[27] The "Concentrate" dance, after Astaire joins it, follows a three-part structure: double-act unison, a series of strange and awkward held poses in shadowy lightboxes, then a return to double act (fig. 42.4). Before the awkward ending, Astaire and Powell

FIGURE 42.3

FIGURE 42.4

touch just once, in insert framing just after he enters (for whispered dialogue explaining Astaire's presence). As discussed in section nine, the first part of "Begin the Beguine" presents a vaguely exotic register typical of MGM: Is this Spanish (as the flamenco-ish tapping and Astaire's form-fitting costume might indicate)? Is this Middle Eastern (as Powell's midriff-revealing costume might suggest)? One passing moment of closed ballroom position is all that pegs Astaire as the male in the pair. Indeed, the whole routine would make sense—and be enhanced sensually along exoticist lines—if done by two women. This puts Astaire in a highly feminized position and shows the power of Powell's persona and the limits of her stereotypically feminine side. The fourth duo dance for Powell and Astaire, the "Jukebox Dance," does contain two sustained sections in closed ballroom position. Noteworthy in both is move a where Astaire stands on one foot and Powell travels around him in a circle, in the process turning Astaire.[28] Powell and Astaire never arrived at a convincingly or conventionally romantic way to dance together—instead, their duos slide toward male-male or female-female pairings.

One dance in Table 7 would seem to be highly gendered in costumes, lyrics, and conceit. "How Could You Believe When I Told You That I Love You When You Know I've Been a Liar All My Life" is perhaps the "lowest" number—in class terms—Astaire did. Astaire and Jane Powell play gum-smacking, down-at-heel types in garish and (for Astaire) ill-fitting costumes. The dance involves among the most physically violent events in the Astaire corpus. I return to it in section forty-seven within a larger discussion of violence in Astaire's work.

Parity before romance with Rogers

Table 8 reveals Rogers's outsized place in the *Astaire dancing* corpus. Fully one-third of all his duos were with her: they dance together for one hour and fourteen minutes. She is also his most iconic screen partner, the dancer with whom he defined his screen dance partnering style in all its parameters. The enduring appeal of the Astaire-Rogers partnership comes into focus when their three dances with the least amount of touching (each of which falls beneath the 80% no-touching benchmark of Table 8) are considered by way of the six types of partner relationships. The seconds-of-touching metric identifies these routines as unusual for the pair. Indeed, the average for the couple was 60% touching. The routine with the least touching, "I'm Putting All My

Eggs in One Basket," has already been considered. The remaining two are exceptional routines worth a closer look.

"Isn't This a Lovely Day?" (11% touching) unfolds as a gradual move across the spectrum of partnering types, moving step by step from contrasting movements to supported partnering and retaining all along the way an almost strictly applied rule of parity: if one partner does something, the other does it as well.[29] (Rogers's stylized male attire tellingly signals reciprocity: she wears riding breeches, tailored tweed coat, and a feminized [and rakishly cocked] bowler.) The dance begins with Astaire strolling in a circle. Rogers joins him of her own volition: she is not pulled into the dance, as in "Night and Day," but chooses to dance. Astaire initially doesn't see her in step behind him. On a turn he registers her there beside him—his pleased double take evidences just one of the ways facial expression in movie dancing tells the story as much as large body movements. The dance continues for a stretch as a double act (unison, side by side, embellished with sidelong glances), but eventually, they end up face to face. The transition to mirroring is upon them and perhaps they might touch—however, they do not do so yet. Instead, they each fold their arms as if to say, "I'm not quite ready to take you in my/fall into your arms." A passage of no-touch mirroring follows, ending with a side-by-side unison move forward that travels from the step up at the back to the step down at the front of the pavilion that frames their dance. Landing in a previously unexplored area of the set, they are primed to go further relationally as well. The first touch happens ninety-five seconds (59% of the way) into the dance and it is the slightest sort of touch and release. Astaire grabs Rogers's hand and spins her around. She immediately reciprocates, touching his hand to set him spinning. These two touches ignite the possibilities: thunder rolls overhead and the tempo of the music picks up. After more excruciating no-touch mirroring—when will they finally *really* partner up?—the pair meet by equal movements toward each other in a closed ballroom position hold and start an exuberant spinning combination that traces a larger circle around the pavilion. All that remains, within our six-type spectrum, is a supported partnering move. "Isn't This a Lovely Day?" does not disappoint. Just before the end, while in closed ballroom position, Astaire swings Rogers momentarily off both her feet. A second later, she swings him off his feet in an identical move. Following this delirious exchange of shared balance, the pair runs off the front of the pavilion into the rain, then backs under the roof, sits cross-legged side by side, and—in token of their new relationship—soberly but with smiles shakes hands. How much of this routine could have been danced with Gene Kelly? Judging from "Babbitt," just about all of it, albeit with slightly different facial interaction (the narrative of shadowing or matching each other would take on a different cast outside a cis-het romance plot). But it was made for Astaire and Rogers and captures a kind of reciprocity between the pair that models heterosexual relations as grounded in complete parity. Of course, this will not be the end of their relationship's trajectory—"Cheek to Cheek" comes next—but at least in *Top Hat*, meeting in this way lays a foundation (if, of course, one watches *Top Hat* from start to finish, which not all the film's original audiences did).

"They All Laughed" from *Shall We Dance* follows an identical trajectory across the spectrum of types, if in a more public and contrived manner. Astaire as a ballet dancer and Rogers as a nightclub star sets up the contrasting moves at the start. They agree on tap as the style they share—Astaire does a tap break that elicits a close-up reaction from Rogers to start the dance proper (exactly as in "Pick Yourself Up"). They dance for a long initial stretch in double-act unison. A shift to no-touch mirroring follows easily. The first touch—coming some seventy-two seconds after the tempo starts—is tentative and formal: Rogers starts a spinning combination under Astaire's arm. The combination travels in a larger circle and goes on longer than expected as the music kicks the energy up a notch. A stretch of playful syncopation follows in double-act side-by-side position: Astaire grabs Rogers's hand for some of it, sustaining the emerging couple narrative. After lifting Rogers onto one of the nearby pianos, Astaire pulls her right back down and they take up closed ballroom position, a sign of increased comfort with each other. A supported partnering move typical of the pair follows when Astaire bounces Rogers in and out of the upholstered bench at the back of the dance floor. The dance ends with the couple sitting side by side on one piano. Given the public context, they don't shake hands at the end but instead turn to the applauding audience and bow (a clear sign they are now in this together).

The pattern of moving methodically from contrasting movements to supported partnering occurs in blunter forms in other Astaire-Rogers numbers as well. The "I Won't Dance" finale to *Roberta* is almost entirely double-act and no-touch mirroring moves. Only at the very end does the pair throw their arms around each other in an embrace. Cut this conclusion and the dance is suitable for any male-male or female-female team. "Bouncin' the Blues" in *Barkleys* puts off touching for the first two-thirds of its duration. Up to that point, it's a marital double act suitable for same-sex doubles or couples. Once near the start, Astaire chucks Rogers under the chin, and later they join inside hands (as Astaire and Garland do in "I Love a Piano")—small touching tokens of romance embellishing an otherwise rigorously equal dance. But the final third of "Bouncin'" grows increasingly hetero—they do a bit of modest swing dancing—and climaxes with a sexy, hip-swinging exit for Rogers (despite her pants), which Astaire watches with a smile. This sort of dance expresses the heart of the Astaire-Rogers partnership. The Astaire-Hayworth duo dance, "The Shorty George" (*You Were Never Lovelier*), also plays around with lots of double-act dancing. Here, it's a kind of dare: each asking the other, can you do this (Black) dance as well as I can? At the close, they fling their arms around each other in a sloppy closed hold as if to exit but then break apart for more double-act dancing before falling into a second hug, this time held as they dance their way out. In all of these dances, the pleasures of double-act dancing are expressed as potentially romantic in their indication of a deeper sympathy between a man and a woman who need not always dance out conventional cis-het gender roles.

43. The Pan Question

How much of the apparent parity between Astaire and Rogers was the result of Astaire building their dances with a man—Hermes Pan—as Rogers's dance-in? Pan is literally present in all their dances: he makes the sound of Rogers's taps at RKO. In his interview with Ronald L. Davis, Pan made a startling claim: "I used to do—well, I would say—fifty-sixty percent of the choreography."[30] Speaking to Joseph McBride, Pan said, "I'd even do Ginger's counter-part, you know, and then finally when it seemed to work, Ginger would come in and we would work with her. Fred would never take Ginger's part. I would always take Ginger's part."[31] And Pan's presence goes beyond RKO. He receives screen credit or appears in the archival record for sixteen Astaire films (just over half the corpus). Speaking forty years after the making of *Broadway Melody of 1940*, Powell confirmed that Pan never visited MGM but she also remembered, "Somebody said that Fred would go at night and show Hermes what we were doing."[32] She intuited Astaire didn't want her to think Pan had too much influence over him. Bob Fosse spoke of Pan's closeness to Astaire physically: "I've never seen a really good imitation of Fred Astaire. I've seen people put on masks and tails and top hat and all the physical things but there's something—except Hermes. Hermes comes as close to dancing like Fred Astaire as anyone I know. They could be twins in a movie."[33] (Pan's similarity to Astaire was already being remarked upon by his Broadway castmates in the early 1930s; when Pan saw Astaire's photo, "fully ten years older than he and already balding," for the first time outside the New Amsterdam Theatre during the run of *The Band Wagon*, he reportedly thought, "I look like *that*?!"[34])

Pan was a gay man who lived very discreetly within the allowances of the open secret in studio Hollywood. Pan's biographers emphasize he was "by [1991 standards] very closeted" up to his death (in 1990) and report only one long-term relationship in the 1960s.[35] Astaire (a straight married man) and Pan (a single gay man, often playing the part of the woman in rehearsals) collaborated in the 1930s on a richly nuanced, historically powerful screen dance representation of heterosexual romance. They made these dances while, literally, in each other's arms—if Astaire and Rogers touch on screen, at some point Astaire and Pan touched in the privacy of the rehearsal hall. As Powell described it, "Pan used to take the girl's part. He would work with Fred, two men together, and Hermes would be whoever the girl was."[36] If some of Astaire's male-female duo dances can be seen as doable by two men, all the male-female dances he made with Pan were, in rehearsal, actually done by "two men together."

Their long working relationship was founded on a shared attraction to "broken rhythms" that both understood to be Black in origin. Pan, who spent his early childhood in Nashville, articulated a direct personal connection to Black music and dance: he told his friend and biographer David Patrick Columbia about his "mammy, a big black woman who was called Aunt Betty," who exposed him to "what was then called 'gut-bucket' jazz and the shuffles and foot-slapping dancing of the local black Americans" in 1915.[37] Astaire never revealed so directly his exposure or connection to Black music and dance, only doing so in more distant terms.[38] So, perhaps, the Astaire/Pan partnership finds its strength in their shared (and common) white love of Black art. But the closeness and longevity of their relationship speaks to more than just professional rapport. Columbia writes, "Hermes' relationship with Fred Astaire was the center of his life. Indeed, it may well have been the most intimate relationship either man ever shared. It was not physical or sexual but they related on a deeply creative level. It also had the depth and political complexities that are found in families. Hermes would never fight Fred on any point.... Fred always came first."[39] While a sexual relationship seems very unlikely (and impossible to determine), Astaire and Pan did have a physical relationship of one sort: they danced together—and not only in rehearsal. In the 1941 film *Second Chorus*, Astaire and Pan danced a duo to the song "Me and the Ghost Upstairs." Cut from the film, Pan saved a copy. In 2010, the number as edited for the film was posted to YouTube by the user *historycomestolife*.[40]

Johnny Mercer's lyric for "Me and the Ghost Upstairs" describes a male ghost who the singer lives near or with (in the same building). The pair share a social life with friends over and parties. The context is intimate, as one line goes "the place is small 'cause you know those spooks don't require no room at all." The word *spooks* evokes Blackness, often on the leading edge in Mercer's work, and Astaire sings this phrase with what sounds like a stereotypical popular music Black accent (of a sort unheard in any released Astaire vocals; the quality of the YouTube audio is admittedly poor). And so, the "ghost" could be read as Black and the song when sung by a white singer as about interracial socializing. Another reading hears the lyric as describing gay men socializing, as they would have had to at the time for safety's sake, in private. The dance Astaire and Pan do seems to confirm the latter. Astaire introduces the tune in a nightclub setting, singing as a band singer. He begins the dance alone, creeping about the dance floor to see if the ghost is nearby. When Pan appears, he wears a ghost costume that reads as a long sheath-like dress with a hip-length, nontranslucent veil that includes gloves for his hands. He appears not to be wearing pants and his shoes may have a low heel. This is not a ghost costume over masculine attire but full-blown ghost drag. The lyric establishes the ghost as male, but the gender of the dancer under the costume is never conclusively indicated (as, for instance, was the case for blackface numbers and men in female drag—see Astaire's male partner in a dress and wig for part of the troop show solo "Hello, Hello, Who's Your Lady Friend?" in *The Castles*). The visual concept for "Me and the Ghost Upstairs" is decidedly queer; in period parlance Pan's ghost is definitely effeminate, especially in the use of his hands.

Pan and Astaire play the number seriously: it's meant to be good and not two guys goofing off (drag was fine at the time in specific contexts, such as fraternity or troop shows; this is not such a setting). After some initial interplay—Pan pantomimes making Astaire a drink (as in the lyric)—Pan stops the dance and whispers repeatedly in Astaire's ear. Astaire initially resists his entreaties, even after Pan gets on one knee to beg, but eventually he gives in and the two men start to jitterbug. They start out pecking (facing each other making jerky forward moves with their heads), then go into closed ballroom position, then do a set of saddle car lifts (facing each other, the flying partner clasps his hands around the base partner's neck and is swung to each of the latter's hips then into a straddle position). Throughout this dance, Astaire plays the girl: Pan leads and lifts Astaire. (Given Pan's costume, reversing the roles seems difficult.) This particularly physical content of the dance confirms that the ghost is played by a male dancer: it's unlikely a woman would be able to lift Astaire as Pan does. Soon, the music changes to the conga. The pair responds accordingly, at one point facing each other and shimmying shoulders—again Astaire takes the female position. They exit together. This truly strange dance casts Astaire as the female and leaves Pan's actual gender identity ambiguous except by deduction from the dance itself. The very concept of the routine—a whispered negotiation, a social dance for two men, all done in private—sits outside the norms of Astaire's other male-male duos, which lean heavily on virtuoso or stylish double-act unison done as a professional performance. Indeed, Pan and Astaire don't even tap much here. This is not a display of "broken rhythms" as we might expect from these two but a comedy routine that plays with gender and same-sex socializing without irony or camp (although the latter quality is very much in the eye of the beholder).

While the Production Code Administration archives contain no correspondence on *Second Chorus*, it's difficult to believe "Me and the Ghost Upstairs" would have been acceptable for release: it's entirely understandable why it was cut. The mystery is why it was made in the first place. Speaking to biographer Bob Thomas in the early 1980s, Astaire dodged the issue: "The 'Ghost' number was cut out of the picture for some reason or other. It wasn't much of a number, didn't mean anything. The idea was all right, but something didn't work out. You wouldn't have seen Hermes anyway. He had a veil over his head throughout the number."[41] Pan reportedly understood the decision to remove the number as Astaire's and was hurt.[42] Cutting "Me and the Ghost Upstairs" seems like a common-sense decision: the number would cast substantial doubt on Astaire's cis-het masculinity at a moment of tenuousness in his career (albeit in a minor film—but who could predict if a given movie might be a hit).

Astaire and Pan often worked with a ghost in the room: before a partner was brought in they had to anticipate what said partner could do. Adjustments once the partner arrived were surely common. Working on solos, Pan could provide critique and ideas. Pan's and Astaire's respective contributions to Astaire's solos cannot be teased apart. This leaves the very strange "Me and the Ghost Upstairs," which fits none of Astaire's practices with male (or female) partners. Confronted with no guiding personas other than their own, Astaire and Pan, following Mercer's lyric, went in a strange direction that crossed several bright lines, such as the normative maintenance of Astaire's straightness. For Pan, it didn't matter: his ghost dress at once disguised his identity and pointed toward his manifest sexuality (he hides in plain sight—one approach to living the open secret). As a limit case, the surviving "Me and the Ghost Upstairs" footage sets Astaire's duo dances in context, showing his screen dance body doing things and presenting in ways beyond the allowances of the clip reel. Of course, if Pan had a copy there's no reason to think Astaire didn't as well—perhaps it was part of his clip reel and thus seen by him again and again over the years.

44. MGM "SHOESHINE BOY"

A memo from R. Monta of the Metro legal department to producer Arthur Freed describes the content of Astaire's *Band Wagon* solo this way: "During a nostalgic visit to Forty-Second Street, the scene of his earlier successes, Mr. Astaire strolls through a Penny Arcade. He ends up at a shoe-shine stand and sings and dances the song 'A Shine on Your Shoes'—using a bootblack as a partner."[43] In a further memo, Monta raised the issue of how the depiction of contemporary Forty-Second Street might reflect on MGM exhibitors who owned theaters in the area: "You are going to show actual theatres and there are very powerful exhibitors running some of these theatres and they would certainly resent the scene as it is now written, calling attention to the honky-tonk, cheap character of 42nd Street and our showing such pictures as 'The Gorilla's Revenge,' 'Savage Princess,' etc., as playing in their theatres."[44] Another memo expressed concerns about possible liability for depicting existing businesses and people on the street. Regarding plans to recreate the "Pokerino and Flea Circus, on 42nd Street set," legal advised that both could be represented "only if action takes place *outside* each of these places, if there are no names shown, and no people identifiable,—(such as a ticket-taker, or barker, for example) who might be able to say we are representing them or pointing to them by reason of one of our actors posing as 'ticket-taker' or 'barker' for one of these places."[45] From this perspective, hiring an actual bootblack to play the "bootblack" in the film was a completely safe choice for a number set in the "real" world that caused much concern.

And so, Leroy Daniels, a Black bootblack with a stand at Sixth and Main, in the Skid Row section of downtown Los Angeles, was hired "as a partner" for Astaire. The MGM personnel department noted on September 2, 1952, "We have engaged [Leroy Daniels] for the role of 'SHOESHINE BOY' at a salary of $350.00 per week with a 1 week guarantee. Starting date 9/3/52."[46] Other "WEEKLY DANCERS" hired for bit parts made around $150 to $175 per week. Daniels rehearsed with Astaire and his *Band Wagon* assistant Alex Romero for ten days over the initial two weeks of rehearsal on the film before the number was ready for prerecording (a sign the choreography was complete). During these same weeks, Astaire was creating "You Have Everything," a number shared with Charisse that was eventually cut. After a few days rehearsing on the set, "Shine on Your Shoes" was the first part of *Band Wagon* to go before the cameras, beginning on September 23, 1952. It took three days to film, as discussed in Part Three. Daniels probably made a maximum of $1,400 on the film (over $13,000 today).

In October 1952, just weeks after filming but months before *Band Wagon*'s release, *Jet*, a national magazine for Black Americans, featured Daniels in a generous two-page spread, including a photo from the number. According to *Jet*, a talent scout suggested Daniels to Astaire, who visited his stand and "watched Leroy dance and make hot rhythm with his rags and brushes, then signed him on the spot." Daniels told *Jet*, "I never had any training. Dancing just comes natural, I guess." Described as "the bebop bootblack," *Jet* attributed Daniels's popularity on a crowded downtown strip of "burlesque houses and risqué theatres, shooting galleries, penny arcades with myriad attractions, bars with sexily-dressed 'B' girls, pawn shops, and numberless bold shoeshine boys" to his "added bebop touch." While Daniels had worked on the street for ten years, *Jet* reported his desire and earlier efforts to get into show business, including performing in "Mexican nightclubs" and on "amateur programs."[47] In the 1960s, Daniels teamed up with Ernest "Skillet" Mayhand as the comedy team Leroy & Skillet. The pair made comedy albums on the LaFF Records label and had recurring roles as themselves on the Black-cast sitcom *Sanford and Son* in 1973.

"A Shine on Your Shoes" is unlike any number Astaire made. It stands alone in his corpus as his only song-and-dance routine done with a Black man as "partner" (to quote the MGM legal department). Beyond this simple distinction, it also finds an awkward fit as to type: it's a solo but also a duo. I vacillated about how to categorize it for months given that Daniels received no billing in the film. Can Daniels be compared to the other performers, all white, who shared a number with Astaire? I strongly believe the only way to understand "Shine on Your Shoes" is as a duo dance on the order of the other ninety-five such routines Astaire made. To think otherwise is to undercount Daniels's extraordinary presence and to endorse the elision of Daniels's contribution by repeating the racism of the *Band Wagon* credits. Furthermore, "Shine on Your Shoes" affords the chance to see Astaire's whiteness in direct danced conversation with Daniels's Blackness. For these reasons, this routine deserves close reading as a duo dance.

That said, Astaire and Daniels's physical relationship is utterly unlike any other Astaire duo dance. The six categories of partnering relationships outlined previously do not apply to "Shine on Your Shoes." Other and contrasting explanatory categories to explain how Astaire and Daniels relate physically in this number are required. This suggests that the reciprocity, telepathy, and double-act parity that define most all Astaire's duos with white men and women are properly understood as expressing whiteness. His sole dance with a Black partner participates in nearly none of the larger tropes of his duo dances. And so, with the admittedly limited data provided by just one number with a Black male partner, we can conclude that the bulk of Astaire's duo dances are not just with male or female partners but also with white male and white female partners. Whiteness inheres as a constitutive element in all those numbers: whatever equity between partners might be seen in these dances is built on a foundation of racial segregation, revealed to be such by way of the contrast offered by the dance with Daniels. "Shine on Your Shoes" stands alone and outside the larger codes of Astaire's duos, which are better seen as Astaire's white duos.[48] "Shine on Your Shoes" differs from all other Astaire duos in the way the partners make and sustain contact, the physical and danced relationship of the pair, and—crucially—the outsized reaction to the shared dance by the crowd of onlookers in the scene, all of whom are white.

In the larger "Shine on Your Shoes" scenario, Astaire and Daniels encounter each other accidentally in a segregated, all-white public place. Daniels is the only Black person in the arcade. From the start, director Vincente Minnelli presents Forty-Second Street as crowded, rowdy, and eccentric in a lower-class way. The denizens of the area are distinct, interesting, and interested characters—brightly dressed, watching each other closely, moving constantly in apparent circles around the arcade, broadly reacting to the busy scene. No other film musical number I know—certainly none in the Astaire corpus—allows for such a diversity of onlookers (within the category white), all of whom share identical reactions to Astaire and Daniels. Throughout the number, these (literal) characters pass behind and in front of Astaire and Daniels as our central focus.

Daniels, wearing a bright-colored, tropical print shirt, is first seen working at his stand in the background between two arcade machines (fig. 44.1). As the camera follows Astaire—perhaps from the point of view of a member of the crowd we never see—Daniels appears two times in this first shot of the number, once each on both sides of the so-called Calliope monster, which has a large question mark emblazoned on its forbidding exterior (fig. 44.2). The camera is stalking Daniels just as much as Astaire, and the hierarchal relationship of the two is already in place: initially with Astaire front, Daniels back. Astaire walks away from the unresponsive machine and, in a cut that significantly resituates him relative to the arcade's layout, engages with a series of attractions: a fortune teller machine, a "Love Appeal" meter (he registers as "GORGEOUS"), and a funhouse mirror. Astaire starts walking one way while looking another and trips over Daniels, who is sitting on the lowest step of his stand, his right leg extended (note the

FIGURE 44.1

FIGURE 44.2

FIGURE 44.3

FIGURE 44.4

lack of taps on Daniels's shoes at this point; fig. 44.3). The initiating action for the number—a meet cute of a sort—is a moment of physical contact between a white man and a Black man in a white public place. Confrontations such as this have proven dangerous for Black men in the United States, and we might expect Daniels to rise and apologize or show some deference or, at the least, offer Astaire a shine. Daniels is, after all, working a service job and Astaire would seem a prime candidate for a shine. But Daniels does not move and the first look the two men exchange shows annoyance on the Black man's part (fig. 44.4). Astaire smiles at Daniels's impassive look and—in an abidingly strange reaction to the moment—proceeds to sing him a song. And not just any song—Astaire sings a song about lifting one's spirits by getting a shoeshine, a lyric that can't really apply to the man *doing* the shining. The first step in the dance involves Astaire leaping over Daniels's unmoved leg on a phrase break. Minnelli adjusts the camera in a recomposition of the two men that recalls the earlier peaking views of Daniels on either side of the question mark machine. The two have been sharing the frame for a while now: this juxtaposition of two bodies in a spatial hierarchy is the visual motif of the number and utterly foreign to any other Astaire duo. Daniels's face remains impassive until the end of the verse, when it becomes evident Astaire is, in fact, looking to have his shoes shined. Daniels breaks out in a smile and the danced vocal of the chorus—danced mostly by Daniels—begins.

A hierarchal, white-over-Black relationship between the pair is maintained throughout the chorus. Their relationship is one of unequal exchanges. Astaire sits atop Daniels's stand (high); Daniels stands or kneels on the floor (low). Astaire sings; Daniels dances. No previous Astaire number uses this distribution of labor. The dance follows the process of an actual shoeshine (polish, brushes, rag) and Daniels makes noise as appropriate (knocking the brushes together in syncopated time, snapping the rag for emphasis). This is the only time in his career Astaire ceded the role of noisemaker to another. The moves Daniels does here likely originated with him during the two weeks of rehearsal with Astaire and surely draw on the "bebop" persona he used on his Skid Row stand to draw customers. Daniels's act of shining Astaire's shoes brings the two men into constant if mediated physical contact for much of the danced vocal and part of the dance that follows. The touch that happens here is of a different order than any found in an Astaire duo with a white partner. The intensity of Astaire's focus on Daniels is palpable. He is singing for him with as much directed energy as Daniels is dancing for Astaire—while, of course, shining his shoes (fig. 44.5).

FIGURE 44.5

When the vocal ends, the dance proper begins. Astaire remains engaged with Daniels and the clear distinction between them is maintained. Astaire poses his way around the chair on the stand while Daniels travels around the stand snapping his rag. Only after traveling once around the stand do the pair face each other and do a two-second no-touch mirroring break (albeit with Astaire still in his elevated position). A return to Astaire in the chair and Daniels on the ground in front of him follows, climaxing in Astaire jumping off the stand and over Daniels. The reframing of the shot reveals that Daniels is now wearing taps on his shoes (he executes an unaccompanied tap break earlier in this shot; fig. 44.6). So, in addition to making noise with his brushes and rag, Daniels also taps. Skip Martin's brassy arrangement makes it hard to distinguish but there are clear moments of foot sounds in the final phrases of the chorus. Who dubbed these sounds? It likely was not Daniels—perhaps Astaire stepped in and did the sound for his only Black partner.

The six types of partner relationship discussed in this part clearly do not apply to "Shine on Your Shoes." We need an entirely new category for duo dancing that emphasizes a division of labor rather than shared identity between the partners. Astaire and Daniels's actions—singing, dancing; sitting, shining shoes; posing, moving through space—are complementary in a hierarchal way, rather than contrasting. They are working together but not in a manner that implies parity or similarity (much less equality): at the level of the shoeshine, Daniels is clearly working *for* Astaire; at the level of the song, Astaire is arguably giving Daniels a gift (even if the address of the lyrics speaks more to Astaire's situation). The differences between their movements are consistent but not so easily ranked. It is extraordinary for Astaire not to make noise with his body in a solo, much less for him to let someone else

FIGURE 44.6

tap instead. The relational quality of complementarity also inheres in the pair's facial interaction: they engage with each other consistently and with enthusiasm.

Having jumped off the stand, Astaire hands Daniels his straw hat, a down payment on their eventual coming back together but also evidence for a service relationship between the two. Daniels initially remains in the frame and watches as Astaire bounces crazily around the arcade repeating the phrase "got a shine on my shoes." He brushes Astaire's hat with his whisk broom, an important prop for later, and seems to enjoy Astaire tormenting the very tall woman in the photo booth, who runs away screaming (she's not shown to be afraid that Astaire and Daniels are singing and dancing to each other; fig. 44.7). If Astaire and Daniels are conceived as buddies here, then Astaire is the crazy one and Daniels is the straight man. The camera proceeds to follow Astaire—completely within historical precedent and one reason it's possible to see this number as a solo—and Daniels disappears from the number for forty-eight seconds. But look closely: he's still there in the background watching as Astaire successfully opens the Calliope monster. A muscular white guy in a yellow shirt with red stripes blocks Daniels's view so he stands up on his shoeshine stand, then moves off screen left so as to reconnect with Astaire at the end of the shot (fig. 44.8).

In the final shot, Astaire and Daniels do a thirty-second dance, only ten seconds of which might be seen to fall into the no-touch mirroring type. A fundamental inequality in their relationship remains evident in Daniels delivering Astaire's hat, as well as brushing off his suit (fig. 44.9). Still, the two men dance the same steps facing each other and even drop to their knees in unison. The forward address of double act, and the accompanying suggestion of equality, is not indicated. Astaire takes his hat and both rise. Daniels brushes

FIGURE 44.7

FIGURE 44.8

FIGURE 44.9

FIGURE 44.10

off Astaire's leg and back, again with a rhythmic figure. Just like Astaire, every move Daniels makes is imbued with syncopated rhythm. They trace a circle, Daniels behind Astaire, and land facing each other, both on one knee, Astaire's back to the camera. On this drop, the pair clasp hands (fig. 44.10).

It's the only moment of physical touching as equals in the number and it's pointedly not a moment of leading. It's an act of man-to-man recognition. The only other person Astaire ever shakes hands with in this way during a dance is Gene Kelly in "Babbitt" (multiple times). (He and Rogers shake hands just after the end of the dance to "Isn't This a Lovely Day?") Having taken Daniels's hand, Astaire immediately rises and takes a piece of paper money out of his pocket and pays for his shine—in rhythm, of course. Astaire makes to leave the arcade and Daniels follows his departure, still on his knees (practically speaking so as not to block our view of Astaire). They salute each other and Astaire exits.

What are we to make of this spectacle of a white man and a Black man dancing together in a Forty-Second Street arcade in 1953? The film itself gives us somewhat hysterical cues. All the white people in the arcade visibly notice and smilingly approve of the white man and the Black man's very public encounter throughout the entirety of the number. Rewatch the number and look only at the many passersby: all bear a consistent and clearly coached reaction of sheer grinning pleasure. At some point in the making of this number, Minnelli must have directed the crowd to look at Astaire and Daniels and register strong facial approval of their routine. Are these smiles an index of concern about movie audience reactions to the number? If so, preview comments provide at least one anecdotal answer as to how this number was received in its time. Among the (presumably white) female responses to *Band Wagon* was the comment, "THE SHOESHINE BOY WAS A BEAUTIFUL DANCER. I'D LIKE TO SEE MORE OF HIM."[49]

"Using a bootblack as a partner" in "Shine on Your Shoes" forced Astaire to invent new ways of relating to another performing body—specifically that of a Black man. He used almost none of the normative ways he related to white men or white women in drag in previous double dances. Dancing with a Black man required a thorough reinvention of his duo dance practices, such that the number is difficult to categorize as either duo or solo. Daniels was not granted the dignity of the double act's enactment of equality (much less inclusion by name in the credits). Instead, a division of performed labor gave Astaire the singing and Daniels the dancing and rhythm making. The embeddedness of the dance in a public situation and a raced character that potentially infantilized, emasculated, and denigrated Daniels—MGM called his role "SHOESHINE BOY"—in the dance as made and done gave the only Black man Astaire ever danced with the opportunity to make rhythm (while Astaire made none) and to shake hands with Astaire. This moment of touching as equals cuts to the mystery at the heart of the number. What were those days in the rehearsal hall like? How much did Daniels contribute to the content of the dance? Who made the decision to have these two men touch in that way?

SIX
NOISY MASCULINITY

I think Fred's greatest contribution to musicals, to movies, and to dancers could be that he was heterosexual.
—Dancer Russ Tamblyn (date unknown)

He was very shy, and much preferred the company of men.
—Douglas Fairbanks Jr. (1988)

Even though [Astaire] didn't look like a truck driver, he was very masculine.
—Actress Carol Lynley (1988)

45. Dancing on Tables for Men

A member of the cast of Astaire's final stage show—the London production of *Gay Divorce*—told the BBC a story about Astaire dancing on a table for a group of men. Renee Gadd wasn't there to see it but she heard tell of her fiancé's bachelor party at Prince's Restaurant, a grand theater district institution in Piccadilly. At the end of the night, with the table cleared except for liqueur glasses, flowers, and candlesticks, Astaire did a tap dance on the long table, three times back and forth, without touching a thing or knocking anything over.[1] Perhaps the stunt was an extension of the table dance from *Gay Divorce* that Astaire was doing nightly—although that one was with his leading lady in his arms, indeed literally hanging on for dear life. But dancing up and over a table is quite different from dancing on a table and for other men.

Astaire dances on a table for a man in *The Sky's the Limit* (1943)—and another man, a figure of masculine authority charged with policing public masculinity, steps up to stop him. In the film, Astaire plays his most hypermasculine character: a Flying Tiger (fighter pilots from the US armed forces who volunteered, with President Roosevelt's approval, to fight for pay under

American command for the Republic of China against Japan in the months before Pearl Harbor). In a version of a familiar Hollywood narrative, the film follows Astaire while he's on leave (actually AWOL from a public relations tour) in New York City, where he meets and pursues Joan Leslie. While wooing her, Astaire intentionally conceals his identity as an elite pilot and one of very few American servicemen already actively fighting in the war. He follows Leslie to a soldiers' canteen and joins her, against her wishes, in a duo dance for the boys to the song "A Lot in Common with You." The song's lyrics, by Johnny Mercer, break the frame of the story by having Leslie and Astaire refer to their most recent costars: James Cagney and Rita Hayworth. In this way, *The Sky's the Limit* opens some distance between Astaire's supposed pilot character and his identity as a dancing movie star. As they take their bows, Leslie asks Astaire, "Where did you learn to dance like that?" He replies, "Arthur Murray." Again, Astaire's dancing star status is poked at a bit: Arthur Murray taught social dancing, nothing like the virtuoso tap routine just completed.

Leslie walks away just before Astaire is hailed by two of his pilot buddies, played by Robert Ryan and Richard Davies. Davies was a tough-guy B-movie actor. Ryan was early in a major career that would be dominated by forceful roles in masculine genres like westerns, war films, and films noir. Both men are appreciably taller than Astaire: Ryan was six foot four (fig. 45.1). Earlier in the film, the three pilots are framed to conceal the height difference between the shorter star and the considerably larger supporting players (fig. 45.2). In the canteen scene, Ryan and Davies's uniforms also put the suited Astaire in a lesser position. They tease him, somewhat menacingly, about his performance: "We came to see you dance." "It was lovely." "How do you bill yourself these days? The Dancing Tiger?" Ryan's underlying menace, key to his

FIGURE 45.1

FIGURE 45.2

FIGURE 45.3

later persona, is already evident. But their real interest is Leslie. They insist on an introduction and push past Astaire in a move that further reinforces Astaire's slight frame (fig. 45.3). *The Sky's the Limit* reverses normal practice in Astaire's films and surrounds the star with supporting men who are aggressive, manly, and strong (rather than silly, effete, and weak). Astaire manages the introductions while keeping his cover. All four sit down to talk. Ryan says to Astaire, "It certainly is swell for you to come up and dance for us, mister." Davies: "Helps our morale." Ryan (looking at Leslie): "You know, I feel better about the whole war already." Astaire: "Thanks. Glad to do my bit." Astaire would face actual soldiers for the first time during a camp tour a few months after filming this scene. (To this point, he had only done a short tour for the Treasury Department promoting war bonds.[2]) This flatly delivered exchange with Davies and Ryan casts movie folks' morale-boosting contributions to the war effort as already cliché. Davies cuts the talk and asks Leslie to dance; she agrees and they peel off to the dance floor, leaving Astaire and Ryan, who says, "I'll wait my turn." Annoyed, Astaire asks Ryan, "Anything I can do to amuse you in the meantime?" Ryan replies, "Yes. You can hop up on the table and do a snake dance."

The "snake dance" in this case likely refers to burlesque routines often involving actual snakes. A nationally known stripper named Zorita was the most famous exponent of the snake dance. Ryan's request boils down to the demand that Astaire play the ultra-feminized role of erotic female dancer in the place of Leslie's wholesome canteen hostess: after all, Astaire had already danced for the troops as a man in a double dance with a woman that, as noted in Part Five, could easily be done by two women. Also implicit here is the feminized position of the male dancer as one who displays their body for any pair of eyes and the direct physical threat a larger man poses to anyone smaller than him (including slight men like Astaire).

Astaire dismisses Ryan's words but Ryan repeats the command, an anticipation of his later menace again registering in his meanly smiling face. Astaire grows concerned after Ryan threatens to "tell the young lady who you are," and he asks Ryan, "What's the matter with you, want me to get thrown in the brig or something?" The dialogue thus registers the real risk to Astaire in any such dancing display. Still, Astaire climbs atop the small square table and faces Ryan. "Now whadda ya want?" asks Astaire. Ryan does a few hula-like hand gestures. Astaire starts to dance; with knees together and legs bent, he wiggles his hips and makes small circular gestures with his hands. Cut to Leslie on the dance floor: she sees Astaire dancing and registers shock. Cut back to Astaire, insert framing from the waist up, making snake-like hand gestures that he treats as actual snakes (responding to a part of his body as if it has its own mind). "That all right?" he asks Ryan below him. Full-figure framing returns just before Astaire kicks toward Ryan's face—he does so on a piano chord in the boogie-woogie music (this is a fragment conceived with all the care of any Astaire number). A cut to Ryan shows his quick reaction to avoid taking Astaire's foot in his face. Ryan responds by stomping on Astaire's foot with his fist. A cut back to Astaire shows him receiving that blow, the table rocking during this exchange. Astaire continues his dance and briefly locks eyes with Leslie in cross-cuts between the two. She is deeply confused; he keeps dancing. Then, the military police (or MP) shows up. Astaire's precarious position shaking his suit jacket—raising his skirts?—for Ryan while a stocky MP looks on would seem to call Astaire's projection of a straight masculinity completely into question (fig. 45.4). Indeed, the MP lifts Astaire down off the table like he's a teenage boy (or girl). The look on Astaire's face when the appreciably bigger and taller man gives him a quick talking to is

FIGURE 45.4

FIGURE 45.5

serious and shut down (fig. 45.5). Why would a major male movie star *who danced* submit to this scene, which is in no way required by the plot of the film? (Ryan briefly returns in a later scene to deliver the news they are all being called back to duty.) *The Sky's the Limit* is a decidedly minor Astaire film. The snake dance is a fragment only—it doesn't make the clip reel. Yet in important ways this confrontation between a dancing man and men in uniform captures the precarity of any claim to a danced straight masculinity that isn't contextualized as courtship or professional work as a song-and-dance man. The context of the war operates here to push Astaire into, for him, odd and tricky territory, showing directions he did not go in fully made numbers (and adding to the sense that "Me and the Ghost Upstairs," the cut duet with Hermes Pan from *Second Chorus* [1941], was simply unreleaseable).

Table dancing for men was, at least in part, what Astaire was doing all the time: presenting himself as a dancer to audiences, female and male, for their assessment—of his dancing, yes, but also of his manliness, his whiteness, and his straightness. As noted earlier, almost 50% of cutaways in the corpus feature men looking at Astaire dancing. In one case, the content of Astaire's dance responds to this male gaze. In the "Audition Dance" in *You Were Never Lovelier* (1942), Astaire dances solo for Adolph Menjou's hotel owner to a medley of Latin hits by a small group from Xavier Cugat's big band. Twice Astaire briefly shakes his hips—an entirely appropriate instance of Latin motion given the music. Both times, Astaire responds to his own very modest hip-shaking by stiffening his body into a position of strength, invoking a matador (a hypermasculine Latin type) or just objecting to any incipient objectification. In one case, he directs an indignant look toward Menjou, as if challenging any gaze that might objectify his hips. But both times Astaire follows said show of strength with a release to more relaxed carriage and a sort of "who cares" dismissal that allows him to go on dancing (as he must). The dialogue into this dance expresses Astaire's frustration at not being immediately ushered in to dance for Menjou: "I've been trying for days to dance for you. You're the only living man who's ever refused to see my work and I want you to know that I resent it." When the angry Menjou tries to send Astaire out, he replies, "You can't talk that way to me. I'm an important guy. Now you're gonna see me dance and like it." This film from 1943, similar to the snake dance imbroglio in *The Sky's the Limit*, acknowledges in dialogue and dancing the especially precarious position faced by the straight white dancing man when dancing for other men. Astaire's ability to thread the needle and present as a thoroughly cis-het white man—one of his signal cultural achievements in his time—is called into question. The audition dance ends with an angry "Well?" from Astaire (subtext: have I not demonstrated by mastery?) to which Menjou replies (shouting, as he does throughout this film), "Excellent. Beautiful. But I don't want it." The risk that male viewers "don't want it" endures for Astaire. How they might receive his dancing is crucial. (A 1941 *Life* magazine profile featuring Astaire wrote of his "special brand of airy charm that women love and men admire"; in 1996 in *People* magazine, dancer Paula Abdul opined, "Men like Fred Astaire, with his top hat and elegance, but women love Gene Kelly. He's so handsome, so sexy, and so self-assured."[3]) The snake dance puts Astaire on (literally) shakier, more exposed ground, denying him the chance to demonstrate his dancing skill and in a context packed with big men in uniform—for a wartime audience, no less. Still, the snake dance fragment, unlike the "Audition Dance," contains select elements—hypermasculine moves like a kick to the face or a stomp on the toe masquerading as dance steps (or vice versa)—that point toward some of Astaire's regular strategies for asserting strength and straightness and eliciting admiration.

The final part of this book considers specific ways Astaire projected a noisy and strong masculinity, often while dancing with men or with women dressed as men. Masculinity is fragile and always at risk. Astaire's noisy masculinity, founded on tap dancing and its notion of the body as an instrument in conversation with the floor, works across his corpus to suggest a kind of forceful male energy. This energy was given off with pronounced vehemence—Astaire's jazz tap style involves pounding the floor—but also with decided nonchalance. Astaire understood that every move he made would be judged, and so he thought about his walking, which he understood to also be a form of the dance. I begin by quantifying Astaire's use of foot sounds and close by detailing his use of recognizable tap steps (the time step and the double flap) in a manner that casts these common moves as components of an assertively and insistently masculine character. Along the way, I quantify an entire class of Astaire dance moves that are *not* dance moves but instead common physical expressions of an aggressively physical masculinity. Larding his dancing with everyday acts of aggression—some positively boyish—kept Astaire near to everyday actions such as walking and helped him, in Pan's words, to create dances that "look like nothing." Central to Astaire's masculine style is a minimizing of dance as dance. As critic Gilbert Seldes wrote of *The Belle of New York* (1952), "Astaire himself is miraculously good in his dances, adding to one of them the kind of excitement Harold Lloyd used to generate on the side of a skyscraper, but always dancing when he is doing stunts and always characterizing when he dances."[4] Astaire's noisy masculine dancing always includes "characterizing" (a strategy supported by the power that screen dance grants to a dancer's facial expressions) just as much as it's made of steps—and even his steps, when broken down into components, are insistently *not* just about dancing. As critic Brian Seibert writes, "Astaire's toe has a tip, and his heel may drop, but he loved nothing better than to stamp a flat foot. Even at high speeds, his tap steps are, to a surprising extent, just that—steps, the foot lifted off the ground and set back down audibly."[5]

As noted in Part One, compared to the other male dancers on the big screen, Astaire does comparatively modest moves. Pan acknowledged this in 1959, noting, "There are many beautiful dancers who can do more fabulous things than Fred, such as Vladimir Vasiliev of the Bolshoi Ballet. Vasiliev can make fantastic leaps, and so forth, but Fred has an uncanny quality of timing that Vasiliev doesn't have."[6] There is, however, one quasi-screen dancer

Astaire always out-moves: Bing Crosby. In the Astaire-Crosby duo's two numbers, Astaire plays his modest dancing self while Crosby makes motions like he might dance but never really does. "I'll Capture Your Heart" (a not-quite-dance number in *Holiday Inn* [1942]) and "A Couple of Song and Dance Men" (*Blue Skies* [1946]) alike invite Crosby to copy or match Astaire in low-key double dances. Crosby dances along a bit but he has an unfailing sense for which moves are just too much effort for him—jumps and quick turns of any kind are out of bounds; instead he pretends to do the former (prepares but doesn't follow through, remaining firmly on the ground) and makes turning hand gestures while Astaire actually turns. Crosby's sense of timing is always on display—he is, in short, a fine dancer—but he just can't (won't?) put in the physical effort, which is also, of course, risky physical display. (Crosby displays decidedly different masculine style when partnered with others, such as Bob Hope or Danny Kaye—with the latter he even does the quasi-drag number "Sisters" in *White Christmas*.) Thus, Astaire's default style lies between Crosby—not dancing but showing he could, if he cared to try—and the other dancing men of the studio-era musical, who go all out and show their muscles, flexibility, and strength, manifesting unmistakably dancer moves, training, and bodies. Astaire's middle ground helps secure his cis-het masculinity and his potential as a leading man other men might like and admire (as opposed to just some guy who shows up and shows off).

Pan's description of Astaire's dancing—"That's the art—to make it look like nothing, so everybody has the feeling, 'Oh, I could do that, if I could just dance a little' "—is very much to the essence of Astaire's style.[7] Critic Gregg Kilday's comparative perspective—"Gene Kelly was always intent on *demonstrating* his masculinity, but Astaire just *assumed* his"—is similarly to the point.[8] Kelly's defensive and argumentative posture toward dance and masculinity took the form of insistence, as in his 1958 television special *Dancing: A Man's Game*. Kelly opens the show with a tracking shot across a room full of men in motion—some dancers, some athletes (including gymnasts, boxers, golfers, tennis and football players, and baseball star Mickey Mantle at the height of his career). Kelly begins, "So, all these men, dancers and athletes alike, possess something very much in common: skill and physical movement, and more important than that, physical movement in rhythm." As to the difference between athletes and dancers, Kelly argues, "The athlete uses his body skills and control in a competitive manner but the dancer must have something to say." Astaire's insistence he had nothing to say, that his dancing has no meaning (at least that *he* was aware of), situates him outside

Kelly's definition of the dancer. Kelly continues, "That is why most dance movements have their counterpart in sports." On the reverse side, Kelly says, "Mickey Mantle throwing a ball is dancing. And even though he's not doing it to music, it's still a beautiful and rhythmic thing to watch." Mantle here tosses the ball to Kelly, who catches it and tosses it back: surely many men and boys watching envied Kelly's chance to play catch with Mantle (Or did they? Who watched this? Would "Male, 18-30" from the *Barkleys* preview cards tune in to a show called *Dancing: A Man's Game*?). Kelly then collects a sports move from each of a series of famous athletes (ending with Mantle, who demonstrates sliding to steal second base) and reinterprets these moves "to music" in an eighteen-second dance. The music— a brassy big band arrangement of one chorus of the twelve-bar blues—would work for a female stripper: the moment Kelly starts dancing the conceit of the show falls apart; clearly a man dancing is making a spectacle of himself, importantly to music (which carries its own meanings separate from a dance), in a way athletes do not. Writing more generally about athletics and men's bodies, masculinity scholar R. W. Connell speaks directly to the contrast between the athletes on Kelly's show and Kelly's dance made of athletic moves: "Sport provides a continuous display of men's bodies in motion. Elaborately and carefully monitored rules bring these bodies into stylized contests with each other. . . . [These] bodily performances are called into existence by these structures. Running, throwing, jumping or hitting outside these structures is not sport at all. The performance is symbolic and kinetic, social and bodily, at one and the same time, *and these aspects depend on each other.*"[9] Kelly's strategy of stylizing sports moves into dance steps as a way to analogize between male dancers and male athletes ends up emphasizing the gap between these two sorts of masculine bodily performers—the latter group, of course, not situated as performing at all but instead competing within Connell's "elaborately and carefully monitored rules." By this measure, a man who dances is, in effect, violating the "rules" of the masculinity game.

Astaire had answered Kelly's sports-derived dance some two decades earlier: his "Golf Solo" from *Carefree* (1938) includes actual golf shots framed so the viewer can assess Astaire's golf skills. Astaire drives the ball and it's a dance step; alternately, Astaire does a dance step that happens to be the act of driving an actual golf ball on an actual golf course. It doesn't look like dancing because so much of it is engaged with the environment or with objects and also—crucially—because it isn't a stylized golf swing dance step; it's an actual golf swing with a club and a ball done on a tee at a golf course. (The screaming hot jazz accompanying the dance also resonates as masculine.[10]) As noted earlier, the context of the "Golf Solo" as showing off for a woman is undercut at the end when Rogers is revealed to have lost interest and left. Such self-mocking moves are common with Astaire. They position his masculinity as never taken quite seriously, as never fully achieved (since any suggestion of that would have been unconvincing). Such moves admit Astaire will never quite measure up to any standard masculinity standard—after all, he is dancing. A comment by MGM art director Jack Martin Smith helps locate Astaire's negotiation of masculine comparison against athletes: "[Astaire] always made his feats unathletic looking; in other words, he didn't do them the way a pole vaulter or a tumbler or a gymnast or a football player or anybody would do. He always did them like Fred Astaire should do them, which was interesting to me."[11] Preserving a kind of inimitability seems key here: Astaire doesn't dance like a dancer, nor does he golf like a golfer; in all things, he's simply Astaire. As Astaire himself said, "I was a weird looking character anyway. And I never liked the way I photographed particularly. I don't think many of them did either when they saw tests of me at the beginning. But they got so used to it that it didn't matter then as long as you had some sort of personality that worked. That's what counted. You know you didn't have to be a handsome dog anymore. . . . That was not my racket. I don't have to explain that [laughing]."[12] This careful setting of his persona relative to good looks begs the question of what was his "racket."

One element of Astaire's "racket" is not trying too hard. The contrast between the original and retake versions of "I Wanna Be a Dancin' Man" (*Belle of New York*) offers a case in point. In the vocal, Astaire delivers the lyric "I'll leave a few creations to show that I was dancing by" in markedly different ways. In the original, he makes tight fists with both hands: the tension comes off as an uncharacteristic insistence on the importance of his dancing in this self-reflexive lyric (fig. 45.6). The retake, besides reframing the shot, shows a much more relaxed Astaire, with nonchalant open hands and relaxed shoulders, an insouciant attitude that communicates ease, of course, but also a general sense of lightness about the proceedings—a song and a dance for the popular screen (fig. 45.7). Yet, much of this part of the book is not about Astaire's easy posture. It is, instead, about the ways he projected an assertive and insistent masculinity. To borrow Kilday's terms, the moves highlighted here mark a strain of demonstration rather than assumption of masculinity in Astaire's work. Such demonstrations often involve the potential of the body to make noise, a potential tapped into with particular power

FIGURE 45.6

FIGURE 45.7

by tap dancing, a dancing style that, in the film musical, required dedicated hours adding a final layer to the soundtrack: foot sounds. After quantifying the extent of Astaire's use of foot sounds, I detail his communicative use of tap in a mode I call *trash-talk taps*. Then, I track the occurrence of six hypermasculine dance moves that strain definition as dance moves: full-body contact, stomped toes, kicks in the pants (or elsewhere), hand-to-hand combat, stick and gun play, and all sorts of tripping, slipping, and falling. Astaire's use of these moves defines a subcorpus of duo and trio dances with men and women (and women dressed as men) that present a singular register in Astaire's dancing notably lacking in the romantic duos (which should not be taken as his only or even primary expressive mode). Then, for stark contrast, I consider a unique instance when Astaire presents a sustained exoticized masculinity by way of racial and ethnic play: the yellowface "Limehouse Blues" from *Ziegfeld Follies* (1946), a routine that lacks foot sounds entirely. Returning to the noisy norm for Astaire, I close by parsing his use of two standard tap steps—time steps and double flaps—in ways that express a danced masculinity with sharp edges, be they confrontational, sarcastic, or maliciously mischievous.

46. Trash-Talk Taps

Foot sounds were a pain. Astaire and Pan separately recalled recording taps to the BBC in 1973. Astaire: "There was a time when you recorded all the taps live and once or twice in the early part we did that but it wasn't practical. And to get every tap was a little difficult because the microphone might not be where it should be and it would miss or you wouldn't get a pure track. So we got a guide track out of it and then added the real sound to it." Astaire reveals here that even the numbers with ostensibly live sound were supplemented in postproduction. On set, he recorded a "guide track"; later, he "added the real sound"—a telling turn of phrase that shows Astaire thinking of the finished film as its own reality. But regardless of the process, he embraced the technological project of making the screen dance body a sounding as well as moving thing. Pan, who did Rogers's taps, also recalled the process, which—like breaking a number into shots—was best done parceled out in pieces: "It was tremendously difficult. Naturally you wouldn't do it the first time, you'd have to do it over and over again. Sometimes you'd get half of the routine done and that would be all right and then you'd have to concentrate on the next half. You'd do it in sections usually because it was almost impossible to go right through a routine with perfectly matching." And so, just as the image of the screen dance body is collaged together, so are the sounds that body makes. Astaire: "It's not a pleasant job. Some people let other people do it. I could never do it because they couldn't do what I was doing. My style was different than most. Mine were not just what you'd call routine tap steps. They were in between beats and they were very important and accented beats that were very important and had to be done by me to get what I thought and to make them look right. I hated that job. I used to sit up with the cutters all night doing that."[13] Astaire provides an aesthetic reason grounded in authentic personal expression for why he had to do his own foot sounds: his steps were unique, not just "routine"; no one else could know how they should sound. (And even when he used "routine tap steps," he did so within a highly personal idiom—see section forty-nine.)

Left unsaid here is Astaire's larger commitment to the use of foot sounds. The extent of this commitment to the sounding screen dance body can be quantified by sorting the 159 dances in the corpus into three groups: those with foot sounds throughout (42%), those lacking foot sounds entirely (21%), and those using foot sounds for some portion but not all of the number (37%). As this data shows, Astaire's most common choice was to include foot sounds for the entirety of a dance; nearly as often he added foot sounds to a portion of the dance. The all and none categories are graphed in chart 21, which gives the percent of numbers in each by period. Astaire's practice of adding foot sounds for the entirety of a dance remains fairly stable in his three Academy periods (above 40%). Only in the widescreen films does this category drop markedly (down to 27%). This shift reflects the waning of tap in 1950s film musicals and the particular dance skills of Astaire's widescreen partners (Leslie Caron, Audrey Hepburn, Cyd Charisse).

Foot sounds work as both a conceit of verisimilitude—dancing bodies jumping about make noise (unless the floor is carpeted, as in six dances)—and an element of aesthetic mood. For instance, dances that lack foot sounds entirely are overwhelmingly (82% of 33 dances) for Astaire and a romantic partner. The lack of foot sounds for romantically entangled heterosexual bodies maps aesthetically onto dances of high romance, whether local to a given number (the Continental milieu of "Let's Face the Music and Dance" in *Follow the Fleet* [1936]) or germane to a larger film plot (the hypnosis informing "Change Partners" in *Carefree* or the sad farewells of "Never Gonna Dance" in *Swing Time* and "The Last Waltz" in *The Castles* [1939]). Highly stylized numbers—like the duos with Lucille Bremer in *Ziegfeld Follies* and *Yolanda and the Thief* (1945)—similarly dispense entirely with foot sounds, as does Astaire's ostensibly ballet duo with Harriet Hoctor in *Shall We Dance* (1937) and the *Daddy Long Legs*

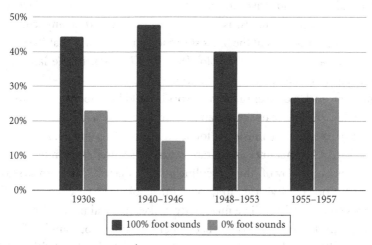

CHART 21 Numbers using 100% and 0% foot sounds as percentage of all numbers (by period)

(1955) dream ballet segments where Astaire plays a guardian angel (with Caron) and an (again, European) international playboy. None of these numbers grant the dancers' bodies any sonic presence: they float instead in a mise en scène (fantastic or a literal dreamscape) that lacks acoustic depth, an airless and unreal zone of weightless motion that supports traditional, strongly dichotomous gender roles (except in "Limehouse Blues") and heightened and intense emotion, often including a sort of romantic despair. "Beautiful Faces," the failed duo for Astaire and Garland in *Easter Parade* (1948), treats such high romantic conceits to comedy and does so without foot sounds—this lack being essential to the joke while also preserving a measure of decorum (Garland's graceless plop to the floor at the end receives no slapstick thud).

More prosaically, some dances have no foot sounds because they are done on carpet ("Stereophonic Sound" in *Silk Stockings*) or grass ("He Loves and She Loves" in *Funny Face* [1957]). When Astaire and Garland discover their ideal shared style in the initial living room section of "I Love a Piano" in *Easter Parade*, their foot sounds precisely match the pair stepping onto and off of a bearskin rug (see also the carpeted floor and hard walls and ceiling of "You're All the World to Me" in *Royal Wedding* [1951]; Astaire's feet only make noise when he's defying gravity). But such literalism is surprisingly rare. Foot sounds might go away during a context shot ("Seeing's Believing" [*Belle of New York*]) or when the music gets loud ("Dancing in the Dark" [*Band Wagon*] and "All of You" [*Silk Stockings*])—both choices indicating a sort of auditory perspective (complicated by the unclear status of playback as nondiegetic music)—but just as often remain audible beyond any sense of realism no matter how loud the brass starts screaming ("Slap That Bass" [*Shall We Dance*] and the "Concert Solo" [*Second Chorus*]). In the latter cases, Astaire sustains the musical contribution of the jazz tap dancer beyond the point when such a dancer in the real world would have to rely on movement only: Astaire has more options than the band tap dancer, who usually shifted to flash steps when the music got too loud for taps to compete. As I argue in *Music Makes Me*, Astaire's use of tap (crucially secured by film technology) underpins his display of "the masculine power of jazz."[14] His body is seldom simply "an object of vision," to quote film scholar Steven Cohan.[15] Rather, Astaire's consistently audible male body makes musical noise within a gendered cultural realm: jazz. The dances where Astaire's foot sounds effectively compete with an entire jazz band—courtesy of the technology of the mixing desk (which prioritizes Astaire's sounding body over the music)—present a supercharged jazz masculinity only possible in the synthetic realm of the cinema and the screen dance body.

Tap as a dance style related to musical style finds consistent illustration in partial foot sound routines that slide into tap during a stretch of dynamically softer or lighter orchestration (as in the B phrase of "Cheek to Cheek" in *Top Hat* [1935]). Other numbers with similar moments of the abrupt addition of foot sounds include "Smoke Gets in Your Eyes" (*Roberta* [1935]) and "Be Careful, It's My Heart" (*Holiday Inn*). These romantic duos can easily be imagined without the tap section. The expressive result of just a touch of tap is a move toward a more informal energy, often with a shift to side-by-side, double-act partnering, which, in itself, indicates a kind of parity (as discussed in the previous part). By contrast, musical sections with strings only often lack foot sounds in numbers where jazzier passages get foot sounds regardless of the music's volume (the "Concert Solo" and "Mr. and Mrs. Hoofer at Home" from *Three Little Words* [1950]). To sum, Astaire's addition of foot sounds is generally pervasive—four of five routines include this audio supplement to his dancing body—but highly situational and often driven by considerations of musical and dance style.

Noisy foot sounds prove a foundational element of Astaire's character. The early RKO films reiterate again and again that Astaire is a noisy man. Before Astaire really starts dancing his first solo, "Music Makes Me," in *Flying Down to Rio* (1933), he demonstrates an undeniable urge to fill musical silences with tapped syncopation: Astaire fills a break in the band's arrangement with a stomping tap combination that combines anger at the band for taunting him this way and a deeper tendency toward "broken" rhythms. Astaire's identification with jazz tap—a heavily syncopated and loud, heavy style (associated with some Black tappers, such as John W. Bubbles)—is forwarded here as Astaire's way of being in the world. His noisy break for the maître d' in the first scene of *The Gay Divorcee* (1934) makes the same point, as do his first two moves in his *Roberta* solo, "I Won't Dance," when Astaire uses a stamping combination to send the two tall Cossacks who carried him to the dance floor scurrying away. It's important to qualify some aspects of Astaire's default tap style: it's heavy and into the floor (with lots of flat-foot stamps with his full body weight behind them); it's grounded in highly syncopated invention (standard tap steps, such as the time step, are avoided); it's identified with Black sources but is not the only Black tap style (not all Black tappers did jazz tap; Bill Robinson, for example, did not); it's not necessarily an expression of aggression (Astaire adds this aspect in select scenes, such as the three instances just mentioned). *Top Hat*, the first leading-man film role written especially for Astaire, makes his proclivity for noise making with his feet the defining aspect of Astaire's specifically American character. In the first scene, Astaire is awaiting Edward Everett Horton at the Thackery Club, a stuffy all-male British institution where noise of any kind—even the rustling of a newspaper in the smoking room—is simply out of order. Astaire initially plays the polite guest. But on his exit from the club he executes a furious tap break that stirs up a ruckus among the old men. The moment sets Astaire up as a boyish prankster, a man who causes mischief. Decades later, Hollywood gossip columnist Joyce Haber pegged this aspect of Astaire: "I have known Fred socially now for a decade and I'd say he's more of an imp. An imp with class."[16] Astaire's "imp" side returns throughout *Top Hat*—for instance, he takes a further parting shot at the Thackery Club men by "shooting" them with his cane during his bows for the title number; they duck in delight at this game with the unpredictable young American visitor.

The two tap attacks on the Thackery Clubbers speak two languages: the dance language of rhythm tap and the visceral language of sheer noise, specifically body noise—an insistent form of body language that stakes a claim to attention by disrupting the sonic realm. In a social dance instruction book from the mid-1930s published in Britain, Astaire wrote about the power of "Talking with Your Feet!"

> Remember that old song "Every Little Movement has a Meaning All Its Own"? There was a lot of truth in that title, especially when applied to dancing. Whole conversations can be carried out on the dance floor, without a word being spoken. A formal sign language for the feet never has been compiled, but when you stop to think of it, it is remarkable how accurately the feet express certain sentiments. For instance, it isn't necessary to have a translator to tell one that a tapping foot means impatience. A stamp means anger in any man's language. Shuffling feet connote embarrassment and lack of self-confidence. Wiggling toes can tell more about small boy ecstasy than volumes of words. So much for the lesson in foot language. It's really possible to carry on a specific conversation with the feet in a Tap Dance routine. There's the conversation sequence in the "I'll Be Hard to Handle" number with Ginger Rogers and I dance in the RADIO musical feature "Roberta" for example. I imagine audiences will have little difficulty in translating that little tap talk.

> After all, the Morse Code is based on a series of dots and dashes, and conversations have been flashed across continents and beneath seas that way. It isn't necessary to know a Morse Code to read the message of foot taps, however, if one has a vivid imagination and can see the facial expressions of the persons doing the tapping. Pantomime and sign language have sufficed for centuries to bridge the gap between tongues. The Tap Dance combines features of both, with the feet doing the heavy language duty.
>
> And if you're sensitive to music, you won't need much coaching in doing "hot dances." The music should take care of your feet. There really isn't much advice I can give about this kind of dancing. You either get it or you don't. I can't say anything about sticking to simple steps, because you make your own steps, or adapt them, as the music moves you. One thing I can advise, though. The place not to do a "Hot Dance" is a crowded ballroom floor. There's nothing more annoying than to be bumped, stepped on or jostled by a couple attempting to out-Harlem Harlem on a floor that is trying to accommodate 500 dancers where there should be but 100. Of course, if it is a free-for-all, with each couple trying to out-hotcha the others, it's all right....
>
> My parting advice, however, is to save the "Hot Dance" for your own home, the exhibition floor, the uncrowded ballroom or for parties where you are sure the host won't mind if his china and glassware are shattered.[17]

Astaire lays out his philosophy of foot sounds in some detail here. First, foot sounds communicate meaning directly, no dance style knowledge or translation needed. The examples he gives of body language that makes noise and carries meaning are distinctly masculine—impatience, anger (a "stamp" that any man will understand), lack of confidence, the ecstasy of a small boy. Second, the key to understanding the "Morse Code" of "foot taps" is seeing the dancer's face, something screen dancing considerably increased in power. Third, talking with your feet is personal—the dancer makes up his own words "as the music moves you." The tapper's imperative to be original flows here not from any shared body of dance-specific knowledge but rather from day-to-day body language translated into dancing—moves that aren't dance steps so much as just steps, like walking. Fourth, in the final part of the passage Astaire elides "Tap Dance," where "the feet do the heavy language duty," and "Hot Dance," a category of music and dance he connects elsewhere in this source to Black spaces, such as Harlem.[18] Tap and "Hot" dancing—essentially the same thing—are then situated as not especially polite, as potential disruptions of the social dance floor. These are (Black) styles for self-assertion and display—at parties if the host is willing to risk some collateral damage to "his china and glassware." Astaire's bachelor party performance at Prince's comes to mind as just such an occasion (Gadd's story of that night emphasizes Astaire didn't break a thing).

Several "conversation[s] with the feet" stand out as defining moments for Astaire's masculinity. The "conversation sequence" in "I'll Be Hard to Handle," referenced by Astaire, has him and Rogers arguing with each other while the band and the beat fall silent. She gets angrier than him and, to end the talk, she both slaps his face and stomps his foot then does a little self-satisfied step celebrating her accomplishment. A bugle call brings them both back in step. Nondance moves—like slaps and stomps—are treated in the next section as a common thread across Astaire's dances. In several RKO numbers, Astaire talks in tap with a chorus. In "I'd Rather Lead a Band" (*Follow the Fleet*), the band and beat again stop for a long stretch while Astaire plays drill sergeant and issues commands with his feet. The first matches the command "about face" (which is how the sailors respond), but the rest are unspecific. The sailors undercut Astaire's authority by collectively kicking him in the butt—another nondance dance step that recurs. In two further RKO solos with chorus, Astaire and the chorus exchange rhythms in a conversational manner, albeit in the context of an ongoing beat. The chorus as a responding collective agent seems to be the point: the women in "Bojangles of Harlem" (*Swing Time*) do a break that kicks a static Astaire into action; Astaire reacts visibly when the men in "Top Hat, White Tie, and Tails" match his fancy tap break solo (perhaps their effrontery initiates his mission to shoot them all down later in the number). Astaire uses facial expressions to lend all these exchanges a sense of spontaneity—these aren't prestaged numbers presented to the audience but conversations between the star and the mass of dancers behind him, a group that exists to support him but who also can serve as a foil for his masculinity (out-tapping them projects his larger presence). And Astaire's foot sounds always remain foremost in the mix. In the shadows portion of "Bojangles," Astaire only notices the three large shadows behind him when he pauses and they execute a tap break. The sound of their feet is hollow and only ever heard here—the shadows are otherwise not given the sonic reinforcement Astaire consistently receives (and intentionally gave himself). Foot sounds make insistent claims on the world, indeed on specific territory. Astaire's larger goal was to say something new and the process of finding such novelty was violent (Astaire: "Dance steps are very hard to get that look fresh. That sort of thing you just have to beat the floor til [sic] you get what you're after.") and analogous to other manly pursuits, such as hunting (Astaire: "This search for what you want is like tracking something that doesn't want to be tracked.").[19] The result is an unrelentingly noisy foot sound persona, demanding attention in a way Astaire's larger body movements do not. Astaire's aggressive sound—Seibert describes it as "not a graceful sound. . . . Astaire's stamped rhythms have the logic of tantrums, impatient, sputtering"—disrupts and dominates, as often as not coming off as in-your-face (ear?) trash talk.[20]

47. The Matrix of Violent Nondance Dance Moves

"The Babbitt and the Bromide" (*Ziegfeld Follies*) stages an encounter on a park bench between two cis-het white men—both of whom dance for a living. Astaire and Gene Kelly initially meet by way of a bit of very polite trash-talk taps: Astaire taps a bit, and then the guy next to him on the bench (Kelly, blocked by the newspaper he's reading) taps back. This leads to a verbal exchange rife with (perhaps false) politeness and (thinly veiled) threat. Kelly recognizes Astaire immediately. Astaire pretends not to know who Kelly is—at this point he had but one substantial credit: *Cover Girl*, released mid-March 1944. ("Babbitt" was filmed in May 1944, but *Ziegfeld Follies* was not released until April 1946, by which time Kelly had appeared in MGM's *Anchors Aweigh* with Frank Sinatra.) When Astaire asks Kelly what he does, Kelly replies, "I dance." Searching for Kelly's name after the mention of *Cover Girl*, Astaire says with a smile, "You're not Rita Hayworth?" Kelly chuckles with annoyance and replies, "No, I'm not—Ginger." They respond together with a "hannn" sound (through smiling clenched teeth) and rise from the bench. Each man, it turns out, has "a little number to do." Astaire suggests they "ad lib a little something together." Kelly says, "Just whip it up on the spot," then continues "like the one we've been rehearsing for two weeks." (In fact, they rehearsed the number for three-and-a-half weeks; it took four days to film.) After another shared "hannn," they turn to the camera and begin a double-act dance filled with masculine aggression. (The shift from dialogue to lip-syncing is especially brilliant—the vocal begins with no instrumental cue; both men are masters of the musical's peculiar production methods.)

Conflict begins early in the first dance section. Astaire and Kelly stride forward confidently and after just four steps turn toward each other and nearly collide. Having avoided a full-body collision, they immediately do run into each other. The tap break that follows has each hit the other's foot—the flats of their feet bang hard against each other. Both react as if in pain. These opening seconds establish motifs developed across the number: Astaire and Kelly each demand right of way (with false politeness) and their respective (and parallel) efforts to assert independence only lead to pain for themselves (an admission they're not so tough after all). Direct physical contact, framed as mistakes (but, of course, well rehearsed), make this point in a way that limiting the dance to just "dance" steps could not. The theme of (minor) self-inflicted wounds is returned to at the end of the first dance section, when, after a successful bit of double-act tap, each man does a high forward kick that hits his own hand. Each registers an "ouch," and then they grasp each other's hands in one of the seven handshakes in the number. The second dance section, done in brown sack suits, bowler hats, and mustaches, begins as an easy soft shoe. But soon enough, the conflict returns. Kelly stomps Astaire's toe; Astaire responds with a high kick that appears to kick (or just barely miss) Kelly's nose. Escalation is the name of the game. They clasp hands—another handshake but this time part of the dance—and Kelly pulls Astaire across front, reversing their position with a supported partnering step. Looks between the two men ensure this dance continues to be also a study in masculine challenge. After a stretch of double-act close-position moves, Kelly restarts the game and knocks Astaire's hat off; Astaire reciprocates to end this section. The pair move toward each other, initially with hands on hips as if in angry challenge. But it's all in fun, say their smiles: they clasp hands and turn to sing the final verse-chorus pair. "Babbitt" is never mean-spirited—it is, however, not about cooperation or deference. Instead, the theme of masculine competition plays out throughout in small (nondance) acts of aggression. Heaven, the location of the third and longest dance section, is a place of waltzes. After waltzing about singly with harps in hand, the two men boldly throw their harps away and fall into closed ballroom position for a few steps. (The continuity of the cut here is poor—the match on action off a noticeable amount.) After separating for a turn, they bump full into each other back to back, bow with mock courtesy, and start waltzing in closed position again. But then the music changes to swing and, taking advantage of a step, Kelly kicks Astaire in the butt twice. The game is back on. Astaire responds with three kicks to Kelly's rear. With miffed looks on their faces, the two walk side by side and proceed to both trip over an unseen object on the floor. The dance stops briefly as they think over this shared loss of physical control. A return to waltz time cues the third passage for the pair in closed ballroom position, but another slide toward swing in the music leads them to open their position; still clasping hands, they dance, for a bit, like a swing couple. Then Astaire releases Kelly's hand and Kelly falls to the floor (discussed earlier under contrasting movements). One wonders if Kelly's remark about "Babbitt" to the BBC recalls this moment: he called Astaire "the senior partner" and said, "Frankly I didn't like the number."[21] Only after Astaire disses Kelly by making him fall does the number turn toward virtuoso dance without male-male conflict. The tempo picks up and they dance with increased speed and size, for one stretch arm in arm. A final handshake seals the number, their harps return—dropped from above—and they walk forward into insert framing for a final pose, Astaire with a fraternal hand resting on Kelly's shoulder.

The content of the "Babbitt" choreography shows a discomfort with simply dancing with each other. A relation of equality or cooperation—a united front—is not the plan for these two professional dancing men. They resist double-act comity (which Kelly gleefully shares with Sinatra and Donald O'Connor in multiple numbers), defer to each other only mockingly, and never show mutual pride in the other's skill (as the Nicholas Brothers do). Astaire and Kelly shake hands at the start and finish of each vocal chorus, but this gesture of nonaggression never does the trick: their relationship cannot sustain civility; a masculine bent toward violence (however interpreted) obtains almost up to the end. Crucially, their conflict plays out not by way of dancing challenges but through the incorporation of dance steps that are not properly dance steps but instead actions typical of two ordinary (nondancing) men fighting—full-body contact (face to face and back to back), stomping each other's toes, kicking each other, knocking each other's hats off (a sublimated punch to the head), and letting the other man fall to the floor. The aggressive moves in "Babbitt"—stomped feet and kicks to the face included in the "Snake Dance"—recur in a subcorpus of twenty-two Astaire dances. Table 9 offers a matrix of these routines that include hypermasculine nondance dance moves involving bodily contact and/or physical aggression of some kind. Any loss of physical control (tripping, slipping, falling) is also counted. These numbers are ranked in the table by the total number of nondance dance moves used. "Babbitt," along with "Please Don't Monkey with Broadway," "Shoes with Wings On," and "How Could You Believe Me..." top the list with five of the six moves. Three distinct types of violent nondance dance moves are discussed in this section (use of a weapon, toe stomps, kicks) with an eye and ear to how each shapes Astaire's "characterizing" and sets the tone for social interaction in his dances with men and with women.

TABLE 9 Matrix of nondance dance moves

	Tally	Bodily Contact	Stomped Toes	Kick in the Pants (or Elsewhere)	Hands as Weapons; as Greeting	Stick and Gun Play	Tripping, Slipping, Falling
"Please Don't Monkey with Broadway" (*BM40*)	5	X		X	X	X	X
"The Babbitt and the Bromide" (*ZF*)	5	X	X	X	X		X
"Shoes with Wings On" (*BB*)	5	X	X	X		X	X
"How Could You Believe Me..." (*RW*)	5	X	X	X	X		X
"Oh, Them Dudes" (*LD*)	4	X		X		X	X
"Oops" (*BNY*)	4	X	X	X			X
"Girl Hunt" opening (*BW*)	4			X	X	X	X
"Girl Hunt" bop joint (*BW*)	4			X	X	X	X
"Put Me to the Test" (*DD*)	4	X	X	X		X	
"I'm Putting All My Eggs in One Basket" (*FF*)	3	X			X		X
"Mr. and Mrs. Hoofer at Home" (*TLW*)	3		X		X	X	
"By the Light of the Silvery Moon" (*SVIC*)	2	X			X		
"Hello! Hello! Who's Your Lady Friend?" (*SVIC*)	2	X		X			
"I've Got My Eyes on You" finale (*BM40*)	2		X		X		
"A Couple of Swells" (*EP*)	2	X					X
"Can't Stop Talkin'" (*LD*)	2		X		X		
"Triplets" (*BW*)	2		X	X			
"I'll Be Hard to Handle" (*R*)	1				X		
"Top Hat, White Tie, and Tails" (*TH*)	1					X	
"I'd Rather Lead a Band" (*FF*)	1			X			
"Audition Dance" (*YWNL*)	1					X	
"A Lot in Common with You" (*STL*)	1						X

As discussed in section thirty-five, Astaire plays with a stick-like object in twenty-four dances. Sometimes he uses these sticks as intended—as with the golf clubs that facilitate golf swings as dance steps. Canes, walking sticks, or furled umbrellas are the most common class of stick Astaire carries. Astaire affects this manly prop of an earlier time with dismissive annoyance and boyish flare. When angry or provoked, he throws his cane aside (see "Please Don't Monkey with Broadway" [*Broadway Melody*] and "I Guess I'll Have to Change My Plan" [*Band Wagon*]). His default relation to sticks is an urge to play—tossing or knocking canes or umbrellas into the air (so as to catch them again) or hitting them on the ground (so as to make more noise than his two feet can do without it). Astaire also tosses drumsticks and walking sticks against walls and floors so as to catch them again, with an added bonus in the added noise. He also relishes tossing stick props into a can: a trick Astaire included in both the "Audition Dance" and "Let's Kiss and Make Up" from *Funny Face* (1957)—as Dick Cavett pointed out to him in their 1970 television interview to challenge Astaire's claim he never repeated steps (Cavett's highly selective clip reel revealed his failure to live up to what he claimed the clip reel was intended to prevent: repetition of steps).

Of course, sticks easily stand in for weapons. Astaire and George Murphy build most of the dance in "Please Don't Monkey with Broadway" on an interpretation of their dancing canes as swords. After stabbing Astaire, Murphy carefully wipes Astaire's blood off his cane/sword. Having caught a drum major's baton in "Shooting the Works for Uncle Sam" in *You'll Never Get Rich* (1941), it takes Astaire just seconds to literalize the song's title and pretend it's a gun. Astaire shoots a stick prop as if it were a gun in two major solos. The broom in "Shoes with Wings On" becomes a machine gun in one of the instances of a lack of synchronization between Astaire and the disembodied shoes (the trajectory of his broom/gun doesn't match the shoes leaping out of its way). In "Top Hat, White Tie, and Tails," his cane morphs into several kinds of guns: initially a sniper's rifle as he picks off individual chorus boys, then a machine gun as he mows them down. "Talking taps" provide appropriate sound effects for each sort of gun, in effect filling in for the verbal "pow pow" or "ratatatatata" a boy might add. Indeed, Astaire's stick play often hints at boyish pleasures. Performer Larry Adler recalled the Broadway inspiration for "Top Hat" in the 1930 stage musical *Smiles*. For the song "Say, Young Man of Manhattan," Astaire created a routine set in the Bowery, a rough neighborhood in lower Manhattan. Adler played a Bowery Kid. Astaire arrived in this lower-class neighborhood with twenty-four chorus boys—all in white tie and tails. The staging suggests a group of wealthy white men slumming—though pointedly they go downtown instead of uptown to Harlem, the more common destination at the time (which would have required Black adversaries). In the course of the number, Astaire shot down the twenty-four chorus boys and Adler as well.[22] The extreme violence of this dance—on Broadway and in Hollywood—warrants pointing out. It's a musical number, yes, but it's also an instance of a privileged white man indiscriminately killing others in an urban context ("Top Hat" is set in Paris). If not for the bright music and assumed "lightness" of the musical as a genre, the narratives of "Say, Young Man of Manhattan" and "Top Hat" alike resemble episodes from Bret Easton Ellis's novel *American Psycho*, with Astaire cast as a gleeful Patrick Bateman. Astaire's killing of the last surviving chorus boy in "Top Hat" with a bow and arrow adds to this comparison: when guns repeatedly don't work, Astaire reaches for more primitive weapons (as does Bateman). Trudy Wellman, the assistant director on *Top Hat*, recalled ordering thirteen canes for the number because Astaire kept breaking them. The violence with which he treated these props shouldn't be underestimated. She added, "He gets very annoyed with himself, just with himself."[23]

Astaire's distinction as an especially violent musical star is confirmed by his use of actual guns in both "Oh, Them Dudes" (*Let's Dance*) and "Girl Hunt" (*Band Wagon*). The former has Astaire and Hutton shoot out a television set where high-class folks—the "dudes" of the title—are square dancing (Hutton names their offense in a terrific Johnny Mercer lyric as "jumping our claim on 'The Turkey in the Straw'"). Multiple gunshots follow as part of the dance (discussed later for their connection to literal ass-kicking dance steps). The western saloon milieu of "Oh, Them Dudes" explains the appropriateness of the danced gunplay by way of generic blending. Astaire's use of a handgun in "Girl Hunt" is similarly understood: he's a musical star doing a film noir sendup. Astaire's capacity to pull off playing private eye Rod Riley needs underlining and his success doing so opened a recurring theme: several of his television dances reprise the gritty atmosphere of the genre.[24] He would not have been convincing in the part had he not already established a persona as an assertive, taciturn, potentially violent screen figure. The distance between Astaire and film noir, albeit a musicalized version of the genre, was much shorter than that traveled by Dick Powell, who went from fresh-faced boy singer in the 1930s to hard-boiled leading man after *Murder, My Sweet* (1944). By a twenty-first-century measure, Astaire earns a singular place for musical film stars among Hollywood tough guys: he has an entry in the user-generated wiki imfdb.com—the Internet Movie Firearms Database. Here we learn that the heat Astaire packs in "Girl Hunt" is a Smith & Wesson Model M&P, a "classic police revolver used by police and military on most continents from the early 1900s until this day. According to the FBI, . . . the most purchased handgun in the U.S."[25]

Toes are an easy target in any tap dance and stomps in a partner's direction might easily start an aggressive tit for tat. Astaire gets his foot stomped more often than he does the stomping, and most toe stomping in the clip reel involves women. At the height of their "talking taps" argument in "I'll Be Hard to Handle," Rogers stomps Astaire's foot. It has a musical effect, suddenly shifting Astaire into triplet motion. Toe stomps are juvenile. It comes as no surprise that they turn up in Astaire's trio dances, which place Astaire in company with one man and one woman. The mood in the trios is friendly rivalry: each can be understood as a dance for siblings. This is literally the case in "Triplets," the brief number in *Band Wagon* that rated highest with the film's preview audience. The very short but visually satisfying dance break in "Triplets" ends with Astaire and Jack Buchanan, in the outside positions, simultaneously stomping Nanette Fabray's toes (fig. 47.1). She cries out "Ow!" just as the vocal tag begins. Astaire receives a double stomp from the first two pairs of disembodied shoes in "Shoes with Wings On," the first indication his magical encounter will skew toward attack (fig. 47.2). Fabray's exclamation in "Triplets" raises the importance of response to foot stomping as a "characterizing" dance move. Response tells the viewer physical contact has occurred: it's unlikely dancers are literally treading on each other's toes—although in *Belle of New York* Vera-Ellen visibly lands and stands on Astaire's toe during "Oops" (he grimaces; she smiles). And the reaction need not be pain: in the short trio dance finale to *Broadway Melody of*

FIGURE 47.1

FIGURE 47.2

FIGURE 47.3

1940, Eleanor Powell reacts to Astaire's stomp toward her toe with a look of amused shock (she had been indulging in a smug little solo; fig. 47.3). In "Put Me to the Test" (*A Damsel in Distress* [1937]), Astaire and the husband-wife team George Burns and Gracie Allen get in a frenzied stamping fight that briefly ignores the beat—Astaire would translate the effect as "anger in any man's language."

Toe stomps can start a chain reaction. Kelly stomps Astaire's toe in "Babbitt." Astaire responds with a kick that catches Kelly in the face. Multiple kicks in the butt are soon exchanged between the pair. The same pattern obtains in "Put Me to the Test," with the stamp fight followed by Astaire and Burns alternately kicking Allen. She gets them back by kneeing both in the butt simultaneously, a double jump kick Astaire repeats with drums at the end of the "Drum Dance" and just after the number to close a plot strand in *Damsel in Distress* (he kicks two servant characters in the derrières and seems more interested in exacting this revenge than strutting out his girl). Kicks to the behind occupy much of the closing section of "Put Me to the Test." Having exchanged initial kicks, all three begin turning, in constant fear of being gotten again. They move to a new area in the room, a wall with three suits of armor. Anyone can see the punchline coming: dancing in front of the armor, Astaire, Burns, and Allen all get kicked by the armor at the same time (fig. 47.4). Fending off further blows from the armor leads to the trio kicking their metal foes and injuring themselves. Cue the trio's exit: limping. If stomps need a reaction from the stompee, kicks allow for a reaction from the kicker. As noted, the notion that acts of physical aggression might backfire and hurt the aggressor recurs in "Babbitt." Kicking as an unassailably masculine form of touch-and-release partnering finds an apogee of sorts in "Oh, Them Dudes," an especially physical routine. After having lifted Astaire full off the ground only to drop him violently, Hutton and Astaire begin to kick each other in the butt in time to the music. The tight blue jeans Hutton wears suggest the force of the kicks—this is a contact routine. To climax the dance, shooting is added to the kicking in a kind of canon: each dances the same pattern of kicks and shots in alternation, turning their backs to the camera in turn to receive repeated kicks from the other. It's a bizarre set of steps but, given Astaire's frequent use of kicks in the past, in no way out of character. The low-class, western conceit of the number—the pair gets progressively drunker as it unfolds—and Hutton being in drag allowed for this routine in the first place. There's no threat things will really get out of hand given it's a broadly comic dance with a woman in drag. How the same scenario might play out with Kelly can only be imagined (suggesting the necessity of the mock politeness of "Babbitt").

A succession of enough physically aggressive moves edges a dance toward the status of a fight. This devolution away from dancing happens near the end of "How Could You Believe Me . . .," another low-class routine. The dance halts when Astaire has a second violent attack, which he ends by throwing his

FIGURE 47.4

straw hat to the floor. Jane Powell proceeds to jump on the hat with both feet, crushing it flat. Astaire picks it up, walks forward into insert framing, and holds it out to the camera in a bid for sympathy amplified by a whiny violin line. But Powell is far from done with him. After Astaire puts the hat back on his head, she promptly pulls the brim down over his head. He pulls back his arm, as if to strike her, but she is too quick and herself administers a series of double blows—first to his gut, then to his chin. Then the big setup: Powell positions Astaire's left hand against his own chin, his left knee against his left elbow, and then she in turn kicks his left foot (fig. 47.5). Astaire knocks himself to the ground, from which position he scoots off stage on his back, pursued by a scolding Powell. Each of these hits and kicks is matched by drums in a vaudeville "catching the falls" style—the effect is intentionally cartoonish. With a background beat going the whole time and a vocal tag that has to be caught by lip-syncing, this is indeed a choreographed fight done in rhythm (and yet another virtuoso shot executed by Astaire and Powell in *Royal Wedding*). The routine turns domestic violence on its head—with a shrewish (but cute) woman beating up a boyfriend who is all talk.

"Girl Hunt" has several stretches of fight choreography that don't follow a prescribed beat but function more like simulated fighting in action movies. This overlap between musicals and action movies again suggests the continuity between these genres. Both are body genres and a male musical star of sufficient masculinity can occupy a position where the two overlap, provided the emphasis remains on the fight (not the dance). The fights in "Girl Hunt" are fast and furious with few punches actually landed, although Astaire does break bottles over two thugs' heads during the free-for-all after his bop joint dance with Charisse. Also of note in this sequence is his response to a thug who, in typical 1950s male dancer fashion, literally comes toward him doing

FIGURE 47.5

FIGURE 47.6

flips. Minnelli and Kidd set up the encounter in its own shot, which begins on and follows the flipping thug, momentarily making him the focus of the fight. Astaire, as Rod Riley, stands there and shoots the thug down—like a precursor to Harrison Ford as Indiana Jones calmly shooting an exoticized Arab male foe who confronts him while swinging a scimitar in the first film in the series (fig. 47.6). In the bop joint fight, Astaire puts aside dance moves—which he only does with the hypersexualized Charisse—and limits himself to fight choreography that removes any taint of dancing connected to the word *choreography*. The flipping thug he fells with one shot "deserves to die" and Astaire administers cold justice with not a dance move but a bullet.

48. Silent Yellowface

In Part One, I counted a total of nine Astaire numbers (from the larger count of 207) in which white performers appear in nonwhite racial guises. As noted, Astaire retains his whiteness in a slight majority of these numbers—he's the white guy in a Western suit in a foreign place where the natives wear body-revealing, bright-colored clothes.[26] Astaire himself performs a nonwhite racial type in four numbers—the blackface "Bojangles," the brownface "Steppin' Out with My Baby" (*Easter Parade*), the yellowface "Limehouse Blues," and the vaguely exotic first part of "Begin the Beguine" (*Broadway Melody*).

The only time Astaire set aside his whiteness for the entirety of a number and took on a nonwhite, not-Black racial persona was "Limehouse Blues," a long dance pantomime in *Ziegfeld Follies* directed by Vincente Minnelli and choreographed by Robert Alton. This extraordinary routine finds a place in this section of the book for its complete lack of foot sounds and its extreme alteration of Astaire's physical person—his yellowface makeup is foregrounded in a close-up early in the number. Setting aside his white man's wardrobe, his "outlaw" (largely Black-derived) dance style and his use of foot sounds make this number as close as we get to answering critic Alexander Bland's question of "how [Astaire] would have fared in choreography not especially created for [him]."[27] "Limehouse" was, of course, created for Astaire. But the conception and execution of the number fall as far outside his normal limits as he ever allowed. Largely ignored in the scholarship on musical film, "Limehouse" deserves close reading.[28]

"*Limehouse Blues*—big number for Astaire" appears on the earliest extant rundown of *Ziegfeld Follies*. Also on the list were a "*Follies Minstrel Number*" (for a while slated as the big finale) and "Lena Horn [sic] and Avon Long in *Big Colored* number."[29] As the contents of the film took shape, Astaire was variously imagined in several numbers that did not get made: as the interlocutor in the minstrel show (perhaps in blackface), in a "high yella" duo with Judy Garland set in "Smoky Joe's Colored Night Club" in Harlem, and as one of "three Indian braves" (with Gene Kelly and Mickey Rooney) in "Pass That Peace Pipe" ("Possibly Fred and Gene will abuse Mickey; and every time he gets fighting mad, they stuff a peace pipe into his mouth and sing, 'Pass that Peace Pipe and bury that hatchet, etc.' This *might* be a running gag during dance").[30] All these unmade numbers traffic in noxious stereotypes of nonwhite others and white racial presumption to re-perform said tropes for white audiences. Two Astaire numbers that did get made project specific sorts of whiteness. Robert Alton's detailed scenario for "The Babbitt and the Bromide" sets the scene in Central Park and pegs the number's array of white masculine types as "young smart elecs [sic]" and "Wall Street brokers."[31] "This Heart of Mine," in one document described as a "Nineteenth-century number,"[32] grew around the figure of Raffles, a gentleman-thief from the pages of Sir Arthur Conan Doyle. The final scenario for the number, which accurately describes the finished version, located it at "A magnificent estate in Southern France, or a colonial possession of France, such as Martinique" on "A beautiful, moonlit summer evening in 1850."[33] Astaire's Continental jewel thief initially sports a monocle and cigarette holder, although they are quickly revealed to be props along with the fake military decorations he dons before entering the ballroom. As all these numbers suggest, *Ziegfeld Follies* was, from the start, conceived as a parade of racial and ethnic stereotypes. The final film offers as much with a decided slant toward whiteness. Only two numbers are nonwhite: Lena Horne's "Love" (a Black-cast number) and "Limehouse Blues" (a yellowface extravaganza).[34]

The song "Limehouse Blues" launched British stage star Gertrude Lawrence's career. Astaire surely saw her sing it in yellowface on Broadway in 1924 in *André Charlot's Revue*. Astaire reportedly asked to do the song in *Ziegfeld Follies* and biographer Peter Levinson notes Astaire said it was his favorite routine in his speech at the 1973 Film Society of Lincoln Center event (where it was part of the clip reel Astaire helped assemble).[35] An initial description of the concept for the number in the Freed papers describes it as "*Limehouse Blues* big dance number with 'broken blossom' background."[36] *Broken Blossoms* was a 1919 film directed by D. W. Griffith set in London's Chinatown—the Limehouse wharf district on the river Thames—about a Chinese immigrant named Cheng Huan (played by the white actor Richard Barthelmess in yellowface) who tries and fails to protect a young white girl named Lucy (played by Lillian Gish) from her abusive prizefighter father. In the final scene, Cheng brings Lucy's dead body back to his home, where he had previously sheltered her, and then kills himself in grief. The source for *Broken Blossoms* was British author Thomas Burke's story "The Chink and the Child" in the 1916 collection *Limehouse Nights*. In 1934, Paramount released a film titled *Limehouse Blues* set in Burke's foggy milieu. The plot turns on a half-white, half-Chinese American cabaret owner and smuggler played in yellowface by George Raft, a tough guy leading man who danced in several films just prior to the start of Astaire's career.[37] Raft's character falls in love with a young white female pickpocket from the neighborhood. She resists his attentions, but in the end, Raft takes a police bullet and dies to avert his own plan to kill the white man she loves—a white Canadian who runs a dog store (his profession opens the way to conversations about mutts and thoroughbreds). Raft's sacrificial death for love of a white girl he cannot have is the film's final tableau. Earlier in the film, he performs a violent Apache dance with Chinese American star Anna May Wong while wearing the costume of a coolie—similar to what Astaire wears in *Ziegfeld Follies*. What little is seen of this routine is sexually fraught and violent in implication. Raft is not a passive or gentle figure like Barthelmess in *Broken Blossoms* or Astaire in "Limehouse Blues."

Indeed, the scenario and dance for Astaire's yellowface routine lies well outside the narrative tropes of the Limehouse district in popular culture. Astaire plays a Chinese man in a simple black Tang suit with a Western-style brimmed hat (fig. 48.1). He wanders a bit, encounters a rich white man

FIGURE 48.1

FIGURE 48.2

(who tips him for picking up his cane; Astaire drops the coin dismissively), then sees Lucille Bremer. Also in yellowface, she wears a form-fitting, bright yellow qipao and projects a fashionable figure in the otherwise dingy mise en scène—indeed, she fairly glows (fig. 48.2). Astaire gazes at her from close range somewhat creepily; she doesn't notice him. Cross-cutting close-ups of both allow for close scrutiny of their makeup.

Astaire proceeds to follow Bremer—more properly stalk, given his stylized steps behind her back—as she wanders through the Limehouse neighborhood. He sees a Chinese gangster-type man (Robert Lewis in yellowface) stop her and offer his arm, which she refuses. The gangster makes a threatening gesture with his thin cane but she moves on and he does not pursue. Bremer then wanders into a shop and inquires about an antique fan in the window. After she leaves, Astaire asks about the fan's price but it is too costly for him. At this moment, the shop is robbed by a group of rough, mustachioed, burly white men familiar from Limehouse stories. The street erupts in chaos but Astaire, oblivious to it all, dreamily steps into the street to pick up the fan. He is caught in the crossfire of a Limehouse gun battle and falls to the ground, reaching toward the fan. A dissolve takes the number into Astaire's imagination for the dance routine proper in a Chinoiserie fantasyland (considered for its unrealistic "jump" cuts in section thirty-six). Before turning to the nature of the duo dance done by Astaire and Bremer in these Orientalist confines, it's useful to finish out the story of the framing narrative. On the return back to the "real" Limehouse, Astaire is laying on a couch in the exact position of Lillian Gish in the iconic final scene of *Broken Blossoms* (the elderly Chinese shopkeeper watches over him). Bremer and the gangster enter the shop—clearly together (their spat on the sidewalk evidence of a combative relationship)—seeking to buy the fan. It is, however, ripped and ruined. Bremer drops it in disgust and leaves smiling with her underworld beau. Astaire follows this action throughout as the camera seeks out the white cabaret singer in the window across the street who sings the song "Limehouse Blues" at the start and finish of the whole sequence.

This narrative shares little more than the Limehouse location and atmosphere with previous tales of the area. Minnelli claimed in his 1974 memoir that "the precision Chinese fan dance around which the sequence was built had already been choreographed and the music recorded" when he created the framing narrative on sets built for *The Picture of Dorian Gray* (1945). The "fantasy section" derived its visual inspiration from the costume sketches of Irene Sharaff, who Minnelli credits with the "eighteenth-century Chinoiserie artifacts."[38] The keynote to all previous Limehouse stories was interracial sex or sympathy, most often between white women and Chinese or "Oriental" men. As Burke scholar Anne Veronica Witchard writes, "*Limehouse Nights* displays what seems an unusual racial tolerance to say the least," specifically "the absence of moral censure regarding miscegenation" between white English girls and Chinese men.[39] A more expected "Limehouse" narrative, if Astaire is to be in yellowface, would be for Bremer to be a blushing English rose (albeit from the gutter)—an easier fit to Bremer's type. But, instead, she was also put in yellowface. Her character—a stylish "Oriental" woman strolling the area, not apparently a prostitute (Limehouse prostitutes are generically white)—has no precedent in the tropes of this sort of story (Wong's character in *Limehouse Blues* is Raft's business associate). Behind it all, of course, is the intention to have Astaire and Bremer dance together. Where and when such an encounter might occur and how they might dance are fundamental problems for any "big number" in this larger milieu and using this song. An extant scenario for "Limehouse" that predates start of work on the number by about three months contains a different plan. "NOTE: This dramatization of 'Limehouse Blues' takes the form of a dance pantomime. The singing voices of Fred Astaire and a mixed choir occasionally punctuate the movement which is projected realistically at first and then in a stylized fashion, as the mood dictates, varying in the degree of its exaggeration from slightly formalized dance pantomime to pure dancing."[40] The narrative casts Astaire as Tai Long, an outcast and shifty figure having a romance, contextualized as memory, on the streets of Chinatown with Bremer as Moy Ling. (Burke's collection includes a character named Tai Ling.) The love of these two "Oriental" denizens of the area is interrupted by a shootout that leaves Moy Ling dead. No journey into a hyper-aestheticized world of the fan is included. So, from the start the plan was for both white performers to be in yellowface—really the only option from the perspective of the Motion Picture Association of America (MPAA) Production Code, which would have frowned on an extended interracial dance number. The challenge—given a commitment to the song "Limehouse Blues"—became creating an occasion for Astaire and Bremer to dance together and framing an understanding of what romance and romantic dancing between two "Oriental" characters might look like. The answer to this question would, of course, be seen in direct comparison with "This Heart of Mine," a fantasy of white romance danced by the same leading players that could hardly be more generic in plot or excessive in execution.

The dream sequence locates a fantasyland of yellow and blue Chinoiserie inside Astaire's imagination: as a projection of an "Oriental" male mind—at least, as the all-white team at MGM imagined such a place might be. Initially, Astaire, now clad in fitted bright red Chinese garb including a cap, literally pursues the fan as it appears to float through a dark space filled with half-seen figures in outlandish costumes. Astaire was self-conscious about his—to him—overly large hands. The initial dream section of "Limehouse" seems designed to emphasize their size (fig. 48.3). His pursuit of the fan leads to the return of Bremer, now wearing a matching red outfit, distinguished from Astaire's by the addition of small white pom-poms on her pants, a slightly longer flounce to her fitted jacket, and a white Hawaiian lei-type decoration on her top. Bremer's elaborate hairdo makes her appreciably taller than Astaire. After Astaire reaches Bremer and the fan, all the lights suddenly come up on the Chinoiserie dreamscape discussed in Part Four. Astaire and Bremer initially do a series of poses similar to Astaire and Powell in "I Concentrate on You" from *Broadway Melody of 1940*, another high-exotic MGM spectacle, then move through this space a bit by way of

FIGURE 48.3

space-defying cuts. Sometimes the conceit of Bremer leading Astaire by the fan is retained; sometimes they're just traveling through a set so packed with stimulation it's hard to concentrate. Visible lighting fixtures in some shots suggest Minnelli was confident audiences would not have time to digest all the details. Decoration overwhelms any narrative reason for being here: or, put another way, Astaire and Bremer's characters, such as they are, are little more than ornamental elements—perhaps the most important (they are in red) but also perhaps just accents in a scene meant to envelope us in sensuous Orientalist sensation. Astaire and Bremer's characters lack any interiority, much less narrative relationship: they are decorative in the manner of European Chinoiserie, "merely physical and exotic" figures in a florid and baroque nonwhite realm. All the principles Astaire adhered to that give space-making power to the dancing body are set aside: he is, here, a nonwhite design element moving silently through an environment, rather than a white agent making noise and producing space as he moves.

The first shot of the dance proper involves precise use of a reframed shot to place props in the dancers' hands. Beginning in context framing, Astaire and Bremer run into a waist-up insert. Careful attention to their arms shows them being handed the large red and white fans they will use throughout the three-and-one-quarter-minute double dance that begins in this shot (fig. 48.4). Appearing magically in their hands when the camera pulls back, they begin the routine by opening their fans in time to big chords in the music. It's a gimmicky touch atypical of Astaire's use of objects. Use of the fans continues throughout the dance, inevitably limiting the amount and types of touching (21%; almost all arms linked or around waists). The music complicates this dance as well. A swing-style beat comes and goes, suggesting the popular song roots of the tune and breaking the Orientalist tone of the preceding

FIGURE 48.4

FIGURE 48.5

exploration of the fantasyland. With fans in their hands and no sexualized hierarchy evident in the setup or their clothes, it's difficult to find any thread of heterosexual meaning in the dance. One moment has Astaire behind Bremer, holding her and swaying—perhaps a kind of lovey-dovey movement (fig. 48.5)—but other than this it's mostly furious arm motion (enlarged by the fans); one partner moving around the posing other (Bremer and Astaire each take both positions); movement in and out of static positions that use the fans in a picturesque fashion (fig. 48.6); and even, at the end, Astaire doing a hurried (not very good) cartwheel. The partnering categories discussed in Part Five hardly apply—mainly because of the lack of any straight white male ballast in the number. They both swing the other off the ground at the end, perhaps analogous to Astaire and Rogers at the end of "Isn't This a Lovely Day?" (*Top Hat*), but with no grounding in heterosexual romance it's difficult to read this moment as a culmination of any relationship. These characters are (decorative) ciphers that do not easily map onto any legible Asian stereotypes—except perhaps notions of the Asian male as passive and feminine. Indeed, the

FIGURE 48.6

entirety of the "Limehouse" dance could be done by two women. The patterns the pair make are consistently collaborative, balanced, and frontal—this is a dance presenting their bodies forward (though there is no evident viewer within the film). Adding to the sense of spectacle is the lack of foot sounds throughout the entire "Limehouse" sequence.

There are several ways to read Astaire's screen dance body in "Limehouse Blues." One way might see a general queering of his persona initiated by his loss of whiteness: Astaire's yellowface masculinity (fundamentally shaped by his costuming as much as his makeup) tilts his every move toward effeminacy. He is denied the cool menace of Chinese criminals (like Raft in *Limehouse Blues*) and left with the passivity of Barthelmess in *Broken Blossoms*, a weakness compounded by the lack of any ennobling plot to save a young white girl. Indeed, Astaire isn't even rejected by Bremer in the framing narrative—she doesn't recognize he exists (even when he stands right in front of her). When she appears in red in the dreamland he seems unsure of what to do with her and so they do a slightly jazzy double dance with fans that has no manifest heterosexual content. The camp potential of their dance is tremendous—even if scholars of camp have avoided this number entirely. The Gish-like sickbed of the closing narrative section solidifies Astaire's ineffectual masculinity in this routine. For some viewers, this might not be a negative shift, making "Limehouse" a signal moment when Astaire's ability as a dancer can be assessed from a unique angle. A second reading finds evidence for Astaire's inherent slippage toward effeminacy when foot sounds, modern dress, and other accoutrements of whiteness (such as visible anger or self-directed interiority) are withheld. Particularly damning (or praiseworthy) is the lack of foot sounds. Astaire floats in "Limehouse" as he rarely does when he's on his straight white male home turf.

49. Sarcastic and Aggressive "Routine Tap Steps"

In the run-up to *The Barkleys of Broadway* (1949) one fan magazine noted, "Since there is no effective method of scoring dance steps, Ginger has probably contributed to the culture of the nation by inventing names for the Astaire creations as she copes with them. Various attitudes are labeled 'The Point Step,' 'The Trained Seal Hop,' and 'The Chinese Hop,' as Ginger happens to think of them. These terms are employed throughout production."[41] Dancing an "outlaw" style in part meant not using standard terminology or set steps. But Astaire did use some recognizable steps. Two are considered here—the time step and the double flap—for the window their use opens on Astaire's noisy masculinity as it relates to codified tap moves. He uses both moves in very limited amounts—I count six routines with time steps (plus three further uses outside of dance numbers) and nineteen routines with double flaps. Astaire's use of these steps is almost always in the interest of "characterizing" his masculine persona as a dancing man of a certain self-aware type. He uses time steps—among the most basic of steps—in sarcastic or openly corny ways. His relation to the move is consistently ironic or parodic. On the rare occasion when he does them in earnest, Astaire intellectualizes the time step, turning it into a mathematical problem that expresses playful interaction with an equal partner (Eleanor Powell). The much more concise double flap shows up in a few combinations but finds distinctive use as an expression of either finality or teasing aggression directed at men (and even boys) who are already weaker than him. The move is often that of a bully.

Time steps

"That's Entertainment" in *The Band Wagon* doesn't really have a dance break but instead uses its instrumental section to stage a sequence of silly bits. Yet there are some dance steps in this paean to old-time show biz values. At the very start of the instrumental break, Astaire, Nanette Fabray, and Jack Buchanan (the "Triplets" threesome) bust out with four time steps. The step is often done serially in this fashion and the trio works it hard. Often taught using the words *hop, step, fl-ap* (two syllables), *ball change*, the duple meter time step is a recognizable staple of American tap. The typical motion of the arms—at the sides throughout, raising the hands with elbows bent on the *hop*, lowering the hands slowly on the *step, flap, ball change*—gives this move a distinctive upper-body identity as well. It's the first step Gene Kelly demonstrates in his "danse Americain" for the French kids in "I Got Rhythm" from *An American in Paris* (1951).

Astaire's commitment to original steps precluded the time step as a regular part of his dancing. He rarely does serial time steps, and when he does, as in "That's Entertainment," it's in a context where overly insistent, even desperate show biz references are being made. It marks a pushy striving to please that Astaire only ever parodies. For instance, Astaire and Jane Powell do a series of time steps in "How Could You Believe Me . . .," a "low" number where the step matches their garish costumes. He also does serial times steps atop an upright piano during the "Ad Lib Dance" (*Let's Dance*). This use of the step follows a comic but directly aggressive attack on the piano (kicking it, slamming the damper bar and lid) itself preceded by a serious boogie-woogie blues piano solo. The time steps on the narrow top of the upright—Astaire lifts his trouser legs like a swing dancer—are followed by a move to the adjacent grand piano where he plays a glissando with his foot (filling in the roar in the "Tiger Rag"), which ends with several cats bursting forth from inside the piano, a peak of craziness not matched elsewhere in his solitary solos but typical, as we have seen, of the film *Let's Dance*, which is tonally and expressively on the wild side (see also Astaire's primal scream while perched inside a grand piano early in the "Ad Lib Dance"). The time steps atop the upright piano make sense as part of this entirely over-the-top routine.

Astaire also used time steps outside of musical numbers. The familiar motion serves several purposes. For instance, after the disastrous dress rehearsal of "You and the Night and the Music" in *Band Wagon*, Charisse asks Astaire, "Are we really supposed to open tomorrow night?" Astaire starts laughing; Charisse joins in. And then Astaire starts doing time steps. Charisse joins but not in sync with him. (This is the only time Charisse taps in her films.) As they dance and laugh, Astaire repeats the cue line for the number that just crashed and (literally) burned, "Dance, fools, dance." Astaire had used time steps like this to signal foolishness before—as a silly or sarcastic response to a situation rather than an expression of his own danced identity. In *Flying Down to Rio*, two policemen tell Astaire and company that they are forbidden to dance on the hotel terrace (precipitating moving the dancing girls to the wings of airplanes in flight). The policemen start repeating the phrase "non puo de dansar" (no dancing permitted). The band picks up the beat and Astaire starts doing time steps. Astaire also uses serial time steps as an "attack" of "St. Vitus dance" during his first meeting with Rogers in a hotel hallway just after "No Strings" in *Top Hat*. Again he just starts time stepping away—on carpet no less. The ubiquity of the time step and its upper-body signature—even without foot sounds—supports this bit: here, comically trying too hard (a subtext for serial time steps in Astaire's work) operates as cheeky romantic aggression, the very definition of being fresh.

Astaire's only serious use of the time step complicates the regularity of the step by adding a changing rhythmic element that lends the step both expressive freshness and the potential for competitive characterization. In the second, swing-style treatment of "Begin the Beguine," Astaire and Eleanor Powell treat serial time steps to an additive process—an additional, forward-traveling ball change is added to the end of each of a pair of time steps. With each trade of the move, Astaire and Powell add one more ball change. By the end each is doing six extra ball changes, which lengthens the distance they travel forward. A step done in place is thereby transformed into a traveling step that moves rapidly forward unpredictably both in timing (when the move happens) and in distance (how far the step travels). Astaire and Powell alternate here, so there's a competitive nature to the exchange centered on catching an idea and extending it rather than showing each other up. We might consider these as time steps for intellectuals, with the interplay of added beats working along a mathematical formula to produce a sophisticated version of an otherwise basic step. These additive serial time steps are the antithesis of the nostalgic, old-timey, corny show biz values of Astaire's typical time steps. Still, the initial standard time steps set up the combination in a way informed 1940 movie audiences could have appreciated. Those audiences would not have the chance to isolate the combination, to watch it closely and repeatedly, to try and understand its workings. Astaire and Powell transform the time step into mathematical art, showing an advanced form of doing. Their musical star texts are alike made of virtuoso creation and execution surpassing the commonplace moves of others, at moments such as this activating the viewer's intellect—again, showing how Astaire's work might be framed as projecting "intelligence."[42]

Double flaps

The flap is a basic tap step. Done one foot at a time, a dancer brushes the ball of the foot forward then back. If the time step (which includes a flap) suggests a word, the flap on its own works more like a syllable (or phoneme). Flaps can be done while standing on the opposite foot or serially on alternating feet while traveling or in place. The double flap consists of one flap on each foot in such rapid succession that the effect is a quick burst of sound: four very quick taps as a unit, an expression of the whole body not each foot. By my count, Astaire used the double flap in some nineteen dances, usually in a way that marks closure and/or asserts dominance. By analogy to punctuation marks, Astaire's double flaps function as both emphatic periods at the end of combinations (or sentences) and isolated exclamation marks often intended to scare another (weaker) man. Astaire also uses variants of the double flap that function similarly.

The double flap as Astaire does it pulls the dancer up onto the balls of the feet, with the legs stiff. It's an aggressive stance that commands attention. (In response to my presentation of Astaire's double flaps at a conference in Paris, Hollywood dance and canine scholar Adrienne L. McLean compared the move to a dog making themselves larger to forestall or signal an attack.[43]) Indeed, several of Astaire's double flaps are direct commands. The most insistent comes in the special effects sections of "Puttin' on the Ritz." Just before Astaire and the chorus line of doubles behind him repeat the trick of making a cane rise from the floor into their hands, all of them do three double flaps in succession. Here, the step functions as a spell. In a more prosaic application, Astaire ends the first section of "I'd Rather Lead a Band" with a double flap that ends the music and calls the sailors behind him to attention. His turn as a taps-talking drill sergeant follows.

The double flap is a relational step for Astaire. He only rarely uses it in an inner-directed way, where it functions as a kind of pause for thought.[44] Most of the time, the step is directed at someone else in the scene, and among these, only twice does Astaire treat the double flap in a neutral manner and make nice with others with the step. In both "The Babbitt and the Bromide" and "Bouncin' the Blues," Astaire exchanges double flaps with his partner—Kelly and Rogers, respectively—in a friendly way, each taking a turn. The step can be done with a variety of characterizations: in these rare instances for Astaire, the double flap is just a burst of four even taps in a tight cluster. The shared double flaps that end the "Jukebox Dance" with Eleanor Powell in *Broadway Melody* might be thought of as friendly, except for the finality of their sound (a precisely modulated aesthetic choice made in postproduction) and the look of implicit challenge the two share just after the dance (and the step), which seems to ask, with no trace of sexual attraction, "So you're that good are you?" The double flap Astaire does by himself to mark the end of the danced vocal of "A Couple of Song and Dance Men" is polite by comparison. With Crosby standing by—and not even nodding toward doing this difficult step—Astaire treats the double flap as a period full stop on this section of the number and a quick illustration of the lyric "and my feet hit the ground" that makes a claim for his own mastery of the form. These examples show that Astaire knew how to dance civil double flaps. This was not, however, his preferred use of the step.

Far more often Astaire used the double flap to assert masculine power in a commanding way: either by celebrating some rascally act or by directly disturbing, scaring, or even "killing" another man. Consider these double flaps, which end tap combinations (emphatic periods) or drop like bombs out of nowhere (isolated exclamations).

- Just before the start of the "I'll Be Hard to Handle" dance, Astaire does an isolated exclamatory double flap to punctuate his joke about helping Rogers win a prize by handing out pictures of Lillian Russell. The move brings Rogers to her feet.
- In the middle section of the "Firecracker Dance" (*Holiday Inn*), Astaire pauses to light firecrackers he had stuffed in his pants pockets just before going on. After an insert shot of Astaire lighting a little string of firecrackers, the number cuts back to Vitruvian for his reaction—a crazy combination that's both response to the explosions and victory dance. This danced reaction ends with a double flap. On a return to insert framing, Astaire pulls out a very long string of firecrackers, which now promise excessive flashes and bangs.
- As described earlier, near the conclusion of "Babbitt," Astaire lets go of Kelly's hand, causing Kelly to fall to the floor. Astaire keeps dancing—now alone—and the combination he does (another victory dance) ends with a double flap, after which Astaire notices Kelly's position and helps him up for the end of the routine. Kelly has no similarly triumphant moment over Astaire's prostrate figure.
- *Top Hat*, discussed earlier for its importance establishing Astaire as an aggressively noisy man, is especially replete with double flaps. Astaire uses one as the final exclamatory punctuation to his noisy break that disturbs the quiet of the Thackery Club smoking room. His third victim in the shooting section of the title routine falls to a double flap. A further double flap fails on his second attempt to fell the last man standing

(the one dispatched with a bow and arrow). Astaire's potential to use a double flap to randomly disturb even a friend is evident in "No Strings." While watching Astaire dance, near the start of the dance proper, Horton rises and walks into the open area where Astaire is dancing. When Horton turns his back, Astaire inserts a double flap that visibly discombobulates Horton (fig. 49.1). Astaire visibly relishes this unmotivated practical joke.

- A double flap behind another man's back has an explosive follow-up in "A Shine on Your Shoes" (*Band Wagon*). While hopping about after the danced vocal, Astaire travels over to a shooting gallery (the only time this particular area of the arcade is used in the number). A double flap on a syncopated beat from Astaire causes a man readying his aim to shoot prematurely (fig. 49.2). The characteristic up-on-the-balls-of-the-feet posture of the step gives it away, as does the distinct cluster of four taps—added in selectively during this stretch when, otherwise, Astaire's body makes no sound.

FIGURE 49.1

FIGURE 49.2

- In an intensified repeat of his attack from behind on Horton in "No Strings," Astaire does a single flap plus a scuff (forward with one leg hitting the heel) to definitively end Sonny Lamont's dance in "By the Light of the Silvery Moon" in *The Castles* (fig. 49.3). Astaire distracts Lamont just before scaring him from behind by literally dancing a ring around him. Later in the dance, he invades Lamont's personal space (pulling on his tie) and sends Lamont skittering to the sidelines by traveling rapidly backward (the portly fellow must scramble to avoid the threat of full-body contact with Astaire). Rogers cheers Astaire on throughout and no one comes to Lamont's defense. Indeed, after the number Lamont gets his hat knocked off by another man in the crowd. By any measure, Astaire has been a bully and his actions encourage others to make fun of Lamont as well.

A final double flap is worth close examination for its prominent (and silent) use in another number where Astaire asserts himself physically against a weaker male counterpart. The narrative of *Easter Parade*'s "Drum Crazy" is odd—and unimaginable had Gene Kelly done the number as planned.[45] Astaire enters a toy shop to buy a stuffed bunny he sees in the shop's window, another of the many Easter gifts for Ann Miller he purchases in the film's opening sequence. As he walks into the store, Astaire discovers that a little blond boy has just chosen the bunny for himself. "Drum Crazy" unfolds as Astaire's successful effort to pry the stuffed animal out of the boy's clutches. Astaire finally achieves this objective—perhaps a questionable one for an adult, especially in a feel-good genre like the musical—by seating the boy on a drum (at which point he finally releases his hold on the bunny, setting it beside him on the floor). Then, Astaire immobilizes the child by stacking

FIGURE 49.3

a set of smaller drums on his lap, in his arms, and, to cap it off, on his head. (Just before doing this, Astaire does a single time step directly at the boy—it's a mean moment, as much as admitting he's preparing to hoodwink this kid into giving up the bunny.) After playing what amounts to a trick on the poor kid, Astaire dances in a little circle, briefly doing a move he often does as a sort of celebration (one arm extended forward, the other up, with his hand behind his head and shaking, perhaps as if holding a hat [see a similar use of this move with his hat on his exit from the number]). Then, just before walking over to pay for the bunny, Astaire does a double flap embellished with a teasing gesture toward the kid of both hands open to either side of his head (fig. 49.4). Astaire's foot sounds fall silent just after the time step, so this double flap relies for its impact on the physical stance (the attack pose) rather than the making of noise with the feet. If we didn't think "Drum Crazy" was rude before, Astaire makes no bones about it here. Thinking stereotypically, who might enjoy seeing a stuffed bunny (candy) taken from a boy (baby)? This juvenile trick—likely condemned by all responsible adults—surely appeals primarily to hoodlums. Tough guy movie star James Cagney famously commented that Astaire had "a little bit of the hoodlum" in him: "Drum Crazy" offers solid evidence. And yet, the two women watching when Astaire goes over to pay for the bunny are all smiles—such is the power of this particular dancing man. For all its highly colored MGM prettiness, "Drum Crazy" is among the most hypermasculine dances in the clip reel. Astaire's virtuoso victory dance after having claimed the bunny—an apotheosis of hits and kicks climaxing with a golf swing connecting with a bass drum—hints at the underlying meaning of any Astaire dance where he hits or throws things: this is a man in control of the world, expressing himself by hitting every surface in sight and absolutely ready to steal from a child.

FIGURE 49.4

Parsing Astaire's use of "routine tap steps" reveals how he danced in a manner that asserted masculine superiority over other men, made satirical comedy out of show dance clichés, and drew attention to the intricacies of his creative art in ways an audience familiar with tap could directly appreciate. The collective body of tap Astaire committed to film—his star text located in the clip reel—coheres aesthetically and expressively around just these sorts of recurring tropes that combine danced movement, noisy sound, and "characterization." Astaire's time steps and double flaps offer a means to define in precise danced terms his screen identity as a dancer, as a man, and as that rare Hollywood product, the self-fashioned musical movie star, one who affords us the pleasure of watching him do.

CONCLUSION

To participate in, even generate, one of the legion moments of profound presence that can be found in screen history: what is that? And since, with cinema, every moment visible on the screen betrays simultaneously an opening into an actor's actual life (lived, while the camera turns, before the camera), we must seek to wonder not only what an actor *does* in making performance but also who an actor *is*.
—Murray Pomerance (2013)

The feeling of strangeness that overcomes the actor before the camera, as Pirandello describes it, is basically of the same kind as the estrangement felt before one's own image in the mirror.
—Walter Benjamin (1935)

He isn't doing that right—that was very important to me. It was what Astaire claimed he was thinking whenever he watched himself onscreen, and I noted that third-person pronoun. This is what I understood by it: that for Astaire the person in the film was not especially connected with him. And I took this to heart, or rather, it echoed a feeling I already had, mainly that it was important to treat oneself as a kind of stranger, to remain unattached and unprejudiced in your own case. I thought you needed to think like that to achieve anything in this world.
—Zadie Smith (2016)

Astaire spent more time watching himself in the mirror than in any other position. The weeks spent creating and rehearsing before shooting numbers involved hours and hours of looking at himself. Pan recalled his and Astaire's use of a mirror and their intentional turning away from the sight of themselves at a particular moment in their creative process: "At first we had a big ceiling-to-floor portable mirror. We like to work out in front of it to see how we looked in the mirror as we did the dance. But we'd get so used to looking at ourselves, which is dangerous because we wanted to be able to do the routine completely naturally without being stuck on that mirror! So, during the last week or so before shooting, we covered it so we couldn't watch ourselves dance."[1] (Pan's use of *we* is telling: he clearly understood Astaire's performance as, in some way, also his own.) As noted earlier, Astaire hated watching dailies and resisted seeing himself on screen while in the midst of shooting—a period when, to use Zadie Smith's words, he absolutely did need to look at "the person in the film" and perhaps struggled to see this dancing figure as "not especially connected with him." Recording foot sounds also required sustained time watching himself but always to a specific purpose—the syncing of a new audio track to the existing image track (which had already been synced to the prerecorded music). The practical work of adding a layer to the synthetic screen dance body likely presented its own highly focused challenge—and it was too late for second guessing and a certain amount of rechoreographing was surely involved (he could not do the actual steps his body did on screen while recording foot sounds on a four-by-four-foot floor). And while Astaire didn't like to look at his films—"I certainly don't want to see my own old films; when people tell me at the racetrack 'I saw you on TV at 3 a.m.' well, I'm happy if they want to see them"—he did, on occasion, suggest his own retrospective reading of his own work. In a 1976 oral history interview, he noted: "But, you see yourself not like others see you. And after a while, many of the pictures that I've done I've seen things that I didn't realize were as good as, as they were. Because this time I saw it, said, 'I didn't know we did that. That wasn't bad, was it! No!'"[2] (Again the use of *we*—Astaire seems to understand his screen dance body as always the result of collective labor.)

Astaire's career as a dancing man was built on repeated and sustained acts of looking at himself dancing, whether in the mirror or on the screen. Such looking, and the necessary self-critique and self-editing involved, recalls the many occasions in his films when Astaire dances before the gazes of other men watching. Still, the topic of the dancer looking at himself in the mirror is largely absent from Astaire's numbers. Indeed, he comes in contact with a mirror only eight times in the clip reel, and among these he only regards himself in the mirror six times.[3] The six occasions when Astaire looks at himself in the mirror prove mostly unhelpful in any effort to plumb the depths of Astaire's self-understanding. The funhouse mirror section in "Stiff Upper

Lip" (*A Damsel in Distress* [1937]), danced throughout with Burns and Allen, can be quickly set aside: it's a gag that goes on too long. The start of *Shall We Dance* (1937) briefly captures Astaire looking at himself while dancing—as noted, the position in which he spent the most total time across his career (fig. 1). The framing doesn't show us what Astaire sees, only that he's looking at himself, intent on perfecting his dancing (no news there). Like Astaire's deflection of basic interview questions—who's your favorite partner? what does your dancing mean?—this framing adds little to our sense for Astaire as a self-reflective creator. There may, of course, be nothing much to say on the matter.

Four numbers where Astaire confronts and responds to himself in a mirror prove only slightly more revealing, with most—again—emphasizing a lack of self-reflection. The glass-shattering climax of "One for My Baby (and One More for the Road)" in *The Sky's the Limit* (1943) is initiated when Astaire jumps to the bar behind the bar and cannot avoid running into himself in a wall of mirrors (fig. 2). With no room to escape, he

FIGURE 1

FIGURE 2

starts trashing the joint: kicking at shelves of glasses, then, having slipped this narrow perch, throwing a barstool to take out the mirrors on the wall behind the bar. Gene Kelly repeated such rage at his own image in psychological fashion in his "Alter Ego" dance in *Cover Girl* (conceived and shot just after *The Sky's the Limit* opened). Kelly's relentless search for meaning in dance finds a fairly naïve start here. By contrast, Astaire's glass-breaking destruction reads as oddly unmotivated. As Brian Seibert writes, Astaire's "tapping and marvelous gliding along the bar's surface seem more an expression of what-the-hell than of rage, yet the outright destruction must have been startling at the time, exposing the violence of Astaire's style."[4] (Indeed, the number was criticized as wasteful destruction in the context of wartime rationing.) Still, Astaire's violence in "One for My Baby" can be read as simple rage—not at all uncommon for straight white men, apparently even those who dance for a living. Astaire's deflection of the "meaning" question leaves him both silent and prey to the most stereotypical judgments (which may, of course, be accurate).

If men "work to appear masculine to other men," then a look in the mirror promises useful self-assessment as well as potentially harsh judgment: as Travis Bickel asks himself in *Taxi Driver* (1976), "You talking to me?"[5] Working in the lighter vein of musical comedy, Astaire makes one such confrontation an occasion for self-deprecation in "No Strings" (*Top Hat* [1935]). The shot in question begins with a trick framing of a "full figure" Astaire in a round wall mirror, a kind of Vitruvian frame at a rakish angle (fig. 3a). But once he dances up to the mirror, Astaire's reaction is negative. He looks at himself, grimaces, and pulls away (fig. 3b). It's a rare admission he has limits (here simply physical—how his face looks) and it's meant to

FIGURE 3

be funny (analogous to the tough guys who hurt themselves in "The Babbitt and the Bromide" in *Ziegfeld Follies* [1946] and elsewhere). But this is performed: Astaire knew he was good and knew his looks didn't matter; his confidence to "just dance" had to have been tremendous. A refusal of sentiment underlines his cool front to the world—which can shade to cold: his comments to the crowd at the American Film Industry (AFI) tribute to his career included the remark, "I could cry, I really could. If I had a little thing that I could squirt in my eye, I could cry."[6]

But men cannot escape themselves, as the spatially odd transition between the two sections of "Puttin' on the Ritz" (*Blue Skies* [1946]) suggests. Astaire meets himself duplicated in two mirrors, perhaps as if being fitted at a tailor's shop, where examining one's self-presentation is surely in order (fig. 4). Movement through these mirrors—double doors he kicks open—doesn't succeed in removing the necessity of confronting himself, for in the abstract space beyond, Astaire finds a chorus of himself staring back at him (fig. 5). They beckon and he shares a short dance with them, including the

FIGURE 4

FIGURE 5

cane levitating trick from the number's first section. This underimagined gimmick with a chorus of rather boring selves who offer no challenge (as the male choruses often do in Astaire numbers) has little of the resonance of the three looming black shadows in "Bojangles of Harlem" (*Swing Time* [1936]). The latter, even though clearly danced by Astaire, raise the specter of Blackness as a constituent part of Astaire's persona and creative identity. Faced literally with himself in color in "Puttin' on the Ritz," Astaire punts and remains on the surface—where we might expect a dancing man always intent on shoring up his "I just dance" credentials to remain. The striking lack of psychological depth in Astaire's work comes into view here, in a special effects dance that fails to explore the dynamics of a man confronting a group made up of himself (as opposed to Astaire's consistently aggressive stance toward groups of men in his solos with male chorus [see his murderous glee in "Top Hat, White Tie, and Tails"]). Indeed, his lack of expressive engagement with the "Puttin' on the Ritz" doppelgängers might be read as an expression of Astaire's straight white male pose. The lack of depth secures his status as one who "just" dances and is "lucky" he's "not well educated enough to think that deeply about it."[7]

A final mirror confronts Astaire in "A Shine on Your Shoes" (*The Band Wagon* [1953]). This Times Square arcade mirror distorts, such that when he first looks into it Astaire goes back to the "Love Appeal" machine to question its verdict of "GORGEOUS." Passing by the mirror a second time, he repeats the gesture of self-horror from "No Strings," a too easy move and a repetition in the clip reel (fig. 6). But on a third pass by the mirror—the camera's position now changed as it follows his magnetic body—we get a glimpse of Astaire looking and seeing in the mirror what he imagined in every rehearsal

FIGURE 6

FIGURE 7

hall mirror: a movie camera, here the one filming him at this moment (fig. 7). The words "Take Your Own Photo," visible in these shots of the arcade mirror, might easily stand as a slogan for Astaire's entire screen dance career, a four-word instruction for how to make your own screen dance body (first, find a major movie studio . . .).

Of course, the clip reel is a mirror—and one Astaire returned to repeatedly. For a screen dancer like Astaire, the camera is a recording mirror. All dancing for the self is trying on possible selves to see if they work toward the intended effect—which Astaire articulated as "trying to make a buck and make it look good and knock a lot of people on their ass in the aisle."[8] He was apparently never after self-discovery or meaning (much less "art") but instead connection with the masses in the dark. In 1976, Astaire reflected, "I think I must have some other style than others to have been noticeable. I don't know, I'm never aware, really, of what I do. I just sort of *do* it. And if it doesn't look good to me—I look at it in the mirror when I'm rehearsing and change it if necessary. I have never analyzed anything like that. I really didn't. . . . I was just . . . *doing* it."[9] The sum of Astaire's screen dances must, then, reflect what he thought looked good to him and *on* him.

Thus, if Astaire is unreflective, his work taken in toto can be made to speak for him. As this study has shown, Astaire consistently put his own body at the center and built a world within the frame on the surface of the screen outward from there. His body makes the space through which it moves. His control over the film-dance-making process secured this priority. His control over how his body moved set consistent limits that hold off potentially emasculating associations ("sissy" ballet) and draw freely if selectively from racial others (Black jazz tap), always in a context of deniability buttressed by claims to "outlaw" status (made from a position of tremendous power).

The data underlying this project begs to be contextualized beside similar data for the other dancers and dance makers in the classical Hollywood musical and beyond. Such comparison would open new insights into Astaire's stylistic choices and relative efficiency as a film dance maker. I presented limited data for comparison in the introduction, where I noted that Kelly's clip reel clocks in at less than half the length of Astaire's and Eleanor Powell's at about a third as long, and that the Nicholas Brothers and Bill Robinson danced as much in their entire careers as Astaire did on average in two of his twenty-nine films. Further quantitative study of star dancers in the Hollywood musical might apply the analysis of framing and cuts used here for Astaire to the work of others, but it remains that only Astaire created enough film dance to serve as a basis for a data-driven definition of normative practices and analysis of change over an extended period of time (almost a quarter century). His status as the first on the scene also establishes his priority in any comparative historical study. In this, as in so much, Astaire stands alone and demands accounting for (as I have done here) before others are brought into the picture (as I hope later scholars will do).

The prospects for comparative data drawn from studio archives proves limited but not without promise. Near-complete survival of RKO and MGM Freed unit assistant director (AD) reports puts Astaire, again, in a favorable position for historical scholarship grounded in quantitative research and eyewitness archival evidence (rather than later musings or gossip). Access to these reports from the studio shop floor provide granular insight into Astaire's practice and, as shown in Part Three, helps us to better understand the situational dynamics informing finished films and specific numbers. A comparative study of Kelly's MGM films or of the Freed unit generally through a systematic approach to the AD reports in the Freed collection at USC awaits future scholarship and could help put Astaire's time at the studio, as discussed in this book, into comparative perspective. Furthermore, the musical output of other studios for which production records survive—such as Paramount—could open new and wider understandings of the musical film production process. The significance of the musical as a genre that toggles between musical and nonmusical actions—each sort produced by different industrial processes—suggests that a close-grained, eminently practical view of how these films were made awaits further quantitative scholarship. Again, the quantity of such data counts and the always spotty, fortuitously surviving archival record will limit both the films and performers to be studied and the conclusions that can be made. This situation rules out quantitative study of Black musical stars in Hollywood: Robinson and the Nicholas Brothers simply made too few numbers for quantitative analysis of their work to yield much insight. Their dances can, however, be read through Astaire's practices as discussed in this book: for instance, cutting a dance number to isolate risky tricks (such as flips) proves a normative practice in several Nicholas Brothers routines.[10] At the same time, multiple or repeated physically difficult moves in one shot—see the Nicholas Brothers' famous descent of a stairway by way of leaping splits in "The Jumpin' Jive" (*Stormy Weather* [1943])—suggests audiences registered (and register) the cuts in dance numbers as indications of dancers' physical labors and achievements. Astaire's longevity and his consistent attachment to a particular kind of musical number—at the "welcome limit" of just over two minutes of dance—makes his case eminently available for quantitative study. Work on other musical film figures would likely dwell less on the dancing body and more on musical numbers generally speaking. And the result might be less than revelatory: it's doubtful a data study of Bing Crosby's vocal numbers would yield much change over time as to length, visual style, production process, or efficiency.

Astaire's position of power—analogous to his access to the studio movie-making machine—exercised over years and years yielded a whiteness marked by Black music and dance and a cis-het masculinity made by dancing often with women and by often using dance steps that read as everyday movements, like walking. Astaire's achievement has been called "transcendent." By now, it should be apparent I do not think it to be so. It is the product of tremendous hard work by a fantastically privileged straight white male dancer who had and seized the opportunity to be great in the medium of motion pictures across a particular stretch of Hollywood history. The clip reel captures this privilege and affords to us today the chance to spend hours and hours watching Astaire as he keeps on "doing something else." My hope for this book is that it offers new tools to evaluate Astaire's clip reel and see it anew as physical evidence for an "actual life (lived, while the camera turns, before the camera)" in the powerful light of dominant social categories—whiteness, masculinity, heterosexuality—that continue to disproportionately shape our world.

APPENDIX ONE

Astaire Films Corpus

				A	B	C	D	E	F	G	H	I	J
				\multicolumn{4}{c}{Duration in H:MM:SS}	\multicolumn{3}{c}{% of Total Duration}	\multicolumn{3}{c}{Count of Musical Numbers}
	Film (in production order)	Studio	Release Month and Year	Total	All Musical Numbers	All Musical Numbers Including Astaire	Astaire Dancing	All Musical Numbers	All Musical Numbers Including Astaire	Astaire Dancing	All Musical Numbers	All Musical Numbers Including Astaire	Astaire Dancing
	CORPUS TOTAL			49:07:00	16:10:13	11:32:42	6:34:50	33%	24%	13%	324	207	64%
	CORPUS AVERAGE/FILM			1:41:37	0:33:27	0:23:53	0:13:37	33%	23%	13%	11	7	67%
	1930s at RKO												
FDR	Flying Down to Rio	RKO	Dec. 1933	1:29:00	0:30:25	0:17:07	0:03:15	34%	19%	4%	6	3	50%
GD	The Gay Divorcee	RKO	Oct. 1934	1:47:00	0:31:07	0:23:12	0:11:18	29%	22%	11%	8	5	63%
R	Roberta	RKO	Feb. 1935	1:46:00	0:36:40	0:27:37	0:08:25	35%	26%	8%	12	8	67%
TH	Top Hat	RKO	Aug. 1935	1:41:00	0:26:05	0:26:05	0:15:06	26%	26%	15%	7	7	100%
FTF	Follow the Fleet	RKO	Feb. 1936	1:50:00	0:33:20	0:25:03	0:13:25	30%	23%	12%	11	6	55%
ST	Swing Time	RKO	Sept. 1936	1:43:00	0:27:45	0:25:26	0:13:34	27%	25%	13%	11	9	82%
SWD	Shall We Dance	RKO	April 1937	1:49:00	0:38:56	0:28:43	0:13:51	36%	26%	13%	16	12	75%
DD	A Damsel in Distress	RKO	Nov. 1937	1:41:00	0:29:38	0:26:23	0:14:56	29%	26%	15%	11	8	73%
C	Carefree	RKO	Aug. 1938	1:23:00	0:15:08	0:15:08	0:10:36	18%	18%	13%	5	5	100%
SVIC	The Story of Vernon & Irene Castle	RKO	March 1939	1:33:00	0:23:30	0:20:21	0:10:50	25%	22%	12%	14	10	71%
	1940–1946: The Peripatetic Years												
BM40	Broadway Melody of 1940	MGM Cummings	Feb. 1940	1:42:00	0:40:38	0:26:10	0:16:56	40%	26%	17%	10	6	60%
SC	Second Chorus	Boris Morros	Jan. 1941	1:24:00	0:21:50	0:17:02	0:05:40	26%	20%	7%	12	10	83%
YNGR	You'll Never Get Rich	Columbia	Sept. 1941	1:28:00	0:19:08	0:19:08	0:13:17	22%	22%	15%	7	7	100%
HI	Holiday Inn	Paramount	June 1942	1:40:00	0:41:20	0:23:07	0:12:38	41%	23%	13%	18	9	50%

YWNL	You Were Never Lovelier	Columbia	Oct. 1942	1:37:00	0:25:54	0:15:26	0:09:42	27%	16%	10%	12	6	50%
STL	The Sky's the Limit	RKO	July 1943	1:29:00	0:15:45	0:13:25	0:06:47	18%	15%	8%	6	5	83%
ZF	Ziegfeld Follies	MGM Freed	April 1946	1:50:00	1:11:08	0:38:06	0:19:46	65%	35%	18%	10	4	40%
YT	Yolanda and the Thief	MGM Freed	Nov. 1945	1:48:00	0:24:13	0:20:37	0:16:45	22%	19%	16%	5	3	60%
BS	Blue Skies	Paramount	Dec. 1946	1:44:00	0:39:42	0:19:39	0:17:32	38%	19%	17%	17	4	24%
1948–1953: Mostly MGM Freed													
EP	Easter Parade	MGM Freed	May 1948	1:47:00	0:48:56	0:32:00	0:20:09	46%	30%	19%	17	10	59%
BB	The Barkleys of Broadway	MGM Freed	March 1949	1:49:00	0:39:31	0:30:00	0:15:40	36%	28%	14%	11	9	82%
LD	Let's Dance	Paramount	Aug. 1950	1:52:00	0:24:42	0:22:11	0:16:19	22%	20%	15%	9	8	89%
TLW	Three Little Words	MGM Cummings	July 1950	1:42:00	0:28:14	0:18:19	0:10:50	28%	18%	11%	16	8	50%
RW	Royal Wedding	MGM Freed	Feb. 1951	1:33:00	0:35:49	0:28:19	0:23:07	39%	30%	25%	10	7	70%
BNY	The Belle of New York	MGM Freed	Feb. 1952	1:22:00	0:37:37	0:28:10	0:20:17	46%	34%	25%	11	8	73%
BW	The Band Wagon	MGM Freed	July 1953	1:52:00	0:41:32	0:33:43	0:15:34	37%	30%	14%	16	11	69%
1955–1957: Widescreen Coda													
DLL	Daddy Long Legs	Twentieth Century-Fox	May 1955	2:06:00	0:43:04	0:25:18	0:14:44	34%	20%	12%	12	7	58%
FF	Funny Face	Paramount	March 1957	1:43:00	0:36:03	0:23:27	0:10:45	35%	23%	10%	10	6	60%
SS	Silk Stockings	Arthur Freed Production	May 1957	1:57:00	0:42:33	0:23:30	0:13:06	36%	20%	11%	14	6	43%

APPENDIX TWO

Astaire Dancing Corpus by Number

DO: dance only
DP: dance portion of larger number
S,D: vocal, then dance
DS,D: danced vocal, then dance
-DS-: danced vocal

Film	Number	A Duration (seconds)	B # of Shots	C Average Shot Length (ASL)	D Longest Shot (seconds)	E Participants	F Content	G Timecode Start in Complete Film
FDR	The Carioca (1st dance)	112	14	8	19	Romantic Duo (Rogers)	DP	43:41
FDR	The Carioca (2nd dance)	27	2	14	20	Romantic Duo (Rogers)	DP	50:43
FDR	Music Makes Me	56	6	9	16	Solo	DO	1:07:11
GD	Nightclub Solo	81	10	8	28	Solo	DO	6:59
GD	A Needle in a Haystack	86	1	86	86	Solo	DO	20:05
GD	Night and Day	176	12	15	40	Romantic Duo (Rogers)	S,D	53:29
GD	The Continental (1st dance)	147	7	21	57	Romantic Duo (Rogers)	DP	1:20:31
GD	The Continental (2nd dance)	105	7	15	58	Romantic Duo (Rogers)	DP	1:31:01
GD	Table Dance	83	5	17	25	Romantic Duo (Rogers)	DO	1:43:15
R	I'll Be Hard to Handle	169	1	169	169	Romantic Duo (Rogers)	DO	32:33
R	I Won't Dance (solo)	147	3	49	90	Solo	S,D	1:12:05
R	Smoke Gets in Your Eyes	138	2	69	121	Romantic Duo (Rogers)	DO	1:39:19
R	I Won't Dance (duo)	51	1	51	51	Romantic Duo (Rogers)	DO	1:43:55
TH	No Strings	163	16	10	50	Solo	S,D	9:27
TH	No Strings (sand dance)	82	7	12	25	Solo	DO	14:46
TH	Isn't This a Lovely Day (to Be Caught in the Rain)	160	4	40	97	Romantic Duo (Rogers)	S,D	25:10
TH	Top Hat, White Tie, and Tails	193	10	19	43	Solo with Chorus	S,D	42:11
TH	Cheek to Cheek	183	5	37	71	Romantic Duo (Rogers)	S,D	1:05:46
TH	The Piccolino	125	1	125	125	Romantic Duo (Rogers)	DP	1:33:47
FTF	Let Yourself Go	193	16	12	43	Romantic Duo (Rogers)	DO	24:57
FTF	I'd Rather Lead a Band	264	11	24	53	Solo with Chorus	S,D	48:03
FTF	I'm Putting All My Eggs in One Basket	180	4	45	78	Romantic Duo (Rogers)	S,D	1:24:06
FTF	Let's Face the Music and Dance	168	1	168	168	Romantic Duo (Rogers)	S,D	1:45:53
ST	Pick Yourself Up	123	5	25	96	Romantic Duo (Rogers)	DO	28:10

ST	Waltz in Swing Time	156	1	156	156	Romantic Duo (Rogers)	DO	51:38
ST	Bojangles of Harlem (part 1: chorus)	187	1	187	187	Solo with Chorus	S,D	1:14:43
ST	Bojangles of Harlem (part 2: shadows)	170	6	28	59	Solo	DP	1:17:51
ST	Never Gonna Dance	178	2	89	151	Romantic Duo (Rogers)	S,D	1:31:09
SWD	Slap That Bass	175	6	29	55	Solo	S,D	21:02
SWD	They All Laughed	237	8	30	117	Romantic Duo (Rogers)	DO	55:29
SWD	Let's Call the Whole Thing Off	139	2	70	102	Romantic Duo (Rogers)	S,D	1:12:31
SWD	Shall We Dance (part 1: duo with Hoctor)	153	8	19	43	Romantic Duo (Hoctor)	DO	1:38:45
SWD	Shall We Dance (part 2: solo)	92	8	12	29	Solo	S,D	1:45:34
SWD	Shall We Dance (part 3: duo with Rogers)	35	1	35	35	Romantic Duo (Rogers)	DP	1:47:07
DD	I Can't Be Bothered Now	71	5	14	29	Solo	DS,D	11:49
DD	Put Me to the Test	179	3	60	146	Trio	DO	39:28
DD	Stiff Upper Lip (part 1: opening)	181	11	16	33	Trio	S,D	49:15
DD	Stiff Upper Lip (part 3: mirrors)	134	9	15	41	Trio	DP	54:27
DD	Things Are Looking Up	118	5	24	62	Romantic Duo (Fontaine)	S,D	1:06:16
DD	Drum Dance	213	1	213	213	Solo	DO	1:36:06
C	Golf Dance	166	8	21	76	Solo	DO	12:48
C	I Used to Be Color Blind	112	1	112	112	Romantic Duo (Rogers)	S,D	26:10
C	The Yam	249	17	15	66	Romantic Duo (Rogers)	S,D	49:58
C	Change Partners	109	2	55	80	Romantic Duo (Rogers)	DO	1:16:15
SVIC	By the Light of the Silvery Moon	97	5	19	58	Solo	DO	13:52
SVIC	Waiting for the Robert E. Lee	95	1	95	95	Romantic Duo (Rogers)	DO	32:00
SVIC	Too Much Mustard	93	2	47	66	Romantic Duo (Rogers)	DO	53:09
SVIC	Medley Montage (tango)	56	1	56	56	Romantic Duo (Rogers)	DO	56:12
SVIC	Medley Montage (polka)	36	1	36	36	Romantic Duo (Rogers)	DO	58:58
SVIC	Medley Montage (maxixe)	65	1	65	65	Romantic Duo (Rogers)	DO	1:00:37
SVIC	Hello! Hello! Who's Your Lady Friend?	80	5	16	56	Solo with Chorus	S,D	1:08:51
SVIC	The Last Waltz	128	2	64	85	Romantic Duo (Rogers)	DO	1:17:44

Film	Number	A Duration (seconds)	B # of Shots	C Average Shot Length (ASL)	D Longest Shot (seconds)	E Participants	F Content	G Timecode Start in Complete Film
BM40	Please Don't Monkey with Broadway	105	5	21	51	Nonromantic Duo (Murphy)	S,D	6:33
BM40	I've Got My Eyes on You (solo)	177	7	25	47	Solo	S,D	1:00:25
BM40	Jukebox Dance	110	2	55	64	Romantic Duo (E. Powell)	DO	1:07:25
BM40	I Concentrate on You	215	6	36	82	Romantic Duo (E. Powell)	S,D	1:20:24
BM40	Begin the Beguine (part 1: flamenco)	187	8	23	70	Romantic Duo (E. Powell)	S,D	1:33:00
BM40	Begin the Beguine (part 2: swing)	161	2	81	132	Romantic Duo (E. Powell)	S,D	1:37:10
BM40	I've Got My Eyes on You (trio finale)	61	5	12	46	Trio	DO	1:40:15
SC	I Ain't Hep to that Step but I'll Dig It	133	1	133	133	Romantic Duo (Goddard)	S,D	16:13
SC	Concert Solo	207	9	23	64	Solo	DO	1:18:52
YNGR	Rehearsal Duet	31	1	31	31	Romantic Duo (Hayworth)	DO	4:15
YNGR	Boogie Barcarolle	106	7	15	31	Exception	DO	5:02
YNGR	Shootin' the Works for Uncle Sam	112	5	22	42	Exception	S,D	29:53
YNGR	Since I Kissed My Baby Goodbye	79	2	40	47	Romantic Duo (Hayworth)	S,D	42:06
YNGR	A-stairable Rag	132	4	33	74	Romantic Duo (Hayworth)	DO	51:16
YNGR	So Near and Yet So Far	193	3	64	84	Romantic Duo (Hayworth)	S,D	58:41

YNGR	The Wedding Cake Walk	144	13	11	34	Exception	S,D	1:23:11
HI	You're Easy to Dance With	168	4	42	79	Romantic Duo (Dale)	-DS-	18:27
HI	Drunk Dance	123	7	18	50	Romantic Duo (Reynolds)	DO	34:28
HI	Be Careful, It's My Heart	141	5	28	60	Romantic Duo (Reynolds)	S,D	53:19
HI	I Can't Tell a Lie	160	26	6	27	Romantic Duo (Reynolds)	S,D	58:54
HI	Firecracker Dance	166	8	21	55	Solo	DO	1:18:53
YWNL	Audition Dance	129	7	18	29	Solo	DO	35:15
YWNL	I'm Old-Fashioned	145	3	48	76	Romantic Duo (Hayworth)	S,D	52:59
YWNL	The Shorty George	239	14	17	68	Romantic Duo (Hayworth)	DS,D	1:04:11
YWNL	You Were Never Lovelier (finale)	69	7	10	33	Romantic Duo (Hayworth)	DO	1:35:47
STL	A Lot in Common with You	115	13	9	17	Romantic Duo (Leslie)	DS,D	35:23
STL	My Shining Hour	159	4	40	69	Romantic Duo (Leslie)	DO	1:01:07
STL	One for My Baby	133	10	13	40	Solo	S,D	1:21:10
ZF	This Heart of Mine	508	12	42	84	Romantic Duo (Bremer)	DS,D	47:51
ZF	Limehouse Blues	382	7	55	124	Romantic Duo (Bremer)	DP	1:23:42
ZF	The Babbitt and the Bromide	296	9	33	64	Nonromantic Duo (Kelly)	other	1:44:39
YT	Will You Marry Me? (part 1: washerwomen)	197	3	66	103	Exception	DP	41:04
YT	Will You Marry Me? (part 2: duo with Bremer)	202	4	51	96	Romantic Duo (Bremer)	DS,D	44:54
YT	Will You Marry Me? (part 3: bad crowd to end)	290	4	73	109	Exception	DP	48:15

		A	B	C	D	E	F	G
Film	Number	Duration (seconds)	# of Shots	Average Shot Length (ASL)	Longest Shot (seconds)	Participants	Content	Timecode Start in Complete Film
YT	Yolanda	75	4	19	53	Solo	S,D	1:05:52
YT	Coffee Time	241	4	60	102	Romantic Duo (Bremer)	DO	1:29:38
BS	A Pretty Girl Is Like a Melody	95	5	19	39	Solo with Chorus	S,D	3:39
BS	Puttin' on the Ritz	272	8	34	79	Solo	DS,D	25:46
BS	A Couple of Song and Dance Men	294	15	20	143	Nonromantic Duo (Crosby)	DS,D	42:53
BS	Heat Wave (part 1: duo with San Juan)	216	4	54	103	Romantic Duo (San Juan)	DS,D	1:32:42
BS	Heat Wave (part 2: solo)	74	1	74	74	Solo	DP	
BS	Heat Wave (part 3: conclusion)	101	7	14	29	Romantic Duo (San Juan)	DP	1:37:31
EP	Drum Crazy	175	5	35	61	Solo	S,D	4:56
EP	It Only Happens When I Dance with You (apartment)	85	1	85	85	Romantic Duo (Miller)	S,D	10:34
EP	Beautiful Faces	72	6	12	24	Romantic Duo (Garland)	DO	28:49
EP	I Love a Piano	59	3	20	29	Romantic Duo (Garland)	S,D	41:18
EP	Ragtime Violin	41	2	21	26	Romantic Duo (Garland)	DS,D	43:21
EP	When the Midnight Choo-Choo Leaves for Alabam	79	3	26	36	Romantic Duo (Garland)	DS,D	44:35
EP	Steppin' Out with My Baby (part 1: partner dances)	213	5	43	69	Romantic Duo (3 partners)	DS,D	1:10:21
EP	Steppin' Out with My Baby (part 2: solo)	114	4	29	57	Solo	DP	1:13:53
EP	A Couple of Swells	259	7	37	74	Romantic Duo (Garland)	DS,D	1:16:20

EP	It Only Happens When I Dance with You (nightclub)	112	6	19	33	Romantic Duo (Miller)	DO	1:27:18
BB	Swing Trot	99	3	33	82	Romantic Duo (Rogers)	DO	00:12
BB	Bouncin' the Blues	123	3	41	63	Romantic Duo (Rogers)	DO	25:09
BB	My One and Only Highland Fling	78	1	78	78	Romantic Duo (Rogers)	S,D	35:48
BB	Shoes with Wings On	343	11	31	86	Solo	other	56:47
BB	They Can't Take That Away from Me	166	3	55	86	Romantic Duo (Rogers)	DO	1:23:23
BB	Manhattan Downbeat	131	10	13	31	Romantic Duo (Rogers)	S,D	1:46:11
LD	Can't Stop Talking	110	5	22	29	Romantic Duo (Hutton)	DS,D	2:47
LD	Ad Lib Dance	235	15	16	43	Solo	DO	22:55
LD	Jack and the Beanstalk	35	1	35	35	Solo	S,D	38:47
LD	Oh, Them Dudes	352	16	22	61	Nonromantic Duo (Hutton)	DS,D	50:05
LD	Why Fight the Feeling	106	3	35	51	Romantic Duo (Hutton)	DO	1:28:45
LD	Tunnel of Love (part 1: danced vocal)	104	5	21	24	Romantic Duo (Hutton)	-DS-	1:46:54
LD	Tunnel of Love (part 2: duo)	37	3	11	15	Romantic Duo (Hutton)	DP	1:50:29
TLW	Where Did You Get That Girl?	111	3	37	70	Nonromantic Duo (Vera-Ellen)	DS,D	1:47
TLW	Mr. and Mrs. Hoofer at Home	248	11	23	51	Romantic Duo (Vera-Ellen)	DO	14:23
TLW	Test Solo	89	2	45	53	Solo	DO	36:43
TLW	Nevertheless	65	4	16	25	Romantic Duo (Vera-Ellen)	S,D	43:36
TLW	Thinking of You	137	3	46	67	Romantic Duo (Vera-Ellen)	S,D	1:08:55
RW	Ev'ry Night at Seven	173	8	22	49	Romantic Duo (J. Powell)	DS,D	2:59
RW	Sunday Jumps	247	6	41	84	Solo	DO	16:24
RW	Open Your Eyes	154	7	22	61	Romantic Duo (J. Powell)	S,D	23:20

Film	Number	A Duration (seconds)	B # of Shots	C Average Shot Length (ASL)	D Longest Shot (seconds)	E Participants	F Content	G Timecode Start in Complete Film
RW	How Could You Believe Me …	234	7	33	45	Romantic Duo (J. Powell)	DS,D	52:40
RW	You're All the World to Me	247	4	62	100	Solo	DS,D	1:05:22
RW	I Left My Hat in Haiti (part 1: danced vocal)	242	6	40	55	Solo with Chorus	DS,D	1:14:47
RW	I Left My Hat in Haiti (part 2: duo)	90	4	23	43	Romantic Duo (J. Powell)	DP	1:19:24
BNY	Bachelor Dinner Song	62	4	16	18	Solo with Chorus	S,D	8:44
BNY	Seeing's Believing	182	11	17	37	Solo	S,D	17:33
BNY	Baby Doll	169	5	34	50	Romantic Duo (Vera-Ellen)	DS,D	26:56
BNY	Oops	234	10	23	64	Romantic Duo (Vera-Ellen)	S,D	34:44
BNY	A Bride's Wedding Day (spring)	86	4	48	49	Romantic Duo (Vera-Ellen)	S,D	44:27
BNY	A Bride's Wedding Day (winter, ice skating)	73	3	24	39	Romantic Duo (Vera-Ellen)	DP	46:23
BNY	A Bride's Wedding Day (summer, Boardwalk Dance)	166	6	28	60	Romantic Duo (Vera-Ellen)	DP	47:41
BNY	I Wanna Be a Dancin' Man	245	5	49	81	Solo	DS,D	1:12:34
BW	A Shine on Your Shoes	259	5	52	123	Nonromantic Duo (Daniels)	DS,D	13:19
BW	Dancing in the Dark	193	3	64	136	Romantic Duo (Charisse)	DO	59:03
BW	I Guess I'll Have to Change My Plan	107	3	36	51	Nonromantic Duo (Buchanan)	DS,D	1:24:16

BW	Triplets	80	1	80	80	Trio	DS,D	1:32:22
BW	Girl Hunt Ballet (Charisse entrance, attack)	69	7	10	16	Romantic Duo (Charisse)	DP	1:36:39
BW	Girl Hunt Ballet (subway duo)	76	1	76	76	Romantic Duo (Charisse)	DP	1:40:33
BW	Girl Hunt Ballet (club duo)	150	10	15	42	Romantic Duo (Charisse)	DP	1:43:28
DLL	History of the Beat	76	10	8	17	Solo	S,D	6:37
DLL	Daydream (part 1: Texas millionaire)	102	4	26	46	Solo	DO	44:16
DLL	Daydream (part 2: international playboy)	72	4	18	29	Solo with Chorus	DO	46:10
DLL	Daydream (part 3: guardian angel)	247	10	25	54	Romantic Duo (Caron)	DO	47:36
DLL	The Sluefoot	188	12	16	49	Romantic Duo (Caron)	DS,D	1:05:12
DLL	Something's Gotta Give	199	6	33	60	Romantic Duo (Caron)	S,D	1:19:29
FF	Funny Face	60	3	20	36	Romantic Duo (Hepburn)	S,D	30:00
FF	Let's Kiss and Make Up	183	13	14	25	Solo	S,D	51:46
FF	He Loves and She Loves	193	10	19	28	Romantic Duo (Hepburn)	S,D	1:07:10
FF	Clap Yo' Hands	209	9	23	47	Nonromantic Duo (Thompson)	-DS-	1:26:43
SS	Too Bad	86	2	43	50	Romantic Duo (3 dancers)	S,D	10:46
SS	Stereophonic Sound	112	4	28	41	Nonromantic Duo (Paige)	DS,D	37:02
SS	All of You	212	13	16	44	Romantic Duo (Charisse)	DO	47:52
SS	Fated to Be Mated	173	10	17	33	Romantic Duo (Charisse)	S,D	1:23:05
SS	The Ritz Roll and Rock	203	9	23	55	Solo	DS,D	1:48:50

APPENDIX THREE

Astaire Dancing Corpus by Shot

Film	Number	Shot Number in Routine	Duration (seconds)	Framing Type	Reframed Subtypes	Uses Crane
FDR	The Carioca (1st dance)	1	19	Vitruvian		
FDR	The Carioca (1st dance)	2	8	Vitruvian		
FDR	The Carioca (1st dance)	3	7	context		
FDR	The Carioca (1st dance)	4	16	Vitruvian		
FDR	The Carioca (1st dance)	5	6	cutaway		
FDR	The Carioca (1st dance)	6	12	context		
FDR	The Carioca (1st dance)	7	8	Vitruvian		
FDR	The Carioca (1st dance)	8	6	insert		
FDR	The Carioca (1st dance)	9	7	Vitruvian		
FDR	The Carioca (1st dance)	10	6	cutaway		
FDR	The Carioca (1st dance)	11	5	Vitruvian		
FDR	The Carioca (1st dance)	12	4	context		
FDR	The Carioca (1st dance)	13	6	Vitruvian		
FDR	The Carioca (1st dance)	14	2	cutaway		
FDR	The Carioca (2nd dance)	1	7	Vitruvian		
FDR	The Carioca (2nd dance)	2	20	context		
FDR	Music Makes Me	1	16	Vitruvian		
FDR	Music Makes Me	2	11	Vitruvian		
FDR	Music Makes Me	3	5	cutaway		
FDR	Music Makes Me	4	8	Vitruvian		
FDR	Music Makes Me	5	6	insert		
FDR	Music Makes Me	6	10	Vitruvian		
GD	Nightclub Solo	1	20	Vitruvian		
GD	Nightclub Solo	2	1	cutaway		
GD	Nightclub Solo	3	28	Vitruvian		
GD	Nightclub Solo	4	2	insert		
GD	Nightclub Solo	5	11	Vitruvian		
GD	Nightclub Solo	6	4	insert		
GD	Nightclub Solo	7	2	cutaway		
GD	Nightclub Solo	8	4	Vitruvian		
GD	Nightclub Solo	9	5	cutaway		
GD	Nightclub Solo	10	4	Vitruvian		
GD	A Needle in a Haystack	1	86	Vitruvian		
GD	Night and Day	1	4	context		
GD	Night and Day	2	4	context		
GD	Night and Day	3	5	context		
GD	Night and Day	4	5	context		

APPENDIX THREE

Film	Number	Shot Number in Routine	Duration (seconds)	Framing Type	Reframed Subtypes	Uses Crane
GD	Night and Day	5	40	Vitruvian		
GD	Night and Day	6	6	context		
GD	Night and Day	7	12	Vitruvian		
GD	Night and Day	8	7	context		
GD	Night and Day	9	30	Vitruvian		
GD	Night and Day	10	7	context		
GD	Night and Day	11	36	Vitruvian		
GD	Night and Day	12	20	Vitruvian		
GD	The Continental (1st dance)	1	27	context		
GD	The Continental (1st dance)	2	4	cutaway		
GD	The Continental (1st dance)	3	8	context		
GD	The Continental (1st dance)	4	39	Vitruvian		
GD	The Continental (1st dance)	5	57	Vitruvian		
GD	The Continental (1st dance)	6	5	insert		
GD	The Continental (1st dance)	7	7	Vitruvian		
GD	The Continental (2nd dance)	1	10	reframed	initial pull	
GD	The Continental (2nd dance)	2	2	cutaway		
GD	The Continental (2nd dance)	3	2	insert		
GD	The Continental (2nd dance)	4	1	cutaway		
GD	The Continental (2nd dance)	5	23	Vitruvian		
GD	The Continental (2nd dance)	6	9	context		
GD	The Continental (2nd dance)	7	58	context		
GD	Table Dance	1	8	Vitruvian		
GD	Table Dance	2	12	Vitruvian		
GD	Table Dance	3	25	Vitruvian		
GD	Table Dance	4	20	Vitruvian		
GD	Table Dance	5	18	Vitruvian		
R	I'll Be Hard to Handle	1	169	Vitruvian		
R	I Won't Dance (solo)	1	40	reframed	varies	
R	I Won't Dance (solo)	2	90	Vitruvian		
R	I Won't Dance (solo)	3	17	reframed	closing push	
R	Smoke Gets in Your Eyes	1	121	Vitruvian		

APPENDIX THREE 377

Film	Number	Shot Number in Routine	Duration (seconds)	Framing Type	Reframed Subtypes	Uses Crane
R	Smoke Gets in Your Eyes	2	17	Vitruvian		
R	I Won't Dance (duo)	1	51	Vitruvian		
TH	No Strings	1	50	Vitruvian		X
TH	No Strings	2	11	cutaway		X
TH	No Strings	3	18	Vitruvian		
TH	No Strings	4	6	cutaway		
TH	No Strings	5	8	Vitruvian		
TH	No Strings	6	7	cutaway		
TH	No Strings	7	2	cutaway		
TH	No Strings	8	8	cutaway		
TH	No Strings	9	9	Vitruvian		
TH	No Strings	10	8	cutaway		
TH	No Strings	11	8	reframed	closing danced in	
TH	No Strings	12	8	cutaway		
TH	No Strings	13	11	Vitruvian		
TH	No Strings	14	2	cutaway		
TH	No Strings	15	5	Vitruvian		
TH	No Strings	16	2	insert		
TH	No Strings (Sand Dance)	1	25	Vitruvian		
TH	No Strings (Sand Dance)	2	7	cutaway		
TH	No Strings (Sand Dance)	3	13	Vitruvian		
TH	No Strings (Sand Dance)	4	3	cutaway		
TH	No Strings (Sand Dance)	5	9	Vitruvian		
TH	No Strings (Sand Dance)	6	4	cutaway		
TH	No Strings (Sand Dance)	7	21	Vitruvian		
TH	Isn't This a Lovely Day	1	6	context		
TH	Isn't This a Lovely Day	2	23	Vitruvian		
TH	Isn't This a Lovely Day	3	97	Vitruvian		
TH	Isn't This a Lovely Day	4	34	Vitruvian		
TH	Top Hat, White Tie, and Tails	1	15	insert		
TH	Top Hat, White Tie, and Tails	2	26	Vitruvian		
TH	Top Hat, White Tie, and Tails	3	7	context		
TH	Top Hat, White Tie, and Tails	4	43	Vitruvian		
TH	Top Hat, White Tie, and Tails	5	21	Vitruvian		
TH	Top Hat, White Tie, and Tails	6	19	Vitruvian		
TH	Top Hat, White Tie, and Tails	7	43	context		

Film	Number	Shot Number in Routine	Duration (seconds)	Framing Type	Reframed Subtypes	Uses Crane
TH	Top Hat, White Tie, and Tails	8	6	Vitruvian		
TH	Top Hat, White Tie, and Tails	9	7	Vitruvian		
TH	Top Hat, White Tie, and Tails	10	6	Vitruvian		
TH	Cheek to Cheek	1	17	context		
TH	Cheek to Cheek	2	71	Vitruvian		
TH	Cheek to Cheek	3	7	context		
TH	Cheek to Cheek	4	39	Vitruvian		
TH	Cheek to Cheek	5	49	Vitruvian		
TH	The Piccolino	1	125	reframed	midway pull	
FTF	Let Yourself Go	1	30	reframed	initial pull	
FTF	Let Yourself Go	2	7	context		
FTF	Let Yourself Go	3	2	cutaway		
FTF	Let Yourself Go	4	15	Vitruvian		
FTF	Let Yourself Go	5	4	cutaway		
FTF	Let Yourself Go	6	8	Vitruvian		
FTF	Let Yourself Go	7	3	cutaway		
FTF	Let Yourself Go	8	12	Vitruvian		
FTF	Let Yourself Go	9	5	cutaway		
FTF	Let Yourself Go	10	2	insert		
FTF	Let Yourself Go	11	3	cutaway		
FTF	Let Yourself Go	12	43	Vitruvian		
FTF	Let Yourself Go	13	14	Vitruvian		
FTF	Let Yourself Go	14	19	Vitruvian		
FTF	Let Yourself Go	15	2	cutaway		
FTF	Let Yourself Go	16	24	Vitruvian		
FTF	I'd Rather Lead a Band	1	16	Vitruvian		
FTF	I'd Rather Lead a Band	2	21	Vitruvian		
FTF	I'd Rather Lead a Band	3	47	Vitruvian		
FTF	I'd Rather Lead a Band	4	14	context		
FTF	I'd Rather Lead a Band	5	40	Vitruvian		
FTF	I'd Rather Lead a Band	6	21	insert		
FTF	I'd Rather Lead a Band	7	15	Vitruvian		
FTF	I'd Rather Lead a Band	8	53	Vitruvian		
FTF	I'd Rather Lead a Band	9	16	Vitruvian		
FTF	I'd Rather Lead a Band	10	10	context		
FTF	I'd Rather Lead a Band	11	11	reframed	closing push	
FTF	I'm Putting All My Eggs in One Basket	1	41	Vitruvian		
FTF	I'm Putting All My Eggs in One Basket	2	37	Vitruvian		
FTF	I'm Putting All My Eggs in One Basket	3	24	insert		

Film	Number	Shot Number in Routine	Duration (seconds)	Framing Type	Reframed Subtypes	Uses Crane
FTF	I'm Putting All My Eggs in One Basket	4	78	Vitruvian		
FTF	Let's Face the Music and Dance	1	168	Vitruvian		
ST	Pick Yourself Up	1	18	Vitruvian		
ST	Pick Yourself Up	2	1	cutaway		
ST	Pick Yourself Up	3	5	Vitruvian		
ST	Pick Yourself Up	4	3	cutaway		
ST	Pick Yourself Up	5	96	Vitruvian		
ST	Waltz in Swing Time	1	156	Vitruvian		
ST	Bojangles of Harlem (part 1: chorus)	1	187	reframed	varies	X
ST	Bojangles of Harlem (part 2: shadows)	1	16	Vitruvian		
ST	Bojangles of Harlem (part 2: shadows)	2	25	Vitruvian		
ST	Bojangles of Harlem (part 2: shadows)	3	59	Vitruvian		
ST	Bojangles of Harlem (part 2: shadows)	4	9	Vitruvian		
ST	Bojangles of Harlem (part 2: shadows)	5	14	Vitruvian		
ST	Bojangles of Harlem (part 2: shadows)	6	47	Vitruvian		X
ST	Never Gonna Dance	1	151	reframed	varies	X
ST	Never Gonna Dance	2	27	Vitruvian		
SWD	Slap That Bass	1	45	Vitruvian		
SWD	Slap That Bass	2	8	Vitruvian		
SWD	Slap That Bass	3	38	Vitruvian		
SWD	Slap That Bass	4	55	Vitruvian		
SWD	Slap That Bass	5	22	Vitruvian		
SWD	Slap That Bass	6	7	Vitruvian		
SWD	They All Laughed	1	33	Vitruvian		
SWD	They All Laughed	2	4	insert		
SWD	They All Laughed	3	37	Vitruvian		
SWD	They All Laughed	4	2	insert		
SWD	They All Laughed	5	13	Vitruvian		
SWD	They All Laughed	6	4	insert		
SWD	They All Laughed	7	117	Vitruvian		
SWD	They All Laughed	8	27	Vitruvian		
SWD	Let's Call the Whole Thing Off	1	102	reframed	closing danced in	
SWD	Let's Call the Whole Thing Off	2	37	context		

380 APPENDIX THREE

Film	Number	Shot Number in Routine	Duration (seconds)	Framing Type	Reframed Subtypes	Uses Crane
SWD	Shall We Dance (part 1: duo with Hoctor)	1	7	context		
SWD	Shall We Dance (part 1: duo with Hoctor)	2	18	context		
SWD	Shall We Dance (part 1: duo with Hoctor)	3	13	Vitruvian		
SWD	Shall We Dance (part 1: duo with Hoctor)	4	16	context		
SWD	Shall We Dance (part 1: duo with Hoctor)	5	43	Vitruvian		
SWD	Shall We Dance (part 1: duo with Hoctor)	6	22	context		
SWD	Shall We Dance (part 1: duo with Hoctor)	7	30	context		
SWD	Shall We Dance (part 1: duo with Hoctor)	8	4	Vitruvian		
SWD	Shall We Dance (part 2: solo)	1	28	Vitruvian		
SWD	Shall We Dance (part 2: solo)	2	7	context		
SWD	Shall We Dance (part 2: solo)	3	17	Vitruvian		
SWD	Shall We Dance (part 2: solo)	4	2	insert		
SWD	Shall We Dance (part 2: solo)	5	2	insert		
SWD	Shall We Dance (part 2: solo)	6	2	insert		
SWD	Shall We Dance (part 2: solo)	7	29	Vitruvian		
SWD	Shall We Dance (part 2: solo)	8	5	insert		
SWD	Shall We Dance (part 3: duo with Rogers)	1	35	Vitruvian		
DD	I Can't Be Bothered Now	1	16	insert		
DD	I Can't Be Bothered Now	2	15	Vitruvian		
DD	I Can't Be Bothered Now	3	2	cutaway		
DD	I Can't Be Bothered Now	4	29	Vitruvian		
DD	I Can't Be Bothered Now	5	9	Vitruvian		
DD	Put Me to the Test	1	146	Vitruvian		
DD	Put Me to the Test	2	22	Vitruvian		
DD	Put Me to the Test	3	11	Vitruvian		
DD	Stiff Upper Lip (part 1: opening)	1	33	reframed	initial pull	

Film	Number	Shot Number in Routine	Duration (seconds)	Framing Type	Reframed Subtypes	Uses Crane
DD	Stiff Upper Lip (part 1: opening)	2	17	Vitruvian		
DD	Stiff Upper Lip (part 1: opening)	3	12	context		
DD	Stiff Upper Lip (part 1: opening)	4	4	Vitruvian		
DD	Stiff Upper Lip (part 1: opening)	5	14	Vitruvian		
DD	Stiff Upper Lip (part 1: opening)	6	12	Vitruvian		
DD	Stiff Upper Lip (part 1: opening)	7	19	context		
DD	Stiff Upper Lip (part 1: opening)	8	24	Vitruvian		
DD	Stiff Upper Lip (part 1: opening)	9	5	context		
DD	Stiff Upper Lip (part 1: opening)	10	27	context		
DD	Stiff Upper Lip (part 1: opening)	11	14	Vitruvian		
DD	Stiff Upper Lip (part 3: mirrors)	1	3	Vitruvian		
DD	Stiff Upper Lip (part 3: mirrors)	2	27	Vitruvian		
DD	Stiff Upper Lip (part 3: mirrors)	3	15	Vitruvian		
DD	Stiff Upper Lip (part 3: mirrors)	4	4	Vitruvian		
DD	Stiff Upper Lip (part 3: mirrors)	5	41	Vitruvian		
DD	Stiff Upper Lip (part 3: mirrors)	6	3	Vitruvian		
DD	Stiff Upper Lip (part 3: mirrors)	7	6	cutaway		
DD	Stiff Upper Lip (part 3: mirrors)	8	22	Vitruvian		
DD	Stiff Upper Lip (part 3: mirrors)	9	13	reframed	entirely danced	
DD	Things Are Looking Up	1	62	context		
DD	Things Are Looking Up	2	23	context		
DD	Things Are Looking Up	3	17	context		
DD	Things Are Looking Up	4	9	Vitruvian		
DD	Things Are Looking Up	5	7	context		
DD	Drum Dance	1	213	Vitruvian		
C	Golf Solo	1	12	insert		

APPENDIX THREE

Film	Number	Shot Number in Routine	Duration (seconds)	Framing Type	Reframed Subtypes	Uses Crane
C	Golf Solo	2	76	Vitruvian		
C	Golf Solo	3	30	Vitruvian		
C	Golf Solo	4	23	Vitruvian		
C	Golf Solo	5	10	Vitruvian		
C	Golf Solo	6	7	Vitruvian		
C	Golf Solo	7	2	cutaway		
C	Golf Solo	8	6	insert		
C	I Used to Be Color Blind	1	112	Vitruvian		
C	The Yam	1	66	Vitruvian		
C	The Yam	2	5	context		
C	The Yam	3	4	insert		
C	The Yam	4	5	context		
C	The Yam	5	4	insert		
C	The Yam	6	18	reframed	entirely danced	
C	The Yam	7	3	Vitruvian		
C	The Yam	8	4	cutaway		
C	The Yam	9	5	cutaway		
C	The Yam	10	5	cutaway		
C	The Yam	11	27	Vitruvian		
C	The Yam	12	7	Vitruvian		
C	The Yam	13	23	Vitruvian		
C	The Yam	14	36	Vitruvian		
C	The Yam	15	13	reframed	entirely danced	
C	The Yam	16	17	Vitruvian		
C	The Yam	17	7	reframed	closing push	
C	Change Partners	1	80	Vitruvian		
C	Change Partners	2	29	reframed	initial pull	
SVIC	By the Light of the Silvery Moon	1	58	context		
SVIC	By the Light of the Silvery Moon	2	7	insert		
SVIC	By the Light of the Silvery Moon	3	20	Vitruvian		
SVIC	By the Light of the Silvery Moon	4	2	cutaway		
SVIC	By the Light of the Silvery Moon	5	10	Vitruvian		
SVIC	Waiting for the Robt E Lee	1	95	Vitruvian		
SVIC	Too Much Mustard	1	66	Vitruvian		
SVIC	Too Much Mustard	2	27	Vitruvian		
SVIC	Medley Montage (tango)	1	56	Vitruvian		
SVIC	Medley Montage (polka)	1	36	Vitruvian		

APPENDIX THREE 383

Film	Number	Shot Number in Routine	Duration (seconds)	Framing Type	Reframed Subtypes	Uses Crane
SVIC	Medley Montage (maxixe)	1	65	Vitruvian		
SVIC	Hello! Hello! Who's Your Lady Friend?	1	3	Vitruvian		
SVIC	Hello! Hello! Who's Your Lady Friend?	2	5	cutaway		
SVIC	Hello! Hello! Who's Your Lady Friend?	3	56	Vitruvian		
SVIC	Hello! Hello! Who's Your Lady Friend?	4	7	Vitruvian		
SVIC	Hello! Hello! Who's Your Lady Friend?	5	9	Vitruvian		
SVIC	The Last Waltz	1	85	Vitruvian		
SVIC	The Last Waltz	2	43	reframed	closing push	
BM40	Please Don't Monkey with Broadway	1	37	Vitruvian		
BM40	Please Don't Monkey with Broadway	2	3	insert		
BM40	Please Don't Monkey with Broadway	3	5	Vitruvian		
BM40	Please Don't Monkey with Broadway	4	9	insert		
BM40	Please Don't Monkey with Broadway	5	51	Vitruvian		
BM40	I've Got My Eyes on You (solo)	1	25	Vitruvian		
BM40	I've Got My Eyes on You (solo)	2	4	cutaway		
BM40	I've Got My Eyes on You (solo)	3	30	Vitruvian		
BM40	I've Got My Eyes on You (solo)	4	37	Vitruvian		
BM40	I've Got My Eyes on You (solo)	5	3	cutaway		
BM40	I've Got My Eyes on You (solo)	6	47	Vitruvian		
BM40	I've Got My Eyes on You (solo)	7	31	reframed	varies	
BM40	Jukebox Dance	1	64	Vitruvian		
BM40	Jukebox Dance	2	46	Vitruvian		
BM40	I Concentrate on You	1	12	context		
BM40	I Concentrate on You	2	27	reframed	varies	
BM40	I Concentrate on You	3	6	insert		
BM40	I Concentrate on You	4	57	Vitruvian		
BM40	I Concentrate on You	5	82	Vitruvian		

384 APPENDIX THREE

Film	Number	Shot Number in Routine	Duration (seconds)	Framing Type	Reframed Subtypes	Uses Crane
BM40	I Concentrate on You	6	31	Vitruvian		
BM40	Begin the Beguine (part 1: flamenco)	1	13	context		
BM40	Begin the Beguine (part 1: flamenco)	2	10	Vitruvian		
BM40	Begin the Beguine (part 1: flamenco)	3	24	context		
BM40	Begin the Beguine (part 1: flamenco)	4	70	context		
BM40	Begin the Beguine (part 1: flamenco)	5	9	context		
BM40	Begin the Beguine (part 1: flamenco)	6	28	Vitruvian		
BM40	Begin the Beguine (part 1: flamenco)	7	11	context		
BM40	Begin the Beguine (part 1: flamenco)	8	22	Vitruvian		
BM40	Begin the Beguine (part 2: swing)	1	132	Vitruvian		
BM40	Begin the Beguine (part 2: swing)	2	29	Vitruvian		X
BM40	I've Got My Eyes on You (trio finale)	1	12	Vitruvian		
BM40	I've Got My Eyes on You (trio finale)	2	1	insert		
BM40	I've Got My Eyes on You (trio finale)	3	1	insert		
BM40	I've Got My Eyes on You (trio finale)	4	1	insert		
BM40	I've Got My Eyes on You (trio finale)	5	46	Vitruvian		
SC	I Ain't Hep to That Step but I'll Dig It	1	133	Vitruvian		
SC	Concert Solo	1	10	context		
SC	Concert Solo	2	8	context		
SC	Concert Solo	3	8	context		
SC	Concert Solo	4	19	Vitruvian		
SC	Concert Solo	5	16	Vitruvian		
SC	Concert Solo	6	21	Vitruvian		
SC	Concert Solo	7	24	Vitruvian		
SC	Concert Solo	8	64	Vitruvian		
SC	Concert Solo	9	37	Vitruvian		
YNGR	Rehearsal Duet	1	31	Vitruvian		
YNGR	Boogie Barcarolle	1	31	reframed	varies	
YNGR	Boogie Barcarolle	2	18	Vitruvian		

Film	Number	Shot Number in Routine	Duration (seconds)	Framing Type	Reframed Subtypes	Uses Crane
YNGR	Boogie Barcarolle	3	7	insert		
YNGR	Boogie Barcarolle	4	12	reframed	closing push	
YNGR	Boogie Barcarolle	5	9	Vitruvian		
YNGR	Boogie Barcarolle	6	6	Vitruvian		
YNGR	Boogie Barcarolle	7	23	context		X
YNGR	Shootin' the Works for Uncle Sam	1	22	Vitruvian		
YNGR	Shootin' the Works for Uncle Sam	2	15	context		
YNGR	Shootin' the Works for Uncle Sam	3	7	cutaway		
YNGR	Shootin' the Works for Uncle Sam	4	42	context		
YNGR	Shootin' the Works for Uncle Sam	5	26	reframed	closing push	
YNGR	Since I Kissed My Baby Goodbye	1	47	reframed	initial pull	
YNGR	Since I Kissed My Baby Goodbye	2	32	Vitruvian		
YNGR	A-stairable Rag	1	74	Vitruvian		
YNGR	A-stairable Rag	2	3	cutaway		
YNGR	A-stairable Rag	3	49	Vitruvian		
YNGR	A-stairable Rag	4	6	Vitruvian		
YNGR	So Near and Yet So Far	1	84	Vitruvian		
YNGR	So Near and Yet So Far	2	56	Vitruvian		
YNGR	So Near and Yet So Far	3	53	Vitruvian		
YNGR	The Wedding Cake Walk	1	11	Vitruvian		
YNGR	The Wedding Cake Walk	2	6	Vitruvian		
YNGR	The Wedding Cake Walk	3	7	context		
YNGR	The Wedding Cake Walk	4	8	Vitruvian		
YNGR	The Wedding Cake Walk	5	3	cutaway		
YNGR	The Wedding Cake Walk	6	4	context		
YNGR	The Wedding Cake Walk	7	27	Vitruvian		
YNGR	The Wedding Cake Walk	8	11	reframed	initial pull	X
YNGR	The Wedding Cake Walk	9	34	reframed	varies	X
YNGR	The Wedding Cake Walk	10	7	Vitruvian		
YNGR	The Wedding Cake Walk	11	16	context		
YNGR	The Wedding Cake Walk	12	6	Vitruvian		
YNGR	The Wedding Cake Walk	13	4	context		
HI	You're Easy to Dance With	1	79	reframed	closing push	
HI	You're Easy to Dance With	2	38	Vitruvian		
HI	You're Easy to Dance With	3	3	insert		

Film	Number	Shot Number in Routine	Duration (seconds)	Framing Type	Reframed Subtypes	Uses Crane
HI	You're Easy to Dance With	4	48	Vitruvian		
HI	Drunk Dance	1	15	reframed	initial pull	
HI	Drunk Dance	2	4	insert		
HI	Drunk Dance	3	50	Vitruvian		
HI	Drunk Dance	4	8	insert		
HI	Drunk Dance	5	23	Vitruvian		
HI	Drunk Dance	6	10	insert		
HI	Drunk Dance	7	13	Vitruvian		
HI	Be Careful, It's My Heart	1	60	Vitruvian		
HI	Be Careful, It's My Heart	2	11	Vitruvian		
HI	Be Careful, It's My Heart	3	38	Vitruvian		
HI	Be Careful, It's My Heart	4	14	Vitruvian		
HI	Be Careful, It's My Heart	5	18	Vitruvian		
HI	I Can't Tell a Lie	1	14	Vitruvian		
HI	I Can't Tell a Lie	2	2	cutaway		
HI	I Can't Tell a Lie	3	10	context		
HI	I Can't Tell a Lie	4	2	cutaway		
HI	I Can't Tell a Lie	5	2	Vitruvian		
HI	I Can't Tell a Lie	6	2	insert		
HI	I Can't Tell a Lie	7	2	cutaway		
HI	I Can't Tell a Lie	8	2	insert		
HI	I Can't Tell a Lie	9	21	Vitruvian		
HI	I Can't Tell a Lie	10	3	cutaway		
HI	I Can't Tell a Lie	11	6	Vitruvian		
HI	I Can't Tell a Lie	12	3	insert		
HI	I Can't Tell a Lie	13	2	cutaway		
HI	I Can't Tell a Lie	14	9	Vitruvian		
HI	I Can't Tell a Lie	15	2	insert		
HI	I Can't Tell a Lie	16	2	cutaway		
HI	I Can't Tell a Lie	17	11	Vitruvian		
HI	I Can't Tell a Lie	18	3	insert		
HI	I Can't Tell a Lie	19	2	cutaway		
HI	I Can't Tell a Lie	20	3	insert		
HI	I Can't Tell a Lie	21	6	Vitruvian		
HI	I Can't Tell a Lie	22	2	cutaway		
HI	I Can't Tell a Lie	23	13	Vitruvian		
HI	I Can't Tell a Lie	24	7	insert		
HI	I Can't Tell a Lie	25	27	Vitruvian		
HI	I Can't Tell a Lie	26	2	insert		
HI	Firecracker Dance	1	55	Vitruvian		
HI	Firecracker Dance	2	15	Vitruvian		
HI	Firecracker Dance	3	6	insert		
HI	Firecracker Dance	4	5	Vitruvian		
HI	Firecracker Dance	5	8	insert		
HI	Firecracker Dance	6	50	Vitruvian		

APPENDIX THREE   387

Film	Number	Shot Number in Routine	Duration (seconds)	Framing Type	Reframed Subtypes	Uses Crane
HI	Firecracker Dance	7	20	Vitruvian		
HI	Firecracker Dance	8	7	Vitruvian		
YWNL	Audition Dance	1	29	Vitruvian		
YWNL	Audition Dance	2	23	Vitruvian		
YWNL	Audition Dance	3	22	Vitruvian		
YWNL	Audition Dance	4	13	Vitruvian		
YWNL	Audition Dance	5	15	Vitruvian		
YWNL	Audition Dance	6	2	cutaway		
YWNL	Audition Dance	7	25	Vitruvian		
YWNL	I'm Old-Fashioned	1	76	Vitruvian		
YWNL	I'm Old-Fashioned	2	57	Vitruvian		
YWNL	I'm Old-Fashioned	3	12	Vitruvian		
YWNL	The Shorty George	1	32	Vitruvian		
YWNL	The Shorty George	2	9	insert		
YWNL	The Shorty George	3	22	Vitruvian		
YWNL	The Shorty George	4	10	insert		
YWNL	The Shorty George	5	5	insert		
YWNL	The Shorty George	6	4	insert		
YWNL	The Shorty George	7	8	Vitruvian		
YWNL	The Shorty George	8	3	insert		
YWNL	The Shorty George	9	68	Vitruvian		
YWNL	The Shorty George	10	6	context		
YWNL	The Shorty George	11	22	Vitruvian		
YWNL	The Shorty George	12	19	Vitruvian		
YWNL	The Shorty George	13	4	cutaway		
YWNL	The Shorty George	14	27	Vitruvian		
YWNL	You Were Never Lovelier (finale)	1	33	reframed	varies	
YWNL	You Were Never Lovelier (finale)	2	2	cutaway		
YWNL	You Were Never Lovelier (finale)	3	8	context		
YWNL	You Were Never Lovelier (finale)	4	3	Vitruvian		
YWNL	You Were Never Lovelier (finale)	5	2	cutaway		
YWNL	You Were Never Lovelier (finale)	6	5	context		
YWNL	You Were Never Lovelier (finale)	7	16	Vitruvian		
STL	A Lot in Common with You	1	17	Vitruvian		
STL	A Lot in Common with You	2	7	insert		

APPENDIX THREE

Film	Number	Shot Number in Routine	Duration (seconds)	Framing Type	Reframed Subtypes	Uses Crane
STL	A Lot in Common with You	3	8	Vitruvian		
STL	A Lot in Common with You	4	4	insert		
STL	A Lot in Common with You	5	17	Vitruvian		
STL	A Lot in Common with You	6	4	insert		
STL	A Lot in Common with You	7	17	Vitruvian		
STL	A Lot in Common with You	8	4	Vitruvian		
STL	A Lot in Common with You	9	12	Vitruvian		
STL	A Lot in Common with You	10	4	Vitruvian		
STL	A Lot in Common with You	11	6	Vitruvian		
STL	A Lot in Common with You	12	4	Vitruvian		
STL	A Lot in Common with You	13	11	Vitruvian		
STL	My Shining Hour	1	58	Vitruvian		
STL	My Shining Hour	2	69	Vitruvian		
STL	My Shining Hour	3	25	Vitruvian		
STL	My Shining Hour	4	7	Vitruvian		
STL	One for My Baby	1	40	Vitruvian		
STL	One for My Baby	2	9	Vitruvian		
STL	One for My Baby	3	6	Vitruvian		
STL	One for My Baby	4	9	Vitruvian		
STL	One for My Baby	5	14	Vitruvian		
STL	One for My Baby	6	10	Vitruvian		
STL	One for My Baby	7	19	Vitruvian		
STL	One for My Baby	8	10	Vitruvian		
STL	One for My Baby	9	5	Vitruvian		
STL	One for My Baby	10	11	context		
ZF	This Heart of Mine	1	56	reframed	varies	
ZF	This Heart of Mine	2	34	reframed	closing push	
ZF	This Heart of Mine	3	60	reframed	varies	
ZF	This Heart of Mine	4	25	insert		
ZF	This Heart of Mine	5	26	Vitruvian		
ZF	This Heart of Mine	6	84	reframed	varies	X
ZF	This Heart of Mine	7	77	Vitruvian		
ZF	This Heart of Mine	8	61	reframed	varies	X
ZF	This Heart of Mine	9	18	context		

APPENDIX THREE   389

Film	Number	Shot Number in Routine	Duration (seconds)	Framing Type	Reframed Subtypes	Uses Crane
ZF	This Heart of Mine	10	33	context		
ZF	This Heart of Mine	11	24	reframed	varies	
ZF	This Heart of Mine	12	10	reframed	entirely danced	
ZF	Limehouse Blues	1	72	reframed	varies	
ZF	Limehouse Blues	2	58	reframed	varies	X
ZF	Limehouse Blues	3	27	Vitruvian		
ZF	Limehouse Blues	4	20	insert		
ZF	Limehouse Blues	5	124	reframed	varies	X
ZF	Limehouse Blues	6	44	Vitruvian		X
ZF	Limehouse Blues	7	37	Vitruvian		
ZF	The Babbitt and the Bromide	1	33	Vitruvian		
ZF	The Babbitt and the Bromide	2	18	insert		
ZF	The Babbitt and the Bromide	3	16	insert		
ZF	The Babbitt and the Bromide	4	64	Vitruvian		
ZF	The Babbitt and the Bromide	5	18	insert		
ZF	The Babbitt and the Bromide	6	38	reframed	midway pull	
ZF	The Babbitt and the Bromide	7	42	reframed	initial pull	
ZF	The Babbitt and the Bromide	8	42	Vitruvian		X
ZF	The Babbitt and the Bromide	9	25	reframed	closing danced in	X
YT	Will You Marry Me? (part 1: washerwomen)	1	103	reframed	entirely danced	
YT	Will You Marry Me? (part 1: washerwomen)	2	44	reframed	varies	X
YT	Will You Marry Me? (part 1: washerwomen)	3	50	reframed	varies	X
YT	Will You Marry Me? (part 2: duo with Bremer)	1	96	reframed	varies	
YT	Will You Marry Me? (part 2: duo with Bremer)	2	29	insert		
YT	Will You Marry Me? (part 2: duo with Bremer)	3	34	context		
YT	Will You Marry Me? (part 2: duo with Bremer)	4	43	reframed	varies	X

390 APPENDIX THREE

Film	Number	Shot Number in Routine	Duration (seconds)	Framing Type	Reframed Subtypes	Uses Crane
YT	Will You Marry Me? (part 3: bad crowd to end)	1	53	reframed	varies	X
YT	Will You Marry Me? (part 3: bad crowd to end)	2	69	reframed	varies	
YT	Will You Marry Me? (part 3: bad crowd to end)	3	109	reframed	varies	
YT	Will You Marry Me? (part 3: bad crowd to end)	4	59	reframed	varies	X
YT	Yolanda	1	13	insert		
YT	Yolanda	2	3	cutaway		
YT	Yolanda	3	6	insert		
YT	Yolanda	4	53	reframed	varies	
YT	Coffee Time	1	39	Vitruvian		
YT	Coffee Time	2	102	reframed	closing pull	
YT	Coffee Time	3	85	reframed	midway push	X
YT	Coffee Time	4	15	reframed	closing push	X
BS	A Pretty Girl Is Like a Melody	1	39	Vitruvian		
BS	A Pretty Girl Is Like a Melody	2	4	insert		
BS	A Pretty Girl Is Like a Melody	3	39	Vitruvian		
BS	A Pretty Girl Is Like a Melody	4	3	cutaway		
BS	A Pretty Girl Is Like a Melody	5	10	Vitruvian		
BS	Puttin' on the Ritz	1	34	reframed	midway push	
BS	Puttin' on the Ritz	2	48	Vitruvian		
BS	Puttin' on the Ritz	3	9	insert		
BS	Puttin' on the Ritz	4	79	Vitruvian		
BS	Puttin' on the Ritz	5	28	Vitruvian		
BS	Puttin' on the Ritz	6	33	Vitruvian		
BS	Puttin' on the Ritz	7	18	Vitruvian		
BS	Puttin' on the Ritz	8	23	Vitruvian		
BS	A Couple of Song and Dance Men	1	143	Vitruvian		
BS	A Couple of Song and Dance Men	2	9	insert		

APPENDIX THREE 391

Film	Number	Shot Number in Routine	Duration (seconds)	Framing Type	Reframed Subtypes	Uses Crane
BS	A Couple of Song and Dance Men	3	14	Vitruvian		
BS	A Couple of Song and Dance Men	4	21	Vitruvian		
BS	A Couple of Song and Dance Men	5	3	insert		
BS	A Couple of Song and Dance Men	6	11	Vitruvian		
BS	A Couple of Song and Dance Men	7	4	insert		
BS	A Couple of Song and Dance Men	8	19	Vitruvian		
BS	A Couple of Song and Dance Men	9	10	Vitruvian		
BS	A Couple of Song and Dance Men	10	5	insert		
	A Couple of Song and Dance Men	11	12	Vitruvian		
BS	A Couple of Song and Dance Men	12	6	insert		
BS	A Couple of Song and Dance Men	13	14	Vitruvian		
BS	A Couple of Song and Dance Men	14	7	insert		
BS	A Couple of Song and Dance Men	15	16	Vitruvian		
BS	Heat Wave (part 1: duo with San Juan)	1	77	reframed	varies	
BS	Heat Wave (part 1: duo with San Juan)	2	5	cutaway		
BS	Heat Wave (part 1: duo with San Juan)	3	31	Vitruvian		
BS	Heat Wave (part 1: duo with San Juan)	4	103	Vitruvian		
BS	Heat Wave (part 2: solo)	1	74	Vitruvian		
BS	Heat Wave (part 3: conclusion)	1	29	reframed	varies	
BS	Heat Wave (part 3: conclusion)	2	11	context		
BS	Heat Wave (part 3: conclusion)	3	17	Vitruvian		
BS	Heat Wave (part 3: conclusion)	4	7	Vitruvian		
BS	Heat Wave (part 3: conclusion)	5	7	context		

Film	Number	Shot Number in Routine	Duration (seconds)	Framing Type	Reframed Subtypes	Uses Crane
BS	Heat Wave (part 3: conclusion)	6	6	context		
BS	Heat Wave (part 3: conclusion)	7	24	Vitruvian		
EP	Drum Crazy	1	61	Vitruvian		
EP	Drum Crazy	2	39	insert		
EP	Drum Crazy	3	20	Vitruvian		
EP	Drum Crazy	4	17	reframed	initial pull	X
EP	Drum Crazy	5	38	reframed	initial pull	
EP	It Only Happens When I Dance with You (apartment)	1	85	reframed	varies	
EP	Beautiful Faces	1	12	Vitruvian		
EP	Beautiful Faces	2	4	insert		
EP	Beautiful Faces	3	12	Vitruvian		
EP	Beautiful Faces	4	5	insert		
EP	Beautiful Faces	5	24	Vitruvian		
EP	Beautiful Faces	6	15	reframed	initial pull	
EP	I Love a Piano	1	29	Vitruvian		
EP	I Love a Piano	2	14	Vitruvian		
EP	I Love a Piano	3	16	reframed	initial pull	
EP	Ragtime Violin	1	26	reframed	initial pull	
EP	Ragtime Violin	2	15	reframed	initial pull	
EP	When the Midnight Choo-Choo Leaves for Alabam	1	36	Vitruvian		
EP	When the Midnight Choo-Choo Leaves for Alabam	2	22	Vitruvian		
EP	When the Midnight Choo-Choo Leaves for Alabam	3	21	reframed	closing pull	
EP	Steppin' Out with My Baby (part 1: partner dances)	1	59	Vitruvian		
EP	Steppin' Out with My Baby (part 1: partner dances)	2	10	reframed	entirely danced	
EP	Steppin' Out with My Baby (part 1: partner dances)	3	45	Vitruvian		
EP	Steppin' Out with My Baby (part 1: partner dances)	4	69	reframed	initial pull	

Film	Number	Shot Number in Routine	Duration (seconds)	Framing Type	Reframed Subtypes	Uses Crane
EP	Steppin' Out with My Baby (part 1: partner dances)	5	30	reframed	initial pull	
EP	Steppin' Out with My Baby (part 2: solo)	1	38	reframed	initial pull	
EP	Steppin' Out with My Baby (part 2: solo)	2	57	Vitruvian		
EP	Steppin' Out with My Baby (part 2: solo)	3	4	cutaway		
EP	Steppin' Out with My Baby (part 2: solo)	4	15	reframed	initial pull	
EP	A Couple of Swells	1	33	insert		
EP	A Couple of Swells	2	20	Vitruvian		
EP	A Couple of Swells	3	74	reframed	midway pull	
EP	A Couple of Swells	4	14	insert		
EP	A Couple of Swells	5	45	reframed	closing push	
EP	A Couple of Swells	6	42	Vitruvian		
EP	A Couple of Swells	7	31	reframed	initial pull	
EP	It Only Happens When I Dance with You (nightclub)	1	33	Vitruvian		
EP	It Only Happens When I Dance with You (nightclub)	2	22	reframed	initial pull	
EP	It Only Happens When I Dance with You (nightclub)	3	4	cutaway		
EP	It Only Happens When I Dance with You (nightclub)	4	24	Vitruvian		
EP	It Only Happens When I Dance with You (nightclub)	5	3	cutaway		
EP	It Only Happens When I Dance with You (nightclub)	6	26	Vitruvian		
BB	Swing Trot	1	82	reframed	varies	
BB	Swing Trot	2	14	Vitruvian		
BB	Swing Trot	3	3	Vitruvian		
BB	Bouncin' the Blues	1	63	Vitruvian		
BB	Bouncin' the Blues	2	25	reframed	initial danced out	
BB	Bouncin' the Blues	3	35	reframed	initial push	X
BB	My One and Only Highland Fling	1	78	Vitruvian		

APPENDIX THREE

Film	Number	Shot Number in Routine	Duration (seconds)	Framing Type	Reframed Subtypes	Uses Crane
BB	Shoes with Wings On	1	81	Vitruvian		
BB	Shoes with Wings On	2	86	reframed	midway pull	
BB	Shoes with Wings On	3	13	insert		
BB	Shoes with Wings On	4	22	Vitruvian		
BB	Shoes with Wings On	5	10	insert		
BB	Shoes with Wings On	6	73	Vitruvian		
BB	Shoes with Wings On	7	2	insert		
BB	Shoes with Wings On	8	15	Vitruvian		
BB	Shoes with Wings On	9	10	insert		
BB	Shoes with Wings On	10	19	Vitruvian		
BB	Shoes with Wings On	11	12	reframed	closing push	
BB	They Can't Take That Away from Me	1	86	Vitruvian		
BB	They Can't Take That Away from Me	2	31	reframed	initial pull	
BB	They Can't Take That Away from Me	3	49	reframed	initial pull	
BB	Manhattan Downbeat	1	14	Vitruvian		
BB	Manhattan Downbeat	2	12	reframed	initial pull	
BB	Manhattan Downbeat	3	3	cutaway		
BB	Manhattan Downbeat	4	31	Vitruvian		
BB	Manhattan Downbeat	5	3	cutaway		
BB	Manhattan Downbeat	6	7	context		
BB	Manhattan Downbeat	7	22	reframed	closing pull	
BB	Manhattan Downbeat	8	7	Vitruvian		
BB	Manhattan Downbeat	9	11	context		
BB	Manhattan Downbeat	10	21	reframed	closing push	
LD	Can't Stop Talking	1	14	Vitruvian		
LD	Can't Stop Talking	2	10	insert		
LD	Can't Stop Talking	3	29	Vitruvian		
LD	Can't Stop Talking	4	29	reframed	initial danced out	
LD	Can't Stop Talking	5	28	reframed	initial pull	
LD	Ad Lib Dance	1	43	reframed	initial danced out	
LD	Ad Lib Dance	2	6	reframed	closing tilt	
LD	Ad Lib Dance	3	13	Vitruvian		
LD	Ad Lib Dance	4	5	Vitruvian		
LD	Ad Lib Dance	5	15	Vitruvian		
LD	Ad Lib Dance	6	5	reframed	closing push	X
LD	Ad Lib Dance	7	24	reframed	closing push	
LD	Ad Lib Dance	8	3	cutaway		
LD	Ad Lib Dance	9	19	insert		
LD	Ad Lib Dance	10	11	insert		
LD	Ad Lib Dance	11	10	insert		
LD	Ad Lib Dance	12	20	Vitruvian		

Film	Number	Shot Number in Routine	Duration (seconds)	Framing Type	Reframed Subtypes	Uses Crane
LD	Ad Lib Dance	13	24	Vitruvian		
LD	Ad Lib Dance	14	24	Vitruvian		
LD	Ad Lib Dance	15	13	Vitruvian		
LD	Jack and the Beanstalk	1	35	Vitruvian		
LD	Oh, Them Dudes	1	61	reframed	varies	
LD	Oh, Them Dudes	2	32	reframed	initial push	
LD	Oh, Them Dudes	3	13	Vitruvian		
LD	Oh, Them Dudes	4	8	insert		
LD	Oh, Them Dudes	5	9	Vitruvian		
LD	Oh, Them Dudes	6	12	insert		
LD	Oh, Them Dudes	7	13	reframed	entirely danced	
LD	Oh, Them Dudes	8	5	insert		
LD	Oh, Them Dudes	9	40	reframed	entirely danced	
LD	Oh, Them Dudes	10	20	insert		
LD	Oh, Them Dudes	11	17	Vitruvian		
LD	Oh, Them Dudes	12	8	Vitruvian		
LD	Oh, Them Dudes	13	29	Vitruvian		
LD	Oh, Them Dudes	14	39	Vitruvian		
LD	Oh, Them Dudes	15	5	insert		
LD	Oh, Them Dudes	16	41	Vitruvian		
LD	Why Fight the Feeling	1	17	Vitruvian		
LD	Why Fight the Feeling	2	38	Vitruvian		
LD	Why Fight the Feeling	3	51	reframed	initial pull	
LD	Tunnel of Love (part 1: danced vocal)	1	19	Vitruvian		
LD	Tunnel of Love (part 1: danced vocal)	2	20	reframed	closing danced in	
LD	Tunnel of Love (part 1: danced vocal)	3	23	Vitruvian		
LD	Tunnel of Love (part 1: danced vocal)	4	24	insert		
LD	Tunnel of Love (part 1: danced vocal)	5	18	Vitruvian		
LD	Tunnel of Love (part 2: duo)	1	8	Vitruvian		
LD	Tunnel of Love (part 2: duo)	2	15	reframed	initial push	
LD	Tunnel of Love (part 2: duo)	3	14	reframed	initial danced out	
TLW	Where Did You Get That Girl?	1	11	reframed	initial danced out	
TLW	Where Did You Get That Girl?	2	70	Vitruvian		

Film	Number	Shot Number in Routine	Duration (seconds)	Framing Type	Reframed Subtypes	Uses Crane
TLW	Where Did You Get That Girl?	3	30	Vitruvian		
TLW	Mr. and Mrs. Hoofer at Home	1	51	Vitruvian		
TLW	Mr. and Mrs. Hoofer at Home	2	41	reframed	midway danced out	
TLW	Mr. and Mrs. Hoofer at Home	3	43	Vitruvian		
TLW	Mr. and Mrs. Hoofer at Home	4	11	Vitruvian		
TLW	Mr. and Mrs. Hoofer at Home	5	9	insert		
TLW	Mr. and Mrs. Hoofer at Home	6	4	insert		
TLW	Mr. and Mrs. Hoofer at Home	7	14	reframed	closing push	
TLW	Mr. and Mrs. Hoofer at Home	8	38	Vitruvian		
TLW	Mr. and Mrs. Hoofer at Home	9	20	Vitruvian		
TLW	Mr. and Mrs. Hoofer at Home	10	6	reframed	closing danced in	
TLW	Mr. and Mrs. Hoofer at Home	11	11	Vitruvian		
TLW	Test Solo	1	53	Vitruvian		
TLW	Test Solo	2	36	reframed	initial pull	
TLW	Nevertheless	1	25	Vitruvian		
TLW	Nevertheless	2	5	cutaway		
TLW	Nevertheless	3	16	Vitruvian		
TLW	Nevertheless	4	19	reframed	closing push	
TLW	Thinking of You	1	67	Vitruvian		
TLW	Thinking of You	2	40	Vitruvian		
TLW	Thinking of You	3	30	Vitruvian		
RW	Ev'ry Night at Seven	1	24	reframed	closing push	
RW	Ev'ry Night at Seven	2	49	reframed	varies	
RW	Ev'ry Night at Seven	3	42	reframed	midway push	
RW	Ev'ry Night at Seven	4	2	cutaway		
RW	Ev'ry Night at Seven	5	6	context		
RW	Ev'ry Night at Seven	6	21	reframed	varies	
RW	Ev'ry Night at Seven	7	14	Vitruvian		
RW	Ev'ry Night at Seven	8	15	reframed	closing pull	
RW	Sunday Jumps	1	61	reframed	varies	
RW	Sunday Jumps	2	84	reframed	varies	
RW	Sunday Jumps	3	52	Vitruvian		

APPENDIX THREE   397

Film	Number	Shot Number in Routine	Duration (seconds)	Framing Type	Reframed Subtypes	Uses Crane
RW	Sunday Jumps	4	10	reframed	initial pull	X
RW	Sunday Jumps	5	30	reframed	closing push	
RW	Sunday Jumps	6	10	Vitruvian		
RW	Open Your Eyes	1	33	Vitruvian		
RW	Open Your Eyes	2	24	reframed	closing push	X
RW	Open Your Eyes	3	6	Vitruvian		
RW	Open Your Eyes	4	3	cutaway		
RW	Open Your Eyes	5	6	Vitruvian		
RW	Open Your Eyes	6	21	reframed	midway pull	
RW	Open Your Eyes	7	61	reframed	closing push	X
RW	How Could You Believe Me...	1	29	reframed	closing push	
	How Could You Believe Me...	2	28	Vitruvian		
RW	How Could You Believe Me...	3	41	reframed	initial pull	
RW	How Could You Believe Me...	4	17	reframed	closing danced in	
RW	How Could You Believe Me...	5	36	Vitruvian		
RW	How Could You Believe Me...	6	45	reframed	initial pull	
RW	How Could You Believe Me...	7	38	reframed	initial pull	
RW	You're All the World to Me	1	63	reframed	varies	
RW	You're All the World to Me	2	100	Vitruvian		
RW	You're All the World to Me	3	80	Vitruvian		
RW	You're All the World to Me	4	4	insert		
RW	I Left My Hat in Haiti (part 1: danced vocal)	1	34	reframed	midway push	X
RW	I Left My Hat in Haiti (part 1: danced vocal)	2	51	reframed	varies	
RW	I Left My Hat in Haiti (part 1: danced vocal)	3	53	reframed	closing pull	X
RW	I Left My Hat in Haiti (part 1: danced vocal)	4	55	reframed	varies	
RW	I Left My Hat in Haiti (part 1: danced vocal)	5	33	reframed	varies	
RW	I Left My Hat in Haiti (part 1: danced vocal)	6	16	reframed	initial pull	

APPENDIX THREE

Film	Number	Shot Number in Routine	Duration (seconds)	Framing Type	Reframed Subtypes	Uses Crane
RW	I Left My Hat in Haiti (part 2: duo)	1	43	reframed	varies	
RW	I Left My Hat in Haiti (part 2: duo)	2	16	Vitruvian		
RW	I Left My Hat in Haiti (part 2: duo)	3	20	reframed	initial danced out	
RW	I Left My Hat in Haiti (part 2: duo)	4	11	reframed	closing push	
BNY	Bachelor Dinner Song	1	18	Vitruvian		
BNY	Bachelor Dinner Song	2	18	Vitruvian		X
BNY	Bachelor Dinner Song	3	13	reframed	varies	X
BNY	Bachelor Dinner Song	4	13	Vitruvian		
BNY	Seeing's Believing	1	18	Vitruvian		
BNY	Seeing's Believing	2	11	Vitruvian		X
BNY	Seeing's Believing	3	37	Vitruvian		
BNY	Seeing's Believing	4	8	Vitruvian		
BNY	Seeing's Believing	5	14	Vitruvian		
BNY	Seeing's Believing	6	6	Vitruvian		
BNY	Seeing's Believing	7	10	Vitruvian		
BNY	Seeing's Believing	8	14	context		
BNY	Seeing's Believing	9	18	Vitruvian		
BNY	Seeing's Believing	10	28	context		
BNY	Seeing's Believing	11	18	Vitruvian		
BNY	Baby Doll	1	45	reframed	midway pull	
BNY	Baby Doll	2	50	reframed	initial pull	
BNY	Baby Doll	3	33	Vitruvian		
BNY	Baby Doll	4	10	reframed	closing pull	
BNY	Baby Doll	5	31	Vitruvian		
BNY	Oops	1	24	reframed	initial pull	
BNY	Oops	2	9	insert		
BNY	Oops	3	23	Vitruvian		
BNY	Oops	4	64	Vitruvian		
BNY	Oops	5	30	reframed	initial pull	
BNY	Oops	6	16	Vitruvian		
BNY	Oops	7	8	insert		
BNY	Oops	8	21	Vitruvian		
BNY	Oops	9	2	cutaway		
BNY	Oops	10	37	Vitruvian		
BNY	A Bride's Wedding Day (spring)	1	12	context		
BNY	A Bride's Wedding Day (spring)	2	21	reframed	varies	
BNY	A Bride's Wedding Day (spring)	3	4	insert		
BNY	A Bride's Wedding Day (spring)	4	49	reframed	varies	

APPENDIX THREE 399

Film	Number	Shot Number in Routine	Duration (seconds)	Framing Type	Reframed Subtypes	Uses Crane
BNY	A Bride's Wedding Day (winter, ice skating)	1	39	reframed	closing danced in	
BNY	A Bride's Wedding Day (winter, ice skating)	2	24	reframed	initial pull	X
BNY	A Bride's Wedding Day (winter, ice skating)	3	10	reframed	closing push	X
BNY	A Bride's Wedding Day (summer, Boardwalk Dance)	1	60	reframed	initial push	
BNY	A Bride's Wedding Day (summer, Boardwalk Dance)	2	18	Vitruvian		X
BNY	A Bride's Wedding Day (summer, Boardwalk Dance)	3	13	Vitruvian		
BNY	A Bride's Wedding Day (summer, Boardwalk Dance)	4	43	reframed	initial pull	
BNY	A Bride's Wedding Day (summer, Boardwalk Dance)	5	25	Vitruvian		X
BNY	A Bride's Wedding Day (summer, Boardwalk Dance)	6	7	Vitruvian		
BNY	I Wanna Be a Dancin' Man	1	20	Vitruvian		
BNY	I Wanna Be a Dancin' Man	2	81	reframed	varies	X
BNY	I Wanna Be a Dancin' Man	3	71	reframed	initial pull	X
BNY	I Wanna Be a Dancin' Man	4	53	Vitruvian		X
BNY	I Wanna Be a Dancin' Man	5	20	reframed	initial pull	X
BW	A Shine on Your Shoes	1	123	reframed	varies	X
BW	A Shine on Your Shoes	2	24	Vitruvian		
BW	A Shine on Your Shoes	3	46	reframed	varies	
BW	A Shine on Your Shoes	4	34	Vitruvian		
BW	A Shine on Your Shoes	5	32	Vitruvian		
BW	Dancing in the Dark	1	136	Vitruvian		
BW	Dancing in the Dark	2	30	Vitruvian		
BW	Dancing in the Dark	3	27	Vitruvian		
BW	I Guess I'll Have to Change My Plan	1	51	reframed	varies	

Film	Number	Shot Number in Routine	Duration (seconds)	Framing Type	Reframed Subtypes	Uses Crane
BW	I Guess I'll Have to Change My Plan	2	39	Vitruvian		X
BW	I Guess I'll Have to Change My Plan	3	17	Vitruvian		
BW	Triplets	1	80	Vitruvian		
BW	Girl Hunt Ballet (Charisse entrance, attack)	1	13	reframed	initial danced out	
BW	Girl Hunt Ballet (Charisse entrance, attack)	2	10	reframed	midway pull	
BW	Girl Hunt Ballet (Charisse entrance, attack)	3	5	cutaway		
BW	Girl Hunt Ballet (Charisse entrance, attack)	4	4	Vitruvian		
BW	Girl Hunt Ballet (Charisse entrance, attack)	5	9	reframed	closing push	
BW	Girl Hunt Ballet (Charisse entrance, attack)	6	16	reframed	closing danced out	
BW	Girl Hunt Ballet (Charisse entrance, attack)	7	12	reframed	initial pull	
BW	Girl Hunt Ballet (subway duo)	1	76	reframed	varies	
BW	Girl Hunt Ballet (club duo)	1	24	insert		
BW	Girl Hunt Ballet (club duo)	2	33	insert		
BW	Girl Hunt Ballet (club duo)	3	42	Vitruvian		
BW	Girl Hunt Ballet (club duo)	4	16	Vitruvian		
BW	Girl Hunt Ballet (club duo)	5	1	insert		
BW	Girl Hunt Ballet (club duo)	6	5	cutaway		
BW	Girl Hunt Ballet (club duo)	7	3	insert		
BW	Girl Hunt Ballet (club duo)	8	13	reframed	closing push	

Film	Number	Shot Number in Routine	Duration (seconds)	Framing Type	Reframed Subtypes	Uses Crane
BW	Girl Hunt Ballet (club duo)	9	4	insert		
BW	Girl Hunt Ballet (club duo)	10	9	reframed	closing push	
DLL	History of the Beat	1	7	insert		
DLL	History of the Beat	2	12	reframed	midway pull	
DLL	History of the Beat	3	2	cutaway		
DLL	History of the Beat	4	7	Vitruvian		
DLL	History of the Beat	5	16	Vitruvian		
DLL	History of the Beat	6	2	cutaway		
DLL	History of the Beat	7	5	Vitruvian		
DLL	History of the Beat	8	17	reframed	midway pull	
DLL	History of the Beat	9	7	reframed	initial pull	
DLL	History of the Beat	10	1	insert		
DLL	Daydream (part 1: Texas millionaire)	1	19	reframed	midway pull	
DLL	Daydream (part 1: Texas millionaire)	2	27	reframed	initial pull	
DLL	Daydream (part 1: Texas millionaire)	3	46	reframed	varies	
DLL	Daydream (part 1: Texas millionaire)	4	10	reframed	initial pull	
DLL	Daydream (part 2: international playboy)	1	29	Vitruvian		
DLL	Daydream (part 2: international playboy)	2	6	insert		
DLL	Daydream (part 2: international playboy)	3	23	Vitruvian		
DLL	Daydream (part 2: international playboy)	4	14	reframed	closing pull	
DLL	Daydream (part 3: guardian angel)	1	23	reframed	midway pull	
DLL	Daydream (part 3: guardian angel)	2	2	insert		
DLL	Daydream (part 3: guardian angel)	3	3	Vitruvian		
DLL	Daydream (part 3: guardian angel)	4	14	insert		
DLL	Daydream (part 3: guardian angel)	5	45	reframed	midway pull	
DLL	Daydream (part 3: guardian angel)	6	10	reframed	entirely danced	
DLL	Daydream (part 3: guardian angel)	7	54	reframed	entirely danced	

402 APPENDIX THREE

Film	Number	Shot Number in Routine	Duration (seconds)	Framing Type	Reframed Subtypes	Uses Crane
DLL	Daydream (part 3: guardian angel)	8	40	reframed	initial pull	X
DLL	Daydream (part 3: guardian angel)	9	38	context		
DLL	Daydream (part 3: guardian angel)	10	18	reframed	initial pull	
DLL	The Sluefoot	1	22	insert		
DLL	The Sluefoot	2	3	cutaway		
DLL	The Sluefoot	3	33	Vitruvian		
DLL	The Sluefoot	4	3	cutaway		
DLL	The Sluefoot	5	3	cutaway		
DLL	The Sluefoot	6	14	Vitruvian		
DLL	The Sluefoot	7	49	Vitruvian		
DLL	The Sluefoot	8	12	reframed	initial pull	
DLL	The Sluefoot	9	19	context		
DLL	The Sluefoot	10	15	reframed	entirely danced	
DLL	The Sluefoot	11	2	cutaway		
DLL	The Sluefoot	12	13	Vitruvian		
DLL	Something's Gotta Give	1	60	reframed	closing push	
DLL	Something's Gotta Give	2	44	Vitruvian		
DLL	Something's Gotta Give	3	28	Vitruvian		
DLL	Something's Gotta Give	4	43	reframed	entirely danced	
DLL	Something's Gotta Give	5	23	Vitruvian		
DLL	Something's Gotta Give	6	1	insert		
FF	Funny Face	1	3	insert		
FF	Funny Face	2	21	Vitruvian		
FF	Funny Face	3	36	reframed	initial pull	X
FF	Let's Kiss and Make Up	1	19	Vitruvian		
FF	Let's Kiss and Make Up	2	12	reframed	varies	
FF	Let's Kiss and Make Up	3	11	insert		
FF	Let's Kiss and Make Up	4	10	Vitruvian		
FF	Let's Kiss and Make Up	5	3	cutaway		
FF	Let's Kiss and Make Up	6	8	context		X
FF	Let's Kiss and Make Up	7	13	reframed	closing push	X
FF	Let's Kiss and Make Up	8	25	Vitruvian		
FF	Let's Kiss and Make Up	9	20	reframed	initial pull	
FF	Let's Kiss and Make Up	10	19	context		
FF	Let's Kiss and Make Up	11	19	Vitruvian		
FF	Let's Kiss and Make Up	12	15	Vitruvian		
FF	Let's Kiss and Make Up	13	9	reframed	entirely danced	
FF	He Loves and She Loves	1	28	reframed	initial pull	X
FF	He Loves and She Loves	2	13	reframed	initial pull	
FF	He Loves and She Loves	3	24	context		

APPENDIX THREE 403

Film	Number	Shot Number in Routine	Duration (seconds)	Framing Type	Reframed Subtypes	Uses Crane
FF	He Loves and She Loves	4	23	Vitruvian		
FF	He Loves and She Loves	5	12	Vitruvian		
FF	He Loves and She Loves	6	22	context		
FF	He Loves and She Loves	7	17	Vitruvian		X
FF	He Loves and She Loves	8	8	Vitruvian		
FF	He Loves and She Loves	9	24	insert		
FF	He Loves and She Loves	10	22	context		
FF	Clap Yo' Hands	1	45	reframed	closing push	
FF	Clap Yo' Hands	2	33	reframed	closing push	
FF	Clap Yo' Hands	3	9	Vitruvian		
FF	Clap Yo' Hands	4	8	reframed	varies	
FF	Clap Yo' Hands	5	47	reframed	midway push	X
FF	Clap Yo' Hands	6	25	Vitruvian		
FF	Clap Yo' Hands	7	14	reframed	initial pull	
FF	Clap Yo' Hands	8	18	reframed	initial pull	
FF	Clap Yo' Hands	9	10	Vitruvian		
SS	Too Bad	1	50	reframed	initial pull	
SS	Too Bad	2	36	reframed	initial pull	
SS	Stereophonic Sound	1	41	reframed	closing push	
SS	Stereophonic Sound	2	30	Vitruvian		
SS	Stereophonic Sound	3	26	Vitruvian		
SS	Stereophonic Sound	4	15	Vitruvian		
SS	All of You	1	9	Vitruvian		
SS	All of You	2	2	cutaway		
SS	All of You	3	4	Vitruvian		
SS	All of You	4	6	cutaway		
SS	All of You	5	10	Vitruvian		
SS	All of You	6	5	cutaway		
SS	All of You	7	29	Vitruvian		
SS	All of You	8	30	reframed	initial pull	
SS	All of You	9	18	reframed	initial pull	
SS	All of You	10	44	reframed	midway pull	
SS	All of You	11	18	reframed	initial pull	
SS	All of You	12	36	reframed	initial pull	
SS	All of You	13	1	insert		
SS	Fated to Be Mated	1	19	Vitruvian		
SS	Fated to Be Mated	2	10	Vitruvian		
SS	Fated to Be Mated	3	11	Vitruvian		
SS	Fated to Be Mated	4	16	reframed	initial pull	X
SS	Fated to Be Mated	5	22	Vitruvian		
SS	Fated to Be Mated	6	28	Vitruvian		
SS	Fated to Be Mated	7	33	reframed	varies	
SS	Fated to Be Mated	8	10	reframed	closing push	
SS	Fated to Be Mated	9	9	reframed	closing danced in	

Film	Number	Shot Number in Routine	Duration (seconds)	Framing Type	Reframed Subtypes	Uses Crane
SS	Fated to Be Mated	10	15	reframed	closing push	
SS	The Ritz Roll and Rock	1	17	context		
SS	The Ritz Roll and Rock	2	6	cutaway		
SS	The Ritz Roll and Rock	3	35	Vitruvian		
SS	The Ritz Roll and Rock	4	55	reframed	varies	
SS	The Ritz Roll and Rock	5	32	Vitruvian		
SS	The Ritz Roll and Rock	6	19	reframed	initial pull	
SS	The Ritz Roll and Rock	7	10	Vitruvian		
SS	The Ritz Roll and Rock	8	17	Vitruvian		
SS	The Ritz Roll and Rock	9	12	Vitruvian		

Acknowledgments

This project began about six years ago when a group of French film scholars, led by Marguerite Chabrol and Pierre-Olivier Toulza, invited me to join an international digital humanities project on the Hollywood musical. Among my colleagues on the team were Jöel Augros, Fanny Beuré, N. T. Binh, Marion Carrot, Steven Cohan, Anne Crémieux, Gaétan Darquié, Gaspard Delon, Claire Demoulin, Laurent Guido, Aurélie Ledoux, Anne Martina, Adrienne McLean, Karen McNally, James O'Leary, Katalin Pór, Caroline Renouard, Doug Reside, Allison Robbins, Robyn Stilwell, and Noah Teichner. I also came to know the wonderful Isabelle Moindrot. Preparing presentations for our five conferences—each a delightful sojourn in Paris, with much in the way of good food and company—and working with the group to assemble a uniform body of data on the corpus of Hollywood musicals led me back to Astaire from a quantitative angle of vision. This book would not have happened without this collaboration with colleagues and friends. Thank you all, especially Marguerite and Pierre-Olivier.

I presented work from this book at the specialist conferences "Music and the Moving Image" (2017) and "Song, Stage and Screen" (2018) and in a lecture for the University of Michigan musicology department (2021).

Thank you to the College of Arts and Sciences at Washington University in St. Louis for research and travel funding.

Caleb Boyd, Daniel Fister, Ward Francis, and Rachel Jones assisted in gathering data from assistant director reports. Rachel Jones and Lisa Mumme helped check my shot-level data.

My friend Nathan Platte asked important "so what" questions.

My editor, Norm Hirschy, was, as always, a calm presence in the midst of the process.

I wrote this book while on leave and in pandemic lockdown with my wife, Kelly, and my younger son, James. My older son, David, was also around some of the time. Sharing movies, music, life, and love with these three remains the deepest pleasure I have known.

Notes

Abbreviations Used in Notes

Archival Collections

BBC	*The Fred Astaire Story*, 13-part radio documentary on BBC Radio 2, produced by John Billingham, aired 1975.
Becker	Paul Becker collection of Ginger Rogers RKO files, Margaret Herrick Library, Los Angeles.
Berlin	Irving Berlin Collection, Library of Congress, Washington DC.
Edens	Roger Edens, USC Cinematic Arts Library, Los Angeles.
Davis	Interview with Fred Astaire, conducted by Ronald L. Davis, 31 July 1976, Southern Methodist University Oral History Project.
Freed	Arthur Freed Collection, USC Cinematic Arts Library, Los Angeles.
McBride	Joseph McBride Papers, Wisconsin Historical Society, Madison.
Paramount	Paramount Collection, Margaret Herrick Library, Los Angeles.
RKO	RKO Collection, Arts Special Collections, UCLA.
Sandrich	Mark Sandrich Collection, Margaret Herrick Library, Los Angeles.

Film Titles

BB	*The Barkleys of Broadway*
BNY	*The Belle of New York*
BS	*Blue Skies*
BW	*The Band Wagon*
C	*Carefree*
DD	*A Damsel in Distress*
DLL	*Daddy Long Legs*
EP	*Easter Parade*
FDR	*Flying Down to Rio*
FTF	*Follow the Fleet*
GD	*The Gay Divorcee*
HD	*Holiday Inn*
LD	*Let's Dance*
R	*Roberta*
RW	*Royal Wedding*
SC	*Second Chorus*
SS	*Silk Stockings*
ST	*Swing Time*
STL	*The Sky's the Limit*
SVIC	*The Story of Vernon and Irene Castle*

SWD	*Shall We Dance*
TH	*Top Hat*
YT	*Yolanda and the Thief*
ZF	*Ziegfeld Follies*

Periodicals

LAT	*Los Angeles Times*
NYT	*New York Times*

INTRODUCTION

1. EPIGRAPHS: Boorstin 1990, 8; Schickel 1962, 143; Erskine Johnson, "The Indestructible Astaire," newspaper clipping, ca. 1959; Manguso 2017, 9.
    Epigraph: Pomerance 2019, 308–309.
    Lincoln Barnett, "Fred Astaire: He Is the No. 1 Exponent of America's Only Native and Original Dance Form," *Life*, 25 August 1941, 74.
2. Quoted in Delamater 1981, 229.
3. Giles 1988, 5.
4. Paul Gardner, "Groups Here to Tip Their Top Hats to Astaire at Champagne Party," *NYT*, 10 February 1973.
5. Carol Saltus, "Fred Astaire," *Interview* 33, June 1973, 16.
6. Joyce Haber, "Astaire's Way to the Stars," *LAT*, 11 May 1975.
7. This count includes twenty-nine films Astaire made between *Flying Down to Rio* (1933) and *Silk Stockings* (1957).
8. Vincent Canby, "Astaire Persona: Urbanity and Grace," *NYT*, 23 June 1987.
9. Alan M. Kriegsman, "Universality of Fred Astaire," *Washington Post*, 6 May 1973.
10. Vincent Canby, "Film View: How Do We Capture a Star's Genius?," *NYT*, 8 May 1983.
11. I visited Anderson and Sheppard with other presenters for "Fred Astaire and Ginger Rogers: A London Celebration," a study day at the Victoria and Albert Museum in September 2015. Warm thanks to Kathleen Riley for this opportunity.
12. Pomerance 2013, 166.
13. Riley 2012.
14. Astaire 1959, 258.
15. David Zeitlin, "Old Dog's New Tricks at 66," *Life*, 29 October 1965, 92; Herb Howe, "Tap Happy," *Photoplay*, 1948.
16. Anna Kisselgoff, "Fred Astaire Perfected a New Art Form," *NYT*, 28 July 1987.
17. Thomson 2016, 42.
18. Remarks at Ninth Annual American Film Institute Life Achievement Award honoring Fred Astaire, 10 April 1981.
19. Bulson 2020, 167.
20. Bulson 2020, 8.
21. Exceptions include Cohan 1993, Craig 2014, and Wood 1979.
22. Pomerance 2016, 103.
23. Giles 1988, 5.

24. Giles 1988, 21.
25. Bland and Percival 1984, 96.
26. Genné 2018, 107–111.
27. Croce 1972; Mueller 1985.
28. Kisselgoff, "Fred Astaire"; Bland and Percival 1984, 110.
29. Quoted in Kisselgoff, "Fred Astaire."
30. Rosenberg 2012, 3.
31. Brannigan 2011, chapter 6.
32. Charness 1977, i.
33. Bulson 2020, 16–17.
34. This team's database on the Hollywood musical can be found at mc2.website.
35. BBC episode 8. Warm thanks to Michael Feinstein for providing a copy of the BBC radio series.
36. Puttnam 1998, 100.
37. Thomson, "Legends of the Lost: The Discreet Charm of Movies We Cannot See," *Harper's* 330/1981, June 2015, 72.
38. Val Adams, "All RKO Movies Sold for TV Use," *NYT*, 27 December 1955.
39. Marcelle Clements, "They Can't Take That Away from Me: Fred Astaire as Metaphor," *Revue* 1/3, 1980, 21.
40. *Million Dollar Movie* ran on WOR TV 9 in New York City from 1955 to 1966 (imdb.com).
41. Rosenberg 2012, 159.
42. Pedullà 2012, 113.
43. Miller 2021, 7–8.
44. Sperb 2016, 16.
45. Bulson 2020, 21.
46. Thomas 1984, 187.
47. Pomerance 2019, xvi.
48. Freed, *EP* AD reports, 24–26 November and 1 December 1947.
49. Sperb 2016, 42.
50. Cavell 1979, 26.
51. Pomerance 2013, 190.
52. Richard Corliss, "Pop Culture: High and Low," *Time*, 8 June 1998.
53. Freed, *BW*, memo, R. Monta, 3 November 1952.
54. Kasson 2001, 10.
55. Mayme Peak, "Insisted the Prince of Wales Eat Corned Beef and Cabbage," *Boston Globe*, 2 December 1934.
56. Giles 1988, 202.
57. The three women Astaire dances with briefly in turn in the numbers "Steppin' Out with My Baby" and "Too Bad" are omitted from this count.
58. Quoted in Delamater 1981, 262.
59. Craig 2014, 30.
60. Giles 1988, 14.
61. Craig 2014, 7.

62. ANTA program book, 1975.
63. Philip K. Scheuer, "Confessions of an Ex-Song-and-Dance Man," *LAT*, 1 October 1978.
64. Gregg Kilday, "Fred Astaire," *Los Angeles Herald Examiner*, 12 April 1981.
65. Riley 2012, 150.
66. Griffin 2018, 115–116.
67. *Broadway Melody of 1940* might be read as emphasizing Astaire's male relationship to George Murphy, with the phrase "who do you love?" passed several times between the pair. Their one dance duet, "Please Don't Monkey with Broadway," includes a duel with canes as swords where Murphy kills Astaire.
68. Two of the eleven, made while Fayard Nicholas was in the military, feature only Harold Nicholas. This count omits the eighteen-second re-appearance of the pair in the finale of *Down Argentine Way* (1940).
69. So 2020, 30, 35.
70. Sullivan 2006, 53.
71. Decker 2011a, especially chapter nine.
72. Decker 2011a, 1.
73. Preciado 2008, 170.
74. Collins and Bilge 2020, 12–15.
75. Dana Burnet, "Watching His Step: A Portrait of Fred Astaire," *Pictorial Review*, January 1936, 40.
76. Jack Kroll, "Never Gonna Dance Again," *Newsweek*, 6 July 1987, 48
77. Collins and Bilge 2020, 167.
78. Connell 2005, 44.
79. Connell 2005, 39, 73.
80. Connell 2005, 75.
81. Connell 2005, 51.
82. Freed, *YT*, contract memo, 9 August 1944.
83. Bulson 2020, 96.
84. Dana Burnet, "Watching His Step: A Portrait of Fred Astaire," *Pictorial Review*, January 1936, 40.
85. Carol Saltus, "Fred Astaire," *Interview* 33, June 1973, 14.
86. RKO, *GD*, letter, Mark Sandrich to Fred Astaire, 26 October 1934.
87. Rapf 2016, 55.
88. BBC episode 9.
89. Freed, *BW*, telegram, Lela Simone to Arthur Freed, 29 April 1953.
90. Decker 2022 considers the complete corpus of studio-made widescreen musicals and provides further context for this abbreviated period in Astaire's career.

ONE

1. USC, Freed.
2. BBC episode 5.
3. Decker 2011a, 2.

4. According to Eleanor Powell on McBride, tape 1036A, interview with Eleanor Powell, 3 March 1981.
5. Baldwin 1998, 500.
6. McLean 2004, 127.
7. Smith 2009, 211.
8. Decker 2011a, 47.
9. Alice Faye opposite Tyrone Power: *In Old Chicago* (1938), *Alexander's Ragtime Band* (1938); opposite Henry Fonda: *Lillian Russell* (1940). Don Ameche, cast opposite Faye in five films, sang but did not dance.
10. Dyer 2012, 69.
11. Leading women in Astaire's films who were usually dubbed include Rita Hayworth, Vera-Ellen, and Cyd Charisse.
12. On use of the term *nonwhite*, philosopher Shannon Sullivan writes, "The drawback to 'non-white' is that it centers on whiteness and can seem to posit white people as the standard against which all others should be measured. But the most satisfactory alternative, 'people of color,' implies that white people do not have a race. And so I use 'non-white' somewhat unhappily, recognizing that the language I utilize to combat racial privilege is complicit with it" (Sullivan 2006, 199).
13. Petty 2016, 9.
14. Friedman 2020.
15. *Ziegfeld Follies* might be understood as an exception here, although the revue format works to separate Astaire's four numbers from Lena Horne's vocal solo.
16. Dyer 2012, 8.
17. Decker 2011a, 123.
18. Brannigan 2011, 152.
19. John T. McManus, "A Sandrich and a Dance or So," *NYT*, 16 May 1937.
20. Sandrich, "Comparative Analysis—Musicals with Fred Astaire and Ginger Rogers."
21. "Music" on Sandrich's chart means scoring for transitions between scenes and during montages.
22. Sandrich, *TH* estimating script, 15 March 1935.
23. Berlin 254/1, emphasis original.
24. 21 April 1949, Bob Fellows to Richard Johnston, Paramount Production Files, AMPAS.
25. See Decker 2011a, 263–270, for a detailed discussion of the "Ad Lib Dance."
26. Edens, *BNY*, memo from Robert Alton to Roger Edens, 16 May 1951.
27. Paramount, *LD* AD reports.
28. Decker 2011b, 476–479.
29. Privately held archival document, *DLL* cue sheet. Special thanks to Chris Bamberger.
30. Berlin 256/13, *EP* cue sheet.
31. Berlin 256/13, *C, EP, HI, TH* cue sheets; privately held archival document, *DLL* cue sheet.
32. Fred Astaire, *Steps in Time* manuscript, USC Cinematic Arts Library, Los Angeles.
33. Letter, Fred Astaire to Mark Sandrich, undated [likely August 1938], Sandrich, emphasis original.

34. Letter, George Gershwin to Mark Sandrich, 3 April 1937, Sandrich.
35. Decker 2011a, 21.
36. Altman 1987 uses the shift to playback sound to make larger claims about the film musical.
37. I exclude the revue film *Ziegfeld Follies*.
38. "The Carioca," "Slap That Bass," "Since I Kissed My Baby Goodbye," "A-stairable Rag," and "A Shine on Your Shoes."
39. McLean 2004, 39–40.
40. Ovalle 2011, 82.
41. Decker 2011a, 199–200.
42. My thanks to Beth Genné and Louise Stein for conversation around the Latin influence in Astaire.
43. Decker 2011a, 191.
44. Pugh 2015, 64.
45. See Decker 2019.
46. Decker 2011a, 201.
47. In addition to the Spanish costume for "Begin the Beguine," Astaire's dancing costumes include a more subdued version for *The Castles*' tango, the quasi-ballet outfit for his duo with Harriet Hoctor in *Shall We Dance*, the red costume for the dream portion of "Limehouse Blues," and the harlequin in "I Concentrate on You."
48. Vinogradov 2013, 13.
49. Moretti 2017, 101–102.
50. So 2020, 4.
51. Dyer 2012, 75.
52. Decker 2011a, 273.
53. Cubitt 2004, 180–181.
54. Cubitt 2004, 168.
55. Decker 2011a, 322.
56. Petty 2016, 3.
57. Freed, *BB* AD report, 19 July 1948.
58. A handful of Astaire numbers are not built on a popular song form. "Mr. and Mrs. Hoofer at Home" and "Ad Lib Dance" are the standout examples. The musical form of both is detailed in Decker 2011a, chapter 8.
59. Astaire's fleeting and nondancing appearances in the second *Daddy Long Legs* dream ballet are not counted here.
60. Decker 2011a, 43–52.
61. *The Gay Divorcee*, *Roberta*, *Shall We Dance*, *Broadway Melody of 1940*, *You Were Never Lovelier*, *The Barkleys of Broadway*, and *Let's Dance* end with a formally complete if generally briefer-than-usual dance—in each film, except *Broadway Melody*—for Astaire and his romantic counterpart.
62. Early in *Blue Skies*, Astaire and Joan Caulfield (who ends the film paired with Bing Crosby) dance briefly together in "A Pretty Girl is Like a Melody" (a number I categorize as a solo). As noted, Astaire joined this film after shooting had already commenced.
63. Paramount, *HI* AD report, 5 February 1942.

64. Paramount, *HI* recording programs, 10 and 21 March 1942.
65. Decker 2011a, 275.
66. McLean 2008, 116.
67. Decker 2011a, 137–138.
68. Three production numbers use pantomime—without dialogue or singing but not quite dancing—to preface song-and-dance content otherwise typical of standalone dance-only or vocal-and-dance numbers: "Let's Face the Music and Dance" (*Swing Time*) and "This Heart of Mine" and "Limehouse Blues" (both *Ziegfeld Follies*).
69. *Roberta* (62% under the average) sits just outside this generalization.
70. Davis.
71. *Ziegfeld Follies*, the only Astaire film without a narrative plot, is omitted: its numbers are unrelated to each other and atypical for Astaire generally.
72. Decker 2011a, 247–248.
73. Edens, *EP*, "PRE-RECORDINGS in 'EASTER PARADE' Production 1418."
74. Freed, *EP* AD reports, 13–16 October 1947.
75. Freed, *EP* talent department memos, 17 and 23 October 1947.
76. RKO, *FDR* AD reports, 21–28 September 1933.
77. See Decker 2011a, 171–177, for more on "The Carioca."
78. Two limit cases for the danced vocal. Astaire and Rogers dance on a crowded dance floor for much of the vocal to "Cheek to Cheek." Their moves are no different in scale from those around them and no foot sounds are added. In the vocal for "Shall We Dance," Astaire marks the syncopated title phrase but little else and there are no foot sounds. Neither of these cases rise to the level of a danced vocal.
79. See Decker 2017 for more on "You're Easy to Dance With."
80. "I Left My Hat in Haiti" (*Royal Wedding*) proves a unique case with a danced vocal followed by a dance in which Astaire is, initially, not involved. Astaire opens with a vocal that is entirely danced and with much camera motion. Then, he moves into a busy scene where he interacts in dance terms with multiple individual chorus members and keeps on singing. Then, Astaire disappears from the number or watches it (his back to the camera) for forty-five seconds as Jane Powell dominates. To close, Powell literally pulls Astaire back into "Haiti" and they do a partner dance (which is here categorized as a dance portion in a longer number). This lengthy routine defies Astaire's standard practice over and over.
81. Two important dances come into focus as complete outliers when considering the shift from song to dance. The "Shoes with Wings On" vocal occurs midway through the number as a voiceover to which Astaire moves. This unique choice was likely driven by the number's larger narrative that has Astaire dance, then "sing" in his head, then dance some more—all the while negotiating a radically unstable situation where shoes unconnected to any visible bodies dance with and attack him. Counting its fully danced vocal, "Shoes with Wings On" is the longest solo Astaire made. Astaire's duet with Gene Kelly in *Ziegfeld Follies*, "The Babbitt and the Bromide," also has a unique structure: the pair sings, then dances, then sings, then dances, then—yet once more—sings, then dances. The number builds on the structure of the Gershwins' song: each of three verse-chorus units takes the same bland bourgeois pair through the same ritual greetings (twice on earth, the last time in heaven). The understood passage of time between each vocal-dance pair works to make this an episodic dance with

three song then dance structures. While the duration of the vocal portions is set by Ira Gershwin's lyrics, the length of each dance segment increases—from thirty-three to sixty-four to 130 seconds.

82. This count includes the fifty-six vocal then dance numbers, the twenty-seven danced vocal numbers with discrete dance sections, and all three transitions from singing to dancing in "Babbitt" discussed previously. Subtracted from these numbers are ten instances when Astaire is not himself singing, making the performance mode transition from singing to dancing a moot question in his case.

83. The second segments described earlier in "Bojangles" and "Steppin' Out" similarly count among the dance portions in larger numbers: viewers experience these dances as bonus segments, add-ons to numbers that had otherwise already met expectations for a substantial dance routine.

84. A new stretch of singing—something like an alternate verse or trio section—interrupts "The Yam" midway through its dance section. Mostly sung by Rogers, this proves a unique moment in Astaire's corpus. But even here, the return to singing is contained in its own shot and a further cut announces the shift back to dancing.

85. RKO, *SWD*, letter, George Gershwin to Mark Sandrich, 7 April 1937.

86. Nelson, "Oh Me, Oh My, Oh You" (*Tea for Two*, 1950) and "The Lately Song" (*Three Sailors and a Girl*, 1953); O'Connor, "Bounce Right Back" (*Anything Goes*, 1956); the Nicholas Brothers, "The Jumpin' Jive" (*Stormy Weather*, 1943).

87. Thomson 2016, 43.

TWO

1. EPIGRAPH: George Balanchine, "Ballet in Films," *Dance News*, December 1944, 8. Edens, *EP*, "PRE-RECORDINGS in 'EASTER PARADE' Production 1418."
2. Sandrich, letter, George Gershwin to Mark Sandrich, 7 April 1937.
3. Decker 2011a, chapter 7 and 74–76.
4. Bordwell et al. 1985, 60.
5. Benjamin 1978, 230.
6. Jack Anderson, "Fred Astaire's Dances Seen Frame by Frame," *NYT*, 30 January 1986
7. Gentry 2017, 61.
8. Garth Greenwell, "Making Meaning: Against 'Relevance' in Art," *Harper's* 341/2046, November 2020, 61–66.
9. Craig 2014, 55.
10. Gentry 2017, 154.
11. See, for instance, Gabler 1988.
12. *Yolanda and the Thief* sits on the RKO average at fifty-four seconds.
13. The career ASL of forty seconds is here averaged by film average. Averaged by the 159 numbers in the clip reel, Astaire's career ASL is thirty-nine seconds.
14. Wood 1979, 31.
15. McBride 93/5.
16. McBride 93/5.

17. Carol Saltus, *Interview* 33, June 1973, 12, 14.
18. Davis.
19. McBride 93/5.
20. See Decker 2011b, 489–497.
21. Quoted in Delamater 1981, 261–262.
22. Paramount, *LD* AD report, 1 July 1949.
23. Decker 2011a, 7–8.
24. The shots of Crosby at the harpsichord could perhaps be understood as inserts. As Crosby's hands on the keyboard are never seen, I consider these shots to be cutaways.
25. BBC episode 7.
26. Genné 2018, 138.
27. Quoted in Delamater 1981, 67–69.
28. My use of *reframed* departs from that of Bordwell et al. 1985 (51), which uses the word *reframing* in reference to "a slight pan or tilt to accommodate figure movement." Such movement is a default aspect of Vitruvian framing and was facilitated by the so-called Astaire dolly, which allowed for subtle adjustments side to side and forward and back.
29. The first partner/shot is immediately preceded by insert framing of Astaire and the partner in question.
30. *Daddy Long Legs* contains a fourth use of this move across the lower horizontal to bring Caron into her own dream ballet.
31. Mueller 1985, 29, discusses this shot.
32. Willis 2009, 52.
33. Decker 2011a, 175.
34. Wood 1979, 29–30.

THREE

1. Epigraphs: McBride, tape 1036A, interview with Eleanor Powell, 3 March 1981; Giles 1988, 10; Fred Astaire quoted by Sam Goldwyn Jr. in Giles 1988, 79.
   AMPAS, typescript of Gladys Hall, *Modern Screen*, 8 March 1937.
2. Dana Burnet, "Watching His Step: A Portrait of Fred Astaire," *Pictorial Review*, January 1936, 11.
3. Burnet, "Watching His Step," 40.
4. RKO, budgets for *FDR, GD, R, TH, FTF, ST, SWD*, and *SVIC*; Becker, "Astaire Pictures—Comparative Costs," 29 April 1938, and memo, Ross Hastings to J. R. Grainger, 6 April 1953.
5. RKO, *STL* budget; Freed, memo, "approximate accumulation on *Ziegfeld Follies* using the five numbers already estimated," 1 March 1944; Paramount, *LD*, agreement to hire Astaire, 15 March 1949; Freed, *SS*, Astaire contract memo, 22 August 1956.
6. Paramount, *HI*, memo, Chas. Woolstenhulme, 17 December 1941, emphasis original.
7. Freed, *RW*, talent department memo, 1 December, and AD report, 30 November 1950.
8. Freed, *BW*, contract memo, 23 May 1952.
9. Pomerance 2013, 186.

416 NOTES

10. The data behind the stats that follow is taken from a range of sources: daily assistant director reports and call sheets, budget and overage notices, contracts (the date when Pan started on a film indicates when Astaire started rehearsing), and music department pay records.
11. This statistic is generated by dividing total hours by total workdays for each film then averaging the film averages. Standard deviation for the film averages is .1.
12. RKO, *GD* AD report, 6 August 1934.
13. RKO, *FDR* AD report, 23 September 1933, and *SWD*, AD report, 13 March 1937.
14. John Mueller writes that the second shot of "Never Gonna Dance" was "shot forty-seven times during a ten-hour shooting day, and Rogers' feet were bleeding before it was over" (Mueller 1985, 112). AD reports show work started at 10:00am and the number completed at 8:00pm. Astaire and Rogers shot publicity stills until 8:55pm, after which production on *Swing Time* closed. RKO, *ST* AD reports, 31 July 1936.
15. Freed, *YT* AD report, 27 January 1945, and *ZF* AD report, 17 August 1944. The *Yolanda* shoot included four days of nighttime exterior shooting of dialogue for the fiesta scene, starting around 8:00pm and ending around 5:00am.
16. Freed, *YT*, memo, H. Boswell to Lennie Hayton, 2 March 1945.
17. RKO, *SWD*, music department memo, 24 February, and AD report, 25 February 1937.
18. *SS* prerecording and scoring schedules, MGM Music Department Collection, Cinematic Arts Library, USC.
19. McBride 93/5.
20. Carol Saltus, *Interview* 33 June 1973, 14.
21. Freed, *BB* AD report, 10 November 1948.
22. Paramount, *White Christmas*, folder 8, memo by Frank Caffrey, 2 July 1952.
23. Becker, *C*, memo, Pandro S. Berman to Mark Sandrich, 24 February 1938.
24. RKO, *R* AD report, 28 November 1934.
25. RKO, *ST* AD report, 5 June 1936.
26. Freed, *YT* AD report, 9 February 1945.
27. Freed, *YT* AD report, 16 February 1945.
28. Quoted in Delamater 1981, 230.
29. Giles 1988, 20.
30. RKO, *STL* AD report, 16 March 1943.
31. RKO, *GD* AD report, 30 July 1934.
32. Duration of this number in the film is taken from the extant prerecorded music track.
33. Freed, *YT*, letter, 31 August 1944.
34. RKO, *TH* AD report, 29 and 30 April and 1 May 1935.
35. RKO, *C* AD report, 6 June 1938.
36. RKO, *C*, "Loss Caused by Illness of Mark Sandrich, June 6–7–8, 1938."
37. Becker, *C*, memo.
38. Freed, *BW* AD report, 3 November 1952.
39. Freed, *BNY* AD report, 18 June 1951.
40. Freed, *SS* AD report, 15 January 1957.
41. Freed, *YT* AD reports, 19 and 26 January 1945.
42. Numbers in this subcorpus are "Firecracker Dance," "Got a Bran' New Suit" (cut from *Band Wagon*), "Shoes with Wings On," "Seeing's Believing," "I Wanna Be a Dancin'

Man" (first version), "The Ritz Roll and Rock," "You're All the World to Me," "Ad Lib Dance," "A Shine on Your Shoes," and "If Swing Goes I Go Too" (cut from *Ziegfeld Follies*).
43. Freed, *ZF* AD report, 18 and 19 April 1944.
44. Freed, *BNY* AD report, 19 June 1951.
45. Freed, *BNY* AD report, 7 September 1951.
46. Freed, *BB* AD report, 22 July 1948.
47. AMPAS, Eddie Mannix Ledger.
48. Davis.
49. Croce 1972, 108.
50. Delamater 1981, 260–261.
51. Paramount, *HI* recording program, 15 November 1941.
52. See Decker 2011a, 117–120, on the word *hot* as a description of musical content in Astaire's corpus.
53. Freed, *BW* AD report, 14 January 1953.
54. BBC episode 11.
55. Freed, *EP* AD report, 3 and 4 December 1947.
56. Freed, *BB* AD report, 20 and 21 July 1948.
57. Freed, *BW* AD reports, 23 and 25 September 1952.
58. Freed, *BB* AD report, 23 July 1948.
59. Paramount, *HI* AD report, 30 January 1942.
60. McBride 93/5.
61. See Decker 2011a, 136, for discussion of the piecemeal construction of the "Girl Hunt" soundtrack.
62. In further evidence that this was the section reshot, only "8 Dancing Men" were called to the retake; none were apparently used as there are no shots in the number with only eight men visible.
63. Paul Gardner, "Groups Here to Tip Their Top Hats to Astaire at Champagne Party," *NYT*, 10 February 1973.
64. Freed, *BB* AD report, 21–24 July 1948.
65. RKO, *SVIC* AD report, 28 December 1938.
66. Freed, *EP* AD report, 4 December 1947.
67. Freed, *EP* AD report, 5 December 1947.
68. Worsley 1997, 48.
69. Freed, *EP* AD report, 9 December 1947.
70. Freed, *EP* AD report, 10 December 1947.
71. Freed, *SS* AD report, 8 November 1956.
72. RKO, *ST* AD report, 21 May 1936.
73. Freed, *EP* AD report, 8 January 1947.
74. Freed, *EP* AD report, 4 December 1947.
75. Freed, *BNY* AD report, 21 June 1951.
76. Freed, *SS* AD report, 29 January 1957.
77. Freed, *BNY* AD report, 6 September 1951.
78. Freed, *BB* AD report, 22 July 1948.
79. Freed, *BB* AD report, 23 July 1948.
80. Freed, *YT* AD report, 18 May 1945.

81. Freed: *BNY* AD report, 19 June 1951; *BB* AD report, 20 July 1948; *BW* AD report, 14 January 1953; *EP* AD report, 6 December 1947; *YT* AD report, 18 May 1945.
82. Freed, *BB* AD report, 19 July 1948.
83. RKO, *ST* AD report, 11 May 1936.
84. RKO, *ST* AD report, 12 May 1936.
85. Freed, *EP* AD report, 4 December 1947.
86. Freed, *BNY* AD report, 6 September 1951.
87. Freed, *EP* AD report, 25 November 1947.
88. Freed, *SS* AD report, 29 January 1957.
89. Freed, *BW* AD report, 23 September 1952.
90. Freed, *BW* AD report, 12 January 1953.
91. Freed, *BB* AD report, 20 August 1948.
92. McLean 2017. Warmest thanks to Adrienne McLean for engaging with my earlier work on this topic in Decker 2017.
93. McLean usefully adds that Eleanor Powell's unique persona was built on her frequent appearance in men's attire.
94. Freed, *BB* AD report, 22 and 23 July 1948.
95. RKO, *DD* AD report, 3 August 1937.
96. Freed, *RW* AD report, 7 September 1950.
97. Freed, *RW* AD report, 6 July 1950.
98. RKO, *SVIC* AD report, 19 December 1938.
99. Freed, *RW* AD report, 7 September 1950.
100. Freed, *RW* AD report, 7 September 1950.
101. Freed, *BB* AD report, 20 August 1948.
102. *Weekend at the Waldorf* (1945), produced by Arthur Hornblow Jr.
103. Freed, *BW* AD report, 25 September 1952.

MIDPOINT

1. Epigraph: Genné 2018, 153.
   Bill Davidson, "Fred Astaire: Just Beginning to Live," *Look*, 10 November 1959, 45.
2. McBride 93/2, "additional quote copy for program book."
3. "Finklea & Austerlitz, Alias Charisse & Astaire," *Newsweek*, 6 July 1953, 48.
4. BBC episode 9; Giles 1988, 51.
5. Giles 1988, 44.
6. Albert Johnson, "Conversation with Rogers Edens," *Sight and Sound* 27/4, Spring 1958, 180.
7. Giles 1988, 51.
8. BBC episode 1.
9. BBC episode 13.
10. Thomson 2016, 43.
11. Richard F. Shepard, "Fred Astaire, the Ultimate Dancer, Dies," *NYT*, 23 June 1987.
12. Marcelle Clements, "They Can't Take That Away from Me: Fred Astaire as Metaphor," *Revue* 1/3, 1980, 21–22,

13. The routine is "See See Rider" on an April 1966 episode of *The Hollywood Palace*.
14. Joe Hyams, "Hollywood's Ageless Stars: Fred Astaire at 57 Still 'Improves on Perfection,'" *NY Herald Tribune*, 1957.
15. John O'Hara, "There's No One Quite Like Astaire," *Show*, October 1962, 76.
16. Martin and Charisse 1976, 203.
17. McBride 93/4.
18. O'Hara, "There's No One Quite Like Astaire," 139.
19. Bill Davidson, "Fred Astaire," 38.
20. Derek Conrad, "Two Feet in the Air," *Films and Filming*, December 1959, 35.
21. Paul Gardner, "Groups Here to Tip Their Top Hats to Astaire at Champagne Party," *NYT*, 10 February 1973.
22. Helen Lawrenson, "It's Better to Remember Fred," *Esquire*, August 1976, 106.
23. Davis, emphasis original.
24. Kathleen Carroll, "Astaire: The Amiable Hoofer," *Sunday News*, 6 May 1973.
25. Astaire 1959, 325.
26. BBC episode 11.
27. Quoted in Delamater 1981, 230.
28. McBride 93/2, cards for Astaire, emphasis original.
29. McBride 93/5.
30. Hungerford 1946, 221–222.
31. Stearns and Stearns 1968, 224.
32. Hill 2010, 115.
33. Seibert 2015, 226.
34. Seibert 2015, 225.
35. McBride 93/4, quoting Fosse from PBS special on Astaire.
36. Quoted in Stearns and Stearns 1968, 227.
37. Thomas 1984, 60.
38. Decker 2019.
39. Pugh 2015, 124. I would add "The Shorty George" and "The Yam" to the list of Astaire numbers that make race an explicit theme.
40. Obama and Springsteen cocreated a podcast and book titled *Renegades: Born in the U.S.A.*

FOUR

1. Epigraph: Schickel 1962, 140.
   Derek Conrad, "Two Feet in the Air," *Films and Filming*, December 1959, 11.
2. Graham Greene, review of *FF*, 1936.
3. Thomson 2019, 305.
4. Thomson 2019, 322.
5. Smith 2018, 139.
6. Sullivan 2006, 150.
7. BBC episode 10.
8. Morton Eustis, "Fred Astaire: The Actor-Dancer Attacks His Part," *Theatre Arts*, 21 May 1937, 378.

9. Rosenberg 2012, 69.
10. *SS* AD report, 16 January 1957.
11. Astaire, *Steps in Time* manuscript.
12. Keating 2019, 93.
13. Harry Burdick, "David Abel Evolves New Technique," *American Cinematographer* 14/3, July 1936, 293.
14. Spoken introduction to "Fast Dances" on Fred Astaire with the Jazz at the Philharmonic All Stars, *The Astaire Story*, Clef MGC 1001-4, 1953.
15. RKO, *STL* overage report, 7 January 1943.
16. I count only shots with noticeable up or down movement that exceeds a tilt; shots from a high angle that required a crane to attain their camera position but that do not move are not classified as crane shots here.
17. BBC episode 5.
18. Freed, *BW* preview cards, 26 March 1953.
19. Riley 2012, 26.
20. Library of Congress, Ira Gershwin home movies, https://www.loc.gov/item/mbrs02062506/ (17:23–19:23).
21. Alan M. Kriegsman, "Universality of Fred Astaire," *Washington Post*, 6 May 1973.
22. BBC episode 5.
23. A similar cut in "I Won't Dance" may have been made to facilitate coordination with the live band on set.
24. Giles 1988, 5.
25. Decker 2011a, 247.
26. McBride 93/4.
27. McBride 93/4, quoting Fosse from PBS special.
28. BBC episode 4.
29. BBC episode 4.
30. "He Loves and She Loves" in *Funny Face*, shot outdoors in France, works a similar sleight of scene between two anchoring structures seen in the far background—the Château de la Reine Blanche and a Roman aqueduct—by way of crane shots that frame the couple against a field of green grass.
31. Rachel Jones found the fourth (in the "Table Dance") during group research viewing to check my data.
32. Hungerford 1946, 45.
33. Viola Hegyi Swisher, "A Special for the Special: Fred Astaire and Partner Barrie Chase," *Dance Magazine*, January 1968, 25.
34. Giles 1988, 20
35. Bland and Perceval 1984, 110, 112.

FIVE

1. Epigraph: Zeitlin, "Old Dog's New Tricks at 66," 92.
   Riley 2012, 26, 36–38, 43–44.
2. Astaire says of Adele, "she wasn't a tap dancer." Thomas 1984, 60.

3. Decker 2019, 98.
4. Riley 2012, 65.
5. Kilday, "Fred Astaire."
6. BBC episode 11.
7. Kobal 1974, 30.
8. I exclude the three women he dances with in turn in "Steppin' Out with My Baby" and "Too Bad" from these totals.
9. Heights for Astaire's partners were gathered from Google searches. No information available for Lucille Bremer, Harriet Hoctor, or Leroy Daniels.
10. Quoted in Barbara Berch Jamison, "The Ageless Astaire," *NYT*, 2 August 1953.
11. Astaire wears his hat throughout "Girl Hunt." See also the duos "Ragtime Violin," "Steppin' Out with My Baby" (first part), "Manhattan Downbeat," and "How Could You Believe Me . . . ." Astaire's hat in "I'm Putting All My Eggs in One Basket," "Let's Call the Whole Thing Off," and the *Belle of New York* skating routine are explained by the outdoor setting of these numbers.
12. Scheuer, "Confessions of an Ex-Song-and-Dance Man."
13. Becker, *FTF*, letter, Navy Department to MPPDA, 7 October 1935, and Pandro S. Berman to Navy Department, 23 October 1935.
14. This subcorpus excludes the serial-partner routines "Steppin' Out with My Baby" and "Too Bad," the danced vocal to "Tunnel of Love," the final section of "Heat Wave," and the all-pantomime summer portion of "Currier and Ives."
15. This group includes the four duo dances with men (Murphy, Kelly, Crosby, and Buchanan, respectively); three with women dressed as men (in chronological order: "A Couple of Swells," "Oh, Them Dudes," and "Where Did You Get That Girl?"); and two with women who are Astaire's professional colleagues (Kay Thompson in *Funny Face*; Janis Paige in *Silk Stockings*).
16. Zeitlin, "Old Dog's New Tricks at 66," 92.
17. Dyer 2012, 91–92.
18. Genné 2018, 37.
19. For a discussion of the musical content of "Dancing in the Dark," see Decker 2011a, 80–82.
20. Freed, *BW* preview cards, 26 March 1953.
21. BBC episode 6.
22. The final section of "Heat Wave" omitted.
23. BBC episode 9.
24. Astaire 1959, 242.
25. McBride, tape 1036A, interview with Eleanor Powell, 3 March 1981.
26. Kobal 1974, 30.
27. AMPAS, Jack Cummings papers, f.9, note, Astaire to Jack Cummings, no date.
28. Mueller 1985, 172, notes several other Astaire duos where this or similar moves recur.
29. This paragraph owes a debt to John Mueller's beautiful analysis of "Isn't This a Lovely Day" at Fred Astaire and Ginger Rogers: A London Celebration at the Victoria and Albert Museum, in September 2015.
30. Davis.
31. McBride 93/5.
32. McBride, tape 1036A, interview with Eleanor Powell, 3 March 1981.

33. McBride 93/4.
34. Columbia 1991b, 848.
35. Columbia 1991b, 849; Franceschina 2012, 209.
36. Kobal 1974, 30.
37. Columbia 1991a, 759.
38. For example, to a London newspaper in 1924 ("Why, man, the 'Blues' is nigger music." Quoted in Riley 2012, 93) and in a 1951 article in *Esquire* magazine (Astaire noted how the Charleston and jazz both mark a "manifestation of the Negro influence" on American culture. Fred Astaire, "Long Live the Beat," *Esquire* 63/3, December 1951, 190).
39. Columbia 1991b, 850.
40. https://www.youtube.com/watch?v=bgSUDWZPRYs, video title: "Me and the Ghost Upstairs Second Chorus out-take" (accessed 8 March 2021).
41. Thomas 1984, 168.
42. Columbia. 1991b, 850
43. Freed, *BW*, memo, Monta to Edens, 9 December 1952.
44. Freed, *BW*, memo, Monta to Edens, 3 September 1952.
45. Freed, *BW*, memo, Monta to Edens, 24 September 1952.
46. Freed, *BW*, memo, Monta to Edens, 2 September 1952.
47. "Bebop Bootblack Lands Movie Role with Astaire," *Jet*, 23 October 1952, 60–61.
48. Astaire's second partner dance in "Steppin' Out with My Baby" can be read as a duo for two Black characters. Astaire and his partner, Patricia Jackson, are both in brownface makeup (as documented in the AD reports). Their bluesy routine (with perhaps Freudian undertones; she steals his cane) signals a raw sexuality stereotypically mapped onto Black subjects and almost entirely lacking elsewhere in Astaire's couples dances.
49. Freed, *BW* preview cards, 26 March 1953.

SIX

1. Epigraphs: Levinson 2009, 423; Giles 1988, 170 and 25.
    BBC episode 3.
2. AMPAS, Motion Picture Association of America Hollywood office files, volunteer card listing Astaire's activities for the MPAA.
3. "Astaire," *Life* 1/6, 28 December 1936, 36; "No False Moves," *People*, 19 February 1996, 37.
4. Gilbert Seldes, review of *BNY*, *Saturday Review*, 22 March 1952, 30.
5. Seibert 2015, 240.
6. Bill Davidson, "Fred Astaire: Just Beginning to Live," *Look*, 10 November 1959, 45.
7. McBride 93/2, "additional quote copy for program book."
8. Kilday, "Fred Astaire."

9. Connell 2005, 54.
10. See Decker 2011a, 218–219, for more on the jazz content of the "Golf Dance" arrangement.
11. Delamater 1978, 253.
12. BBC episode 5.
13. BBC episode 8.
14. Decker 2011a, 123.
15. Cohan 1993, 55.
16. Haber, "Astaire's Way to the Stars."
17. *The Fred Astaire Top Hat Dance Album* 1936, unpaginated.
18. For more on this connection as articulated by Astaire in this source, see Decker 2011a, 118.
19. BBC episode 5; Zeitlin, "Old Dog's New Tricks at 66," 92.
20. Seibert 2015, 226.
21. BBC episode 10.
22. BBC episode 4.
23. BBC episode 6.
24. See "Man with the Blues" (*An Evening with Fred Astaire*, 1958) and the routine to blues choruses sung by Joe Williams (*Astaire Time*, 1960).
25. http://www.imfdb.org/wiki/Smith_%26_Wesson_Military_%26_Police (accessed 12 February 2021).
26. Among the imitations in "A Couple of Song and Dance Men," Bing Crosby does a Pullman porter "rushing to help you catch the five o'clock train" (Crosby walks very slowly in a rolling gait). Pullman porters were African American men. The job was coveted in the Black community—it secured a middle-class income—and the porters, organized in the Brotherhood of Sleeping Car Porters led by A. Philip Randolph, were among the most politically active and powerful of Black groups.
27. Bland and Percival 1984, 96.
28. Genné 2018, 197–201, and Harvey 1989, 60–61, are exceptions.
29. Freed, ZF, Al Lewis, "Tentative ideas for numbers and specialties," 7 September 1943.
30. Freed, ZF: Al Lewis, "Tentative ideas for numbers and specialties," 7 September 1943, and Robert Alton, "IDEA SUGGESTED FOR ZIEGFELD FOLLIES . . . Sand," 2 February 1944; AMPAS Turner/MGM Scripts, ZF, Robert Alton, "IDEA SUGGESTED FOR ZIEGFELD FOLLIES" "PASS THAT PEACE PIPE."
31. Freed, ZF, Robert Alton, "IDEA SUGGESTED FOR ZIEGFELD FOLLIES" "Title of Number: 'Babbitt and Bromide,' " 31 March 1944.
32. Freed, ZF, "Proposed Order," 21 January 1944.
33. Freed, ZF script, cover dated 31 March 1944.
34. Horne and dancer Avon Long's "Big Colored Number," to the Gershwin tune "Liza" (with a lyric in a stereotypically Black popular music idiom), was shot but ultimately cut from the film. Black newspapers reported on the decision, noting that Horne was "brilliantly costumed" in an "old-fashioned gown being wooed by Avon Long." Surviving stills suggest the high-romantic style of "This Heart of Mine," only here executed in an "all-white and all-paper" set and starring two Black performers. Horne's

remaining number in *Ziegfeld Follies* was, Black newspapers reported, "a torrid blues ballad" set "in a dingy café on the waterfront." Dolores Calvin, " 'Liza' Number Out of Lena's New Picture," *California Eagle*, 24 May 1945.
35. Carrick 1984, 108; Levinson 2009, 145.
36. Freed, ZF, Al Lewis, "Tentative ideas for numbers and specialties," 7 September 1943.
37. Decker 2011a, 23–25.
38. Minnelli 1974, 142–143.
39. Witchard 2009, 3.
40. Freed, ZF, script, cover dated 31 March 1944, insert describing "Limehouse Blues" #17 dated 4-1-44.
41. Clipping from unknown fan magazine, c. 1949.
42. Astaire reprised additive times steps in his 1960 television special *Astaire Time*. Dancing with the Earl Sisters, before the routine the viewer is given just enough information to follow the permutations of a dance stated by the sisters as a kind of mathematical formula. Astaire describes the approach as interlocking time steps. The sisters reveal that partners in this formula are separated by one beat and "each add a beat alternately as we go on and it gets wilder and wilder." The notion that so intellectualized a combination yields danced wildness suggests a very tame context indeed. The trio does a dance that demonstrates the approach then wraps up with a *pas de trois*, all in service of solid entertainment. No childish foot stamps or kicks in the rear here. The routine demonstrates the resilience of tap in the skill and style of the sisters—Astaire plays the hip uncle who doesn't feel bad that he has nothing to teach them and just wants to make them (and himself) look good.
43. Warm thanks to Adrienne McLean for clarifying this step as a double flap.
44. See "Bojangles of Harlem," "One for My Baby," and "A Pretty Girl Is Like a Melody."
45. Kelly had completed choreography on his "Drum Crazy" as of September 29, 1947. There was no boy involved. Jimmie Bates was hired as "Bit Boy with Astaire" on November 7, 1947, three weeks after Astaire joined the film. Freed, EP AD report, 29 September 1947, and talent memo, 7 November 1947.

CONCLUSION

1. Frank 1994, 83.
2. Joyce Haber, "Astaire's Way to the Stars," *LAT*, 11 May 1975; Davis.
3. Astaire dances near but does not regard mirrors in "A Needle in a Haystack" (*The Gay Divorcee*) and "The Ritz Roll and Rock" (*Silk Stockings*).
4. Seibert 2015, 282.
5. Craig 2014, 7.
6. Remarks at Ninth Annual American Film Institute Life Achievement Award honoring Fred Astaire, 10 April 1981.
7. Davis.
8. McBride 93/3, interview with Fred Astaire, 6 January 1981.
9. Davis.
10. See, for instance, "I've Got a Gal in Kalamazoo" (*Orchestra Wives*, 1942).

References

Newspaper and magazine articles referenced only once appear solely in the endnotes.

Altman, Rick. 1987. *The American Film Musical*. Bloomington: Indiana University Press.
Astaire, Fred. 1959. *Steps in Time*. New York: Harper and Brothers.
Baldwin, James. 1998. *Collected Essays*. Toni Morrison, ed. New York: Library of America.
Benjamin, Walter. 1968. *Illuminations: Essays and Reflections*. Hannah Arendt, ed. New York: Schocken Books.
Bland, Alexander, and John Percival. 1984. *Men Dancing: Performers and Performances*. New York: Macmillan.
Boorstin, Jon. 1990. *The Hollywood Eye: What Makes Movies Work*. New York: Cornelia & Michael Bessie Books.
Bordwell, David, Janet Staiger, and Kristin Thompson. 1985. *The Classical Hollywood Cinema: Film Style & Mode of Production to 1960*. New York: Columbia University Press.
Brannigan, Erin. 2011. *Dancefilm: Choreography and the Moving Image*. New York: Oxford University Press.
Bulson, Eric. 2020. *Ulysses by Numbers*. New York: Columbia University Press.
Carrick, Peter. 1984. *A Tribute to Fred Astaire*. Salem, NH: Salem House.
Cavell, Stanley. 1979. *The World Viewed: Reflections on the Ontology of Film, enlarged edition*. Cambridge, MA: Harvard University Press.
Charness, Casey. 1977. "Hollywood Cine-Dance: A Description of the Interrelationship of Camerawork and Choreography in Films by Stanley Donen and Gene Kelly." PhD dissertation, New York University.
Cohan, Steven. 1993. "'Feminizing' the Song-and-Dance Man: Fred Astaire and the Spectacle of Masculinity in the Hollywood Musical." In *Screening the Male: Exploring Masculinities in Hollywood Cinema*, ed. Steven Cohan and Ina Rae Hark. New York: Routledge, 46–69.
Collins, Patricia Hill, and Sirma Bilge. 2020. *Intersectionality, second edition*. Medford, MA: Polity.
Columbia, David Patrick. 1991a. "The Man Who Danced with Fred Astaire." *Dancing Times* 81/968, May, 759.
Columbia, David Patrick. 1991b. "The Man Who Danced with Fred Astaire: Part Two." *Dancing Times* 81/969, June, 848–850.
Connell, R. W. 2005. *Masculinities, second edition*. Berkeley: University of California Press.
Craig, Maxine Leeds. 2014. *Sorry I Don't Dance: Why Men Refuse to Move*. New York: Oxford University Press.
Croce, Arlene. 1972. *The Fred Astaire and Ginger Rogers Book*. New York: Galahad Books.
Cubitt, Sean. 2004. *The Cinema Effect*. Cambridge, MA: MIT Press.
Decker, Todd. 2011a. *Music Makes Me: Fred Astaire and Jazz*. Berkeley: University of California Press.
Decker, Todd. 2011b. "On the Scenic Route to *Irving Berlin's Holiday Inn* (1942)." *Journal of Musicology* 28/4, 464–497.

Decker, Todd. 2017. "Fred Astaire, Captain America, and the Cyborg: The Technological Body of a Musical Star." In *Stars of Hollywood Musicals* (French and English editions), Marguerite Chabrol and Pierre-Olivier Toulza, eds. Paris: Presses du reel, Grande Collection du Labex Arts-H2H (Paris), 24–41.

Decker, Todd. 2019. "Broadway in Blue: Gershwin's Broadway Scores and Songs." In *The Cambridge Companion to George Gershwin*, Anna Celenza, ed. New York: Cambridge University Press, 80–101.

Decker, Todd. 2022. "Singing and Dancing in Widescreen: The Extreme Aesthetics of the Mid-1950s Studio Musical Number." In *The Oxford Handbook of the Hollywood Musical*, Dominic McHugh, ed. New York: Oxford University Press, 72–101.

Delamater, Jerome. 1981. *Dance in the Hollywood Musical*. Ann Arbor, MI: UMI Research Press.

Dyer, Richard. 2012. *In the Space of a Song: The Uses of Song in Film*. New York: Routledge.

Franceschina, John. 2012. *Hermes Pan: The Man Who Danced with Fred Astaire*. New York: Oxford University Press.

Frank, Rusty E. 1994. *Tap!: The Greatest Tap Dance Stars and Their Stories*, revised edition. New York: Da Capo Press.

The Fred Astaire Top Hat Dance Album: A Comprehensive Compendium on Ballroom Dancing, second edition. 1936. London: Queensway Press.

Friedman, Ryan Jan. 2020. "By Herself: Intersectionality, African American Specialty Performers, and Eleanor Powell." In *Hollywood at the Intersection of Race and Identity*, Delia Malia Caparoso Konzett, ed. New Brunswick, NJ: Rutgers University Press, 122–140.

Gabler, Neil. 1988. *An Empire of Their Own: How the Jews Invented Hollywood*. New York: Random House.

Genné, Beth. 2018. *Dance Me a Song: Astaire, Balanchine, Kelly, and the American Film Musical*. New York: Oxford University Press.

Gentry, Philip M. 2017. *What Will I Be?: American Music and Cold War Identity*. New York: Oxford University Press.

Giles, Sarah. 1988. *Fred Astaire: His Friends Talk*. New York: Doubleday.

Griffin, Sean. 2018. *Free and Easy?: A Defining History of the American Film Musical Genre*. Hoboken, NJ: Wiley Blackwell.

Harvey, Stephen. 1989. *Directed by Vincente Minnelli*. New York: Museum of Modern Art and Harper & Row.

Hill, Constance Valis. 2010. *Tap Dancing America: A Cultural History*. New York: Oxford University Press.

Hungerford, Mary Jane. 1946. "Dancing in Commercial Motion Pictures." PhD dissertation, Columbia University.

Kasson, John F. 2001. *Houdini, Tarzan, and the Perfect Man: The White Male Body and the Challenge of Modernity in America*. New York: Hill and Wang.

Keating, Patrick. 2019. *The Dynamic Frame: Camera Movement in Classical Hollywood*. New York: Columbia University Press.

Kobal, John. 1974. "Eleanor Powell: 'I Would Rather Dance that Eat.'" *Focus on Film* 19, Autumn, 22–31.

Levinson, Peter J. 2009. *Puttin' on the Ritz: Fred Astaire and the Fine Art of Panache, A Biography*. New York: St. Martin's Press.

Manguso, Sara. 2017. *300 Arguments*. Minneapolis: Graywolf Press.

Martin, Tony, and Cyd Charisse. 1976. *The Two of Us*. New York: Mason/Charter.

McLean, Adrienne L. 2004. *Being Rita Hayworth: Labor, Identity, and Hollywood Stardom.* New Brunswick, NJ: Rutgers University Press.
McLean, Adrienne L. 2008. *Dying Swans and Madmen: Ballet, the Body, and Narrative Cinema.* New Brunswick, NJ: Rutgers University Press.
McLean, Adrienne L. 2017. "'A Nice Easy Dance' (Part 1): Managing the Musical's Working Bodies." Paper given at Le film musical hollywoodien en contexte médiatique et culturel/The Hollywood Film Musical in Its Mediatric and Cultural Context. MSH Paris Nord, December.
Miller, D. A. 2021. *Second Time Around: From Art House to DVD.* New York: Columbia University Press.
Minnelli, Vincente, with Hector Arce. 1974. *I Remember It Well.* Garden City, NY: Doubleday and Company.
Moretti, Franco, ed. 2017. *Canon/Archive: Studies in Quantitative Formalism from the Stanford Literary Lab.* New York: n+1 Books.
Mueller, John. 1985. *Astaire Dancing.* New York: Wings Books.
Ovalle, Priscilla Peña. 2011. *Dance and the Hollywood Latina: Race, Sex, and Stardom.* New Brunswick, NJ: Rutgers University Press.
Pedullà, Gabriele. 2012. *In Broad Daylight: Movies and Spectators after the Cinema.* New York: Verso.
Petty, Miriam J. 2016. *Stealing the Show: African American Performers and Audiences in 1930s Hollywood.* Berkeley: University of California Press.
Pomerance, Murray. 2013. *The Eyes Have It: Cinema and the Reality Effect.* New Brunswick, NJ: Rutgers University Press.
Pomerance, Murray. 2016. *Moment of Action: Riddles of Cinematic Performance.* New Brunswick, NJ: Rutgers University Press.
Pomerance, Murray. 2019. *Virtuoso: Film Performance and the Actor's Magic.* New York: Bloomsbury Academic.
Preciado, Paul T. 2008. *Testo Junkie: Sex, Drugs, and Biopolitics in the Pharmacopornographic Era.* Translated by Bruce Benderson (2013). New York: Feminist Press at the City University of New York.
Pugh, Megan. 2015. *America Dancing: From the Cakewalk to the Moonwalk.* New Haven: Yale University Press.
Puttnam, David. 1998. *Movies and Money.* New York: Alfred A. Knopf.
Rapf, Johana E. 2016. "Classical Hollywood, 1928–1946." In *Producing*, Jon Lewis, ed. New Brunswick, NJ: Rutgers University Press, 36–62.
Riley, Kathleen. 2012. *The Astaires: Fred and Adele.* New York: Oxford.
Rosenberg, Douglas. 2012. *Screendance: Inscribing the Ephemeral Image.* New York: Oxford University Press.
Schickel, Richard. 1962. *The Stars.* New York: Bonanza Books.
Seibert, Brian. 2015. *What the Eye Hears: A History of Tap Dancing.* New York: Farrar, Straus & Giroux.
Smith, Zadie. 2009. *Changing My Mind: Occasional Essays.* New York: Penguin Books.
Smith, Zadie. 2016. *Swing Time.* New York: Penguin Books.
Smith, Zadie. 2018. *Feel Free: Essays.* New York: Penguin Books.
So, Richard Jean. 2020. *Redlining Culture: A Data History of Racial Inequality and Postwar Fiction.* New York: Columbia University Press.
Sperb, Jason. 2016. *Flickers of Film: Nostalgia in the Time of Digital Cinema.* New Brunswick, NJ: Rutgers University Press.

Stearns, Marshall, and Jean Stearns. 1968. *Jazz Dance: The Story of American Vernacular Dance*. New York: Macmillan.

Sullivan, Shannon. 2006. *Revealing Whiteness: The Unconscious Habits of Racial Privilege*. Bloomington: Indiana University Press.

Thomas, Bob. 1984. *Astaire: The Man, The Dancer*. New York: St. Martin's Press.

Thomson, David. 2016. *The New Biographical Dictionary of Film, sixth edition*. New York: Alfred A. Knopf.

Thomson, David. 2019. *Sleeping with Strangers: How the Movies Shaped Desire*. New York: Alfred A. Knopf.

Vinogradov, Oren. 2013. "Dressing Both Sides: American Masculinity in the Films of Fred Astaire." MA thesis, University of North Carolina at Chapel Hill.

Willis, Corin. 2009. "Blackface Minstrelsy and Jazz Signification in Hollywood's Early Sound Era." In *Thriving on a Riff: Jazz & Blues Influences in African American Literature and Film*, Graham Lock and David Murray, eds. New York: Oxford University Press, 40–61.

Witchard, Anne Veronica. 2009. *Thomas Burke's Dark Chinoiserie: Limehouse Nights and the Queer Spell of Chinatown*. Burlington, VT: Ashgate.

Wood, Robin. 1979. "Never Never Change, Always Gonna Dance." *Film Comment* 15/5, September–October, 28–31.

Worsley, Sue Dwiggins. 1997. *From Oz to E.T.: Wally Worsley's Half-Century in Hollywood*. Charles Ziarko, ed. Lanham, MD: Scarecrow Press.

Index

For the benefit of digital users, indexed terms that span two pages (e.g., 52–53) may, on occasion, appear on only one of those pages.

Tables and figures are indicated by *t* and *f* following the page number

Abel, David, 198–200
"Ad Lib Dance" (*LD*), 37, 39, 57, 102, 343
Adler, Larry, 327–28
Alexander's Ragtime Band, 36–37
"All of You" (*SS*), 94, 120, 121–22, 126–28, 196–97, 222–23, 242, 278, 318–19
Alton, Robert, 65, 94–95, 103, 144–46, 167–68, 204–5, 253, 333–35
"Am I in Love," 51–52
American in Paris, An, 342–43
American Psycho, 327–28
Anchor's Aweigh, 323
Andre Charlot's Review, 335
Assistant director reports, 14–15, 76–77, 147, 160–74
    at MGM, 149
    at Paramount, 148
    at RKO, 147–48
"A-stairable Rag" (*YNGR*), 98–99
Astaire Story, The, 79
Astaire, Adele, 4, 19–20, 178, 214–15, 251, 253–55, 267, 274
Astaire, Fred
    access to films of, 11–13, 229–31
    attitude towards his work, 131–32, 140–41, 175–77
    average duration of dances, 66–71
    average shot length of dances, 83–85, 84*f*
    and Blackness, 21, 33–34, 50, 181–82, 291–92, 319–20, 321–22, 355–56, 357, 422n.38, 422n.48
    body of, 3–4, 6–7, 13–15, 24, 170–72
    career periods, 28–30
    clip reel of (*Astaire dancing* corpus), 1–4, 10, 11, 55, 66–71, 246–47, 357
    dancing style
        and ballet, 61–62, 180–81, 357
        and foot sounds, 25–26, 99, 311, 316–23, 317*f*
        modesty of, 77–79, 78*t*, 248
        "outlaw" claim, 21–22, 180–81, 182–83, 214–15, 333–34, 342, 357
        and social/ballroom dancing, 181, 259–66, 267
        and tap dancing, 181–82, 316–23, 357
        and walking, 17, 42–43, 52, 62, 88, 158–59, 175–77, 183, 311, 321–22, 359
    discourse around, 19, 21–22, 146, 255
    height, 3–4, 255–57
    heterosexuality of, 17–20, 23, 181–53, 255, 261–62, 280–82, 305, 359
    interest in scripts, 140–41
    and jazz, 21, 57, 61–62, 318–19
    as leading man, 15–16, 17–18, 19–20, 21–22, 51*t*, 52, 79, 258–59, 311–12
    longest (in duration) shots in dances, 85–88, 86*f*, 91–92
    masculinity of, 4–5, 15–16, 17, 19, 22–23, 34, 42–43, 62, 82–83, 171–72, 175, 192, 270–72, 293, 305–50, 359
    and mirrors, 351–57
    one-shot dances, 88–90, 91–92, 216–17
    partner dances, 17–18, 18*f*, 25–26, 32–33, 251–304, 252*f*
    pay, 132–33, 258–59
    playing a musical instrument, 57
    reluctance to view dailies/rushes, 164–65, 168, 188–89
    screen dance body of, 5, 6–9, 14, 24, 81–82, 122–23, 187–92, 246–47, 248–49
    singing, 43–44, 55*f*, 63*f*, 72–79, 72*f*

Astaire, Fred (*cont.*)
   singing while dancing, 72–74, 72*f*, 74*f*
   solo dances, 153–55, 251–53, 252*f*
   studio era career, 26–30
   sweat of, 4, 76–77, 166, 170–72
   theatrical career of, 4
   trio dances, 252*f*, 253
   use of "context" shots, 112–14, 113*f*, 120–21, 123
   use of crane shots, 86–87, 107, 204–9
   use of cutaway shots, 93*t*, 94–100, 97*f*, 104–6
   use of cuts, 217–24, 229–46
   use of double flaps, 342, 344–50
   use of frame edges, 192–202
   use of "full-figure" shots, 92–94, 93*t*, 106–7
   use of "insert" shots, 93*t*, 100–6, 121–22
   use of non-white and ethnic stereotypes and caricatures, 47–49, 60–61, 333–41
   use of noise, 25–26
   use of props, 97–98, 101–2, 216–17, 224–29
   use of "reframed" shots, 93*t*, 114–20, 115*f*–19*f*, 124–28, 127*f*, 415n.28
   use of shadows, 184–85, 185*f*, 186*f*
   use of spinning, 76, 242
   use of time steps, 342–44
   use of violence, 251–53, 323–33, 346–48, 353–54
   use of "Vitruvian" shots, 93*t*, 107–12, 110*f*, 111*f*, 124–25, 128
   watched by white men, 100, 305–15
   weight, 3–4, 255–57
   whiteness of, 20–22, 23, 25–26, 50, 82–83, 128–30, 192, 296, 334–35, 359
   working methods of, 27–28, 82–92, 107–8, 132–33, 134–60, 138*f*, 351–52
      desire for further takes, 172–74
      efficiency of, 149–60, 169–70
      making sound recordings, 135–37, 316, 351–52
      rehearsing, 137–39, 141–46
      retakes, 165–66
      sets used for dance numbers, 202–3, 206–8, 210–16, 247
      shooting dialogue, 140–41, 144
      shooting numbers, 139–40, 141–46
Audition Dance" (*YWNL*), 215–16, 226–27, 232, 233, 326*t*, 327

"Babbitt and the Bromide, The" (*ZF*), 12–13, 67–68, 75–76, 125–26, 144–46, 156*t*, 177, 204–5, 221–22, 227–28, 257, 265–66, 266*f*, 267, 267*f*, 270*f*, 274*f*, 279–80, 279*f*, 283*t*, 298*f*, 301–3, 323–25, 326*t*, 330–31, 345–46, 354–55, 413–14n.81
"Baby Doll" (*BNY*), 242
"Bachelor Dinner Song" (*BNY*), 118–20, 119*f*, 251–53
Balanchine, George, 7–9, 80, 181–82, 248
Baldwin, James, 32
Band Wagon, The, 15–16, 25–26, 30, 33–34, 56–57, 65, 67–68, 73–74, 75–76, 88, 100, 103–4, 105*f*, 213, 221–22, 234–35, 242, 253, 256*f*, 262–63, 264*f*, 268, 271*f*, 274–76, 274*f*, 283*t*, 294–304, 297*f*–302*f*, 318–19, 326*t*, 327, 328–30, 329*f*, 332–33, 333*f*, 342–44, 347, 347*f*, 356–57, 356*f*–57*f*
   production history, 138*f*, 139–40, 141–42, 153–54, 156*t*, 162–63, 165, 169–70, 171, 174
Barkleys of Broadway, The, 31, 54, 67–68, 79, 111*f*, 121–22, 127*f*, 196–97, 198*f*, 200–2, 201*f*, 204, 222–23, 228–29, 237–38, 242, 262–63, 268, 271*f*, 274*f*, 276–77, 289–90, 325, 326*t*, 327–28, 330*f*, 345–46, 413–14n.81
   production history, 137, 138*f*, 139–40, 142–43, 150–51, 153–55, 163–64, 169–70, 171, 172, 174
Barthelmess, Richard, 335, 336–37, 341
Baryshnikov, Mikhail, 5, 7
"Be Careful, It's My Heart" (*HI*), 219–20, 239–41, 319
"Beautiful Faces" (*EP*), 102, 102*f*, 116–17, 117*f*, 278–79, 284–85, 317–18
"Begin the Beguine" (*BM40*), 48–49, 48*f*, 70–71, 88, 222–23, 283*t*, 285–87, 298*f*, 333, 344

Belle of New York, The, 17, 37, 66, 75–76, 113*f*, 118–20, 119*f*, 184–85, 205–9, 206*f*, 226–28, 242, 251–53, 314–15, 318–19, 326*t*, 329–30
   finale, 112–14, 113*f*
   production history, 63–64, 138*f*, 141–42, 153–55, 156*t*, 157–58, 165, 168–70
Benjamin, Walter, 80–81, 351
Berkeley, Busby, 204
Berman, Pandro S., 28–29, 257
Bland, Alexander, 7, 248, 333–34
Blue Skies, 19–20, 26–27, 29, 44–45, 45*f*, 47–48, 66, 67–68, 69–70, 88, 96, 97*f*, 101, 110*f*, 112–14, 124*f*, 213, 219–20, 228–29, 251–53, 265–66, 266*f*, 283*t*, 311–12, 345–46, 355–56, 355*f*, 412n.62
   production history, 36–37
"Boardwalk Waltz" (*BNY*). *See* "Bride's Wedding Day, A (Currier and Ives)" (*BNY*).
Bogart, Humphrey, 32
"Bojangles of Harlem" (*ST*), 47, 70, 86–87, 141–42, 156*t*, 158, 181–82, 184–85, 186*f*, 205–6, 207, 242, 251–53, 322–23, 355–56
"Boogie Barcarolle" (*YNGR*), 74–75, 103, 117–18, 118*f*, 205
Bordwell, David, 80–81, 415n.28
Born to Dance, 51–52
Borne, Hal, 28–29
"Bouncin' the Blues" (*BB*), 79, 111*f*, 142–43, 171, 174, 200–2, 201*f*, 204, 289–90, 345–46
Brando, Marlon, 15–16
Bremer, Lucille, 18*f*, 144–46, 198–200, 199*f*, 262–63, 335–41
"Bride's Wedding Day, A (Currier and Ives)" (*BNY*), 63–64, 141–42, 156*t*, 157–58, 168–69, 205
Broadway Melody of 1940, 48–49, 48*f*, 51–52, 68, 70–71, 88, 97–98, 101–2, 101*f*, 104–5, 213, 215–16, 222–23, 224–25, 226*f*, 227–28, 244–46, 274–76, 275*f*, 283*t*, 285–87, 298*f*, 325–28, 326*t*, 329–30, 330*f*, 333, 338–39, 344, 345–46

   trio finale dance, 102–3, 104–5, 326*t*, 329–30, 330*f*
Broken Blossoms, 335, 336–37, 341
Brown, Kelly, 97–98, 98*f*, 100
Bubbles, John W., 33–34, 319–20
Buchanan, Jack, 255–57, 271*f*, 274*f*, 329*f*
Burke, Thomas, 335, 337–38
Burns and Allen, 115*f*, 331*f*
Butterworth, Charles, 60–61, 271*f*
"By the Light of the Silvery Moon" (*SVIC*), 153, 326*t*, 348, 348*f*

Cagney, James, 305–6, 348–49
"Can't Stop Talking" (*LD*), 37, 39, 267, 274–76, 274*f*, 326*t*
Carefree, 41–42, 88–90, 97–98, 121–22, 125–26, 126*f*, 147–48, 213–14, 221–22, 225–27, 262–63, 265–66, 272–73, 273*f*, 313–14, 317–18, 414n.84
   production history, 132–33, 138*f*, 139–40, 150–51
"Carioca, The" (*FDR*), 56–57, 65, 70–71, 74–75, 100–1, 112–14, 113*f*, 128–29, 134, 192–93, 194*f*, 203–4, 211
Caron, Leslie, 18*f*, 51*t*, 53*f*, 63–64, 78*t*, 104*f*, 127*f*, 171–72, 281, 316–17
   on Astaire, 175–77, 224
Castles, The. *See The Story of Vernon and Irene Castle.*
Champion, Marge and Gower, 51–52, 51*t*, 53*f*, 78*t*
"Change Partners" (*C*), 125–26, 126*f*, 213–14, 272–73, 273*f*, 317–18
Charisse, Cyd, 51*t*, 52–53, 53*f*, 58–59, 78*t*, 88, 94, 105*f*, 162–63, 171, 198*f*, 255–57, 256*f*, 262–63, 264*f*, 316–17, 343–44
   on Astaire, 178
Chase, Barrie, 168
"Cheek to Cheek" (*TH*), 80, 107–8, 112–14, 113*f*, 192–93, 192*f*–93*f*, 196, 196*f*, 221–22, 276–77, 284–85, 288–89, 319, 413n.78
Churchill, Sarah, 58–59, 68
"Clap Yo' Hands" (*FF*), 67–68, 73, 213, 278, 283*t*, 298*f*
"Coffee Time" (*YT*), 47–48, 121–22, 156*t*, 169–70, 205, 268

Comden, Betty, 175–77, 255–57
"Concert Solo" (*SC*), 196–97, 244–46, 318–19
"Continental, The" (*GD*), 56–57, 65, 74–75, 102–3, 143–44, 211, 213
"Couple of Song and Dance Men, A" (*BS*), 67–68, 88, 265–66, 266f, 283t, 311–12, 345–46
"Couple of Swells, A" (*EP*), 163, 166–67, 168–69, 170, 253, 283t, 284–85
Cover Girl, 323, 353–54
Crawford, Joan, 26
Crosby, Bing, 19–20, 29, 32, 36–37, 44, 88, 160–62, 255–57, 265–66, 266f, 311–12, 423n.26
   on Astaire, 178–79
cue sheets, 39–40
Cummings, Jack, 285–87

Daddy Long Legs, 30, 39–40, 58, 97–98, 98f, 100, 103, 104–5, 104f, 121–23, 126, 127f, 200–2, 201f, 205, 222–23, 251–53, 262–63, 272–73, 278–79, 280–82, 283t, 298f, 317–18
   dream ballet (Daydream), 56–57, 63–64, 200–2, 201f, 205, 251–53, 272–73, 283t, 298f, 317–18
   production history, 171–72
Dale, Virginia, 18f, 160–62, 265–66, 265f
Damsel in Distress, A, 70–71, 72–73, 74–75, 84–85, 87, 88–90, 110f, 114–15, 115f, 192–93, 215–17, 225, 244, 245, 326t, 329–31, 331f, 352–53
   production history, 138f, 141–42, 143–44, 150–51, 156t, 158–59, 165, 172
"Dancing in the Dark" (*BW*), 88, 213, 221–22, 234–35, 268, 318–19
Dancing Lady, 26, 51–52
Dancing: A Man's Game, 312–13
Daniels, Leroy, 88, 121–22, 163, 174, 253, 255–57, 294–304, 297f–302f
Darktown Strutters Ball" (*SVIC*), 173–74
Davies, Richard, 306–8
Davis, Bette, 32
"Dig It" (*SC*), 84–85, 88–90
digital humanities methods. *See* quantitative methods
Donen, Stanley, 7–9, 43–44, 123, 172–73, 204
   on Astaire, 1

Dorsey, Jimmy, 61–62, 135
Drake, Tom, 32–33
Draper, Paul, 36–37, 96
"Drum Crazy" (*EP*), 43–44, 57, 126, 127f, 137–39, 215–16, 348–49, 349f, 424n.45
"Drum Dance" (*DD*), 87, 88–90, 110f, 150–51, 215–17, 225, 244, 245, 330–31
Dyer, Richard, 32–33, 171–72, 260–61

"Easter Parade" (*EP*), 43–44, 326t
Easter Parade, 26–27, 36, 40, 43–44, 47, 56–57, 63–64, 66, 69–70, 73–75, 77, 80, 97–98, 102, 102f, 116f–17f, 116–17, 120–21, 124–25, 124f, 126–28, 127f, 213–14, 215–16, 222–23, 253, 270–72, 270f, 278–79, 283t, 284–85, 298f, 317–19, 326t, 333, 348–49, 349f, 422n.48, 424n.45
   production history, 13–14, 70, 136, 137–39, 138f, 143–44, 153–54, 163, 166–70
   rehearsal scene, 40, 58–59, 167–68
   vaudeville medley, 56–57, 63–64, 284–85
Easton Ellis, Bret, 327–28
Edens, Roger, 175–77
Ellis, Anita, 63–64
"Ev'ry Night at Seven" (*RW*), 97–98, 132–33, 173, 200–2, 202f

Fabray, Nanette, 77, 329f
"Fated to Be Mated" (*SS*), 136, 156t, 162–63, 169, 171, 196–97, 198f, 214–15
Faye, Alice, 32–33
Finian's Rainbow, 26
Firecracker Dance" (*HI*), 94–95, 163–64, 226–27, 243–44, 346
"Fit as a Fiddle," 298f
"Flying Down to Rio" (*FDR*), 35–36, 65
Flying Down to Rio, 26–27, 35–36, 56–57, 65, 66–67, 69–71, 74–75, 97–98, 100–1, 112–14, 113f, 128–29, 192–93, 194f, 203–4, 211, 319–20, 343–44
   production history, 70–71, 134, 138

INDEX   433

"Foggy Day (in London Town), A" (*DD*), 165
Follow the Fleet, 56–57, 69–70, 74–75, 85–86, 98–99, 100, 101, 118–20, 121–214, 222–23, 251–53, 257, 265–66, 276–77, 279–80, 279*f*, 283*t*, 298*f*, 317–18, 322–23, 326*t*, 345
   production history, 35–36
Fontaine, Joan, 18*f*, 84–85, 87–88, 192–93
Ford, Harrison, 332–33
Fosse, Bob, 51–52, 51*t*, 53*f*, 78*t*
   on Astaire, 178, 181–82, 224–25, 290–91
fragments, 40, 57–62
Freed Unit, 29–30
Freed, Arthur, 152–53, 172–73
"Funny Face" (*FF*), 75–76, 265–66
Funny Face, 26–27, 30, 43–44, 67–68, 73, 75–76, 88, 97–98, 120, 122–23, 122*f*, 205, 213, 226–27, 229–31, 230*f*, 265–66, 278, 280–82, 283*t*, 298*f*, 318–19, 327
   production history, 136

Gable, Clark, 32
Garland, Judy, 18*f*, 29–30, 32–33, 43–44, 58–59, 63–64, 77, 97–98, 102*f*, 117*f*, 142–43, 163, 166–67, 168, 170, 270*f*, 284–85, 334–35
Gay Divorce, 4, 214–15, 224–25, 253–55, 305
Gay Divorcee, The, 26–27, 56–57, 65, 74–75, 85–86, 102–3, 184–85, 185*f*, 194–95, 195*f*, 196, 211, 213, 214–15, 216–17, 224–25, 227–28, 242, 244, 249–50, 249*f*, 272–73, 273*f*, 278, 319–20
   production history, 134, 138*f*, 143–44, 165–66, 249*f*
Gershe, Leonard, 140–41
Gershwin, George, 41–42, 62, 80, 253–55
Gielgud, John, Sir, 163
"Girl Hunt" (*BW*), 56–57, 65, 67–68, 100, 103–4, 105*f*, 141–42, 156*t*, 162–63, 165, 169–70, 171, 256*t*, 262–63, 264*f*, 326*t*, 328–29, 332–33, 333*f*
Gish, Lillian, 335, 336–37
Goddard, Paulette, 60–61, 84–85, 88

"Golf Solo" (*C*), 41–42, 97–98, 139–40, 221–22, 225–27, 313–14
Gould, Dave, 65
Greene, Graham, 186
Griffith, D.W., 335

Having Wonderful Time, 140
Hayworth, Rita, 18*f*, 29, 45–47, 48–49, 117–18, 118*f*, 268*f*, 274*f*, 305–6
"He Loves and She Loves" (*FF*), 43–44, 122–23, 122*f*, 205, 280–82, 318–19
"Heat Wave" (*BS*), 44–45, 45*f*, 47–48, 67–68, 96, 97*f*, 110*f*, 112–14, 213
"Hello! Hello! Who's Your Lady Friend?" (*SVIC*), 141–42, 153, 326*t*
Hepburn, Audrey, 18*f*, 43–44, 97–98, 122*f*, 131, 255–57, 316–17
"History of the Beat (*DLL*), 100, 121–22, 222–23
Hoctor, Harriet, 18*f*, 70–71, 105–6
Holiday Inn, 19–20, 29, 36, 67–68, 73, 94–95, 102–3, 104–5, 200–2, 219–20, 224, 226–27, 239–41, 243–44, 265–66, 265*f*, 278–79, 311–12, 319, 346
   Hollywood montage, 59–60
   opening, 61–62
   production history, 132–34, 138*f*, 139, 153–54, 160–62, 163–64
Hollywood
   conversion to widescreen, 30
   musical genre, 10, 11, 24, 31–35, 66–67, 68, 198–200, 210–11
   production methods, 10–11, 24, 27–28, 35–40, 59–60, 63–64, 80–81, 133–34, 160–74, 210–11
   studios, 14–15, 26–30
      Columbia, 29
      MGM (Metro), 29–30, 149, 150–51, 150*t*
      Paramount, 29–30, 36–37, 139, 148
      RKO, 28–29, 147–48, 150–51, 150*t*
   and whiteness, 20–21, 33–34, 44–54, 70–71, 82–83, 247–48, 285–87
Hollywood Palace, The, 278
Honolulu, 214–15
Hope, Bob, 19–20, 257, 311–12
Horne, Lena, 33–34, 334–35, 423–24n.34
Horton, Edward Everett, 61–62, 346–47, 347*f*

"How Could You Believe Me When I Said I Love You When You Know I've Been a Liar All My Life" (*RW*), 75–76, 150–51, 278–79, 283*t*, 287, 325, 326*t*, 331–32, 332*f*, 343
Hutton, Betty, 18*f*, 37, 38–39, 263–64, 264*f*, 274*f*

"(I Ain't Hep to that Step But I'll) Dig It," *See* "Dig It"
"I Can't Be Bothered Now" (*DD*), 72–73, 141–42, 143–44
"I Can't Tell a Lie" (*HI*), 102–3, 104–5, 200–2, 278–79
"I Concentrate On You" (*BM40*), 101, 213, 244–46, 285–87, 338–39
I Dood It, 33–34, 51–52
"I Got Rhythm," 342–43
"I Guess I'll Have to Change My Plan" (*BW*), 271*f*, 274*f*, 274–76, 283*t*, 327
"I Left My Hat in Haiti" (*RW*), 47–48, 156*t*, 158, 173–74, 227–28, 283*t*, 413n.80
"I Love a Piano" (*EP*), 63–64, 166–67, 222–23, 284–85, 318–19
"I Used to Be Color Blind" (*C*), 88–90, 150–51, 262–63, 265–66
"I Wanna Be a Dancin' Man" (*BNY*), 37, 75–76, 154–55, 165, 169, 170, 184–85, 206–9, 227–28, 314–15
"I Won't Dance" (duo, *R*), 195–96, 196*f*, 213, 283*t*, 289–90
"I Won't Dance" (solo, *R*), 107–8, 118–20, 221–22, 319–20
"I'd Rather Lead a Band" (*FTF*), 118–20, 121–22, 222–23, 251–53, 322–23, 326*t*, 345
"I'll Capture Your Heart" (*HI*), 160–62, 224, 311–12
"I'm Old Fashioned" (*YWNL*), 235–37, 242, 280
"I'm Putting All My Eggs in One Basket" (*FTF*), 101, 265–66, 279–80, 279*f*, 283*t*, 298*f*, 326*t*
"I've Got My Eyes on You" (*BM40*), 88, 97–98, 215–16, 224–25, 226*f*
ice skating routine (*BNY*). *See* "Bride's Wedding Day, A (Currier and Ives)" (*BNY*).

"If Swing Goes (I Go Too)" (*ZF*), 144–46, 154–55, 156*t*, 157–58, 224
"I'll Be Hard to Handle" (*R*), 84–86, 195–96, 196*f*, 320, 322–23, 326*t*, 329–30, 346
intersectionality, 6–7, 16–17, 21–23
"Isn't This a Lovely Day (to Be Caught in the Rain)" (*TH*), 43–44, 196, 213–14, 276–77, 283*t*, 288–89, 301–3, 339–41
"It Only Happens When I Dance with You" (apartment, *EP*), 278
"It Only Happens When I Dance with You" (nightclub, *EP*), 74–75
"It's All in the Cards" (*ST*), 59, 169–70

"Jack and the Beanstalk" (*LD*), 38, 141–42
Jackson, Patricia, 70, 116*f*, 422n.48
"Jukebox Dance" (*BM40*), 244–46, 285–87, 345–46
"Jumpin' Jive, The" 358–59

Kaye, Danny, 311–12
Kelly, Gene, 4–5, 7–9, 19–20, 29–30, 32, 51–53, 51*t*, 53*f*, 70, 77–79, 78*t*, 144–46, 171–72, 208–10, 248, 251, 255–57, 266*f*, 267*f*, 270*f*, 279*f*, 298*f*, 301–3, 312–13, 323–25, 334–35, 342–43, 353–54, 358–59, 424n.45
Kidd, Michael, 262–63, 332–33

Lady, Be Good!, 253–55
Lamont, Sonny, 153, 348, 348*f*
"Last Waltz, The" (*SVIC*), 242, 262–63, 317–18
Lawrence, Gertrude, 335
Leonardo da Vinci (Vitruvian man), 108–12, 109*f*, 211
Leslie, Joan, 18*f*, 111*f*, 150–51, 277*f*, 305–9
"Let Yourself Go" (*FTF*), 56, 74–75, 98–99, 100
"Let's Call the Whole Thing Off" (*SWD*), 87, 139–40
Let's Dance, 21–22, 26–27, 29–30, 67–68, 73–74, 102, 253, 263–64, 264*f*, 267, 274–76, 274*f*, 298*f*, 326*t*, 328–29, 330–31, 343
production history, 37–39, 141–42, 153–54, 165

"Let's Face the Music and Dance" (*FTF*), 56–57, 85–86, 213–14, 276–77, 317–18
"Let's Kiss and Make Up" (*FF*), 88, 97–98, 136, 226–27, 229–31, 230*f*, 327
Levant, Oscar, 31, 142–43
Lewis, Robert, 336–37
Limehouse Blues, 335, 341
"Limehouse Blues," 335
"Limehouse Blues" (*ZF*), 25–26, 47, 56–57, 67–68, 144–46, 156*t*, 238, 239, 317–18, 333–41
Limehouse Nights, 335, 337–38
Long, Avon, 423–24n.34
Loring, Eugene, 253
   on Astaire, 1, 140–41, 180–81
"Lot in Common with You, A" (*STL*), 111*f*, 150–51, 196–97, 283*t*, 298*f*, 326*t*
"Love," 334–35

Mamoulian, Rouben, 178–79
Manhattan Downbeat" (*BB*), 142–43, 150–51, 222–23
Mantle, Mickey, 312–13
Martin, Skip, 103–4
masculinity, 15–16, 22–23, 312–13
Mayer, Louis B., 168
Mayhand, Ernest "Skillet," 295
McAllister, Helen, 70
McCain, John, 182–83
McLean, Adrienne L., 32, 45–47, 61–62, 171–72, 345
"Me and the Ghost Upstairs" (*SC*), 291–94, 308–9
Meet Me in St. Louis, 32–33, 49–50
Mercier, Louis, 173–74
Merman, Ethel, 278
"Michigan" (*EP*), 167–68
Miller, Ann, 18*f*, 74–75, 255–57
Minnelli, Vincente, 29, 65, 124–25, 140–41, 204, 296–97, 303, 332–33, 337–39
   on Astaire, 188–89
Moore, Victor, 59
Morgan, Frank, 140–41
"Mr. and Mrs. Hoofer at Home" (*TLW*), 222–23, 262–63, 278–79, 319, 326*t*

Murder, My Sweet, 328–29
Murphy, George, 255–57, 274–76, 275*f*, 285–87, 330*f*, 410n.67
"Music Makes Me" (*FDR*), 97–98, 319–20
"My One and Only Highland Fling" (*BB*), 142–43, 150–51, 262–63, 271*f*, 274*f*
"My Shining Hour" (*STL*), 150–51, 196–97, 244–46, 276–77, 277*f*

"Needle in a Haystack, A" (*GD*), 165–66, 216–17
Nelson, Gene, 51–52, 51*t*, 53*f*, 77–79, 78*t*, 171–72, 251
"Never Gonna Dance" (*ST*), 86–87, 88, 141–42, 156*t*, 158–59, 202, 202*f*, 213, 242, 268, 269*f*, 276–77, 276*f*, 278, 317–18
"Nevertheless" (*TLW*), 244–46
New Moon is Shining (Russian Cafe), The" (*SC*), 60–61
Nicholas, Harold and Fayard (the Nicholas Brothers), 20–22, 33–34, 51–52, 51*t*, 53*f*, 77–79, 78*t*, 274–76, 358–59
"Night and Day" (*GD*), 194–95, 195*f*, 196, 213, 242, 249–50, 249*f*, 272–73, 273*f*, 278
"Nightclub Solo" (*GD*), 74–75, 102–3, 134, 211, 319–20
"No Strings (I'm Fancy Free)" (*TH*), 43–44, 99, 104–5, 211–12, 212*f*–13*f*, 343–44, 346–47, 354–55, 354*f*

O'Connor, Donald, 51–52, 51*t*, 53*f*, 77–79, 78*t*, 298*f*
O'Hara, John, 177
Obama, Barack, 182–83
"Oh, Them Dudes" (*LD*), 38, 39, 253, 263–64, 264*f*, 274–76, 298*f*, 326*t*, 328–29, 330–31
"One for My Baby (And One More for the Road)" (*STL*), 75–76, 141–42, 156*t*, 196–97, 202–4, 203*f*, 215–16, 219–20, 221–22, 353–54, 353*f*
"Oops" (*BNY*), 165, 326*t*, 329–30
"Open Your Eyes" (*RW*), 95–96, 150–51, 265–66

Paige, Janis, 77, 277f
Pan, Hermes, 28–29, 70–71, 86–87, 88,
    91, 92–94, 114–15, 136–37, 168,
    192–93, 196, 206, 214–15, 253–55,
    259–60, 290–94, 308–9
  quoted, 91–94, 105–6, 164–65, 175–77,
    180–81, 205, 221–22, 279–80, 290–
    92, 311–12, 316, 351–52
"Piccolino, The" (TH), 56–57, 65, 85–86,
    141–42, 211, 212f, 213, 216–17,
    217f, 280
"Pick Yourself Up" (ST), 56, 74–75, 86–87,
    100, 200–2, 201f, 257f
Picture of Dorian Gray, The, 337–38
"Please Don't Monkey With Broadway"
    (BM40), 101–2, 101f, 227–28, 274–
    76, 275f, 283t, 325–28, 326t
Pomerance, Murray, 1, 3–4, 6–7, 13–15,
    133–34, 351
Potter, H.C., 107–8
Powell, Dick, 328–29
Powell, Eleanor, 17, 18f, 29, 33–34, 47, 48–
    49, 48f, 51–52, 51t, 53f, 70–71, 78t,
    97–98, 137, 214–15, 284–87, 330f,
    344, 345–46
  on Astaire, 131, 175–77, 255–57, 290–91
Powell, Jane, 18f, 68, 95–96, 202f, 332f
"Pretty Girl is Like a Melody, A" (BS), 101,
    412n.62
Priest, Bobbie, 70
"Put Me To the Test" (DD), 74–75, 326t,
    329–31, 331f
"Puttin' on the Ritz" (BS), 44, 219–20,
    228–29, 251–53, 345, 355–56, 355f

quantitative methods, 3, 5–6, 9–10, 12–13,
    14–15, 20–21, 24, 25–26, 40, 358–59
  analyzing partner dances, 258–59,
    260–61
  defining musical numbers, 43–44, 54–
    57, 63–65, 66–68, 74–75
  defining shots, 80–81
  and race, 49, 54
  using assistant director reports, 24,
    133–34, 139, 142–43, 149–50

Raft, George, 335, 337–38, 341
"Ragtime Violin" (EP), 63–64, 283t, 298f

Reagan, Nancy, 175–77
"Rehearsal Duet" (YNGR), 274, 274f, 283t,
    298f
Reynolds, Marjorie, 18f, 59–60
Rhapsody in Blue, 253–55
"Ritz Roll and Rock, The" (SS), 149–50,
    156t, 158, 184–85, 186f, 191–92,
    231–32
Robbins, Jerome, 7–9
Roberta, 80–81, 84–87, 88, 107–8, 118–20,
    195–97, 196f, 211, 213, 221–22,
    233–34, 276–77, 283t, 289–90,
    319–20, 322–23, 326t, 329–30, 346
  production history, 132–33, 136–37,
    138f, 140–41
Robinson, Bill "Bojangles," 20–21, 33–34,
    51–52, 51t, 53f, 77–79, 78t, 214–15,
    319–20
Rogers, Ginger, 18f, 28–29, 58, 62, 70–71, 77,
    100–1, 111f, 113f, 127f, 132–33, 137,
    140, 142–43, 166–67, 174, 192f–97f,
    201f, 202f, 212f, 249f, 255–57, 257f,
    258–60, 261–62, 269f, 271f–73f,
    276f, 279f, 287–90, 323, 342
Ross, Herbert, 247–48
Royal Wedding, 47–48, 51–52, 66, 68,
    73–76, 95–96, 97–98, 110f, 200–2,
    202f, 224–25, 227–28, 243, 265–66,
    278–79, 283t, 287, 318–19, 325,
    326t, 331–32, 332f, 343, 413n.80
  audition scene, 58–59
  production history, 132–33, 138f, 150–
    51, 153–54, 156t, 158, 159–60,
    166–67, 172–74
Ryan, Robert, 306–9

"'S Wonderful" (FF)
Sablon, Jean, 173–74
San Juan, Olga, 18f, 36–37, 44–47, 48–49,
    96
Sandrich, Mark, 28–29, 35–36, 41–42,
    143–44, 147–48, 160–62
Sanford and Son, 295
"Say, Young Man of Manhattan," 327–28
Scott, Hazel, 33–34
Second Chorus, 29, 57, 58, 60–61, 66–67,
    68, 69–70, 84–85, 88–90, 196–97,
    244–46, 291–94, 308–9, 318–19

"Seeing's Believing" (*BNY*), 17, 154–55, 168–70, 205–6, 206*f*, 226–28, 318–19
Seibert, Brian, 181–82, 311, 322–23, 353–54
Seldes, Gilbert, 311
Seven Brides for Seven Brothers, 51–52
"Shall We Dance" (*SWD*), 70–71, 77, 105–6, 134, 156*t*, 276–77, 317–18, 413n.78
Shall We Dance, 41–42, 54, 56, 62, 70–71, 75–76, 77, 80, 84–85, 87, 100, 101, 105–6, 181–82, 184–85, 185*f*, 203–4, 215–16, 221–23, 242, 244–46, 276–77, 283*t*, 289, 317–19, 352–53, 353*f*, 413n.78
   opening, 61–62, 353*f*
   production history, 132–33, 134, 135, 136–37, 138*f*, 139–40, 143–44, 156*t*
Sharaff, Irene, 337–38
Shaw, Artie, 29, 60–61
She's Working Her Way Through College, 51–52
"Shine on Your Shoes, A" (*BW*), 25–26, 33–34, 88, 139–40, 163, 171–74, 242, 253, 294–304, 297*f*–302*f*, 347, 347*f*, 356–57, 356*f*–57*f*
"Shoes with Wings On" (*BB*), 67–68, 121–22, 139–40, 142–43, 154–55, 163–64, 169–70, 172, 196–97, 198*f*, 228–29, 242, 325, 326*t*, 327–28, 330*f*, 413–14n.81
"Shootin' the Works for Uncle Sam" (*YNGR*), 94–95, 327–28
"Shorty George, The" (*YWNL*), 45–47, 72–73, 289–90
Silk Stockings, 26–28, 30, 75–76, 94, 120–22, 126–28, 184–85, 186*f*, 196–97, 198*f*, 214–15, 222–23, 231–32, 242, 253, 277–78, 277*f*, 283*t*, 298*f*, 318–19
   production history, 136, 149–50, 156*t*, 158, 162–63, 168, 169, 171, 191–92
Sinatra, Frank, 19–20, 323
"Since I Kissed My Baby Goodbye" (*YNGR*), 98–99
Singin' in the Rain, 11, 51–52, 208–9, 298*f*
"Sisters," 311–12

Skelton, Red, 51–52
Sky's the Limit, The, 26–27, 29, 34, 60–61, 66–67, 75–76, 94–95, 111*f*, 124*f*, 196–97, 202–4, 203*f*, 215–16, 219–20, 221–22, 244–46, 276–77, 277*f*, 283*t*, 298*f*, 305–9, 309*f*, 325, 326*t*, 353–54, 353*f*
   production history, 138*f*, 141–42, 150–51, 156*t*, 202–3
"Slap that Bass" (*SWD*), 61–62, 76, 80, 87, 100, 135, 143–44, 181–82, 184–85, 185*f*, 203–4, 215–16, 221–23, 242, 244–46, 318–19
"Sluefoot, The" (*DLL*), 97–98, 98*f*, 100, 103, 104–5, 104*f*, 126, 127*f*, 171–72, 262–63, 278–79
Smiles, 327–28
Smith, Jack Martin, on Astaire, 17, 95–96, 313–14
Smith, Zadie, 32, 187–88, 351–52
"Smoke Gets In Your Eyes" (*R*), 84–85, 86–87, 88, 195–96, 213, 233–34, 276–77, 319
"Snake Dance" (*STL*), 34, 60–61, 305–9, 309*f*, 325
"Snooky Ookums" (*EP*), 63–64, 166–67
"So Near and Yet So Far" (*YNGR*), 45–47, 198, 199*f*, 221–22
"Something's Gotta Give" (*DLL*), 122–23, 222–23, 280–82
"Song of Freedom" (*HI*), 94–95
Spitz, Leo, 168
Springsteen, Bruce, 182–83
"Steppin' Out with My Baby" (*EP*) 13–14, 47, 70, 80, 97–98, 116–17, 116*f*–17*f*, 120–21, 128, 137–39, 170, 213–14, 333, 422n.48
"Stereophonic Sound" (*SS*), 75–76, 120, 277–78, 277*f*, 283*t*, 298*f*, 318–19
"Stiff Upper Lip" (*DD*), 70–71, 87, 114–15, 115*f*, 143–44, 156*t*, 158–59, 352–53
Stormy Weather, 20–21, 358–59
Story of Vernon & Irene Castle, The, 26–27, 58–59, 63–64, 69–70, 86–87, 242, 260–61, 262–63, 265–66, 317–18, 326*t*, 348, 348*f*
   maxixe, 63–64
   montage, 56–57, 63–64, 139–40

Story of Vernon & Irene Castle, The (cont.)
  polka, 63–64, 265–66
  production history, 132–33, 138*f*, 139–40, 141–42, 153, 166–67, 173–74
  tango, 63–64, 262–63
Sullivan, Shannon, 20–21, 187–88, 411n.12
"Sunday Jumps" (*RW*), 51–52, 74–75, 172–73, 224–25, 227–28
Swing Time, 47, 51–52, 56, 59, 69–70, 74–75, 84–85, 86–87, 88–90, 100, 129–30, 181–82, 184–85, 185*f*, 186*f*, 200–2, 201*f*, 202*f*, 205–6, 207, 213, 224–25, 242, 251–53, 257*f*, 268, 269*f*, 276–77, 276*f*, 278, 280, 317–18, 322–23, 355–56
  production history, 132–33, 138*f*, 140–42, 156*t*, 158–59, 168, 169–70
"Swing Trot" (*BB*), 142–43, 237–38

"Table Dance" (*GD*), 214–15, 224–25, 227–28, 244
Taxi Driver, 354–55
Temple, Shirley, 51–52, 77–79
"That's Entertainment" (*BW*), 342–43
"They All Laughed" (*SWD*), 41–42, 56, 75–76, 101, 143–44, 283*t*, 289
"They Can't Take That Away from Me" (*BB*), 127*f*, 142–43, 262–63, 268, 276–77
"Things Are Looking Up" (*DD*), 84–85, 87, 165, 192–93
"Thinking of You" (*TLW*), 221–22
"This Heart of Mine" (*ZF*), 56–57, 67–68, 144–46, 152–53, 156*t*, 158–59, 198–200, 199*f*, 204, 205*f*, 317–18, 334–35
Thompson, Kaye, 77, 278
Thomson, David, 5, 11, 79, 175–77, 187
Three Little Words, 26–27, 221–23, 244–46, 253, 262–63, 274–76, 275*f*, 278–79, 283*t*, 319, 326*t*
"Tiger Rag," 343
"Too Bad" (*SS*), 120–21, 168
"Too Much Mustard" (*SVIC*), 86–87
Top Hat, 35–36, 42, 43–44, 54, 56–57, 65, 80, 85–86, 99, 104–5, 107–8, 112–14, 113*f*, 147–48, 192–93, 192*f*–93*f*, 196, 196*f*, 211–12, 212*f*–13*f*, 213–14, 216–17, 217*f*, 221–23, 229, 251–53, 276–77, 280, 283*t*, 284–85, 288–89, 301–3, 319–20, 326*t*, 327–28, 339–41, 343–44, 346–47, 347*f*, 354–56, 354*f*, 413n.78
  finale, 58, 59–60
  production history, 137–40, 138*f*, 141–42, 165–66
"Top Hat, White Tie and Tails" (*TH*), 42, 139–40, 147–48, 165–66, 222–23, 229, 251–53, 326*t*, 327–28, 346–47, 347*f*, 355–56
"Triplets" (*BW*), 75–76, 326*t*, 329–30, 329*f*
"Tunnel of Love" (*LD*), 38–39, 67–68, 73
Turnell, Dee, 70

Vera-Ellen, 18*f*, 51*t*, 53*f*, 63–64, 78*t*, 113*f*, 255–57, 274–76, 275*f*
Vitruvian man. *See* Leonardo da Vinci

"Walking the Dog" (*SWD*), 62
Walters, Charles, 43–44, 124–25, 167–68
"Waltz in Swing Time" (*ST*), 86–87, 158–59, 184–85, 185*f*, 280
"Way You Look Tonight, The" (*ST*), 129–30
Wayne, John, 19, 32
"Wedding Cake Walk, The" (*YNGR*), 65, 103, 205
West Side Story, 42–43, 88
"When the Midnight Choo-Choo Leaves for Alabam" (*EP*), 63–64, 270–72, 270*f*, 283*t*, 284–85, 298*f*
"Where Did You Get That Girl?" (*TLW*), 253, 274–76, 275*f*, 283*t*
White Christmas, 139, 311–12
whiteness, 20–21, 70–71, 108–9, 128–29, 181–82, 187–88. *See also* Astaire, Fred: whiteness of; Hollywood: and whiteness
"Why Fight the Feeling" (*LD*), 38
Williams, Guinn "Big Boy," 94–95
Wong, Ana May, 335, 337–38

"Yam, The" (*C*) 41–42, 121–22, 262–63, 414n.84
Yolanda and the Thief, 26–27, 29, 47–48, 56–57, 69–70, 121–22, 124*f*, 157–58, 205, 219–20, 253, 262–63, 268, 317–18

dream ballet, 47–48, 56–57, 65, 67–68, 134, 139–40, 152–53, 156t, 157, 165, 219–20, 253, 262–63, 317–18
   production history, 135, 138f, 139–41, 143–44, 152–54, 156t, 157, 165, 169–70
"You and the Night and the Music" (*BW*), 58–59, 343–44
You Were Never Lovelier, 29, 45–47, 72–73, 124f, 213, 215–16, 226–27, 232, 233, 235–37, 242, 267, 268f, 280, 289–90, 326t, 327
   finale dance, 88, 213, 267, 268f
"You'd Be Hard to Replace" (*BB*), 142–43
You'll Never Get Rich, 29, 44, 45–47, 65, 74–75, 94–95, 98–99, 103, 117–18, 118f, 198, 199f, 204–5, 221–22, 253, 274, 274f, 283t, 298f, 327–28

"You're All the World to Me" (*RW*), 110f, 150–51, 156t, 159–60, 172, 173–74, 243, 318–19
"You're Easy to Dance With" (*HI*), 67–68, 73, 102–3, 265–66, 265f

Ziegfeld Follies, 12–13, 25–26, 29, 47, 56–57, 66, 67–68, 75–76, 124f, 125–26, 198–200, 199f, 204–5, 205f, 221–22, 224, 227–28, 238, 239, 257, 265–66, 266f, 267, 267f, 270f, 274f, 279–80, 279f, 283t, 298f, 301–3, 317–18, 323–25, 326t, 330–31, 333–41, 345–46, 354–55, 413–14n.81, 423–24n.34
   bubble number, 134, 144–46
   production history, 134, 138f, 144–47, 152–55, 156t, 157–59, 334–35

Printed in the USA/Agawam, MA
October 5, 2022

799370.032